Pir-o-Murshid Inayat Khan
1882–1927

COMPLETE WORKS
OF
PIR-O-MURSHID
HAZRAT INAYAT KHAN

ORIGINAL TEXTS:
LECTURES ON SUFISM
1925 I: January to May 24
and
SIX PLAYS
c. 1912 to 1926

"Work for the work; not for success.

"Forget the Past; think not of the Future; mind the Now."

INAYAT KHAN.

1925.

JANUARY.						
S	...	4	11	18	25	...
M	...	5	12	19	26	...
T	...	6	13	20	27	...
W	...	7	14	21	28	...
T	1	8	15	22	29	...
F	2	9	16	23	30	...
S	3	10	17	24	31	...

FEBRUARY.						
S	1	8	15	22	...	...
M	2	9	16	23	...	...
T	3	10	17	24	...	...
W	4	11	18	25	...	...
T	5	12	19	26	...	...
F	6	13	20	27	...	...
S	7	14	21	28	...	...

MARCH.						
S	1	8	15	22	29	...
M	2	9	16	23	30	...
T	3	10	17	24	31	...
W	4	11	18	25	...	...
T	5	12	19	26	...	...
F	6	13	20	27	...	...
S	7	14	21	28	...	...

APRIL.						
S	...	5	12	19	26	...
M	...	6	13	20	27	...
T	...	7	14	21	28	...
W	1	8	15	22	29	...
T	2	9	16	23	30	...
F	3	10	17	24	...	...
S	4	11	18	25	...	...

MAY.						
S	...	3	10	17	24	31
M	...	4	11	18	25	...
T	...	5	12	19	26	...
W	...	6	13	20	27	...
T	...	7	14	21	28	...
F	1	8	15	22	29	...
S	2	9	16	23	30	...

JUNE.						
S	...	7	14	21	28	...
M	1	8	15	22	29	...
T	2	9	16	23	30	...
W	3	10	17	24	...	...
T	4	11	18	25	...	...
F	5	12	19	26	...	...
S	6	13	20	27	...	...

JULY.						
S	...	5	12	19	26	...
M	...	6	13	20	27	...
T	...	7	14	21	28	...
W	1	8	15	22	29	...
T	2	9	16	23	30	...
F	3	10	17	24	31	...
S	4	11	18	25	...	...

AUGUST.						
S	...	2	9	16	23	30
M	...	3	10	17	24	31
T	...	4	11	18	25	...
W	...	5	12	19	26	...
T	...	6	13	20	27	...
F	...	7	14	21	28	...
S	1	8	15	22	29	...

SEPTEMBER.						
S	...	6	13	20	27	...
M	...	7	14	21	28	...
T	1	8	15	22	29	...
W	2	9	16	23	30	...
T	3	10	17	24	...	...
F	4	11	18	25	...	...
S	5	12	19	26	...	...

OCTOBER.						
S	...	4	11	18	25	...
M	...	5	12	19	26	...
T	...	6	13	20	27	...
W	...	7	14	21	28	...
T	1	8	15	22	29	...
F	2	9	16	23	30	...
S	3	10	17	24	31	...

NOVEMBER.						
S	1	8	15	22	29	...
M	2	9	16	23	30	...
T	3	10	17	24	...	...
W	4	11	18	25	...	...
T	5	12	19	26	...	...
F	6	13	20	27	...	...
S	7	14	21	28	...	...

DECEMBER.						
S	...	6	13	20	27	...
M	...	7	14	21	28	...
T	1	8	15	22	29	...
W	2	9	16	23	30	...
T	3	10	17	24	31	...
F	4	11	18	25	...	...
S	5	12	19	26	...	...

COMPLETE WORKS OF PIR-O-MURSHID HAZRAT INAYAT KHAN

ORIGINAL TEXTS: LECTURES ON SUFISM 1925 I: January to May 24 and SIX PLAYS c. 1912 to 1926

Source Edition

Omega Publications, Inc.
New Lebanon, New York

Previous volumes in this series:

Biography of Pir-o-Murshid Inayat Khan (1979)

Complete Works of Pir-o-Murshid Hazrat Inayat Khan, Original Texts:
Sayings, Part I (Gayan, Vadan, Nirtan, 1982, rev. ed. 1989)
Sayings, Part II (Bowl of Saki, Aphorisms, Unpublished Sayings,1982, rev. ed. 1989)

Lectures on Sufism:
1922 I: January-August (1990)
1922 II: September-December (1996)
1923 I: January-June (1989)
1923 II: July-December (1988)
1924 I: January-June (2004)
1924 II: June-December (2010)
1926 I: December 1925 to May 12 (2010)
1926 II: March 14 to May 28 (2012)

Published by the Nekbakht Foundation;
the Complete Works are downloadable from
nekbakhtfoundation.org

Printed on acid-free paper with sewn and glued binding
Editorial and production services by Omega Publications Inc.
Printed and bound by Sheridan Books, Inc., Ann Arbor, Michigan
Manufactuered in the United States of America

Inayat Khan (1882–1927)
Complete works of Pir-o-Murshid Hazrat Inayat Khan; Original texts: Lectures on Sufism, 1925 1: January to May 24, 1925 and Six Plays c. 1912 to 1926
1. Inayat Khan, 1882-1927 2. Sufis 3. Sufism

Library of Congress Control Number: 2013931535
ISBN 978–0–930872–99–1

10 9 8 7 6 5 4 3 2 1

TABLE OF CONTENTS

Preface

After the large volume of teachings given in the latter half of 1924 (see Complete Works 1924 II), the beginning of 1925 seems to have been a relatively quiet period. Nevertheless, we have thirty-five texts, and we know about another eighteen which went unrecorded.

During the period 1923-1926, Inayat Khan kept a journal of his activities, particularly noting and praising the work of the many people who, by that time, were involved in arranging his lectures in many places. About early January, 1925, he wrote: "On my coming to Paris I found our venerable friend and worker Baronne d'Eichthal as busy as ever. The wonderful talks that our most trusted worker Murshida Goodenough gave to mureeds and friends in Paris kept up the rhythm of my Message during my absence. I spoke at the Musée Guimet, at the Sorbonne, and gave lectures at the drawing room of Baronne d'Eichthal."[1] The lectures he refers to at the Musée Guimet and the Sorbonne must have been "Is Man the Master of His Destiny" and "Concentration", but there is no indication on the typescripts as to which is which. Inayat Khan also remarked on the difficulty of working in France: "Paris has so many distractions that it is found always difficult to keep the thoughts of the mureeds concentrated on one line. Besides, for many and various reasons, members seemed to be scattered. It is by the most sincere devotion of Mejuffrouw Kismet Stam to the Cause that she made unceasing efforts to keep threads together, thus keeping alive that flame which was once kindled from being blown away by the continual attacks of the sweeping wind." Kismet Stam, cousin of Sakina Furnée, became one of Inayat Khan's three secretaries, and later in the period covered by this book, she organized his visit to Nice and his time in Munich. She also later accompanied him on his 1926 tour of America, and was his travelling companion during his time in India just before his untimely death in 1927.

Also included in this section are two *gatha* lessons (usually dictated to Murshida Sherifa Goodenough), and two other texts of unknown date and place: a text from Nargis Dowland, and a story by Inayat Khan for children, followed by two question and answer sections.

---

1. *Biography of Pir-o-Murshid Inayat Khan* (East-West, London and The Hague, 1979, 202)

The second of these, from Murshida Sherifa Goodenough, contains some of the most telling instructions for guiding *mureed*s, and deserves to be much better known.

Around the middle of January Inayat Khan went to International Headquarters in Geneva, where he lectured and then made a tour of Switzerland, giving fifteen lectures, of which eight went unrecorded. In his journal Inayat Khan mentions Bern, Lausanne, Zurich, Rapperswil and Basel as the lecture tour, and credits Frau Meyer de Reutercrona, the National Representative for Switzerland, as having organized them. It is possible that the lecture entitled "Colour and Sound", known to have been given in Switzerland but without any date, is the same as the missing lecture "The Mystery of Sounds and Colours" of 15 January, given in Geneva. However, the content of the former has no reference to "mystery", making that seem unlikely. The fifteen lectures do not seem to have been conceived as a series, and probably only a few people travelled with Inayat Khan on this journey, probably by train, around this small country. Most of the lectures bore titles which had by now become familiar. However, typically, when one compares two lectures with the same title by Inayat Khan, even when they were given on successive days, the content is quite different. Since he used a limited number of titles over and over again, an interesting exercise might be to compare a dozen or so lectures with the same title given over the course of his last half dozen years or more.

In early February he returned to Italy, which he had visited twice before. He gave three lectures at the British Institute, the Biblioteca Filosofica and the Association for Religious Progress in Florence arranged by Angela Alt, of which two were written down. The next week in Rome eight lectures were given, all arranged by his mureeds Mr. and Mrs. Craig (about whom little is known). We have records of only two, taken down by Angela Alt. The titles of the six missing lectures were, again, quite familiar, and he gave many other lectures, both before and after the visit to Rome, with those same titles.

On his way back to Geneva he gave some lectures in a public hall in Nice. These were arranged by Kismet Stam. He was also invited to speak at the house of Comte and Comtess Prozor, where he was well received. However in his journal Inayat Khan notes that Baron von Howen "took up the work in that part of the country" although Inayat Khan never went there again.

After two weeks in Geneva, where he gave only two or three talks, he went to Munich, where there was already an enthusiastic following, and gave a series of six talks and lectures in various people's houses, all arranged by Kismet Stam. He then returned to Paris, where he had been invited to give a series of three lectures at the Sorbonne in late March.

Early in April he travelled to England, where he spent the first two days in Southampton, where Khalifa Nargis Dowland ran the Polygon House Hotel. Khalifa Nargis Dowland was the United Kingdom National Representative of the Movement from 1921 to 1933. Also in Southampton was Shahbaz Edgar Austin Mitchell, a journalist and lead writer for the Southern Daily Echo (a Southampton newspaper), an active member of the Sufi Movement after he met Inayat Khan in London during the First World War. It was he who took down the lectures in Holland in 1922 which were published as *The Inner Life*, and the family connection remained strong. Much later Inayat Khan's eldest son, Vilayat, was engaged to be married to one of Shahbaz Mitchell's daughters, Myrtle, who tragically died in a motorcycle accident. Inayat Khan then travelled to Bournemouth, where he gave the lecture "The Awakening of the Soul" on April 4th, about which we know only the title. It is likely that this lecture was organised by Dr. Arthur Bodley Scott, whom Inayat Khan mentioned in his Viladat Day speech in 1925: "Khalif Dr. Scott has splendidly worked for the Cause in Bournemouth."

Inayat Khan had intended a lecture tour of England, but due to illness he had to cancel that tour and return to France. He had been ill the previous year in Southampton, and had been in bed for a week. His mureeds were understandably reluctant to speak of or even acknowledge his illnesses, but these both seem likely to have been instances of pneumonia, which became chronic, and for which allopathic medicine had no effective treatment before antibiotics. However, presumably to fulfill commitments to the London mureeds, he returned to England and gave a series of three lectures in London on the 20th to the 24th of April. We have texts for none of these lectures, and we do not know what he was doing for most of the month.

In late May he went to Holland, and in Amersfoort and gave two lectures, probably to a group of his mureeds. The first one concerns the importance of silence gained in repose (known by the odd title "The Fourth Aspect of the Nature which leads to the Path of

Wisdom"); the second, "The Way Reached by Action", investigates what a mystic can gain in the active life.

Late May and early June appear to have been a period of repose for Inayat Khan, no doubt in preparation for the intensive period of teaching in the Summer School, which began on June 14. The numerous lectures from that annual gathering, as well as the rest of the lectures he gave in Europe before his departure for America in early November, will appear in the next volume, 1925 II.

Editorial History

As Inayat Khan's lectures and talks were given, they were taken down by one or more of his three secretaries: Murshida Sherifa Goodenough, Sakina Furnée, and Kismet Stam. Sherifa Goodenough had become his principal editor very early in the London days, probably by 1916, and she continued to write down what he said in longhand. In the early days, all those present had been encouraged to write down all that was being said, and Inayat Khan spoke very slowly and gave short lessons. As time passed, his English naturally improved, and he began to give more extensive discourses and to speak faster. Eventually, those present were asked not to write but to listen only, while one or more of the three secretaries made a written record. In 1921 Sakina Furnée became the second secretary, and was asked by Inayat Khan to learn shorthand so as to take down his words accurately. Not long after that, Sakina's cousin, Kismet Stam, also become a secretary and was also asked to learn shorthand. Although cousins, these two young women were of very different temperaments. Sakina learned a Dutch shorthand system, Pont, and recorded each syllable of Inayat Khan's speaking. Kismet learned a French system, Aimé, and took down a normal shorthand with many connective words deliberately left out. Thus Sakina's shorthand is the fullest and most accurate record of Inayat Khan's speaking, backed up by Sherifa Goodenough's longhand and Kismet's shorthand. Wherever Sakina's shorthand record exists it forms the solid basis for representing exactly what Inayat Khan actually said.

Editorial Practices

The shorthand records naturally contain no punctuation, but punctuation was added by Sakina Furnée and others in the transcriptions. Throughout the *Complete Works*, the editor has reconsidered the punctuation and altered it when necessary to conform with current practice. The spelling follows British standards, since these volumes are intended for a worldwide audience, but follows the conventions of Oxford University Press, where, for example, "realize" and similar words are spelled with a z rather than an s, the more common British spelling.

The purpose of these volumes is to come as close as possible to the actual words spoken by Inayat Khan , and to relegate all editorial "improvements" to the footnotes. For this reason we do not correct grammatical errors. We do standardize spelling, and the punctuation is added, sometimes but not always following the old manuscripts. The primary focus always remains the spoken words of Inayat Khan.

Footnotes

The footnotes represent mostly the differences between the shorthand text and the written-out text, whether in handwriting or typed. The reason for this careful footnoting is to give readers complete information about the contents of the shorthand record, so that it is not necessary to learn this abstruse (and now obsolete) system of notation to determine what Inayat Khan actually said, the main concern of this publication.

The footnote numbers in the text have been repeated in the following instances:
1. When the note refers to a lengthy set of words rather than just a few, the note number appears both at the beginning and the end;
2. When the same information applies in more than one instance.

References to the various works of ancient Sufis and to scriptures, particularly the Bible and the Qur'an, have been included whenever they could be found. Many works of ancient Sufis still await translation into English or other European languages. Where Biblical references begin with "See", the quotation cited by Inayat Khan does not correspond exactly to standard translations. Often references to the Qur'an prove difficult or impossible to identify precisely, since translations differ dramatically, and it is not always clear which translation, if any, Inayat Khan is referring to.

Table of Contents

In the Table of Contents, the lectures have been listed under the title which appears in the basic text. As far as books and classified series of lectures are concerned, these later titles can be found by consulting the appendix. The dates will be found at the top of the lectures themselves, and are no longer included in the Table of

Contents. However, the lectures appear in chronological order as well as that can be determined.

Explanation of Abbreviations
This list, which follows this preface, offers the general meaning of each abbreviation. The list of documents preceding the notes for each lecture gives the specific meaning of the abbreviation for that particular lecture and are therefore not included in the list. For information about the *mureeds* (initiates) who took down or later edited the lectures, please refer to the List of Persons, or to the *Biography*.

Appendix
The appendix is designed to show what a particular lecture may have become later on. One use for a lecture, of course, was as a chapter for a book. Another very common use was as a lesson to be distributed to Sufi Centres, which included several different series for different purposes. The Gathas, Githas, Sangathas, and Sangithas were texts for mureeds of particular levels of initiation. The various Gatheka series were for a more general use. Those in possession of the books or copies of the lessons will be able to use this appendix to discover the source of the material, and then to compare the edited versions with the original lectures.

Glossary
Even though explanations of foreign (non-English) terms are generally given only in the glossary, in some instances an immediate understanding of a term is so essential to understanding the statement that a brief explanation has been included in the notes. When Inayat Khan seems to have used a term in a special sense, the usual accepted meaning is given first, and his special meaning afterwards marked "(suf)". Standard reference sources have been used to make these entries, but especially Dr. M. C. Monna's *Short Dictionary of the Foreign Words in Hazrat Inayat Khan's Teachings* (revised edition, Alkmaar, 1991). Because of occasional errors in this dictionary, all entries have been further checked in standard sources.

List of Persons, Places and Works
Of the names of deities, persons, peoples, geographical locations, works, etc., mentioned in the lectures in this volume, a short explanation has been given following the Glossary. In many cases, these might appear to be so well-known or readily available in

reference works that no explanation is required. When this series began in the 1980s, finding information on these matters still required access to a reference library. In the intervening years, the development of information technology has made vast amounts of information readily available virtually anywhere through the Internet. Therefore, in this volume we have shortened the entries in the List to just the essential information.

Index

The extensive analytical index at the end of the book may prove useful for private study, for preparing lectures, as well as for scholarly purposes in general. The intent has been to be inclusive and to provide some idea of the content of each reference. Within each entry, a hyphen replaces the word being indexed. The downloadable version of each book, to be found at nekbakhtfoundation.org, is also searchable using Adobe Acrobat Reader.

In conclusion, the objects of this book, and indeed of the whole series, may be summed up as threefold:

— to safeguard for posterity the teachings of Pir-o-Murshid Hazrat Inayat Khan gathered in the Biographical Department;

— to serve as the basis of future publications and translations;

— to make the earliest source materials of Pir-o-Murshid Hazrat Inayat Khan's words available to scholars, researchers, students, and the many persons interested today in finding authentic texts of Sufi spiritual teachings.

Donald Avery Graham, Editor-in-Chief Emeritus
Anne Louise Wirgman, Editor-in-Chief
Nekbakht Foundation
34, rue de la Tuilerie
92150 Suresnes, France
website: nekbakhtfoundation.org

Acknowledgements

The largest part of the work on this volume was done by Juliane Jasmine Damm, who keyboarded the lectures, carefully compared the manuscripts and participated in the several rounds of proofreading necessary for each volume. Her meticulous work forms the basis of the entire volume.

Professor Donald Sharif Graham has overall responsibility for the work. He prepared the critical apparatus, including an analytical index, and in the Preface has attempted to give the reader an overview the historical context. He was aided in the Preface, in the final proofreading of this book, and especially with the plays by Anne Louise Wirgman, who, as of July, 2012, became the new Editor-in-Chief, as Professor Graham has now retired and returned to the United States.

The Reverend Berthi van der Bent Hamel has continued the challenging work of transcribing Sakina Furnée's shorthand, has provided the footnotes regarding the shorthand record, and has also participated in the proofreading and corrections. She is assisted by Margaret Lesley who turns the transcriptions into computer files and then works with Anne King, meticulously checking and re-checking the documents.

As with the other volumes, the Glossary and List have benefited from a check by Shaikh-ul-Mashaik Mahmood Maheboob Khan, an Advisor to the Nekbakht Board, and his wife, Ma-Shaika Harunnisa, who is a native speaker of Gujerati and Urdu, just as was Pir-o-Murshid Inayat Khan. They should not, however, be held responsible for any inaccuracies.

We wish also to acknowledge the support, both financial and moral, of the Nekbakht Foundation, a Dutch foundation created by Sakina Furnée for the purpose of preserving the manuscripts and eventually publishing them. It is with sadness that we report the passing of one of the Board members, Johannes Molenaar, in 2012. His kindness and unfailing optimism were an inspiration to all who worked with him. His position as Secretary of the Board has been taken by Jos van den Heuvel, who has rapidly adapted to the demands of the position.

List of Abbreviations

abbr. = abbreviation
a.o.d = all other documents
corr. = corrected
B.v.d.B. = Berthi van der Bent Hamel
hw.= handwriting
lh. = long hand
sh.= shorthand

Sakina Furnée's typescript

Number 4 (no date)

Gatheka: Reincarnation[2]

People have often asked[3], "What has the Sufi to say about reincarnation?" [4]My silence at times, and yes and no at times, has made it vague. Some perhaps thought that I did not believe in it, and that if I did [not][5] believe, then the Sufis do not believe, naturally. This is not the case. Every Sufi is free to believe what he understands to be[6] right and what he can understand. He is not nailed to any particular belief. By believing in any doctrine the Sufi does not go out of his Sufism, as by not believing he does not go out of the Order of the[7] Sufis. There is perfect freedom of belief.

For my yes, there was a reason; for my no, there was also[8] a reason, a reason not for myself, but for the person who asked me the question. People in the world wish to make things rigid which are of the finest nature, which words alone[9] cannot explain. It is just like wanting to weigh the soul, or photograph the spirit, when a person describes the hereafter.[10] You must not depend upon my words. Self-realization is the aim. Belief in doctrines are pills given to ill people for their cure.

In point of fact, all things are true to a certain extent[11], but when compared with the ultimate truth, they fall short in proving themselves existent. Things appear different from every different

---

Documents:

Sk.tp. = typescript prepared by Sakina Furnée.

Hq.tp. = a typescript prepared at Headquarters, Geneva, probably edited by Murshida Sherifa Goodenough.

Hq.st. = a stencil (cyclostyle) identical in wording to Hq.tp., prepared for distribution to Sufi Centres, not included in the notes.

Notes:

2. The classification "Gatheka" added in Hq.tp., followed by the Sufi Invocation
3. Hq.tp.: "me" added
4. Hq.tp.: "and" added, continuing the previous sentence
5. Hq.tp.: "not" added (apparently inadvertently omitted in Sk.tp.)
6. Hq.tp.: "as" instead of "to be"
7. Hq.tp.: "the" omitted
8. Hq.tp.: "also" omitted
9. Hq.tp.: "alone" omitted
10. Hq.tp.: "I, personally, think that you must be able yourself to realize what is the hereafter." added
11. Hq.tp.: "point" instead of "extent"

plane from which you look at them, and when a person standing on the flat part of the[12] earth asks a question of a person standing on the top of a mountain, "Do you also believe something?", he cannot tell you much. The questioner must come on to the top of the mountain and see. There can be no link of conversation between them during that time. The method of the Sufi is quietude and silent progress, and[13] by this one arrives[14] at the stage where one can see for oneself[15]. You may say that patience is needed. Yes, but the spiritual path is for the patient. Patience is the most difficult thing.[16]

---

12. Hq.tp.: "part of the" omitted
13. Hq.tp.: "and" omitted
14. Hq.tp.: "arriving" instead of "one arrives"
15. Hq.tp.: "you can see for yourself" instead of "one can see for oneself"
16. Hq.tp.: "To be read before candidates for initiation in the Sufi Order." added

Sakina Furnée's typescript

(no date)

Story for Children

[1]There was once a little boy whose name was Dildar, which means purity of heart, and he had come to live upon this round ball that we call the earth, and when he was seven years old his mother brought him to the wise one to learn about God, and this is what I think he said.

Once upon a time the sky and the earth and the sea were covered by a great darkness and the darkness was full of silence. No one could say this is the earth, this is sea or sky, for all was hidden by the darkness, in which there was no sound and where nothing moved. The name by which we call that strange world is space, and that space was empty and very still, just waiting.

Then suddenly, there came a movement in space, and a trembling like that of the water when a gentle wind blows upon its surface. And out of darkness there rose the sun in all his glory and the arrows of light shot out in thousands of rays, and the darkness was driven away at their touch.

Then the light of the sun began to work upon the earth, the waters gathered together into the seas and the rivers, and part became dry land where no water was; and they felt the power of the sun and were glad. And in the whole earth there was no life but the life of the sun, for when one part of the round ball was turned away from the sun and praised him with the words, "None exists save he," meaning there is no other living being but the sun.

And the sun looked down upon the earth and when his glance touched it, the trees and flowers, the little plants and all the growing things sprang into being, and lifted their faces to the sun and cried, "None exists save he." And the sun looked deep into the

Documents:

Sk.tp. = a typescript prepared by Sakina Furnée or under her supervision.

Hq.tp. = a typescript from the Headquarters' archive, The Hague.

Notes:

1. Sk.tp.: at the top of the document is written: "This is a story told to children by Hazrat Inayat Khan about creation and about the first Sufi Thought, "There is one God, the eternal, the only being. None exists save He."; Hq.tp.: at the top of the document is written 10 Sufi Thoughts, I, There is One God, the Eternal, the Only Being, none exists save He.

waters of the sea where some of the darkness had hidden under the rocks and in the deep pools, and the rays of the sun became living creatures that played in the waters as the birds play in the air, darting about like living shafts of light, and the fishes and the birds saw the sun and knew his life had made them, and the fishes and the birds saw the sun and knew his life had made them, and again the wonderful words rose up to the sun, "His life is our life! None exists save he."

But this was not the end of that most wonderful work of the sun and his rays of light, for out of the warm earth, and the cool water and the pure air he made a little child and into the little child he sent one ray more beautiful than all the rest. This ray went straight into the heart of the child and became his soul; and it whispered to the child and the child listened and understood. The ray said, "I am your life for ever, for I am also the life of the sun itself. You cannot see me for I have no form that your eyes can see, but you can find me in all the forms there are.

"In the rock, in the flowers, in the fire, in the air, in the tiny insect and in the noble lion or the wise elephant. I gave them all my life through my earthly body, the sun. I give all life; all life is mine. I am the heart of the sun and the heart of the child and[2] man.

"My name is God, the Holy, the Eternal. I am in all beings. None exists save me."

- - - - - - - - - - - - - - - - - - - -

Q.: What does Dildar mean?
A.: Purity of heart.

Q.: What is purity of heart?
A.: The kind of heart which the angels have is pure, in which God sees his face reflected as in a mirror.

Q.: Who is God?
A.: The only being.

Q.: What does that mean?
A.: That God lives in all forms.

---

2. Hq.tp.: "the" added

Q.: What do you mean by forms?
A.: All that we can see: the sun and moon, the stars, trees and flowers, and all living beings.

Q.: Is God[3] *to be found inside all these forms?*
A.: No, his life is inside them, but he is outside as well, just as the sun's life is in them, but he is outside as well; just as the sun's life is in them, yet we can see him in the sky as well.[4]

Q.: Does God ask us to do anything for him?
A.: He asks us to love him.

Q.: How can we love him?
A.: By loving all that is beautiful. As is said in the Qur'an, "God is beautiful and he loves beauty."[5]

Q.: Can we speak to God?
A.: There are two ways of speaking to God, one is called prayer, the other praise. The first is asking, and the second is saying, "Thank you."

Q.: What is a Sufi?
A.: He is someone who is looking for God, who loves him, and sees his light everywhere.[6]

Q.: Can we find him in all the religions of the world?
A.: Yes, as all the spokes of a wheel meet in the middle of the wheel, so do all religions lead their followers to the only being.

There is one God, the eternal, the only being, none exists save he.

- - - - - - - - - - - - - - - - - - - -

3. Hq.tp.: "only" added
4. Hq.tp. adds a citation at the end of this line, "(Gita)" with a footnote "'Having permeated all this with myself' Tremaine.", then "Bhavagad Gita" handwritten
5. Hq.tp. has, instead of "As is said in the Qur'an, 'God is beautiful and he loves beauty'.", a footnote reading: "God is beautiful, and he loves beauty.", and then, handwritten, "Koran" [actually it is a *hadith qudsi*]. For *hadith qudsi,* see Glossary
6. Hq.tp. ends here with "Let us say all together, 'There is One God, the Eternal, the Only Being. None exists save he.'"

Murshida Goodenough's handwriting

Q.: Does the Sufi do work upon the astral plane?
A.: The astral plane is the plane of thought and feeling. The word Sufi means cleaner. Really the brass cleaner should be called the brass Sufi, the window cleaner should be called the window Sufi, the laundry man should be called the laundry Sufi. The work of the Sufi on the astral plane is to clean, to clear off. He clears away all thoughts and feelings. He does this by what we call the[7] *tassawur*[8]. When the king passes, the policeman is placed in the road to keep it clear of all other motors, carts, and carriages, and of all enemies and undesirable people. The Sufi places the policeman on his road, the tassawur of Murshid, the image of the object of his devotion, to keep away all other thoughts and feelings.

Q.: Some complain, as soon as I began the spiritual path, all material things went wrong. How is this?
A.: Initiation is a battery. If his thoughts were success, uplifting[9], through initiation he becomes more successful. And if his thoughts were low down, by initiation he runs low down more quickly. Initiation is a battery behind all power.

Q.: How to approach people?
A.: Human being is proud at first, it is afterwards that he becomes easy, obedient, humble. Human beings are like little doves. Throw grains from a distance, and they will come to take them. But as soon as you stretch your hand to them, even with the intention to help, they fly away, for they feel a prison. Never let anybody understand that you wish to help them; this will frighten them away. Once frightened, they are far away, even if they sit before you.

Q.: If new mureeds tell us that they do not want to say Saum and Salat, but their own prayers, what must we do?
A.: If they do not want to say Saum and Salat, let them say their own prayers. It is our object to make them feel happy, as long as they are happy in their own prayers let them do it. The made prayer said is

---

7. Sk.tp.: "the" crossed out
8. For *tassawur*, see Glossary
9. Sk.tp.: originally "uplifted" typed followed by "(ing?)", then the "ed" of "uplifted" crossed out to indicate "uplifting"

caught by the mind. And even if said once a day, it will continue unnoticed deep in the mind for twenty-four hours.

Q.: How do we cultivate belief in another?
A.: Not by speaking about it, or by showing him his shortcomings. Never do so. An ordinary person judges, an esoteric leader must never do that. But how? By appreciating the little faith he has, trying to find out the little faith he has (everyone has) and appreciating it. Never judge. Even if a person comes and asks you, "Tell me, am I right or wrong?", by judging you always lose your pupil. Show him love and appreciation, but never judge him. A subtle form of judgement may do, if he knows that you love him; but therefore always show love and tolerance and forgiveness and kindness, but never judge. Of course every teacher has his own ways, and the way of the one teacher is as good as that from the other. But every teacher will variate his ways according to the nature of the pupil. Never force a pupil, i.e. never tell him he must do his meditations. Appreciate the little he does. Ask him what he can do. If he says he meditates twice a week, say, "That is very good," but it would be still better if he did it four times a week, and still better if he did it every day. Never force, and always, if someone asks an advice, think about his benefit, his happiness in the first place, and about the furtherance of the Message in the second place.

Q.: How can one learn virtue?
A.: The real virtue is learned by the study of reality, and the true virtue comes by itself. When a person becomes conscious of reality all he does becomes virtuous. He has the light of reality before him, the lantern of Aladdin[10], the guiding light.

---

10. For Aladdin, see List

An old typescript

[1]Switzerland, January, 1925[2]

Colour and Sound[3]

[4]Beloved ones of God,

I am asked to speak this evening on the subject of colour and sound. It is not at all my intention this evening to give a theoretical exposition of this subject, for if I would try to do so it will take a series of lectures for many days in order to cover perhaps the smallest part of the subject. Therefore, I only intend giving this evening the spiritual significance of colour and sound.[4]

It seems what science arrives at realizing in the end, mysticism reaches it[5] from the beginning, according to the saying of Christ that[6], "First seek ye the kingdom of God and it will be added"[7]. When one hears the present discoveries about sound and about colour from scientific directions[8], one begins to be surprised; one says, "What a new discovery, something we have never heard[9]." It is something quite new, and yet, when you open the Bible, there it says, "First was the word, and the word was God."[10] And if you open the still older scriptures of [Vedanta][11] you read in their [verses][12] that in the creator there was that word or that vibration. And when we come to the Qur'an, we read there, "First there was

---

Documents:

od.tp.	=	an old typescript of unknown provenance.
Sk.tp.	=	a typescript made by Sakina Furnée, nearly identical to od.tp.
Hq.tp.	=	a typescript prepared at Headquarters, Geneva possibly edited by Murshida Sherifa Goodenough, showing differences from the other documents.

Notes:

1. Sk.tp.: "public lecture" added; Hq.tp.: "SOCIAL GATHEKA." added, followed by the Sufi Invocation
2. Hq.tp.: "Number 55." instead of the place and the date
3. Hq.tp.: "THE SPIRITUAL SIGNIFICANCE OF COLOUR AND SOUND." added underneath the title
4. Hq.tp.: "Beloved ones of God, I am asked ... colour and sound." omitted
5. Hq.tp.: "it" omitted
6. Hq.tp.: "that" omitted
7. See Matthew 6:33
8. Hq.tp.: "side" instead of "directions"
9. Hq.tp.: "of" added
10. See John 1:1
11. Od.tp., Sk.tp.: a space, indicating missing words; Hq.tp.: "Vedanta"
12. Od.tp., Sk.tp.: a space, missing words; Hq.tp.: "verses"

the word 'be' and then it[13] became."[14] The religions of the world, the prophets and mystics who existed thousands of years before[15] knew it[16] then. Today a man comes with a little plate, a photographic plate, and says, "Here I have a photograph of sound." That shows how important is vibration and its action upon it[17]. He does not know that it is something which has always been known to those who knew it, and has been spoken[18], but in a spiritual term, and[19] therefore, what has been spoken man does not think about. What is being spoken he thinks it is something new, but as we realize, as Solomon has said that there is nothing new under the sun[20], then we begin to enjoy life, seeing how, time after time, the same wisdom is revealed to man. The one who seeks through science, the one who searches through religion, the one who finds it through philosophy, the one who finds it through mysticism, in whatever manner one seeks[21] the truth, he finds[22] it in the end.

I was very amused once. I was introduced in New York to a scientist, to[23] a philosopher, and the first thing he said about it[24], his accomplishments was that[25], "I have discovered the soul." It amused me very much that all scriptures have spoken about it, that thinkers have spoken about it, mystics have spoken about it, the prophets have spoken about it, and the man comes and says, "I have discovered the soul." I thought, "Yes, that was the new discovery that we were expecting, something that we never knew."

Such is the attitude of mind today, the childish attitude. When one sees into the past, the present and[26] future, one sees that it[27] is eternal and what one can discover is that which has always been discovered by those who seek[28]. In the first place philosophy

---

13. Hq.tp.: "there" instead of "it"
14. Sura II, verse 11
15. Hq.tp.: "ago" instead of "before"
16. Hq.tp.: "them" instead of "it"
17. Hq.tp.: "the plate" instead of "it"
18. Hq.tp.: "of" added
19. Hq.tp.: "and" omitted
20. See Ecclesiastes 1:9
21. Hq.tp.: "they seek" instead of "one seeks"
22. Hq.tp.: "they find" instead of "he finds"
23. Hq.tp.: "to" omitted
24. Hq.tp.: "it" omitted
25. Hq.tp.: "that" omitted
26. Hq.tp.: "the" added
27. Hq.tp.: "life" instead of "it"
28. Od.tp.: "by those who seek" written twice but second omitted in Sk.tp., Hq.tp.

or science, mysticism or exotericism[29], they will all agree on one point if they touch the summit of their knowledge, and that point is that behind the whole creation, behind the whole manifestation, if there is any subtle trace of life that can be found, it is motion, it is movement, it is vibration.

Now this motion has its two aspects. There are two aspects for this reason, that we have developed these two principle faculties, sight and hearing. One aspect appeals to hearing, the other to our sight. The aspect of movement or vibration that appeals to our hearing is that aspect which we call audible, and that which we term sound. The aspect which appeals to our sight, we call it light, we call it colour, and we call it visual[30]. In the point of fact, all that is visible, all that is audible, what is it in its origin? It is motion, it is movement, it is vibration. It is one and the same thing and therefore even that which is audible, that which is called sound, those who can see can trace colour in it. And those who can hear, to them, even the sound of the colour is audible.

Is there anything that unites these two things? Yes, there is. And what is it? It is harmony. It is not a particular colour which is harmonious, or which lacks harmony, it is the blending of that colour, it is in which frame it is fixed, how the colour is arranged, in accordance to that it has its effect upon the one who sees.

And so it is with sound. There is not any sound which is harmonious or unharmonious[31], it is the relation of one sound with another sound that creates harmony. Therefore harmony is not such a thing as to[32] point out that this certain thing is harmony. Harmony is a fact, harmony is the result of the relation between colour and colour, the relation between sound and sound, and the relation between colour and sound.

The most interesting aspect of this knowledge is how to different persons different colours appeal, and how different people enjoy different sounds. The more one studies this, the more one finds its relation with the particular advancement of man's evolution, because one will find that at a certain time of one's evolution one had loved a certain colour, and then one lost contact with that colour. With one's growth and evolution in life, one begins

---

29. Hq.tp.: "esotericism" instead of "exotericism"
30. Od.tp.: "visual" written twice, but Sk.tp.: one "visual" omitted and "visible" substituted in Hq.tp.
31. Hq.tp.: "inharmonious" instead of "unharmonious"
32. Hq.tp.: "that one can" instead of "as to"

to like some other colour. It also depends upon one's[33] condition, whether the person[34] is emotional, whether[35] passionate, whether[35] romantic, whether[35] warm or cold, whether sympathetic or disagreeable. Whether be his emotional condition, in accordance to that he has his likes or dislikes in colours. It is therefore that which makes it easy for the seer, for the knower, to read the character of man, even before having seen his face, by only seeing his clothes. His liking for a certain colour expresses what the person is like, what is his liking. His liking for a certain flower, his liking for a certain gem or jewel, his liking for a certain environment in his room, the colour on his wall, that all shows what a person is like, what is his fancy. And as man evolves through life spiritually, so his choice of colour changes. With each step forward he changes, his idea about colour becomes different. And[36] there are then[37] some to whom striking colours appeal, to others pale colours, and the reason is that the striking colours have intense vibrations, the pale colours have smooth and harmonious vibrations, and it is according to the emotional condition of man that he enjoys different colours.

I am[38] now coming to the[39] sound. Every person, whether he knows it or not, has a choice of a certain sound. Although every person does not study this subject and therefore he[40] remains ignorant of that idea, but he[41] has a certain liking for a certain sound. It is therefore that there is a saying, a belief among people, that each person has his note. The thing is that each person has his sound, a sound which is akin to his particular evolution. And besides that, with all the divisions that the singers have made of tenor and bass and of baritone, each person has his particular pitch and each person has his peculiar note in which he speaks, and that particular note is expressive of his life's evolution, expressive of his soul, [42]the condition of his feelings, of his thoughts. And[43] besides this, it does not only make effect upon children to hear certain sounds and to see

---

33. Hq.tp.: "a person's" instead of "one's"
34. Hq.tp.: "he" instead of "the person"
35. Hq.tp.: "whether" omitted
36. Hq.tp.: "And" omitted
37. Hq.tp.: "then" omitted
38. Hq.tp.: "I am" omitted
39. Hq.tp.: "the" omitted
40. Hq.tp.: "mostly man" instead of "he"
41. Hq.tp.: "yet every person" instead of "but he"
42. Hq.tp.: "of" added
43. Hq.tp.: "And" omitted

certain colours, but it also makes effect upon animals. The[44] colours have a great effect and influence upon all living creatures, animals or birds or human beings. Without them[45] knowing[46], the influence of colours works in their lives, turning them to this or that inclination.

An amusing story I remember. Once I was visiting a house which was[47] taken by a certain club and that[48] said that, "It is a very great pity, since we have taken this house, in our committee there is always a disagreement." I said, "No wonder, I see it." They said, "Why?" I said, "The walls are red, they make you inclined to fight. Striking colour from all round[49], it gives you the inclination to disagree, their[50] emotions are touched by it and certainly those inclined to disagreement are helped by it."

And it is these things in view, and it is from this psychological point of view that[51] the ancient customs that one finds in the East, especially in[52] their weddings, that a certain colour is chosen for the time of wedding and[53] for other different times in different festivities. It has all its meaning; it[54] has a psychological significance behind it.

Since colour and sound both are perceived differently, we have different senses to perceive these, we have distinguished between visible and audible things. But in reality, those who meditate, those who concentrate, those who go within themselves, those who trace the origin of life, [they][55] begin to see that behind these outer five senses there is one sense hidden, and that sense is capable of doing all that which we seem to do or to experience. There are our external five senses. We distinguish five senses because we know the five organs of sense. In reality there is one sense. It is that sense which through these five different organs experiences life and distinguishes life into[56] five different forms, and

---

44. Hq.tp.: "The" omitted
45. Hq.tp.: "their" instead of "them"
46. Hq.tp.: "it" added
47. Hq.tp.: "had been" instead of "was"
48. Hq.tp.: "they" instead of "that"
49. Hq.tp.: "around" instead of "round"
50. Hq.tp.: "the" instead of "their"
51. Hq.tp.: "in" added
52. Hq.tp.: "at" instead of "in"
53. Hq.tp.: "certain colours" added
54. Hq.tp.: "all" added
55. Sk.tp.: "that" written then crossed out, "they" added; Hq.tp.: "they" instead of "that"
56. Hq.tp.: "in" instead of "into"

that calls[57] it five senses, but there is one sense, and so all that is audible and all that is visible is one and the same. It is that[58] which is called in Sanskrit [*purusha* and *prakriti*][59]. In the terms of the Sufis it[60] is known [as *zat* and *sifat*][61], the manifestation of it is called [sifat][62], the outer appearance. It is in its[63] manifestation as [sifat][62] that one sees the distinction or the difference of that which is visible and [64]audible. In its[65] real aspect of being, it is[66] one and the same. In[67] that plane of existence where it is[66] one and the same, according to Sufi mystics, that plane of existence[68] is called [zat][69], that knowledge of the inner existence in which one sees the source and goal of all things.

What principally I wish to explain today is this, that the[70] colour and sound is[71] a language, a language which can be understood not only in the external life but also in the inner life. For the physician, the[72] colour has a great significance; for the chemist, the[72] colour has a great significance. The more[73] one goes in the science of medicine, in the science of chemistry, the more one recognizes the value of colour, that each element and the development of every object, or the changement[74] of every object is distinguishable by [75]changing [76]the colour. And[77] the physicians of the old used to recognize diseases by the colour of the face and form. And even today there exist physicians, the[78] principal [79]thing that is in their hand to recognize the principal way through which

57. Hq.tp.: ". They call" instead of "and that calls"
58. Hq.tp.: "this" instead of "that"
59. Od.tp., Sk.tp.: a space, missing words; Hq.tp.: "Purusha and Prakriti". For *purusha* and *prakriti* see Glossary
60. Hq.tp.: "this" instead of "it"
61. Hq.tp.: "as *zat* and *sifat*" added. For *zat* and *sifat* see *dhat* and *sifat* in Glossary.
62. Od.tp., Sk.tp.: a space, missing words; Hq.tp.: "Sifat"
63. Hq.tp.: "the" instead of "its"
64. Hq.tp.: "that which is" added
65. Hq.tp.: "their" instead of "its"
66. Hq.tp.: "they are" instead of "it is"
67. Hq.tp.: "In" omitted
68. Hq.tp.: "that plane of existence" omitted
69. Od.tp., Sk.tp.: a space, missing word(s); Hq.tp.: "zat"
70. Hq.tp.: "What principally I wish to explain today is this, that the" omitted
71. Hq.tp.: "are" instead of "is"
72. Hq.tp.: "the" omitted
73. Hq.tp.: "deeper" instead of "more"
74. Hq.tp.: "change" instead of "changement", French for "change"
75. Hq.tp.: "the" added
76. Hq.tp.: "of" added
77. Hq.tp.: "And" omitted
78. Hq.tp.: "whose" instead of "the"

they recognize[79] the complaint [80]man has is from the colour in his eyes, on the tongue, on the nails, on the skin. In every condition it is colour which is expressive of the condition of the man[81]. Also in the[82] objects [83]and the changement[74] of the object is recognized by the changing[84] of colours[85]. And[86] the psychologists have recognized [87]condition of things, of objects, by the sound, and[88] persons by their voice. What person[89] he is, whether strong or weak, what is his character, and what are his inclinations, what is his attitude to[90] life, his outlook on life, all that is known and understood by his voice.

But colour and sound is[91] not the only[92] language that[93] one communicates with life without, but also this is[94] the language with[95] which one communicates with life within, and[96] one might like to ask how, how is it done? And[97] the answer is that we today see some scientific experiments; some make certain plates. By speaking near their plate, one makes with the sound and with vibrations marks upon that plate and those marks make either harmonious forms or inharmonious forms. If that is true, then every person, from morning till evening, [98]what he says by it[99] is making an invisible form in the space. He is creating invisible vibrations around him. He is, therefore, introducing[100] an atmosphere and[101] it is therefore that one person comes into the house and before he speaks you are tired of him, you wish to get rid of him. Before he has said or done anything,

79. Hq.tp.: "way of recognizing" instead of "thing that is in their hand to recognize the principal way through which they recognize"
80. Hq.tp.: "a" added
81. Hq.tp.: "man's condition" instead of "the condition of the man"
82. Hq.tp.: "the" omitted
83. Hq.tp.: "the condition" added
84. Hq.tp.: "change" instead of "changing"
85. Hq.tp.: "colour" instead of "colours"
86. Hq.tp.: "And" omitted
87. Hq.tp.: "the" added
88. Hq.tp.: "of" added
89. Hq.tp.: "kind of a man" instead of "person"
90. Hq.tp.: "toward" instead of "to"
91. Hq.tp.: "are" instead of "is"
92. Hq.tp.: "only the" instead of "the only"
93. Hq.tp.: "by which" instead of "that"
94. Hq.tp.: "they are" instead of "this is"
95. Hq.tp.: "in" instead of "with"
96. Hq.tp.: "and" omitted
97. Hq.tp.: "And" omitted
98. Hq.tp.: "by" added
99. Hq.tp.: "by it" omitted
100. Hq.tp.: "producing" instead of "introducing"
101. Hq.tp.: a semi colon instead of "and"

you are finished with him, you would like him to go away, for he is creating in his atmosphere[102]; there is a sound going on, a sound which is disagreeable. There is another person with whom you feel sympathy, to whom you feel drawn, whose friendship you value, whose presence you long for. There is harmony which is continually created through him. That is a sound too.

If that is true, then it is not only the external signs, but it is the inner condition also which is audible and visible, though not visible to the eyes and not audible to the ears, and yet it is audible and visible in[103] the soul. We say, "I feel his vibrations, I feel the person's presence," either, "I feel sympathy" or "an antipathy against[104] that person," but there is[105] a feeling, and the person creates a feeling without having said anything or done anything. Therefore, a person who is in a wrong vibration, without doing wrong, without saying wrong, he creates the wrong atmosphere and you find a fault with himself.

It is most amusing and very funny to see in life you meet people who bring to you a complaint, "I have said nothing, I have done nothing, and yet people dislike me, and yet people are against me." That person does not know, it is not saying or doing, what you are[106] says[107] louder than what you speak[108], it is being[109]. It is life itself which has its tone, which has[110] its colour, which has[110] its vibration. It speaks aloud and one may think where it is[111] and what it is[111] and where is it to be found? And the answer is that what little man knows about himself is only about his body. If you tell [112]man to point out where he is, he will point out this arm, this hand, this body. He knows little further than that. There are many whom[113] you ask, "But where do you think? Is your body thinking?"[114] "Yes," he

---

102. Hq.tp.: "a sound" added
103. Hq.tp.: "to" instead of "in"
104. Hq.tp.: "to" instead of "against"
105. Od.tp., Sk.tp.: "is" underlined for emphasis
106. Od.tp., Sk.tp.: "are" underlined for emphasis
107. Hq.tp.: "speaks" instead of "says"
108. Hq.tp.: "say" instead of "speak"
109. Od.tp., Sk.tp.: "being" underlined for emphasis
110. Hq.tp.: "which has" omitted
111. Hq.tp.: "is it" instead of "it is"
112. Hq.tp.: "a" added
113. Hq.tp.: "who, if" instead of "whom"
114. Hq.tp.: "'But where do you think in your body?'" instead of "but where do you think? Is your body thinking?"

says[115], "my brain[116]." [117]He limits himself in that little physical region which is called body, thus making himself much smaller compared to what he really is.[117]

The reality is that man is one individual with two ends, just like one line with two ends. If you look at the ends it is two; if you look at the line it is one. The one end of the line is limited, limitedness, the other end of the line is unlimited. One end is man, the other end God. Man forgets that end and knows only this end of which he is conscious, and it is the consciousness of limitedness which makes him more limited. Otherwise he has a greater scope to approach that unlimited[118] which is within himself, which is only the other end of the same line, the line which he calls, or which he considers to be himself.

And when a mystic speaks of [self-knowledge][119], it is not[120] to know how old I am, or how good I am, or how bad I am, or how right or wrong I am, it is[121] to know the other part of one's being, that deeper, subtler aspect of one's being. It is in[122] the knowledge of that being that the fulfilment of a[123] life depends. And[124] one might ask, "How can one get nearer to it, how can one get closer to it?" The way that the people[125], those who search[126] after truth, those who sought after God, those who wished to analyse themselves, those who wished to sympathize with life, they have found[127] one way and that is the same way of vibrations. It is again the same way of old, that by the help of sound they have prepared themselves. They made these physical atoms which in time became[128] deadened, they made them[129] live again by the help of sound. As [Zeb-un-

---

115. Hq.tp.: "say" instead of "Yes, he says"
116. Hq.tp.: "Thinking, yes, in my brain" instead of "my brain"
117. Hq.tp.: instead of "He limits himself in ..... what he really is.", "They limit themselves to that little physical region which is called body, thus making themselves much smaller compared to what they really are."
118. Sk.tp.: "unlimited" changed by hand to read "unlimitedness"
119. Od.tp., sk.tp.: "self only"; Hq.tp.: "self-knowledge" which seems correct here
120. Hq.tp.: "does not mean" instead of "is not"
121. Hq.tp.: "means" instead of "is"
122. Hq.tp.: "on" instead of "in"
123. Hq.tp.: "a" omitted
124. Hq.tp.: "And" omitted
125. Hq.tp.: "have found" added
126. Hq.tp.: "searched" instead of "search"
127. Hq.tp.: "is" instead of "they have found"
128. Hq.tp.: "had become" instead of "became"
129. Hq.tp.: "they made them" omitted

Nisa][130] says so[131] continually, "That sacred name which will make thee sacred." They have worked with the power of sound. The Hindus have called it [*mantra Yoga*][132]. The Sufis have termed it [*wazifa*][133]. It is the power of [134]word which works upon each atom of [134] body, making it sonorous, making it a communicative medium[135] between [134]external life and between [134]inner life. The[136] first one begins to realize as the first experiment[137] of one's spiritual development is that one begins to feel communicative[138] with living beings, not only with human beings, but with animals, with birds, with trees and with plants. It is not an old tale that people tell that the saints used to speak with the trees and with[139] the plants. You can speak today if you are communicative[140]. It was not the ancient times[141] which were blessed, the blessing which was ancient[142] is today, but the old one is not today old, it is new. It is the same soul[143] that was, that is, and that will be and no privilege was ever limited to a period of the world's history. Man has the same privilege today if he will realize that he is privileged.

When he closes himself[144] his heart, when he makes himself covered by the life within and without, he no doubt becomes exclusive, he no doubt becomes cut away from this whole manifestation which is one whole and which is not divided. It is man himself who divides himself; if not, life is undivided, indivisible. And it is by[145] opening communication with the external life which makes man wider. Then to[146] his friend he[147] does not say that[148],

---

130. Od.tp., Sk.tp.: a space, indicating missing words; Hq.tp.: "Zeb-un-Nisa" added; for Zeb-un-Nisa see List
131. Hq.tp.: beginning of the quote "'Say" instead of "says so"
132. Od.tp., Sk.tp.: a space, missing words; Hq.tp.: "*mantra Yoga*". For *mantra Yoga* see Glossary.
133. Od.tp., Sk.tp.: missing words; Hq.tp.: "Wazifa". For wazifa see glossary
134. Hq.tp.: "the" added
135. Hq.tp.: "medium of communication" instead of "communicative medium"
136. Hq.tp.: "What" instead of "The"
137. Hq.tp.: "experience" instead of "experiment"
138. Hq.tp.: "in communication" instead of "communicative"
139. Hq.tp.: "with" omitted
140. Hq.tp.: "in communication" instead of "communicative"
141. Hq.tp.: "only" added
142. Hq.tp.: "of old" instead of "ancient"
143. Hq.tp.: "old one" instead of "soul"
144. Hq.tp.: "himself closes" instead of "closes himself"
145. Hq.tp.: "by" omitted
146. Hq.tp.: "of" instead of "to"
147. Hq.tp.: "man" instead of "he"
148. Hq.tp.: "that" omitted

"This is my friend, I love him" but [149]says, "This is myself, I love him." That is the time that he can say that he has arrived at the realization of love. As long as he says, "I feel sympathy with him because he is my friend," his sympathy has not yet been fully wakened. The real wakening of his sympathy is on that day when he sees his friend and says this is himself. There[150] the sympathy is wakened.

Then there is the communication within oneself. Man does not close only oneself[151] from the external, but also he closes oneself[152] from the inner[153] which is a still more important part of one's life, and[154] that inner[155] is also sound, the inner[155] is light, [156]and when one gets in touch with this sound and this light[156] [then][157] one knows that language which is the language of [heaven][158], a language which is expressive of the past and the present and of the future, a language which is revealing of[159] the secret and character of nature, a language which is [receiving][160] and giving that divine message which [161]prophets at times have tried to reveal.

Thank you all for your sympathy, response and[162] God bless you.[163]

---

149. Hq.tp.: "he" added
150. Hq.tp.: "Then" instead of "There"
151. Hq.tp.: "himself only" instead of "only one's self"
152. Hq.tp.: "himself" instead of "one's self"
153. Hq.tp.: "part" added
154. Hq.tp.: "and" omitted
155. Hq.tp.: "part" added
156. Hq.tp.: "and when one gets in touch with this sound and this light" omitted
157. Hq.tp.: ". Then" instead of "than"; od.tp., sk.tp.: "than"
158. Od.tp.: "giving"; Hq.tp.: "heaven" instead of "giving"
159. Hq.tp.: "reveals" instead of "is revealing of"
160. Sk.tp., od.tp.: "believing"; Hq.tp.: "receiving" instead of "believing"
161. Hq.tp.: "the" added
162. Sk.tp.: "and" moved before "response"
163. Hq.tp.: "To be read at the Meeting of the World Brotherhood." instead of "Thank you ... bless you."

Murshida Sherifa Goodenough's handwriting

January 1st, 1925

[1]

Pasi Anfas[2]

The mechanism of the human body shows[3] nervous system as its principal battery in which magnetism is prepared by the action of breath. It is[4] when the nervous system cannot function, then[5] this battery[6] gets out of order and does not work properly. Many, in order to make this battery of the nervous system work properly, take drugs and other medicines which stimulate the nervous system. But instead of giving power to it, they take away power from it, and in the end the nervous system becomes accustomed to all such medicines one takes.

The nourishment of the nervous system is what breath attracts from the space. As far as science goes, it says one gets into one's system oxygen. The mystic goes further in saying that[7] not only oxygen but that life and intelligence, that power and radiance which makes the nervous system in perfect order, the result of which is not only good health but ever[8]-increasing[9] magnetism, which comes forth from the person in his thought, speech, movement and action, charging his atmosphere with magnetism which[10] surrounds

Documents:

Gd.hw. =	Murshida Sherifa Goodenough's handwritten report of the lecture.
Gd.tp. =	a typescript made by Murshida Sherifa Goodenough, nearly identical with her handwriting.
Hq.st. =	a stencil, prepared at Headquarters, Geneva, for the Gatha series, identical in wording to Gd.tp.
Hq.tp. =	a typescript, prepared for the Gatha series, identical to Hq.st. and therefore not mentioned in the footnotes.

Notes:

1. Gd.hw.: "Gatha" added; Gd.tp.: date omitted, the Sufi Invocation added, followed by "Series III" and "GATHA." and "Number 8." then in the next line "PASI ANFAS" and "BREATH"; Hq.st.: date omitted, "Series III. GATHA: Number 8." added followed by the Sufi Invocation, followed by "PASI ANFAS." and "BREATH." in the next line
2. Gd.hw.: "III.8" added; for Pasi Anfas, see Glossary
3. A.o.d.: "the" added
4. Gd.hw.: "the lack of" written, then crossed out and omitted in a.o.d.
5. A.o.d.: "that" instead of "then"
6. Gd.hw.: "becomes closed" written, then crossed out and omitted in a.o.d.
7. A.o.d.: "that" omitted
8. Gd.hw.: an illegible word crossed out possibly "springing"
9. Gd.hw.: "ever" and "increasing" written above the line
10. Gd.hw.: "stands" written, then crossed out and omitted in a.o.d.

him as a fortification and protection against all influences, physical and mental, thus making man live a fuller life.

[11]

---

11. Gd.hw.: "A skeleton outline of thought for circulation among the members of the Senior Study Circle only." added; Hq.st.: "A skeleton outline of thought for circulation among the members of the S.S.C." added

Sakina Furnée's shorthand reporting

Baronne d'Eichthal's, Paris
January 3rd, 1925

Science and Psychology

[1]Today I would like to speak on the subject of science and psychology[2]. The day when science and psychology[2] will come to a[3] certain understanding, on that day the knowledge will become complete. But when the word psychology I use,[4] I mean psychology in the sense that I mean[5], not in the sense as is understood by everyone. For the psychology which[6] is known as a new philosophy, it[7] is in its primitive condition. What I mean by psychology is that which bridges material science with esotericism. In order to go[8] further in this subject, I should mention first that the name[9] "matter" and "spirit" are for our convenience. As far as we perceive life as something tangible, we call it matter. And what is not as tangible as a substance, but perceivable, then that we call [spirit][10], the knowledge of which we call psychology. But esotericism is that knowledge which is gained not by perception, nor by tangibility of substance, but by revelation. And so we can divide the three different aspects of science[11] in these three names[12]: science, psychology, esotericism. Science cannot be complete without

---

Documents:

Sk.sh. = Sakina Furnée's shorthand reporting of the lecture, newly transcribed by B.v.d.B.

Km.tp. = a typescript prepared by Kismet Stam.

bk. = the book *Philosophy, Psychology, Mysticism* (Heijnis, Zaandick, Netherlands, 1956).

Notes:

1. Km.tp.: "Beloved ones of God," added
2. Sk.sh.: "sc." and "sy.", abbr. for "science" and "psychology"; bk.: "Today I would ... and psychology" omitted
3. Sh.sh.: "an understate" written, then crossed out
4. Bk.: "But then I use the word psychology in a specific sense" instead of "But when the word psychology I use"
5. Bk.: "intend" instead of "mean"
6. Bk.: "nowadays" added
7. Bk.: "it" omitted
8. A.o.d.: "get" instead of "go"
9. Bk.: "terms" instead of "name"
10. Sk.sh.: "sy." in sh., abbr. for "psychology", apparently written by mistake; a.o.d.: "spirit"
11. Bk.: "knowledge" instead of "science"
12. Bk.: "groups" instead of "names"

psychology, nor psychology can[13] be complete without esotericism. It is these three that make knowledge complete and by this[14] that one can hope to understand life more fully.

There is a vast field of knowledge in the realm of psychology[15]: the knowledge of imagination and the same turning into thought; the knowledge of feeling and the same turning into emotion; the knowledge of passion and the same turning into expression; the knowledge of impulse, [16]its outlet; the knowledge of impulse and its suppression; the knowledge of attraction and the knowledge of its contrary effect; sympathy and antipathy, their origin and source, all these belong to psychology. Therefore, psychology is a knowledge of tangible things, yet not of solid things that one can touch. And therefore it is more difficult to explain the laws of psychology[17] in words than explaining the laws of the material science. A perception must be developed in order to understand psychology better, and insight into life must be obtained in order to understand psychology better. It is the understanding of a law working behind the screen which is real psychology. It is the understanding of cause and effect in everything, in every action, in every aspect, and it is a stepping stone towards esotericism because it is psychological attitude which leads one to esoteric knowledge. The person who cannot see the truth of esotericism or mysticism[18] is[19] because he is backward[20] in psychology. If a person is not able to see the hidden law, he will not be able to see that hidden love which is called in the scripture[21] "God". Esotericism[22], therefore, is quite a contrary process of learning to the process by which science is learned. For science is learned by analysis; esotericism is obtained by synthesis. If a person, while wanting to obtain esoteric knowledge, turns things into bits, he is analysing them. As long as he is analyzing them,[23]he will never come to the understanding of esotericism.

---

13. Bk.: "can" moved before "psychology"
14. A.o.d.: "it is by these" instead of "by this"
15. Sk.sh.: a blank
16. A.o.d.: "and" added
17. Sk.sh.: "sy." indistinctly written, abbr. for "psychology"
18. Km.tp.: "it" added
19. Bk.: "ignorant" added
20. Sk.sh.: "backward" encircled
21. Bk.: "scriptures" instead of "scripture"
22. Sk.sh.: "Esotericism" indistinctly written
23. Sk.sh.: "he will not" written, then crossed out

Psychology needs two things, analyzing and synthesizing. And by understanding psychology better, when one has accustomed oneself to synthesize as well as to analyse, then he[24] prepares himself[25] to[26] synthesize[27] only in order to understand esotericism more fully. Therefore, it is quite different to acquire esoteric knowledge from acquiring the knowledge of science. [28]It is like going to the north in acquiring for[29] one thing and going to the south for acquiring another thing. The ancient people, therefore, made the knowledge of the[30] science of psychology and of esotericism as one knowledge, and they called it alchemy. And it was very convenient to explain to the simpleton; they said: turning [steel][31] into gold. Therefore, many who sought gold in life[32], they went into the pursuit of learning this alchemy. And some who went to the end, instead of finding gold, they became gold.

There is a story told in the East which explains this idea in an interesting form. A king was anxious to find some man who really knew alchemy. Many came, but at[33] the end of examination, they found that they could not make gold. In the end someone told him that there is in a village a person living who is simple, most unassuming[34], but they say that he has the knowledge of alchemy. The king sent for him immediately, and he was brought in the presence of the monarch. When he was brought in the court, the king desired[35] his wish for[36] learning alchemy[37]. And he told him that whatever he will ask for it, he[38] will be given[39].

"No," said the man. "I do not know any such thing as you ask." The king said, "Everyone told me, everyone said that you are

---

24. Bk.: "one" instead of "he"
25. Bk.: "oneself" instead of "himself"
26. Sk.sh.: "right" written (or "write"), but omitted in a.o.d.
27. Sk.sh.: "synthesize" indistinctly written
28. Bk.: This long passage: "It is like going to the North ... The other process through which the king demanded, that was not the right way acquiring that knowledge; that knowledge never came through that process." omitted
29. Km.tp.: "for acquiring" instead of "in acquiring for"
30. Km.tp.: "the" crossed out in hw.
31. Sh.sh.: "silver" written, then crossed out, then "steel" in lh. added above; an illegible sh. symbol below crossed out; Km.tp.: "steel"
32. Sk.sh.: a blank, then "it" added above
33. Km.tp.: "in" instead of "at"
34. Sk.sh.: a semi-circle is drawn around "un"
35. Km.tp.: "expressed" instead of "desired"
36. Km.tp.: "of" instead of "for"
37. Sk.sh.: "alch." abbr. for "alchemy"
38. Km.tp.: "he" omitted
39. Km.tp.: "to him" added

the person who knows it." "No, King," he said. "No,[40] you have found the wrong person; I am not the person who knows it." "Look here," said the king, "I am going to give you a sentence for your whole life in the[41] prison." He said, "Whatever you wish to do, you may do; you have found the wrong person for what you want." "Well," the king said, "I will give you six weeks to think and till then you will be in prison. In the end of the six weeks, I am going to[42] have you put to death." He was put to the[43] prison, and every morning the king came to the prison and said, "Now have you changed your mind, can you teach me? Now death is approaching, take care, give that knowledge to me." He said, "No, King, go to someone else who has got what you want. I am not the person that you are seeking for." And at night every night, the king went as a porter, and swept the floor and dusted the room, and took food for him, and sympathized for[44] him, and did everything he could do for him, as a servant could do for him. He asked him, "Is your head aching? Can I do something for you? Are you tired, can I make your bed for you to lie down? Shall I fan for you to sleep? It is hot, it is warm." Everything that a person could do, he did at that time. And so days passed and one day remained, the next day of which was appointed for this man to be beheaded. The king visited him every morning and told him, "Now you see, there is only one day remaining before your death, and this is your last opportunity of saving your life." He said, "No, King, you are looking for someone else, not for me." But at night when that porter came, this man said, putting his hand on his shoulders[45], he said, "Poor man, poor porter, you are so sympathetic. I will whisper in your ears a word, a word of alchemy, and that alchemy will change you from steel to gold." This porter said, "I do not know what you say, alchemy. I only know to serve you, and only I am sorry that tomorrow you will be beheaded; that is the[46] one thing that tears my heart. I only wish that I would give my life to save yours; [47]I would be most [thankful][48]."

The alchemist said that, "It is better for me to die rather than

40. Km.tp.: "No," omitted
41. Km.tp.: "the" omitted
42. Sk.sh.: "give you a life's sentence" written, then crossed out
43. Km.tp.: "to the" corr. in hw to read "into"
44. Km.tp.: "with" instead of "for"
45. Km.tp.: "shoulder" instead of "shoulders"
46. Sk.sh.: "only" written, then crossed out
47. Sk.sh.: "I will" written, then crossed out
48. Sk.sh.: "grateful" retraced to read "thankful"; Km.tp.: "thankful"

give alchemy to the unworthy. It is the same thing which I give you just now in sympathy, by[49] appreciation, in love, which I do not give to that king which will now tomorrow take my life. Why is it? It is because you deserve it; the king does not deserve." He whispered in his ears the words of secret. Instead making gold, he became gold. In the morning the king came to give him the last warning. He said, "Now there is your last chance. Now that moment has come that you must be beheaded. Now you must give or you go to the place where[50] you ought to be beheaded." He said, "No, not[51]." The king said, "Yes, you have already given me." He said, "Did I give you? I did not give to the king, I gave to the porter."

This beautiful story gives us an insight[52] into the idea. That process through which the king went through[53] as a porter, it is that process through which the knowledge of esotericism is to be gained. The other process through which the king demanded, that[54] was not the right way of acquiring that[55] knowledge; that knowledge never came[56] through that process.[27]

[57]The difficulty of esoteric[58] knowledge at the present time is only this, that man trained in science is not yet capable of attaining to the esoteric knowledge, unless he [went][59] through the process of psychological knowledge. In order to enter the gates of mysticism, the first thing for man is to understand what feeling is, what service is, what[60] sympathy is, what sincerity is.

It is a great fault of the learning today that sentimental side is kept apart, which is the most important side. It is like wanting a person to come, but not with his life, but as a corpse. In order to educate a person, the life should be taken out of him and turn him from a living person to a dead one. Therefore, we find the death of heroism; therefore, we find the death of idealism; therefore, we find the death of souls who have made impressions upon humanity and which have lasted for thousands and thousands of years. What is to

49. Km.tp.: "in" instead of "by"
50. Sk.sh.: "you will be beheaded" written, then crossed out
51. Km.tp.: "no" instead of "not"
52. Sk.sh.: "to the" written, then crossed out
53. Km.tp.: "through" crossed out by hand
54. Km.tp.: "that" crossed out by hand
55. Km.tp.: "that" corr. in hw. to read "this"
56. Km.tp.: "comes" instead of "came"
57. Bk.: "And" added
58. Sk.sh.: "es." in lh abbr. for "esoteric"
59. Sk.sh.: "bent" retraced to read "went"; a.o.d.: "went"
60. Sk.sh.: an illegible symbol crossed out

be revived in the present generation is the capacity of feeling. It is the thinking which is developed today, but not the feeling. Because thinking is not enough, after thinking comes feeling, after feeling comes seeing. And it is this seeing which is known in the English word "seer"[61].

- - - - - - - - - - - - - - - - - - -

Q.: Which[62] is the best way in education to develop that feeling in children?

A.: I think people at home are more responsible for it than at school because this is the first work of home. But if at home such education is given and at school it is spoiled, then of course there is of [63] inharmony[64]. For instance, I will give you an example: a nurse was telling the children that you must keep your toy; you must not take away the toy [of][65] another child when they were quarrelling [over][66] one another's [toys][67]. The nurse taught them, "No, each of you have your own; the other one has not the right to touch the toys of the other." It was just, but it was not love. Then another one came who knew about it and who said to each child, "No, all the toys belong to all of you, and the best thing is to give one's toys to the other, that you all play with each other's toys. Do you not like to see your brother or your sister playing with your[68] toy? You ought to be delighted to see that your brother or sister is playing with it." Well, that is the feeling that must be developed. This crude way in which sometimes people want to work[69] up high ideals by troubling and fighting, that is not the way. The best way is the way of love, of harmony and[70] sympathy. And for that, feeling must be developed instead of thought. The present generation has made a great advancement in thought, but that is not enough. Now what is needed is that battery which stands behind thought, and that is feeling.

---

61. Sk.sh.: "seer" repeated in lh. and encircled
62. Km.tp.: "What" instead of "Which"
63. Km.tp.: "an" instead of "of"
64. Sk.sh.: first "in" in lh. written then "harmony" and encircled together
65. Sk.sh.: "a" apparently written; Km.tp.: "of" instead of "a"
66. Sh.sh.: "of" retraced to read "over"; Km.tp.: "over"
67. Sh.sh.: "choice" retraced to read "toys"; Km.tp.: "toy"
68. Sk.sh.: "your" retraced to read "all", but "your" in Km.tp.
69. Sk.sh.: "work" retraced without creating a readable new sh. symbol
70. Km.tp.: ", of" instead of "and"

Nargis Dowland's handwriting

January 7th, 1925

Absolute Radiance

Absolute is a radiance; this radiance is audible and visible by nature because it is [1]motion, a vibration naturally. Therefore, the same radiance is vibration and vibration is radiance; it is its contraction which centralizes it. The outer physical radiance is centralized in the sun; the inner radiance is centred in the divine spirit.

The sun, therefore, may be called the body of the divine spirit. The ancient peoples worshipped the sun but later on at an advanced stage of humanity the prophets taught[2] the divine spirit to be worshipped and that the sun was only an outer manifestation. Nevertheless, the mystery of the sun reveals the mystery of the divine spirit, for one throws its light upon all things making them visible and the other, namely divine spirit[3], throws its light upon all that is within and without, revealing the earth and the heavens. "God is the light of the earth and heaven"[4] (Qur'an). Life shows the same nature[5] in every aspect of its manifestation, centralizing and then expressing. Thus life acts and reacts, as souls and objects. The planets are the semi-centralization of the sun. Some stars, demi-semi-centres, where the light of the sun functions, though from a scientific point of view different[6] in nature and character from the sun, but still from the[7] view of the mystic the same manifestation in a lesser degree.

Documents:

Nd.hw. = a handwritten document by Nargis Dowland. Munira van Voorst van Beest has a handwritten note in the file: "This could be (a report) annotations by Nargis, made after a lecture or personal talk by Murshid. Or telepathic message?" On the back of the last sheet, an insert "x how mighty was the power of a faithful man", although no insertion point is indicated in the text.

Notes:
1. Nd.hw.: "a" written, then crossed out
2. Nd.hw.: "the Sp." written, then crossed out
3. Nd.hw.: "D.Spt." abbreviation for "Divine Spirit"
4. Sura XXIV (an Noor), verse 35, "God is the light of the heavens and the earth."
5. Nd.hw.: "life shows" written, then crossed out
6. Nd.hw.: actually "diff:" written here
7. Nd.hw.: an illegible word, which looks like "syntheien", possibly meaning "synthetic", followed by, a letter, possibly "p", which is crossed out

Man lives on these planets and is like a drop in the ocean in them, and yet that is his limited self. Man's perfect self is larger, incomparably larger than the planets he lives on, for he is[8] a ray of this divine spirit which is the soul of the sun, of which the physical sun is the body.

– Murshid

---

8. Nd.hw.: "the" written, then crossed out

Sakina Furnée's shorthand reporting

Paris, Baronnne d'Eichthal,
January 10th, 1925

Psychology[1 2]

Beloved ones of God,

I should like to speak [this][3] afternoon on a subject concerning psychology, especially what we may acknowledge[4] and what we may not acknowledge in life.[5] What generally happens is this, that man acknowledges what he must not acknowledge, and he does not acknowledge what he should[6] acknowledge in life. As a rule, it is best never to acknowledge a fact that he[7] does not wish to give life to. For instance, when a person begins to see that his friend is not as kind, is not as affectionate, is not as pleased as he ought to be as a friend, and[8] as soon as he acknowledges it, he at [once][9] gives strength to something which so far has been a shadow. A person who feels that[10], "Everyone in my family, in my surroundings, they [dislike][11] me, they disapprove of me," that,[12] "I have a tiring effect upon them," he certainly gives a[13] life to that fact.

A friend came to me and said, "I do not know what kind of bad planet has its influence upon me, that since last three years,

---

Documents:

Sk.sh.	=	Sakina Furnée's shorthand reporting of the lecture, newly transcribed by B.v.d.B.
Sk.tp.	=	a typescript prepared by Sakina Furnée, showing editorial changes.
Hq.tp.	=	a typescript prepared at Headquarters, Geneva, for distribution to Sufi Centres, showing many editorial changes.
od.tp.	=	an old typescript of uncertain provenance, showing editorial changes.

Notes:

1. Sk.sh.: "Psychology" added above the text; Hq.tp.: "GATHEKA. Number 48." followed by the Sufi Invocation instead of "Psychology"
2. A.o.d.: "What we may acknowledge and what we may not acknowledge in life." added as a subtitle
3. Sk.sh.: "the" retraced to read "this"; Sk.tp.: "this"
4. Sk.sh.: "acknowledge" added in lh.
5. Hq.tp.: "Beloved ones ... not acknowledge in life." omitted
6. Sk.sh.: "not" written, then crossed out
7. Hq.tp.: "one" instead of "he"
8. Hq.tp.: "and" omitted
9. Sk.sh.: "as" retraced to read "once"; a.o.d. have "once"
10. Hq.tp.: "that," omitted
11. Sk.sh.: "dislike" traced through a now illegible symbol; Hq.tp.: "dislikes" instead of "they dislike"
12. Hq.tp.: "that" omitted
13. A.o.d.: "a" omitted

everything I touch goes wrong; nothing do I touch that brings success or pleasure." I asked, "How long?" and she[14] said, "[15]Three years now." I said, "I am very sorry, you have come too[16] late. And yet it is not too late. But for three years you have given fuel[17] to this fire." The friend asked, "How did I give fuel to this fire?" "By your acknowledging[18] it," I answered[19]. What happens is that[20] every little fact that has a bad effect upon one's life, if we acknowledge it, we give a[21] life from our own to that fact and thus make it a living thing. And so it is with many illnesses also. Very often people get in[22] a habit of saying, "Oh, I am so tired." For them it is not necessary that they should cut stones or [cut][23] woods[24] or carry wood or carry stones. You[25] will be tired before doing it. They need not wait for an action, for a thing to make them tired. No sooner they think of tiredness, [26]it is there. There are many cases where there is no need of[27] being tired, and the person is tired by the fact of having acknowledged it. The same thing with sleeplessness. Once you acknowledge to yourself, "I cannot sleep," that is enough as a cause to keep you awake [all][28] night. There are many illnesses of this kind, especially the acknowledging of depression. [To][29] acknowledge that[30] I am depressed, I am sad, that[31] certainly there may be no other reason of[32] being depressed[33], of[34] [being][35] sad; the

---

14. Hq.tp.: "he" instead of "she"
15. Hq.tp.: "For" added
16. Sk.sh.: "too" crossed out, but a.o.d. have "too"
17. Sk.sh.: "fuel" retraced for clarity
18. Sk.sh.: the last syllable "ing" of "acknowledging" is missing; this will not be further mentioned
19. Sk.sh.: "By ... it", "I answered"; these parts are encircled; a.o.d.: "I answered" moved before "'By your acknowledging it,'"
20. Hq.tp.: "this" instead of "that"
21. Hq.tp.: "a" omitted
22. Hq.tp.: "into" instead of "in"
23. Sk.sh.: "get" retraced to read "cut"; a.o.d.: "cut"
24. Hq.tp.: "wood" instead of "woods"
25. A.o.d.: "They" instead of "You"
26. Hq.tp.: "than" added
27. Sk.sh.: "of" crossed out; a.o.d. have "of"
28. Sk.sh.: "of" retraced to read "all"; a.o.d.: "all"
29. Sk.sh.: "Over" appears to be written, but a.o.d. have "To" instead of "Over"
30. Hq.tp.: "that" omitted
31. Hq.tp.: "that" omitted
32. Hq.tp.: "for" instead of "of"
33. Sk.sh.: "depr." abbr. for "depressed"
34. Hq.tp.: "for" instead of "of"
35. Sk.sh.: "being" inserted; a.o.d. have "being"

very fact of acknowledging that[36] I am sad, it[37] will make a person sad.

[38]One who will acknowledge this life[39] to be his friend[40]. [41]The one who will acknowledge this[42] life to be his enemy, this[43] life will prove in every way to be his enemy. There are many who take note[44] of those who are working against them, and[45] especially by taking note[46] of it, they make them do so more, because they make impression upon them. But you might say, "But[47] does there not exist any animosity in persons, without thinking about it?" Yes, there may exist, but[48] by taking note[49] of it, by acknowledging it, you give a[50] life to it. If you do not[51] acknowledge it, it will die in time. For animosity is a fire, but not a perpetual fire. For[52] it is [the][53] acknowledging it which gives the fire the fuel. If you do not acknowledge it, the fire will extinguish[54].

Many might say that it is hypocrisy not to acknowledge a fact, but that hypocrisy[55] is better than the truth. But in fact that cannot[56] be called a hypocrisy when you know its meaning, its worth, its understanding. That doctor is not[57] hypocrite who says to his patient, even seeing that his patient has a[58] high fever, who says,[59] "It is all right, it is all right, it is nothing." By saying that that[60] exists,[61]

---

36. Hq.tp.: "that" omitted
37. Sk.tp.: "it" omitted
38. Hq.tp.: "To the" added
39. Sk.sh.: "this life" written again, then crossed out
40. Sk.tp.: "the life will prove to be his friend" added; Hq.tp.: "life will prove to be his friend"
41. Hq.tp.: "To" added
42. Hq.tp.: "this" omitted
43. Hq.tp.: "this" omitted
44. A.o.d.: "notice" instead of "note"
45. Sk.sh.: "at that" written, then crossed out
46. Sk.sh.: "notice" added in lh.; a.o.d.: "notice"
47. Sk.sh.: an indecipherable sh. symbol
48. Sk.sh.: "but" in sh. indistinctly written
49. A.o.d.: "notice" instead of "note"
50. Hq.tp.: "a" omitted
51. Sk.sh.: "take note" written, then crossed out
52. Hq.tp.: "For" omitted
53. Sk.sh.: "an" retraced to read "the"; a.o.d.: "the"
54. Hq.tp.: "be extinguished" instead of "extinguish"
55. Sk.sh.: "H." abbr. for "hypocrisy"
56. Hq.tp.: "is not to" instead of "cannot"
57. A.o.d.: "a" added
58. Hq.tp.: "a" omitted
59. Hq.tp.: "who says," omitted
60. Sk.sh.: a blank, then "fever" added; Sk.tp.: "that" omitted; Hq.tp.: "it" instead of "that"
61. Sk.tp.: "exists," omitted

there is a high fever, he will certainly increase the fever of the patient, and many doctors do so. [62]Everything a physician or a religious man does to make a person who is in[63] his death[bed][64] think of death, he only encourages him towards death, he is pushing him towards death. One could prove a greater friend to his friend, the one[65] who is up[66] his deathbed, not to acknowledge[67] his trouble, his difficulty, his coming death. I have heard of many people[68] as soon as the doctor thinks that he has given up hope, the whole family begins[69] to talk about it to him[70] and his departure is hastened six months before[71].

And now coming to the question,[72] What must we acknowledge? That which we always escape from acknowledging, and that is our faults. By acknowledging our [faults][73], we shall kill[74] them. When we acknowledge them as our enemies, we shall destroy them. But that is the one thing that we want to hide, and that is the one thing that we want to keep [hidden][75], even from our own sight. To look in the face of one's own faults[76] is the best thing to do: to analyse it, to weigh it, to measure it and to understand it better. By this, either one destroys it, or one understands it, or one does turn the same fault into [a][77] merit. Very often people think it is wise to tell a person that, "No, you are not my friend; no, you have not been very attentive to me, very kind to me." All these things, when a person tells another person[78], even if they were not existing there, he inspires the person with them. Besides, all misfortunes, all dangers that threaten, that frighten man, very often they are not so great as man

62. Hq.tp.: "By" added
63. Hq.tp.: "on" instead of "in"
64. Sk.sh.: "both" retraced to read "bed", "deathbed" added in lh; a.o.d.: "deathbed"
65. Hq.tp.: "the one" omitted
66. Sk.tp.: "in" instead of "up"; Hq.tp.: "on"
67. Hq.tp.: "by not acknowledging" instead of "not to acknowledge"
68. Hq.tp.: "cases where" instead of "people"
69. Sk.sh.: "speaks" added, retraced to an illegible sh. symbol, then both crossed out
70. Hq.tp.: "the patient" instead of "him"
71. Hq.tp.: "by six month" instead of "six month before"
72. Hq.tp.: "And now coming to the question," omitted
73. Sk.sh.: "fault" instead of "faults"
74. Sk.sh.: "kill" added in lh.
75. Sk.sh.: "hid" instead of "hidden"
76. Hq.tp.: "fault" instead of "faults"
77. Sk.sh.: "of" retraced to read "a"
78. Hq.tp.: "When a person tells another these things" instead of "All these ... tells another person"

thinks; [they][79] can be avoided[80] if man did not acknowledge them. For it is[81] the particular pitch to which the heart is tuned that[82] a person feels about the danger. For instance, ten persons standing before the same danger: if one can weigh their fear, one will find that the degree of[83] fear that the persons[84] have is very different, one from the other[85].

There is an interesting story of [86]Prophet Muhammad, when once they were exiled and there[87] their[88] enemies [89]pursuing them in the desert. A disciple was with the Prophet. They were standing behind a rock, and the running of the many horses was being[90] heard. "Oh, Prophet," said the disciple, "they are pursuing us, they are many, they are many —it is an army behind us." "Oh, they are going somewhere else," said the Prophet.[91] "They are coming here; I hear it." "They will go to some other direction," said the Prophet. "But what shall we do if they came[92] here? How many they are and we are only two." "Are we two?" said the Prophet; "No, three —you, I, and God."

For everyone does not look at the[93] danger at[94] the same point of view[95]. To one, the smallest thing is too great; for the other, the greatest thing is nothing. It is as one views it. Once you see the danger great, you will make it more great. And by not acknowledging the greatness of the danger, you will diminish its greatness.[96]

And[97] there is another thing what[98] one must acknowledge. One must acknowledge in one's friend, in one's companion, in those

---

79. Sk.sh.: "which" appears to be written; a.o.d.: "they" instead of "which"
80. Sk.sh.: "avoided" written in lh., then "averted", "eviter", French for "to avoid" in lh. added and crossed out; Sk.tp.: "averted"; Hq.tp.: "avoided"
81. Hq.tp.: "depends upon" instead of "is"
82. Hq.tp.: "how" instead of "that"
83. Sk.sh.: an illegible symbol added and crossed out
84. Hq.tp.: "they" instead of "the persons"
85. Hq.tp.: "in each of them" instead of "one from the other"
86. Hq.tp.: "the" added
87. Sk.sh.: illegible symbols crossed out; a.o.d.: "there" omitted
88. Hq.tp.: "the" instead of "their"
89. Hq.tp.: "were" added
90. Hq.tp.: "being" omitted
91. Sk.sh.: a blank
92. Hq.tp.: "come" instead of "came"
93. Hq.tp.: "the" omitted
94. Sk.tp., Hq.tp.: "at" corr. by hand to read "from"
95. Sk.sh.: "p.o.v." abbr. for "point of view"
96. Hq.tp.: here Gd. inserted an edited version of the 2nd qa. after the lecture
97. Hq.tp.: "And" omitted
98. Hq.tp.: "that" instead of "what"

one wishes to help[99], the good part in their character. By acknowledging it, by noticing it, you will fortify it; it will become greater. And do not think that it is against humility even to acknowledge your own merits, because if you are unconscious of your merits, the plant is suffering there without water. [100]By acknowledging one's merit, one's [virtue][101], it is not that[102] one becomes proud or conceited. If one kept oneself from proud or conceit, one can keep oneself of it ....[103] By recognizing it, one certainly waters that plant which is worth rearing.

And now coming from psychological point of view to esoteric point of view.[104] It is the same method you can carry from psychology to esotericism. In the[105] esotericism you have a problem[106] before you. There is a[107] truth which you have to discover, which is covered by a fact. And if you are accustomed to deny a fact in order to discover[108] a truth, then[109] you are ready then in the esoteric work to deny this[110] fact which hides the truth and discover thereby that truth which is worth discovering.[111] And[112] the one who understands this will understand the meaning of all the concentrations and meditations[113] which are studied and practised by the Sufis, that it is all one thing for one purpose; it is all in order to deny that fact in order to establish truth.[114]

- - - - - - - - - - - - - - - - - - -

115

Q.: What kind of fact is it which obscures the truth, which we remove by meditation?

---

99. Sk.sh.: an indecipherable sh. symbol
100. Hq.tp.: "It is not that" added
101. Sk.sh.: "virtue" traced through a now illegible original sh. symbol
102. Hq.tp.: "it is not that" omitted
103. Sk.sh.: this sentence is left unfinished, and so noted by dashes; Sk.tp.: dots instead of "of it"; Hq.tp.: "free of it" instead of "of it" and dots
104. Hq.tp.: this sentence omitted
105. Hq.tp.: "the" omitted
106. Sk.sh.: "problem" indistinctly written
107. Sk.tp.: "a" omitted
108. Sk.sh.: "discover" indistinctly written
109. Hq.tp.: "then" omitted
110. Hq.tp.: "that" instead of "this"
111. Hq.tp.: here Gd. inserted an edited version of the 1st qa. after the lecture
112. Hq.tp.: "And" omitted
113. Hq.tp.: "concentration and meditation"
114. Hq.tp.: "To be read before Candidates for initiation in the Sufi Order." added
115. Sk.sh.: an editorial note in Dutch "Hier begint" meaning "Here begins" crossed out

A.: By explaining the meaning of the word "fact," I should like to say that the fact is a shadow which for the moment represents something which has [116]certain meaning to it, which we [can][117] witness and which at the same time will not continue its reality forever. For instance, a person says, "Sandow[118], in fact, is a strong man." Yes, it is a fact that he is a strong man, but because he will not be eternally strong, that is a fact; it is not a truth. And, therefore, the knowledge of our own existence and the knowledge of the existence of the others, all this knowledge that we have is a changeable knowledge and since it is changeable, it is a fact. Truth is behind it. But when we discover within our own self, and when we discover [in][119] the others that something which is everlasting and will never change, [that][120] is the truth.

Q.: In great trouble, how is one to dominate one's thoughts?
A.: Of course, when conditions have gone so far that it is most difficult to dominate the trouble, then one has to control them[121]. But at the same time, by making a great excitement over it, we shall not make the trouble any lesser[122]; on the other hand, it will be greater. I will tell you a story which is amusing, but at the same time it explains it. There was a prime[123] minister of Hyderabad not long ago. He was one of the ancient royalties who carried with them a certain kind of ideal, manner and culture. And once, sitting at the table, entertaining some foreign friends, it happened that [a][124] part of his palace was set on fire. Of course, as[125] was the custom of the palace not to come hurriedly to tell a news, the aide-de-camp had to come very gently between the dishes and whisper in his ears what was happening. To the great surprise of the aide-de-camp[126], the prime minister only said, "Yes," and went with the other course which had come. And then when there was the [next][127] course coming, he begged their pardon and said, "I will come in a moment." Gently he

---

116. Sk.tp.: "a" added
117. Sk.sh.: an indecipherable sh. symbol inserted after "we"; Sk.tp.: "can"
118. For Sandow, see List
119. Sk.sh.: "in" inserted
120. Sk.sh.: "there" retraced to read "that"; Sk.tp.: "that"
121. Sk.sh.: "to control them" is followed by a blank and has an editorial underlining
122. Sk.tp.: "lesser" corr. in hw. to read "less"
123. Sk.tp.: "prime" omitted
124. Sk.sh.: "of" inadvertently written for "a"; Sk.tp.: "a" instead of "of"
125. Sk.sh.: "as" indistinctly written
126. Sk.sh.: "a.d.c." abbr. in lh. for "aide-de-camp"
127. Sk.sh.: "other" crossed out, then "next" substituted

went, as if nothing had happened[128], giving orders what to do to extinguish the fire, and then came back gently. A great part of the palace had[129] already burned; everyone, after they went from dinner, they had not known it. [130]Next day in the paper they read that a great part of the building[131] had [132]burned[133]. They were very surprised to see such a thing, such a patience, such a self-control, such a mastery to[134] oneself. It does not mean that he did not feel the loss; he perhaps felt more than anyone could have felt it. He did not show it. It was not his manner to jump about. It was not his manner to run and rush; it was not his manner to make a fuss for nothing. And suppose[135] if he had done as everyone does, what would he have done? He would have excited the other also and made the things worse. It is better that the palace was on fire than the spirit being on fire; that is better[136].

---

128. Sk.sh.: "happened" in sh. clearly written
129. Sk.sh.: "was" written, then crossed out
130. Sk.sh.: "When" written, then crossed out
131. Sk.tp.: "palace" instead of "building"
132. Sk.tp.: "already" added
133. Sk.sh.: "for" clearly written; Sk.tp.: "for" omitted
134. Sk.tp.: "over" instead of "to"
135. Sk.sh.: "as" written, then crossed out
136. Sk.sh.: "better" written, then crossed out, then "better worse still" written and then crossed out, then "better" written again; Sk.tp. has "better"

An old typescript

[1]January 16th, 1925

Is Man the Master of His Destiny?

Beloved ones of God,

My subject this evening, "Is man the master of his destiny?" Often a person wonders if man was meant to be the master of his destiny, for the[2] life's experience has taught men to say, "Man proposes, God disposes[3]," but I will still say that man is[4] the master of his destiny for the very reason that man may be resigned to the destiny, but he cannot be happy with that destiny which he does not wish to have. If man was meant to be the slave to[5] his destiny, then he would have been content with it, he would have been happy in it. For the very reason that he does not wish to be contented, for the very reason that he cannot be contented with his destiny shows that he is seeking for a mastery, and it is in order to get the key to this mastery that man strives through a right way or a wrong way. By going the wrong way he has the same motive, but he does not accomplish it because then, in that way, he goes through an illusion. He thinks that he is striving in order to master his destiny, but he goes the wrong way. The one who goes the right way, he finds that key to that mastery, the mastery over his destiny.

Well, now is the question how far is man granted that power of mastering his destiny and how far he stands in this life helpless? And the answer is that it differs with every man. Every man has a certain degree of that power. But this must be seen in this way, that a soul is born on earth helpless, and out of this helplessness it grows and then learns to help itself. A soul grows from infancy to youth, from helplessness he becomes helping himself, able to help himself. So is the soul. The person, as he evolves, so he develops to help

---

Documents:
- od.tp. = an old typescript of unknown provenance.
- Sk.tp. = a typescript made by Sakina Furnée, nearly identical to od.tp. showing some handwritten corrections.

Notes:
1. Od.tp., Sk.tp.: "Switzerland" added by hand
2. Sk.tp.: "the" placed between parentheses
3. English translation of a Latin saying by Thomas à Kempis in *Of the Imitation of Christ*
4. Od.tp., Sk.tp.: "is" underlined
5. Sk.tp.: "to" placed between parentheses and "of" written in the margin

himself.

Do you not hear sometimes a relation or a friend say about his friend, "He is a child"? He is a child means that he is still helpless. And this shows that in man there are both things, there is part of his being which is helpless, and there is a part of his being which has the mastery.[6] The external part is the part which represents the helplessness of man, it is the inner part of man which represents the mastery.

And since every man is conscious of his external being and rarely one is conscious of his inner being, so rarely is man a master, but everyone experiences helplessness through life. And after all, it is the consciousness of a thing which makes the person possess it, and if the person is not conscious of it, it may belong to him and yet he does not possess it. For an instance, there may be a large sum of money put in the name of a child in the bank, the child still does not possess it, he is not conscious of it, he cannot utilize it. It belongs to him, not to the others. To him it is nothing, it does not belong to him.

And now you will ask me that what explanation have I to give about that belief which has always existed and believed by the wise and foolish, that there exists some such a thing which is called predestination. And I will explain it. That there was an artist and he planned in his mind, he made in his mind, planned that he wants to produce it on a canvas. And no sooner he took the colours and brush in his hand and began to paint his picture, every line he made and every colour he put, it suggested him something, and that altered altogether his plan, the very plan with which he began then became an obscurity to his mind, and what was produced before him was quite a different thing than he had thought before. What does it show? This shows the three stages of the picture. The first stage of the picture is that plan which, before bringing on the canvas, the artist had designed, the artist had planned; and the other aspect is that action of producing that picture which went as changes, right and wrong and right and wrong, and so on it went; and the third aspect is the completion of that plan, the completion of that picture which stood quite different from the plan first conceived. Therefore,

---

6. Od.tp.: "The part of his being which has the mastery is the external part of his being, and that part which has the mastery is the inner part. I will repeat this." written, then placed between parentheses, then crossed out; Sk.tp.: this passage crossed out by hand

what may be called predestination is that plan which is made beforehand, and what may be called *karma* as they say in the Hindustanic tongues, is that process through which the picture is made, and the completion of that picture is what may be called mastery.

It does not always happen that the picture is altogether different from what is[7] was planned, and yet it often happens. And however much different the picture may be from the plan, and[8] yet the foundation remains there as first planned. And therefore, how much different the life may be from that mark of predestination which was before, and yet the life is built, the life is erected upon the same plan which has been first made.

No doubt, the astrologers and the fortune tellers, the future tellers, the prophets, will not always say the thing that is really coming, they may mistake, and yet the predestination is there, the mistake is in their reading, not in the predestination.

And still that saying of the old that the feet of the infant tell what he is going to be will always prove true. It is the lack of seeing, that men cannot see, but the one who can see, can see from infancy what the child is going to be. And that old saying that the fate of the child is written on his forehead, it is the same in reality, every part and particle of the infant is expressive of what he is going to be. The one who can read the eyes and the ears and the features and the form as letters, he can read an infant, a human being, as a letter. He need not consult with planets and mathematics. He need not know other sciences, that intuitive sense can see what the soul is going to be like. And the eyes which are open to see this, they are also open to see the process, that middle part of life's journey, how the person is developing, how the person is going through changes. They can see in the failure of a person a success, there can be in the success of a person a failure. And the one who is capable of doing this also can see that how, when this picture will be complete, what sort of picture it will be. What the picture is going to be, he can see it beforehand.

And in order to support the argument of the fatalist we do not need to go far to find examples. Everyone has examples near him. There are men most qualified and yet fail; there are people most clever, and yet always lose.

In order to support the argument of the one who thinks free

---

7. Sk.tp.: "it" instead of "is"
8. Sk.tp.: "and" placed between parentheses

will is something, there are reasons too, because it is the active, it is the persevering, it is the courageous who attain to the success, and those who lack it can sit and wait, and wait forever. And this teaches us that it is a great mistake to divide destiny from free will, because behind destiny there is a free will, and behind a free will there is destiny. What we call destiny is a kind of cover upon the free will; it is the free will working in the form of free will and yet the spirit of destiny is working.

I am now coming to a question: How does a mystic look upon this question? The mystic thinks that in the being of man there are two aspects, one aspect of his being is like a machine, the other aspect of being is like an engineer. The machine part of his being, which[9] is dependent upon climatic changes, upon what is given to it, what is put into it, upon what it depends in order to keep in working condition. And there is another machine of fine mechanism which works as the inner part of this machine that is finer than its outer part. And that fine part feels atmosphere, feels vibrations, feels pleasures and displeasures, enjoys comforts and rejects discomforts, every kind of feeling exists there. Then the mystic looks on life in this manner: that this machine is made for the use of the other part of one's being, which is the engineer. But as long as that engineer is asleep, and that engineer is unaware of this machine, he does not run it; it is just left to conditions and environment, they run it. And so it means illness, with depressions, with fears, with his failures, with his helplessness when this engineer part of his being is asleep and the inner[10] part of his being is subject to conditions. On the day when this engineer part of man begins to waken, that day he begins to feel mastery over this machine, he begins to know on that day this machine was made for him to work it to the best advantage.

I am coming to a still deeper side of metaphysics. We shall find that God himself, from his own experience, manifests and experiences life through all its aspects, and specially through man. For what is this whole manifestation? This is nothing but the sublime vision of divine being. And with all the beauty that one sees in manifestations[11], the greatest and the most important thing is the fulfilment of this whole creation, and that is to be found in man. And

---

9. Od.tp.: "which" placed by hand between parentheses; Sk.tp.: "which" crossed out
10. Od.tp.: "outer" [probably correct] with a question mark written by hand above the line, and so in Sk.tp.
11. Sk.tp.: "manifestations" changed by hand to "manifestation"

this object is only fulfilled when man has wakened to this part of his being which represents the master, in other words God himself. But as long as man is interested in borrowing all that is necessary for this mechanism which he calls his mind and body from the external world, he depends upon it and he lives in it. And since this becomes his occupation, and this becomes his nourishment, this outer world, then he becomes mortal. In other words it is[12] the immortal being becomes mortal by borrowing all that he needs from the mortal world. The more he depends upon the external life, the more he forgets the inner life, and there comes a time when he entirely forgets that there can exist a life which is above, which is beyond this external life. We do not need to go to see the example of this very far when we see just now the condition of the world. We see that, with all this progress, there is materialism every day on the increase, and all the suffering that humanity has gone through, and just now humanity is going through, has been caused by this ever-increasing materialism.

What man believes in is in all that is external, that which he can touch, which he can see, which he can possess externally. In connection with him it may be said, quite contrary to what is said in the Bible[13], that he lives and moves and makes his life with what is in the material world. And when a person will live like this, his eyes will keep closed to that part of mastery which needs blowing, and by that blowing it can be risen to a blaze which can lighten, which can illuminate the path of man's life.

Therefore, the object of the Sufi Movement just now in this world, and its work, is only to waken in humanity the importance of that side of life which is much more important than the earth side of life. The Sufi Message, therefore, is not a message of a particular creed, it is the message of understanding life better. And the question, how can one attain to it, is to be answered, that it is not one day's work, or two day's work. It is the work of a whole life. As every art and science is the same if one says that, "In ten years I will accomplish learning music," he does not know what music means. If a person says, "In ten years I will be a great poet," he does not know what poetry means. A whole lifetime is not sufficient. If these things are so difficult to attain, one cannot suppose to attain in one day the knowledge of the deeper side of life, and there are some

12. Sk.tp.: "it is" placed between parentheses
13. See Acts 17:28

enthusiastic persons who will talk enthusiasm one day and another day will run away, because they did not see something wonderful. When a person takes the spiritual part[14], he must understand first that he has taken a part for eternity. If eternity he does not know, he should not take his first step, because he is not entitled to take his first step in the spiritual path. And the one who wants to seek that truth, he must not seek it superficially, for truth is not sought, it is discovered. For truth is not something that is to be attained or to be possessed. Truth is the self of one's own being, and it is oneself that is to develop into truth and what is to be found in this whole strife is[15]...

Very often people think that sorrow or pain, that is the sign of spirituality. One must not mistake spirituality for sorrow or pain. Yes, in many cases sorrow or pain becomes a source or a process of attaining quickly spirituality, but for that one must not ascribe to oneself a sorrow or pain, for life has enough of sorrow or pain.

Why does man seek for happiness? Because in reality his real self is happiness. He has lost that self and therefore is unhappy. The greatest tragedy in life is helplessness, limitedness, and the idea is to rise above this limitation in every way possible. And this rising is climbing towards spiritual ideals from materialism. It is the summit of this spiritual ideal which must be climbed, and in the climbing this then[16] is the fulfilment of life's promise.

Thank you for your sympathy, response, and God[17] bless you.

---

14. Sk.tp.: "part" changed by hand to read "path" [probably correct]
15. Od.tp.: a space, indicating missing words; Sk.tp.: a number of dots
16. Od.tp.: "there (?)" substituted by hand; Sk.tp.: "there (?)" written in the margin
17. Sk.tp.: "and response. God" instead of "response, and God"

An old typescript

January 17th, 1925[1]

[2]

Concentration

[3]Beloved ones of God,

My subject of this afternoon will be the concentration.[3] Concentration is a simple word, in practice it is most difficult. Everyone knows the word concentration; if he knows how to do it, he knows everything. Sometimes[4] to sit with closed eyes means concentration, but whether you close your eyes or whether you open your eyes, concentration has nothing to do with it. If you concentrate, you concentrate, with open eyes or with closed eyes, in the middle[5] of the crowd or in the solitude, and if you don't, you don't. But concentration is one state, a state which leads to contemplation, and so one goes through the meditation[6] process to achieve that in which is the fulfilment of every soul's purpose in life. Therefore it is that the ancient people called it alchemy, and[7] from which the word[8] alchemical or chemical[9] or *chimie*[10] come. Only now there are simple persons, even in the East we find many,[11] who by the meaning of[12] alchemy understand the turning of iron into gold. But when we consider it symbolically, the meaning that we find in alchemy is to turn this very personality, which is human

Documents:

od.tp.	=	an old typescript of unknown provenance.
Sk.tp.	=	a typescript made by Sakina Furnée, nearly identical to od.tp.
Hq.tp.	=	a typescript prepared at Headquarters, Geneva for inclusion in the series Social Gatheka, where it became Number 44, showing differences from the other typescripts.
Hq.st.	=	a stencil prepared at Headquarters, Geneva nearly identical in wording with Hq.tp. and therefore only mentioned in the notes where it differs.

Notes:

1. Hq.tp.: "Number 44." added
2. Sk.tp.: "Public Lecture." typed on the left side above the text; Hq.tp.: "SOCIAL GATHEKA." added followed by the Sufi Invocation
3. Hq.tp.: "Beloved ones of God ... will be the concentration." omitted
4. Hq.tp.: "people think" added
5. Hq.tp.: "midst" instead of "middle"
6. Hq.tp.: "meditative" instead of "meditation"
7. Hq.tp.: "and" omitted
8. Hq.tp.: "words" instead of "word"
9. Hq.tp.: "'chemical' or 'chemistry'" instead of "'alchemical' or 'chemical'"
10. *Chimie*, French for chemistry
11. Hq.tp.: "even in the East we find many," placed between parentheses
12. Hq.tp.: "the meaning of" omitted

personality, from the baser metal into gold. But [13]alchemy, it is not the gold which is made in order to possess, the gold of the soul is made, one becomes oneself gold, and it is that gold which is incomparably of greater value than the gold of this mortal world. Then there are people who still remember the stories of the ancient times, the stories of the alchemists, and it is even till now most interesting to get the meaning out of these symbolical stories, for they are always instructive.

There is a story of a king who was very fond of gathering[14] out ways of alchemy, of turning baser metal into gold, and everyone that professed knowing alchemy had a welcome at the palace, but in the end of examination he found their profession futile. And then they found someone, and they said to the king, "Here is a real alchemist," and to the king's great sadness, when this alchemist came before the throne, he said, "No, king, I am not the man which[15] knows the alchemy which you are looking for." The king said, "No, you know it. I feel confident in my heart that you are the person who knows it and you must teach the study to me." The man continued refusing, the king continued persisting, and then he said, "Do you know that I am a king, and here I command you to do so, and if you still refuse, you know what I can do. I give you forty days limit. If during this time you did not tell me, then do you know what is waiting for you? You will be beheaded." The man was taken to a prison and the king visited him every morning, telling him, "Man, change your mind. Remember life is greater than gold. You can still teach me and save your life." And at night the same king came in the form of a working man, in the form of a servant, and he swept the floor and he made the bed for him and he cleaned the table for him and he served his dinner, and he did every little thing possible to make this prisoner feel comfortable. And so every day this went on. In the evening, the king visited as a servant, and in the morning he went as a king, and gave him a warning again and again. And there comes that last day, the day after which was waiting the death of this man and the king gave him the last warning and said, "Now tomorrow is the day, be ready, for a king's command is his command." And in the evening this servant shed tears at the thought of this poor prisoner being taken to be beheaded. "Don't shed tears,"

---

13. Hq.tp.: "by" added
14. Hq.tp.: "finding" instead of "gathering"
15. Hq.tp.: "who" instead of "which"

he said, "life is such, but remember, that which I refused to[16] the king, to you I most willingly give, if you will keep it in confidence. And now you will see that[17] how great a trust it is, how sacred the thing is to me which I have guarded more than my life, that I have sacrificed my life in order to guard this, that you will keep it in the same way." This servant said, "Well, I appreciate most what you give me, although I do not know its value, but[18] at the same time, for you to be killed tomorrow, this I cannot bear, it tears my heart to pieces." "Be not sad, man," he said, "life is such. I give you this secret, gold that will make you gold." And he whispered in his ears and enlightened him with his secret. And the morning came and the king came for his last warning. There soldiers were waiting to take him to be beheaded, and there he was waiting[19] his death, and the king is there to ask him for the last time if he will obey the command. "No," said this prisoner, "find someone else, king, I am not the person you are looking for." But the king said, "But you have given me that, don't you remember?" "Did I?" said the prisoner, "If I have given it, it is to the servant, not to the king."

To the hungry food is given, and to the seeker truth is given. But one who is not hungry, even if the food is given, he cannot eat, and one who does not seek the truth, even the most ultimate truth given to him, he will not appreciate. Those great ones who came to illuminate souls, and who lived on this earth, they have touched millions, but did millions get that illumination? No. What was[20] remained afterwards and[21] modified, lost its fragrance, perhaps after thousands of years. Then, when it was dust, people began to talk, but at the time when it was given, people did not appreciate. It will always prove true, man is the worst enemy of his best friend. Whom he strikes first is his best friend, he has crucified him, he has imprisoned him, he has killed him, he has beheaded him, he has flayed him. And yet, without meaning, without intending, with good will and with reason, what he calls reason in his head.

I am[22] now coming to the actual subject of this alchemy. That[23] what is it and how is it made. What they say in legends is that

---

16. Hq.tp.: "to" omitted
17. Hq.tp.: "that" omitted
18. Hq.tp.: "but" omitted
19. Hq.tp.: "awaiting"
20. Hq.tp.: "was" omitted
21. Hq.tp.: "was" entered
22. Hq.tp.: "I am" omitted
23. Hq.tp.: "That" omitted

alchemists used to take mercury, and by putting some chemicals, they used to still it, and in stilling that mercury, it turned into silver, and then, by putting it into a fire, the very silver[24] turned in the flame and took up that flame colour which we call gold.

I am now[25] coming to the question what is this mercury symbolically. The mercury is a condition of the heart, the condition of the mind. It is never still. Automatically one's mind takes up any impression and thought, and without intention may hold it as a despair, as a depression, but as soon as one intentionally takes up a thought, the mind goes on in its active way and loses it. As soon as man wishes his mind to take up a thought, the mind fails, and that is the nature of mercury. Mercury is never still and the mind is never still. The more you wish the mind to become still, the more active the mind becomes, and therefore, that precise object, this mind can become still, it is that process which is called concentration and it is by this process that this mercury can be turned into silver.

The Sufis have different ways of posture[26], different ways of standing or sitting, all these different things are in order to still that mercury, not only in the mind but also in the body, which keeps mind always active, moving, restless. Hardly one thinks how little power man has upon his body. As soon as you tell a man to sit still, the moment he knows that he must control his body, the body will begin to move and be restless, and since mind and body are connected, one with the other, the stilling of the mind needs stilling of the body at the same time. There are just now many movements, schools where they will teach the way how to move gracefully, but it is not the stilling of the mercury. The stilling of the mercury is how to sit restfully. That is another subject in life to learn and much more important too.

As essential it is to keep awake, so essential it is to sleep, and as important it is to move, so important it is to take a repose. But[27] one's mind is controlled, one's body is made still, still[28] it has made man valuable, it has made that personality precious, and yet it is not gold. For the gold is gold because it has light in it. This tranquillity which one has learned is in order to make one a vessel, a pitcher which can hold, but that pitcher must hold divine light in

24. Hq.tp.: "silver itself" instead of "very silver"
25. Hq.tp.: "I am now" omitted
26. Hq.tp.: "postures" instead of "posture"
27. Hq.tp.: "once" added
28. Sk.tp., Hq.tp.: "still" omitted

it, and when the pitcher has that divine light then there is a value of that pitcher.

This shows that it is not only an intellectual conception of God or of life which is sufficient for man; the first thing is that one must develop that tranquillity in one's body and mind so that this vessel may contain in itself the life and the light of God.

Sometimes it amuses me very much when I meet people who tell me, "Well, what is your conception of God? Please tell me." Here for years and years people have to train their bodies and their minds in order to get in tune, in order to find a glimpse of that truth which a person with his intellect comes and asks, "Please tell me how do you believe in, what way do you consider God?" But this thought,[29] as in other theories and different things that[30] he reads and learns in books every[31]..., he thinks that even God is a conception, an idea which can be explained in a sentence. Sometimes a person comes and asks me, "Well, do you believe in a personal God or do you believe in an abstract God?" and before the answer he tells himself that, "I do not believe in a personal God, I only believe in an abstract. I can[32] only believe in that idea." He comes with his preconceived ideas of which he is not sure. He is asking only to be sure whether that fits in with his ideas. If it does not fit in, then he goes away. Another man comes. He says, "What do you think of the hereafter? What is your idea?" He wants in one sentence what will become[33] after death. And then, whereas that idea that[34] in order to die that death here in life that people spent days and years in studying, in practice, in meditation, in order to experience themselves what is after death, and they have experienced by dying a death here on earth, it is not impossible to know it, but it is not so easy to know as a person thinks. In order to keep man quiet, the wise had to tell them a thousand things in order to fit in with their particular conceptions. Well,[35] that cannot be the truth, and if they say the truth, they cannot say it, truth cannot be said in words. Where[36] is truth? Truth is life itself, and it is the realizing of the life

---

29. Hq.tp.: "But this thought," omitted
30. Hq.tp.: "that" omitted
31. Sk.tp.: "every" is followed by a number of dots, indicating missing words; Hq.tp.: "everything" instead of "every-"
32. Od.tp.: "can" underlined for emphasis and so in a.o.d.
33. Hq.tp.: "be" instead of "become"
34. Hq.tp.: "Whereas" instead of "And then, whereas that idea that"
35. Hq.tp.: "Well," omitted
36. Hq.tp.: "What" instead of "Where"

that is the discovering of the truth. If truth is such a small thing that it can be spoken in words, then truth is no truth. And what are words? Words are something that covers truth. When one comprehends beyond words, it is then that one realizes truth. To become gold is to become light, and the light in this precise sense is truth itself. Light and life are two words; in the[37] point of fact, it is one. In the essence it is one; call it light, because it is knowing, call it life because it is living.

To a dervish a person went and said, "Please tell me what happens after death." The dervish said, "Go to someone who is going to die, who is mortal, he will tell you what happens after death. Neither do I die, nor do I know what happens after death." And that explains the central thought of Sufism, and that thought is that life lives, it is death that dies. In spite of all the great masters, Jesus Christ had to teach to the people to satisfy their fancies, to help them in their lives; the central theme of the master's teaching is one, and that is to distinguish[38] immortality of the soul. [39]Sufi, therefore, is the pupil of wisdom, and since he is the pupil of wisdom he is the pupil of the all wise. He sees the source of wisdom in all its forms, in religious forms, in philosophical form or in mystical form[40], and scientific or artistic form; in all its forms it has one source, and it is that source which is the master. And therefore, he is not in any disagreement with any religion, with any sect or with any community. Those teachers that[41] have adored their own teachers and their own scriptures that they worship and respect, for the Sufi does[42] all the same. The Sufi's church, therefore, is every place where he stands, the dome of that church is the sky, and the floor of that church is his thoughts. The whole scripture of the Sufi is all this life that teaches lessons from morning till evening. Therefore, the literature of all those great prophets and teachers for him is the interpretation which they have taken from this life, interpreted in the language of the people of that time. And yet that wisdom for the Sufi is not limited at a certain period; that wisdom has always been, therefore is and will always be, for he [43]finds the source of that

37. Hq.tp.: "the" omitted
38. Hq.tp.: "the" added
39. Hq.tp.: "The" added
40. Hq.tp.: "forms" instead of "form"
41. Hq.tp.: "People" instead of "Those teachers that"
42. Hq.tp.: "they are" instead of "does"
43. Hq.tp.: "that" added (but not in Hq.st.)

wisdom which he considers most sacred is to be found in the heart of man.

Thank you all for your sympathetic response, may God bless you.[44]

---

44. Hq.tp.: "To be read at the Meetings of the World Brotherhood" instead of "Thank you all ... bless you."; Hq.st.: "To be read at the Meetings of the Universal Brotherhood."

An old typescript

Geneva, January 18th, 1925

A Universe in Man[1]

[2]Beloved ones of God,

My subject of this afternoon is a universe in man. To say that, [3]universe in man, is just like saying the sea in the drop. It is like saying the sun in the atom, and yet[2] it is not absurd, it is not nonsense when you say the tree in a seed. [4]A seed, so[5] insignificant as it seems to be, should have in it that property which makes a tree grow out of it, which makes flower to come[6] out of it, it[7] causes fruits to come forth, and as in the seed one does not see the tree, and as one who is not acquainted with this knowledge may say, "There is no reason for me to believe that out of the seed comes a tree," and[8] so it is when I say[9] universe in man. A person likes to see where it is, he only sees the[10] man.

Man lives in this tiny world which we call the small world, and in this small world man is so insignificant that even this small world does not know him. People used to know their neighbours, but now often one[11] does not know his next door[12]. Man has become more insignificant now than ever before, and yet, in the[13] point of

---

Documents:

od.tp. = an old typescript, possibly from a transcription of a shorthand reporting of a stenographer which has not been found.

Gd.tp.= a copy of the od.tp. with her own handwritten corrections.

Hq.tp.= a typescript which follows exactly the editing of the Gd.tp., as it includes all her handwritten corrections in the typescript.

Sk.tp. = a typescript made by Sakina Furnée or under her supervision, including all editorial changes of the Gd.tp. and some more handwritten corrections.

Notes:

1. Gd.tp.: "written down by a stenographer" added in pencil
2. Gd.tp.: "Beloved ones of God ... It is like saying the sun in the atom, and yet" crossed out and omitted in a.o.d.
3. Gd.tp.: "a" added
4. A.o.d.: "that" added
5. Gd.tp.: "so" crossed out and omitted in a.o.d.
6. Sk.tp.: "flower to come" changed by hand to read "flowers to blossom"
7. Gd.tp.: "which" instead of "it"
8. Sk.tp.: "and" crossed out by hand
9. A.o.d.: "it is said a" instead of "I say"
10. Gd.tp.: "the" crossed out and omitted in a.o.d.
11. A.o.d.: "a person" instead of "one"
12. A.o.d.: "neighbour" added
13. Gd.tp.: "the" crossed out and omitted in a.o.d.

truth, man is larger than the universe. It is his ignorance about himself that keeps man ignorant of that largeness of his own being. Besides, that largeness is of no use to him when he is not conscious of that largeness. What use that wealth is[14] to a little child in whose name it is put in the bank when he is not conscious of his capital, of his property? Nevertheless, man is the owner of that property, that property which is called the universe. And he can only be the owner of that property according to the law of nature when the soul is mature, as the law of the world, also of nations, will not allow an immature soul to own his own property.

There are different points of view from which a person looks at an individual. One point of view is that an individual is a part of all other beings in the world, and that point of view is like saying that a chair in the room is one of the things that are to be[15] in the room. And there is another point of view of[16] looking at it, and that point of view is that when a person says that[17] for this prince it is that this whole palace was made, that[17] this whole palace was decorated and illuminated and supplied with all things of comfort and grandeur for this prince. That is another outlook on life. The difficulty is where to find that prince. When a person goes to find that prince he finds a pauper. If he is, therefore, still more inclined to believe in the prince than he believes[18] in the pauper, [19] who is past (a prince of the story, of the legend)[20], the difficulty is that neither the prince knows of his property, nor the one who goes to look at him finds that capital with him. Then the confusion begins in the mind of the seeker. Is there someone who is really rich? Is there such a thing as to be rich spiritually? And the way of finding it has two steps to be taken in order to come[21], to arrive to[22] the place[23]. In[24] the first step[25] he[26] has to give that pauper the property

14. A.o.d.: "is the wealth" instead of "that wealth is"
15. A.o.d.: "found" added
16. A.o.d.: "for" instead of "of"
17. Gd.tp.: "that" crossed out and omitted in a.o.d.
18. Gd.tp.: "he believes" crossed out and omitted in a.o.d.
19. A.o.d.: "a prince" added
20. A.o.d.: parentheses omitted
21. A.o.d.: "to" added
22. A.o.d.: "at" instead of "to"
23. A.o.d.: "palace" instead of "place"
24. Sk.tp.: "In" crossed out
25. Sk.tp.: "is that" added
26. A.o.d.: "a person" instead of "he"

in order[27] to make a king from his own pocket, and the next step[28], when he takes that property, [29]will become automatically his own.

I have[30] spoken it[31] symbolically, but the understanding[32] is that all beauty, all goodness that there is, will not be seen in its completion unless one completes it oneself. For an[33] instance, there is a young person who says, "All I have, all the love there is to give[34], but I don't find someone to whom I must give it. I am looking for it[35], but I see no one fit to receive it. This admiration which comes out of my heart, who deserves it? To whom it may be given I don't see." Then he says, "But I shall not be deluded, I shall not be deceived, I must give it to the deserving one, and that is the one I don't find." And he may go throughout the whole universe, from land to land, and from planet to planet, he will seek in heaven and on earth, and yet he will find no one unless he did not make[36] his heart so generous that he may give his love to the[37] one with all that is lacking[38], for no one makes an ideal except by giving oneself to that ideal.

Majnun and Leila[39] are the Romeo and Juliet of the East, and in their legend there is a part which is most interesting. Somebody asked[40] Majnun, "How foolish Majnun to long over someone who is not even really beautiful." And Majnun said, "In order to observe Leila, you must have the eyes of Majnun."

It is not in a person itself that[41] is all the property there[42] but one has to give what is lacking. It is in give and take, it is in that reciprocity that there is perfection.

When[43] one[44] dives deep into the nature and character of the

---

27. Gd.tp.: "in order" crossed out and omitted in a.o.d.
28. A.o.d.: "is" added
29. A.o.d.: "it" added
30. A.o.d.: "This is" instead of "I have"
31. Gd.tp.: "it" crossed out and omitted in a.o.d.
32. A.o.d.: "meaning" instead of "understanding"
33. Gd.tp.: "an" crossed out and omitted in a.o.d.
34. A.o.d.: "is there to be given" instead of "there is to give"
35. A.o.d.: "one" instead of "it"
36. A.o.d.: "makes" instead of "did not make"
37. Sk.tp.: "the" crossed out by hand
38. Sk.tp.: "that is lacking" crossed out, "his shortcomings" substituted by hand
39. For Majnun and Leila, see List
40. A.o.d.: "said to" instead of "asked"
41. A.o.d.: "there" added
42. Gd.tp.: "there" crossed out and omitted in a.o.d.
43. Sk.tp.: "When" crossed out
44. Gd.tp., Hq.tp.: "a person" instead of "one"; Sk.tp.: "a person" and "who" added by hand instead of "one"

universe, he[45] will not say, as Darwin[46] says, that man has come from [47]monkey, and then stop there. He goes so far and no further. The sense that man gets by diving deep into life[48], one finds that it is for the sake of man that the universe was made. It is true, according to Darwin, that it is the material from the earth[49] was taken to give man what is called his body, but not his soul. But even[50] that offering [51]the physical plane gives to this princely soul, even in that offering[52] you will see that the body of man cannot be compared with any object, with any other things in the world, whether gold or silver, or pearl or diamond. In its beauty, in its fineness, in its structure, in its radiance and livingness, no pearls, no diamonds, no gold nor silver can be compared[53]. For all that is precious, for[54] all that is beautiful, for[54] all that is strong and for[54] all that is fine, all that in its essence is to be found in the body of man. All the four[55] planes of material existence, such as the mineral kingdom, such as[56] the vegetable kingdom, such as[56] the animal kingdom, all these are represented in the body of man. And it is not necessary to trace as the original[57] of this body only the animal kingdom, or the source as a monkey, but there is nothing in this world which does not constitute [58]body of man; gold or silver or steel or mercury, whatever there is, it is all there. The essence of the fact[59] of the fruit and flower, of the tree and plant is to be found in man also, and in the appearance of man's thoughts and ideals. In the variableness[60] of man's sentiments, man's feelings, you can see the hearts of different metals, of iron, of steel, of gold, of silver. There are hearts who[61] are harder than steel, you cannot penetrate them, and there are hearts from which a valuable treasure comes, a treasure that you can always value, and there are

---

45. Gd.tp.: "he" crossed out and omitted in a.o.d.
46. For Darwin, see List
47. A.o.d.: "the" added
48. A.o.d.: "is that" added
49. A.o.d.: "that" added
50. A.o.d.: "in" added
51. Sk.tp.: "which" written by hand in the margin to be inserted here
52. A.o.d.: "even in that offering" omitted
53. A.o.d.: "with it" added
54. Gd.tp.: "for" crossed out and omitted in a.o.d.
55. Sk.tp.: "four" crossed out
56. Gd.tp.: "such as" crossed out and omitted in a.o.d.
57. A.o.d.: "origin" instead of "original"
58. A.o.d.: "the" added
59. Gd.tp.: "of the fact" crossed out and omitted in a.o.d.
60. Sk.tp.: "variableness" changed by hand to read "variability"
61. A.o.d.: "that" instead of "who"

hearts which are fountains, a fountain from which gold drops. And[62] all this shows that all that is there on earth and in heaven is to be found in man, and the deeper you go[63] in man you will also find that not only the beings known, such as animals and birds and trees and plants, are represented in him, but also beings imagined by man such as jinns and angels are to be found in man.

[64]A child came perplexed from his school and asked me[65] a question[66]. He said, "Do you really think that Santa Claus exists?" I[67] saw from the eyes of the child that he would like to feel very much[68] that Santa Claus existed, for he was very disheartened to have heard in the[69] school some child say, "Do you still believe in Santa Claus? You are too grown up for that!" And I[70] told him to repeat this theory to himself several times, and if anyone says[71] about Santa Claus' existence, then you will[72] repeat the same theory before him, that there is nothing that [73]human mind can conceive of that does not exist. If it does not exist in the spiritual plane, it exists in the sphere of mind. And[74] this was a great consolation to the poor child to think that it exists somewhere.[64]

One very often notices that people who become all wise culminate into[75] being fools. Once I know of an instance that[76] a director of a factory [77]while visiting his people, those who were working there, he[78] saw a girl, most devout in her faith, reading the Bible whenever she had a moment to spare. And then this man went and said, "Why don't you work? Why do you do such a foolish thing? Never such a person existed as Christ, I have read[79] in a

---

62. Gd.tp.: "And" crossed out and omitted in a.o.d.
63. A.o.d.: "as you go deeper" instead of "the deeper you go"
64. Gd.tp.: This paragraph "A child came ... exists somewhere." has been placed between parentheses; a.o.d.: this paragraph omitted
65. Gd.tp.: "me" crossed out
66. Gd.tp.: "of a wise man" added
67. Gd.tp.: "The wise man" instead of "I"
68. Gd.tp.: "very much to feel" instead of "to feel very much"
69. Gd.tp.: "at having heard in" instead of "to have heard in the"
70. Gd.tp.: "he" instead of "I"
71. Gd.tp.: "spoke" instead of "says"
72. Gd.tp.: "to" instead of "you will"
73. Gd.tp.: "the" added
74. Gd.tp.: "And" crossed out
75. A.o.d.: "in" instead of "into"
76. A.o.d.: "There was" instead of "Once I know of an instance that"
77. A.o.d.: "who" added
78. Gd.tp.: "he" crossed out and omitted in a.o.d.
79. A.o.d.: "it" added

thousand books." The girl became so disappointed, [80]simple girl was never[81] trained or educated, that she cried from that time and her tears were never dry. This girl was brought to me[82] to tell her what is right. She was most unhappy and embarrassed, thinking that she had believed in something which did not exist. I[83] told her that[84], "He has read so many books that he has driven out that belief which still is in your heart. Kindle that belief and know and be sure that Christ always exists in your heart." And this simple girl said to me[85] in return that[86], "I was dead, you[87] made me alive."

The difficulty is that man becomes so sure of his brain that he does not know what is behind this old[88] world which he calls mortality. As the horizon stands so far from us that the further we go the further we have to go, so is that object, that spiritual object to attain; the further we go, still[89] more we have to go in order to attain it. The day when man thinks he knows, he knows nothing, for he closes the doors of knowing, a knowing which continually wants to know and can never know enough, and it is that unlimited knowing faculty, it is that faculty which awaits the bliss of perfection. This knowing faculty, there comes a time that it[90] becomes knowledge itself. This living arrives[91] at a certain stage when this[92] living becomes a[93] being, then no more there is[94] living and dying, there is always being[95].

[96]Thank you for your sympathetic response. May God bless you.[97]

---

80. A.o.d.: "a" added
81. A.o.d.: "who had never been" instead of "was never"
82. A.o.d.: "a wise man" instead of "me"
83. A.o.d.: "The wise man" instead of "I"
84. A.o.d.: "that" omitted
85. A.o.d.: "him" instead of "me"
86. A.o.d.: "that" omitted
87. A.o.d.: "have" added
88. A.o.d.: "whole" instead of "old"
89. A.o.d.: "the" instead of "still"
90. Sk.tp.: "This knowing faculty there comes a time that it" changed by hand to read "There comes a time that this knowing faculty"
91. Sk.tp.: "This living arrives" crossed out by hand
92. Sk.tp.: "when this" crossed out
93. Sk.tp.: "a" crossed out
94. Sk.tp.: "no more there is" changed by hand to read "there is no more"
95. Od.tp.: "being" underlined for emphasis and so in a.o.d.
96. Gd.tp.: "Thank you ... bless you." crossed out and omitted in a.o.d.

An old typescript

[1] Geneva, [2]January 19th, 1925

Art and Religion

Beloved ones of God,

My subject this evening is art and religion. A time has come when the life seems so divided that people feel afraid to connect in any way, or in any form, art and religion. In reality art has always done the greatest service to religion. In all ages and to most of the world religions no doubt there has always come a reaction in the great service that art has done to religion; then that reaction has swept away art from religion. But no thoughtful person will ever deny the fact that when the art is taken away from religion, it is just like taking away breath out of body. And if we go still further we shall find that art in itself is a religion, for art fulfils that purpose towards which religion works.

If I were to give a definition of art in words, I would say that art is a harmonious expression of the soul. And what is religion? Religion is the way by which one arrives at that harmonious response. Yes, there are souls who look upon art as something man-made, and then they say, "But art is art, nature is nature." They are right, but this would not be untrue also if I said that art is nature and nature is art. What is produced in the art is a reflection of nature, and besides this, if you will take a philosophic point of view, you will also see that art is an improvement upon nature. It will not be an exaggeration to say that what was not produced in nature was made by the creator through the pen of the artist.

It is primitive to divide works of men from the works of God. If God is the light of the heavens and of the earth, then God's creation it is which we call nature, and God's creation again it is which we call art. As long as the artist is unaware of this truth, his art is only art, but no sooner he is acquainted with this truth, his art

---

Documents:

od.tp. = an old typescript, double-spaced, with a number of corrections, of unknown provenance.

Sk.tp. = a typescript prepared by Sakina Furnée or under her supervision, nearly identical in wording to the od.tp.

Notes:

1. Sk.tp.: "Public Lecture." typed above the text
2. Sk.tp.: "Switzerland" added by hand

becomes religion.

Imagine to what extent the sculptor, the painter, the poet, the musician have inspired men. Suppose there was no music, there was no poetry, no sculpture nor painting to inspire mankind, how far men would have been inspired only by what we call religion? Art has taken a central action, the central activity in each religion. Art has an influence, a power to suggest an idea, an idea which cannot be very well spoken in words, and a person who only can understand an idea through words has not yet arrived at that delicacy to understand an idea without words. For real inspiration comes by communicating with life. When one can communicate with a piece of art, with a picture, with a poetry, with music which can convey to his soul some idea, some feeling, then really he[3] begins inspiration in his life.

When we trace the sense behind the whole creation, we find that the whole creation is working towards one object, and that object is to arrive at a perfect harmony, and it is that harmony which may be called beauty. There is no other explanation of beauty, for everyone sees in an object a beauty, but if you ask him, "What is beautiful, what is in this object which makes you think it is beautiful?" he cannot say it because it is abstract, it is the feeling of harmony which is produced by that object which makes one feel this is beautiful.

There are several notes of music, there are numberless words in different languages, there are numerous colours which have their peculiarities, but what we call beautiful is the harmonious combination, harmonious arrangement, harmonious grouping in all different things.

Therefore the mission of art is to produce harmony, to combine lines or colours or notes or words in a harmonious group, and this is the art. Therefore, if I were asked to explain that what is beautiful in this picture, I would say the music that this picture conveys. Also in the poetry, what gives the sense of beauty is the music of that poetry, the music of its sense, the harmony of its words, rhymes, of the idea.

And what does religion teach us? Religion teaches us also the ways of harmony. The mission of religion is to teach us how to live in the room, outside, with friends, with neighbours, how to be

---

3. Sk.tp.: "he" placed between parentheses

kind, how to be forgiving, and how to harmonize with our creator, how to harmonize with one's soul, with one's mind. Therefore, in the ancient Arabic language there is a name which they give to the deity, and that name is "the artist".

There is a story, a story which is symbolical but expressive of the mission of art for the artist. There was an artist, a young lady who gave her whole life, her thought, to the piece of art, to the little marble piece that she was working on. This was the one piece of art which interested her most than anything else she had ever met in her life. She was such a devotee of art that her studio was her temple; that was the place for her soul's rest; nowhere else she felt at home. It is there that she was working with her art. Her friends, her comrades, all find her quite devoted in one thing and engrossed. She did not mix with others. Though she was in the midst of life, she was quite retired, quite devoted to her art, nothing else would interest her. They used to tease her and they used to dislike her tendency of giving her whole soul to her work; they could not understand. Very often at home and outside, a psychological influence came out of that piece of work that she was accomplishing. As more it became finished, the more that piece of art did influence upon her. She began to see more life in it; she began to see a beauty which was wakening in it; she could no longer consider it a statue. She began to see in this statue life. She says, "I have sought you my friend, my beautiful, that in you I see the beauty that all else in this world is unreliable. I do not feel attracted to it. You have come as the expression of my being; you are my soul, you are my life, nothing else in the world interests me; it is in you that I see there is any real beauty in life." So it is in art. A voice arose in the ears of her heart, "Yes, I am living and I will live, and I can speak and I will speak only on one condition, that you will take a bowl of poison out of my hand. For the condition of my being alive, my coming to life is only one, and that is that you die and that I live." And she said, "Nothing can please me but to see you live—you, the expression of my soul—for in you I see the beauty that is in that soul of my spirit, and I will most gladly take the cup of poison in order to see you alive." And what happened? She took the bowl of poison, and as she was dying this statue became alive, lifted her, and then restored her. This is the picture of all those who have really made the art, those who have found the real benefit from the art.

The musicians such as Beethoven, whose whole life was devoted to their work, to their music, themselves were nothing. To them, self vanished, art begins[4] living. They are dead; the art still lives, and the art kept them alive also. And so it is with the dead poets in the history of the world. Those who have produced a piece of art in their poetry, a work of their poetry which is living till now, they have been dead and yet they are alive. The beauty that they have created when they are creating that beauty they forgot themselves, and after their death they are still alive in the arms of their art.

And this shows what devotion can do. The artist's devotion to his[5] art is just like a devotion of a worshipper to his deity, but if he also knows the secret[6] of the art, then it is no longer art to him, it is the expression of the deity in the form of beauty. [7]For there cannot be a better form than[8] human mind can comprehend and that human mind can love better than art which is expressive of beauty.[7]

And now we come to realize that there are many different aspects of the art, but art is one and the same. What painting cannot express, poetry expresses; what poetry cannot explain, music expresses. But greatest of all arts is the art of personality. No doubt, a devotee of art, without knowing, develops art in his personality, but it is possible also that an artist may be a good artist and yet may miss that something which should be developed in his own personality, and in that case he has not yet perfected his art or his personality would have been developed.

The Mongolian[9] emperors used to have some artists in their court and very often the courtiers, they were very annoyed with that idea, but at the same time they said, "There is something living in the association of the arts." But one might ask that everybody is not born with the gift of the artist, and if they were all artists, then how could the world go on and therefore what could we do with the art? In order to learn art, in order to practise art in life, we need not be painters, we need not be sculptors. Whatever be our condition of life and whatever be our occupation, we have sufficient scope in our everyday life to develop that artistic faculty that is in us. The best expression of artistic faculty can be given by an artistic personality.

---

4. Od.tp.: "becomes" written by hand above "begins"
5. Od.tp.: "this" typed and the 't' crossed out by hand
6. Od.tp.: "secret" typed, then "spirit" typed over it; Sk.tp.: "secret"
7. Sk.tp.: "For there cannot ... expressive of beauty." not included, but later added by hand
8. Sk.tp.: "that" instead of "than"
9. Sk.tp.: "Mongolian" corrected by hand to read "Mogol" [Mughal]

That agreeable manner, that politeness, that fineness which proves a person to be harmonious, of beautiful personality; that is the best art that one can ever learn. A person who lacks this faculty shows that lack in everything he does: writing, reading, walking or sitting, in every action he shows that what he lacks is that artistic faculty. A person who is awkward in his manner, he is awkward in what he says, awkward in what he does, awkward because awkwardness represents lack of harmony. Fineness, beauty, can be expressed in every form. A person who loves beauty, a person who worships beauty, a person who devotes himself to beauty, expresses beauty in everything he does.

In order to arrive at that aim for which every soul is born is not in being perhaps so earthly, or so spiritual as an angel. For on this plane of the earth souls were not created in order to be angels, they were created to be perfect men, and this perfection is not only gained by thinking deep, by realizing deep, by attaining to that harmony in which is the fulfilment of the whole life. A person who cannot get along with those he[10] lives with, a person[11] who cannot live in harmony among those with whom he is put, a person who cannot agree with those he comes in contact with, that person has not yet wakened to that harmony which makes personality.

For it is just like painting a picture which nobody admires, nobody likes. It is like a violin so inharmoniously played that everybody should go out of the room. The greatest art is the art of personality. When man can draw the other men towards him by goodness, by kindness, by fineness, by forgiveness, by understanding, he knows the greatest art there is. It is the same personalities, it is the spiritual personality who did not only attract man, but they attracted beasts and birds to them. Today that power can be developed which is spoken in the Bible, that[12] Daniel, in the cave in the mountains, in the lions' den, the cruel animals in a moment's time were quiet. The great ones who[13] had such charm that they impressed the world with it and for thousands of years, millions of people have read their scriptures, remembered their names as the holy ones. And what had they? They had the art of personality. When Christ said to the fishermen, "Come hither, I will

10. Od.tp.: "who" written, then crossed out by hand, and "he" written above the line;
11. Sk.tp.: "who live with a person" instead of "he lives with, a person"
12. Od.tp.: "with" added by hand
13. Od.tp.: "who" crossed out by hand

make you fishers of men,"[14] what was he going to teach them? It was the art of personality.

Today the time has come when humanity should be wakened to the higher ideal, and there cannot be a better means of elevating the human ideal today better than the idea of harmony, of love and of beauty.

Thank you for your sympathetic response, and may God bless you.

---

14. Matthew 4:19

An old typescript

[1] Lausanne, January 20th, 1925

The Power of the Sacred Word

Beloved ones of God,

My subject of this evening will be the power of the sacred word. A time is coming at the present age that spiritual or material, both kinds of people, are realizing the power of word. For an instance, the Couéism[2] which is talked about among the spiritual and material people, they begin to see what word can do. But when one goes a step further, one will find that a sacred word has a greater importance and a greater phenomenon. Everyone who discovers some new idea feels for the time that he is the discoverer of it, but when we look back we find in the history of the world that they had already known it. And thus we come to realize and believe in the saying of Solomon that there is nothing new under the sun[3].

There was a time, thousands of years before Christ, when Brahmins, when Hindus, used to practise Yogas by the help of word. There were different ways of silence, different ways of concentration and meditation, but the principal way was to help development with the word. Jesus Christ has also considered the importance of it, as all other prophets of Israel have acknowledged the power of word. The Bible says aloud that first was the word and the word was God[4]. But at the same time, it seems very few in the world who perhaps read the Bible very often who stop to think about the meaning of this saying. So on the other hand, few believe in that word of the Bible which says to refrain from vain repetitions[5]. There are more inclined to believe in that rather than to believe in the power of the word. And the reason is that those who interpret the Bible must in the first place know the sense of the Eastern terminology of that time in which it was given. There was a time when it was easy for people in

---

Documents:
od.tp. = an old typescript of unknown provenance.
Sk.tp. = a typescript made by Sakina Furnée, nearly identical with the od.tp.

Notes:
1. Sk.tp.: "Public Lecture." typed above text
2. For Coué, see List
3. See Ecclesiastes 1:9
4. See John 1:1
5. See Matthew 6:7

Syrian Palestine to bring before the name of God in every little conversation. They wanted to prove every line they spoke by the name of God. It is that vain repetition that was prohibited and not the name of God. As a great poet of Persia says, that the repetition of the sacred name will not add sacredness as a sacred thing, but will make your own soul sacred. Now those who understand from the psychological point of view the value of auto-suggestion and the value of saying very often, how it works upon their body and upon their mind, are beginning to understand the elementary aspect of it. But before them there is a large world of sound and mystery which is still closed because they know not that by repeating one word or one thing it might bring about that particular result but it might do harm to something else.

I am now coming to the question of the secret of language, that in all the different languages which we find today in the world there seems to be one central language to be traced as the mother language of all languages. No doubt, it is difficult to distinguish that language as such or such, but at the same time the relation that is between one language and another shows this, that the human race had one language to begin with. Many linguists have said that it was the Sanscrit language. There are other linguists who say that before Sanscrit there was another language. There will be historians who will have different opinions, but the metaphysics teach us one thing, that there was a language which was one language of the human race. Then came from it many languages. A historian cannot be a historian if he does not give the name to a certain language to be the first language; for a metaphysician it does not matter. He only understands, he knows it for proof that there was one language. He does not mind if he does not know the name of that language. And when we come to that language we also understand that that was a more natural language compared to the languages we know today, which are most complicated. For an instance, the language of the birds and animals. These languages are not made from grammar, they are not mechanical languages. They are natural expressions of their real sentiments, of their real needs. And it is by that natural expression that other animals of the same kind understand the warning that they give for the movement, the warning that they give to protect themselves, to leave the place, the warning of death or danger, or of the change of climate, of storm or rain coming. Affection, passion, wrath, anger that they express at that moment, they have a certain way of expressing, and yet it is not a mechanical language; it is [6]natural expression, it is a natural language. The primitive language of mankind, therefore, has been a language of feeling, of natural expression, just like the primitive figures. If we trace back thousands of years before, we shall find that there were pictures, the name of every object was written in a sort of picture which suggested that object. And now that thousands of years have passed and those figures and forms have changed, and the words of the primitive language have been changed, and yet the one who can see into life can trace back some forms at least and some sounds and words which come from the origin of the human race.

Now the outcome of the language which was the original language of humanity was this, that every word, every sound that was expressed did not only convey a meaning to the mind of the person who said it, but it had a sensation which it created in the person who heard it, a sensation of particular expression, of particular feeling or sentiment. And as the ancient people cultivated this domain of science, they arrived to understand that the sound is the main principle in man's life, which is called voice. It is the voice of man which shows whether a person is hard or soft, or wilful, or weak-willed; every character of man can be seen by his voice. The grade of the person's evolution, the person's tendency and the condition of that person at that moment can be realized by his voice. And that shows that before face or expression or movement, word can express a feeling or a condition. This shows that the real being of man, the central point of his life is to be found in breath, because voice is only an expression of breath. And when this voice is expressed outwardly, it expresses in a form of word. It has a kind of reaction inwardly, and that makes an effect upon a person's mind, upon his body, upon his soul. There are certain parts in a person's body, which parts may be considered as the factors of intuitive senses, and when by voice, by word, by breath, those parts of human body are brought to action, are brought to life, man begins to experience a fuller life. If that person is an artist, or a musician, or a writer, or a genius, whatever he is, by cultivating all the natural faculties which are within him he can express his art or his science to its fullest.

It is with this secret in consideration that the ancient people developed the science which they called Yoga[7]. By the repetition of

---

6. Sk.tp.: "a" added
7. Od.tp.: "Iago" typed here; Sk.tp.: "Iago" typed, then corrected to read "Yoga"

certain vowels, by the repetition of certain words, and by the repetition of a particular way of breathing, they touched within themselves those centres which are connected with intuitive faculties. And it is not only a story of the past. The school of the Sufis, the origin of which is the ancient school of Egypt where Abraham was initiated, their school still exists and there are words you use which have their power in form. But at the same time these schools have not made this sacred idea as an ordinary thought. They have not spread among people who would take it and abuse it, because if you give a sharp sword in the hands of a child the consequences will be fatal. A person who has not yet risen above his angers and passions, a person who has not yet risen above greed and above pride and conceit, if that person is given all the power there is, how will he use it? What will he do with it? It is therefore that the school first arranged that the people may be taught the moral culture and the attitude they must have to their fellow men. For any power that was ever attained they believed, and they still believe, that it must be for only one purpose, and that purpose is nearing God, and if it is not for that purpose, if it is for selfish purposes, then it is just as well that man remains without powers. Therefore, in the ancient schools which have the tradition at the back of them, and which are meant to serve humanity for this purpose, there are initiations to be taken.

I am now coming to the question of initiation. What does initiation mean? Initiation means a confidence on the part of the teacher and trust on the part of the pupil. Initiation is not given to the one who is curious, who comes to examine the teacher, or who comes to find out if in this particular culture, in this cult, there is truth or there is not. And if by any chance that person received an initiation, he will go through the whole thing and come back by the same door as he entered without finding anything. For this treasure house, which is so great a treasure, is a magic house, a house where there is every treasure and yet the thief cannot find it. He will go through the house, he will go all round, he will not see anything, and he will go back with his hands empty. For truth is a portion of the sincere one. It is one who is hungry who must be given food; it is one who is thirsty who must be given water. Who is not hungry, to him food will do no good, and to him who is not thirsty, water will not satisfy his need. A person who, in order to develop magnetic power, in order to accomplish his way, in order to get power, or name, or get things more than he can get in his daily life, if he wants to know these things to help him, that is useless. For the word, and especially the sacred word, is the key, as it is said in the Bible, that first was the word, and so the last key is the word also. It is the word which is the beginning of the creation, and it is the word which opens the mystery of creation. The different centres of intuition, of inspiration, of evolution are touched by the sacred word. And now, if they found out by the way of science how wireless can reach through the space without any means between, but they will find still one day when it comes the truth which has been known to the mystic for thousands of years, that man himself is the instrument, the receiver and the sender of that wireless which is above all other ways of wireless. But this wireless can explain to us much more of the possibilities which otherwise are difficult to comprehend. For this explains to us that every word that is spoken once is not lost. It is there and it can be caught. This is the great support for the argument which I have brought today before you for that sacred word which has power that nothing, either distance or space, or air, or sea, can keep it back from entering. It enters and reaches the hearts who can catch it. Only the difference is that the wireless is known to those from one country to another who communicate between themselves to themselves, but this mystery of the word is known to those for whom communication between the world is nothing but the communication between this world and that world. For as the word was the first, and word was at the beginning, therefore, at the beginning there was not this word or that word, there was only one life, there was only one existence and in reality there is one life and there is one existence. What we call this world and that world is for our own convenience. It is our speculation, it is our way of distinguishing between the different dimensions. In reality what is a dimension? Dimension is rather conception. If not, it is existence. It is just like time. There is no such thing as time; it is we who have a certain conception of it. If not, it is only an existence. It is an eternal continuity of life. In the same way, this world and that world is only a matter of our conception of all that hides the other world from our material physical eyes with which we have always accustomed ourselves to look at life. That makes for us that world and this world. There is one existence; there is one life, eternal, everlasting. In short, what I would like to say is this, that if by way of wireless, word can be transferred from one place to another, that gives us a proof that if it is one existence, if it is one life, then we[8] in this world or that world, here or in the hereafter, communication is possible, possible by only one thing, and that is if man has tuned himself, wound himself to that condition where he fully lives.

Since the world has so much falsehood in it, every good thing is imitated, and every writing is made into false. Since there is such a great desire in the mind of every person to do, to know something about reality, it seems that many different institutions, many different societies and groups wish to try and speak about things which they themselves do not know. If we count today we shall count hundreds of institutions which are working in order to give the belief of God by teaching what they call spirit communications. And by doing all these things, they spoil that sacred science and that greatest phenomenon which by attaining to the kingdom of God one realizes. It is for that the Sufi Movement, without pretending to give any power of wonder working, any desire for phenomenon, only helps those seekers after truth to find reality by searching after the kingdom of God.

I thank you for your sympathetic response[9].

God bless you.

---

8. Sk.tp.: "we" crossed out by hand
9. Od.tp., Sk.tp.: "support" written, then crossed out, "response" substituted by hand

An old typescript

Bern, [1]January 21st, 1925

A Universe in Man

When one hears this title, one feels[2] it strange. It is like saying, the sea in the drop, it is like saying, the sun in an atom, and at the same time, when we look at it from a different point of view, there are a thousand things that can prove this to us. And since man is born as a helpless infant, and as he has seen from the moment of his birth nothing but limitation, he cannot think of himself as anything else but a limited, miserable, poor, wretched man. Man has many reasons to prove his limitation, his poorness, his wretchedness. But at the same time, if he saw the other side of the question, he would sooner or later agree in saying that the universe is in man.

The life of man, the life of an individual, may be pictured as a line, a line with two ends. One end may be called limitation, the other end perfection. One end is human, the other end representing the divine. The end which is known to man is that human end, and the end which is unknown to man is that divine end, of which he hears, but that he[3] does not know. And what separates man from God is not life only, it is his ignorance. It is not only so with God, but with all things. A man does not know the treasure that he may have within his reach, but is ignorant of. The treasure is in his own self. If we are connected with one another in all different relationships and yet we are ignorant of one another, we are far apart, and where there is this wall of ignorance people may stay together their whole life and yet there will remain lack of understanding. Someone asked a close friend of a singer, who had perhaps lived with this great singer all his life, "Why do you sing so out of tune, when you have been with this great singer all your life?" He said nothing, but the singer then said that he never understood him. Two persons may start good friends, and then as days pass, as

---

Documents:

od.tp.	=	an old typescript of unknown provenance.
Sk.tp.	=	a typescript made by Sakina Furnée, nearly identical with the od.tp.

Notes:

1. Sk.tp.: "Public Lecture." added by hand
2. Sk.tp.: "feels" crossed out, "thinks" substituted by hand
3. Od.tp.: "he" written by hand above the line

weeks, months, years pass, they understand one another very well; but there are others, as days pass, as weeks, months, and years pass, they are still far apart. And so even man goes far apart from his own self, from his real self. It is ignorance of self which keeps man away from that perfection which is his own, which belongs to man.

The idea of the mystic is that all that exists in this universe, above in heaven or below in the earth, all is to be found in oneself, within oneself. Gold and silver and copper and brass, all things of earth and air and fire, all elements, all can be found within man himself. The mineral, vegetable, animal, all these and all their qualities are to be found within himself. All that man has ever imagined, fairies, genie, or God, all is to be found within himself. Nothing can he imagine, or nothing can anyone imagine, that does not exist in man, within himself. All that man denies, all of which he says, "This does not exist; that does not exist; it is not there," he denies because he does not know himself. If he knew himself, there is not anything that he would deny. All that exists, exists in man and can be found within himself. But there is not a man to be found in this world who becomes acquainted with this fact and becomes convinced of this truth, that it is truth. There is nothing in the whole universe that cannot be traced in some other form within man himself.

What is the reason of it? Why is man ignorant of that self which contains all that is truth? Why is he experiencing that utter wretchedness when the riches and the treasure of the whole existence are within himself? The reason is that the nature of man is to look on one side, and since on one side he has sufficient attraction to hold his eyes, he never has a moment to take away his eyes from this attraction and look at the other side where he can see something else. To make it more plain, man only knows what he wishes to see, to see through his eyes, but never can think of closing his eyes and trying to see, naturally; when a person wishes to hear, his first thought is to hear through his ears, he cannot imagine ever trying to hear without those ears open to the outer world. And what does it show? It shows that man directs his intelligence all outwardly in order to experience, to know, to attain, to gain all that he desires and wants in his life. And since in this way he experiences life, he remains unaware of that part of his being, a part which is a kingdom in himself, a part which may be called perfection, and only knows that part of his being which stands in need of every little thing from outside.

For instance, someone once asked a person about smoking, saying, "Have you ever thought what it is that interests you in smoking?" And the person directed his thought to a reason, a reason which could explain what it is that makes one inclined to smoke. He found a reason, and the right one too. He said, "Smoking helps one to relax. I suppose it automatically or unconsciously makes one concentrate one's mind." This explains to us that it is the need of man to relax, his need in this life to concentrate. It is natural for him to get into the condition of concentration. It is his natural craving to relax and feel that comfort which comes of it. But because he does not know how to concentrate, how to relax, he becomes dependent upon something outside of him instead of making himself self-sufficient, to experience the condition of concentration, of relaxation. Then, coming to the question of a man who drinks. If he is interested in it, he gets some comfort out of it. It is therefore that he seeks for it, and that shows that his nature needs that stimulant, his nature needs that little intoxication which turns his mind away from the immediate troubles and worries and fatigues. Therefore, in order to gratify that desire which is natural to him, he becomes dependent upon something which in other ways does him some harm. These one or two things are said as an example, but there are thousands and millions of things which man strives after in life, and yet he has a reason to strive after them because there is a natural seeking for them, to find them in his own being. Once a person asked a wise man, "What is there in life which is the source of all unhappiness?" The wise man said, "Limitation". Without thinking about it, man always strives in life and wishes to attain things all in order to become more limited. Man seems like a drop in the ocean when we see the whole universe, but at the same time this drop was meant to be the ocean, and instead this drop becomes lesser[4] than the ocean.

There is a story of Buddha known to the people of the East. When he grew up to be a man the first time he was allowed by his parents, who were keeping him away from all misery and trouble, knowing he was too sensitive to it, to go out from the palace, the first thing he did was to go in the midst of the crowd. He was anxious to see the world, he was longing to see humanity. A soul who was always kept from every worry or anxiety, from every sort

---

4. Sk.tp.: "lesser" corrected by hand to read "less"

of pain or trouble, and was always looked after that no miseries of the world might reach him, now stood in the midst of the crowd with amazement. He saw a very aged person, quite bent, and said to his friends, "What is this, what has made it?" They said, "Age." He saw those who are mourning a relation who has passed away, and he said, "What unhappiness is that?" They said, "It is death." He saw a person walking with two sticks, with great difficulty. He said, "What is it?" They said, "Illness." He saw a person unhappy, hungry, without sufficient clothes to wear, and he said, "What is it?" They said, "Poverty." He saw people fighting together, quarrelling, hitting one another, and he said, "What is it?" They said, "Disagreement." This young soul, who had come to heal the wounds and sufferings of this mortal world, looked here and there, and he said, "Poor humanity!" And he asked himself, were[5] all these different pictures of misery, some showing outwardly and some inwardly, and he said, "Misery everywhere." And then came the answer to his question, "What is the cause of it all? Where does it all come from?" The answer arose from the depths of his own heart that the source of all this misery is one and the same, and that source is limitation. Never after that day could the master sleep a whole night. That one impression was enough to keep him busy every moment of his life, thinking whether anything could be found to heal this disease. But then he said, "I must study the malady first in order to find the remedy." In studying the malady he found every desire man has, everything he wants is from the life outside, and instead of being perfect he becomes limited. And if there is anything that can save man, it is for him to realize this and to make his life as independent as possible of this outer world. He found then that it is not one day's work to make oneself independent of it. In order to get to this freedom one must work for the whole of one's life. But it is not this the teaching of this [age][6].

What was the message of Christ? It was the same message, it was the message to rise above all limitations and to get nearer the truth. And those who have come in the history of the world at any time and who have left impressions in the world of their compassionate personality, have always come with this one mission, to awaken man to get nearer to reality, a reality which is to be found

5. Sk.tp.: "were" crossed out by hand and "what are" substituted
6. Od.tp.: a space indicating missing words, then "age" added by hand and a question mark written in the margin; Sk.tp.: "(age)" filled by hand in the space

within himself, that man within[7] can find within himself a universe, all that exists, if he can arrive at the freedom of his soul at that realization which is called truth. Those who have sought solitude in order to get this realization have been called by many different names.

The world today seems further from this idea than ever before. One might ask, "Why do you say that the world is farther away from this idea?" There is a large part of humanity which has lost belief in any life beyond. They live a purposeless life, and know that to eat, drink, and be merry is the only principle of life. Wisdom to them is the common sense of a man who is well qualified to guard his interests against all others. What one wants to be, or wishes his children to be, is not wise but practical, for he knows that this world is a struggle, and the best thing he could do for his children is to make them fit for the strife, and the best thing he can do for himself is to qualify himself best to fight. And it is as a result of this that we have gone through these wars, and such conditions that no one could ever imagine that humanity could give us a destruction to such an extent[8] of the human race. The person who really has wisdom is considered by those people a simple one. A wise person is considered unpractical. They say, "You have no common sense." If we always promote struggle, then strife will get more bitter every day. As it is already, life is very difficult, more difficult than ever before in the world's history. For the rich and poor, for the qualified and unqualified, all, life is difficult. And now they are beginning to say that there are too many people in the world, and that is why it is wrong. The truth is that there are not too many. One hundred persons with understanding could live more peacefully and more comfortably than two persons with competition and with this attitude of strife. They say, "You can't do it because the condition of it is such," but they do not try to help the condition to become different. Verily, the time has come when souls must awaken to that truth and reality which alone can give freedom, which alone can bring happiness and peace. The humble service that the Sufi Movement has to render is in awakening souls to, and to contribute to, the good of humanity.

---

7. Sk.tp.: "within" crossed out by hand
8. Sk.tp.: "a destruction to such an extent" changed by hand to read "to such an extent a destruction"

An old typescript

[1]Bern, January 22nd, 1925

The Journey to the Goal

Beloved ones of God,

This evening I wish to speak on the subject of the journey to the goal. When we picture life as a journey, there are a thousand things which will prove this fact to us when we see in taking a journey we are with a great many people looking at life and going forward. Those who have arrived at their station have got out of the train, and the little friendship or sympathy or antipathy that we had with them only lasted till then. Those who have left, what they have left with us is that impression which we carry of them. Either that impression makes us happy or unhappy; either it makes us love them still in their absence, or hate them, wishing that we shall never see them again. When we think of yesterday, when we think of last week, when we think of last month, and when we think of the years that have passed in our lives, it only shows that they have passed and we have gone through. And at the same time it is the same sensation that one has in the train, as if the train were standing still and the trees were running. In life we have that sensation, that life is passing and we are standing.

And then we also see in this travelling that some are prepared, prepared with all that is necessary in this world. And there are others who are not prepared. Both have to journey just the same, those who are prepared and those who are not. Only the difference is that those who are prepared for the journey, for them this journey is easy. There is a fable of the monkey and the sparrows. When autumn seemed coming closer the sparrows said, "We must have a nest, we must build it, it must be ready because the autumn is coming nearer." A little monkey also heard it and was very

---

Documents:
- od.tp. = an old typescript of unknown provenance.
- Sk.tp. = a typescript made by Sakina Furnée or under her supervision, nearly identical with the od.tp.

Notes:
1. Sk.tp.: "Public Lecture." added

frightened because this was the first time for this young monkey to face autumn. It came with all anxiety to its parents and said, "We must build a home, we must build a nest where we can be protected. I did not know the autumn was coming, but someone told me it was coming." But while they were speaking the sparrows had their nest ready. But the monkeys put it off and went from one tomorrow to another tomorrow. And so it is in this world we find two kinds of personalities. There is one person who says, "What does it matter? We shall see what will come," and when he is faced by a difficulty, by a need, by a want, then he begins to realize that it would have been perhaps better if he had prepared beforehand.

And so it is with education. When a person is learning there is always for a young person an attraction to play, to enjoy life, and when that golden age of childhood which gives facility to learn and acquire knowledge is passed, then it is too late to acquire it. And the same thing is with the youth; the days when he should be careful of what he spends, and the time when he has spent all he has, and not earned, then he begins to feel the loss. And the greatest wealth is health and energy and intelligence and life itself. If this health from youth is not preserved and conserved and looked after, then at that time one does not feel it; but there comes a time when one knows that one did not prepare for it. I once asked a person who was old and strong and healthy, "Sir, will you tell me what blessing you have, what is it that keeps you at this age so strong and healthy?" He said, "This is the conserved energy of youth which is now maintaining my life." Very few young people think about it. Youth is an intoxication. When they are in that intoxication, when they are full of energy, they do not think about it, of what they have to spend in order to go far in the journey of life.

And then[2] we come to the idea of humanity. What we consider today learning or education, it is mostly made of grammar and history and geography and mathematics and calculations. But that education which we have to have as a current coin—a good manner, a strong will, a right attitude of mind—that education seems to be overlooked. We do not find it. And if a man had the education, qualification; if he had rank or position, and yet lacked manner; he lacks a great deal of life. If a man had all these things such as rank and position and qualifications of education, and yet he did not have

---

2. Sk.tp.: "when" instead of "then"

that strength of mind which is necessary to carry him through all his life's path, he is lacking a great deal. A man who lacks money misses little, but the man who lacks a power of mind misses everything in life. Weakness develops, and develops, and develops without man knowing it. When one sees a little spark of weakness in oneself, one says, "What is it, it is nothing," but one does not know that the spark will turn into a glow, and the glow will turn a flame one day. And those who lack manner, those who lack strength of mind, those who lack a right attitude, it is then too late, they cannot be corrected. And the nature of life is such that the thoughtless life will pull into thoughtlessness, and the thoughtful also [will draw thoughtlessness][3] towards itself, and therefore there is more chance of falling than of rising in life. And besides, friends, among thousands of persons there is hardly one who is taking this journey with open eyes, but mostly all journey with their eyes closed. Man so much depends upon his friends, upon his relations, upon those who love him, upon those who admire him, but does not know that any quality missing in him those who love him ask of him.

Therefore what is necessary in life, one must possess oneself, and not think, "Oh, what does it matter, my father was a king and my grandfather was an emperor; it does not matter." What relations you have, how great and good they may be, that is not of any use to you. We each have our journey to make and we have to answer the demands of this journey. How wonderful it is to watch in little journeys we make. One person comes along in a little group of travellers and gives them all pleasure, puts before them all the good he has, shares with them and gives a good impression to all, wins their hearts. When he has gone, what he has left with his friends is joy, that beautiful impression which they will always keep. And there is another one who has hurt or harmed or produced some disturbance among those travelling with him. And when he has gone, they pray that they will never meet him again. A maid said one day to her mistress that there was a funeral passing through the street. She was so much impressed and she said, "Certainly the person who died went to heaven." Her mistress laughed at the idea of this maid's authoritative exclamation that this dead person went to heaven. She said, "Did you see this dead person go to heaven?"

---

3. Od.tp.: "thoughtlessness will draw" written, then changed by hand to read "will draw thoughtlessness"; Sk.tp.: "will draw thoughtlessness"

"It is simple, Madam," she said, "for everyone who was going with the funeral was weeping. Certainly this person made an impression on those among whom he lived."

Man loses all absorbed in his daily life, not knowing that life passes and the call comes before he thinks of it. Man makes great mistakes, but among all mistakes there is one principal mistake, and that mistake is that he goes on through life thinking that he will stay here for ever. And naturally without preparation the call comes to him as a blow instead of coming as an invitation. And when we think, friends, of the journey beyond, we begin to see how many there are in this world who even do not know that there is a hereafter. And if one knows of the hereafter, then he has his preconceived ideas as to the coming of the hereafter: there is either a religious or philosophical belief, but it is not either that can suffice our purpose. What can suffice our purpose is to be acquainted with the road through which we have to pass, and by becoming acquainted with the road one also begins to see that that was the road where the soul descended to come to the earth. This road is that bridge which stands between the physical and the spiritual part of one's being, and therefore the nature of this journey is different. The journey in the world that we make is outside ourselves. This journey which we are making is within ourselves. And it is by being acquainted with this road that leads to that destination where we are meant to go; it is this that is acquired as a divine knowledge by the help of meditation. Many there are in this world curious to know what we shall find beyond this life. And it is this which gives way to those who wish to attract mankind by falsehood, this gives them scope to make up stories and to satisfy man's curiosity. For who can know of this way but the man himself; he is the traveller and his own spirit is the way. It is the man himself who must see his way, and it is with his own eyes that he must see what he will find in this way. Therefore, the teachers of life's secret do not tell that he will see this on the way or that[4] on the way. They say he will find whatever he will find, and your duty is to open your eyes that you may travel on the way and see for yourself. Once a *mureed*[5] asked his teacher; he said, "How I should like to see how it is in heaven and what is the appearance of hell." "Close your eyes," said the teacher "and you will see it." "Shall I see heaven first?" The teacher

---

4. Od.tp., Sk.tp.: "this" and "that" underlined for emphasis
5. Sufis use the word *mureed* for an initiate, see Glossary

said, "Yes." He closed his eyes and he went to his meditation. "And now," said the teacher, "hell, see it also in meditation." And when he opened his eyes, the teacher said, "What did you see?" He said, "Neither did I see in heaven that paradise of which people speak, or those beautiful plants and flowers and all the beautiful things of comfort and luxury, I saw nothing." "And what did you see in hell?" said the teacher. "I saw nothing. I had expected to see fire and people in torture, but I saw nothing. What is the reason, did I see or did I not see it?" "Certainly you have seen, but the brimstone and fire, or the beautiful gems and jewels of paradise, you have to take them for yourself. You do not get them there." And that gives the secret to the saying of Omar Khayyam[6]. He says, "Heaven is the vision of a fulfilled desire. Hell is the shadow of the soul on fire."[7] What is most necessary for us to learn and understand is that from a perfect source we come and to a perfect goal we go. But many seek that source unconsciously, and most of us seek that source wrongly. But few seek that source consciously, and fewer still seek that source rightly.

And now coming to the question of right seeking of that source. The way to seek this is to first learn the psychology of one's own life. What makes him fall, what makes him rise, what makes him fail, what makes him succeed, what gives him happiness, what brings him sorrow. And then to study the nature of pleasure and pain, whether it is lasting pleasure, whether it is lasting pain, or whether it is momentary pleasure, or whether it is momentary pain. And then to find out the deceitful and false nature of one's own impressions, how under a cover of pain there was a pleasure, how under a cover of pleasure there was a pain, and how in the worst persons there is some good to be found, and how in the best person there is something worse to be traced. And this widens the point of view of man, and this prepares the ground of his heart, in order to realize the secret of enjoyment. And the next thing that he has to do is to control his activities, physical and mental, that he must know that this nature of life is to go on, and therefore this suspension of life gives that travelling attitude of life a scope within, instead of giving a scope without. However much a person reads and studies about these things, that does not bring him satisfaction; satisfaction comes out of experience, and experience is gained out of meditation.

---

6. For Omar Khayyam and his Rubaiyat, see List
7. Stanza LXVII of FitzGerald's fourth edition

Besides, in this journey no one asks you what family you come from, what nation, what race you come from, what people, what faith you are coming with. What is asked is that are you prepared for this journey. It is your preparation which is your passport, it is your readiness which is your ticket to show in this path of life. There are no personalities considered here; what is considered is the evolution in the spiritual path. In the East the schools of the Sufis have existed for thousands of years, a school which had its beginning even before the time of Abraham. It is the message of that wisdom which is now being given here in the Western World. And at this time when the need is felt everywhere in the world, the doors of this school are being opened in many different nations of the world, and also in Switzerland. It is to the serious seekers, who do not seek for phenomena or wonder working, or go after this information for the sake of curiosity, but only with a serious mind and with a steady intention of going in this path, it is to these that this school opens the doors of its heart to welcome them.

Thank you for your sympathetic response. God bless you.

A typescript of unknown provenance

[1]Basel, January 30th, 1925

Die Innere Stimme

Heute sprechen wir ueber die innere Stimme. Die Bezeichnung 'die innere Stimme' ist die geeignetste, die man finden kann, um dasjenige zu nennen, worum es sich handelt, denn es ist unleugbar, dass es eine innere Stimme wie auch eine äussere Stimme gibt. Diese innere Stimme wird in jedem Menschen gefunden werden, aber nicht jeder Seele ist es gegeben, diese Stimme zu verstehen, sie wahrnehmen zu können und zwar aus zwei Hauptgründen: der eine Grund ist, dass das Menschenherz sich so verhärtet, dass es wie ein Stein werden kann, der nicht mitschwingen kann. Wenn die innere Stimme spricht, dann tönt dieser Stein nicht mit, kann[2] nicht mittönen und daher vernimmt man diese Stimme nicht.

Wenn wir nun etwa von den 'geistigen Ohren' des Herzens sprechen wollen, so ist es leider so, dass diese Ohren so viele Geräusche von aussen wahrnehmen, so viele Eindrücke von aussen an sich herankommen lassen, dass sie diese eine Stimme nicht mehr vernehmen können; die innere Stimme versinkt unter dem Lärm, der von aussen her hineindringt.

Wenn wir dazu kommen wollen, die innere Stimme zu hören, so müssen wir eben das Herz völlig umgestalten, damit es aufnahmefähig werde. Das Herz muss zu seinem natürlichen Zustand zurückgeführt werden, und dann wird es wieder für die innere Stimme empfänglich, und kann sie erfassen und aufnehmen. Gewiss, verschiedenartige Menschen bezeichnen diese eine Stimme verschiedenartig. Die einen behaupten, sie käme aus den Vorstellungen der verschiedenen Menschen hervor, die anderen sagen, es wäre die Sprache eines Engels der auf Erden etwas zu verkündigen habe. Andere wieder sind der Ansicht, dass die Stimme aus der Tiefe ihres eigenen Wesens kommt und andere wieder, es sei Gott, welcher in ihnen spricht. Welche Benennung auch der inneren

---

Documents:

un.tp. = a German typescript of unknown provenance.

Notes:

1. Un.tp.: "Vortrag von Pir-o-Murshid INAYAT KHAN" typed above text
2. Un.tp.: "kann" underlined for emphasis

Stimme gegeben wird, sie hängt von der Einstellung des Menschen zum Leben und von seinem Enwicklungszustand ab.

Wenn einer sagt, es sei die Stimme der Seele, so ist es so. Für denjenigen, welcher glaubt, es sei die Stimme eines Geistes oder eines Engels, auch für ihn trifft es zu. Und auch im Falle desjenigen, welcher meint, die Stimme komme von einem verstorbenen Menschen, auch der hat recht, wie auch in dem Falle, dass da jemand glaubt, es sei die Stimme Gottes, welche spricht. Auch dieser hat recht. So lange jene Menschen aufrichtig fühlen und glauben, ist dem so, nicht aber wenn sie, aus irgend einem Gedankenvorgang heraus, es sich vorstellen.

Eines Tages kam ein Kind zu mir und fragte mich, ob die Geschichte von Sankt Nikolaus wahr und wirklich wäre und dem Kinde war es vor der Antwort bange. Das Kind hatte nämlich schon an Sankt Nikolaus einen Brief geschrieben, aber in der Schule hatte ein Klassenkamerad gefragt, "Gibt es denn ein Sankt Nikolaus?" Darum war es dem Kinde bange, es fürchtete, dass der Brief zwecklos wäre. Das Kind wurde aber über die Antwort, die es bekam, sehr froh, eine Antwort, die jenes Menschenkind sicher auf seinen Lebensweg mit sich trägt. Die Antwort lautete zusammengefasst folgendermassen: alles, was des Menschen Geist sich denkt, das besteht, das ist, alles, wenn nicht auf dem physischen Plane, so doch auf einer mentalen Ebene. Jene, welche leicht behaupten, dies und jenes ist unmöglich, sie sind nicht zu einem tieferen Verständnis vorgedrungen. Ebensogut wie für den einen ein gewisses Etwas nicht lebt, nicht existiert, so ist das für einen anderen die Wirklichkeit. Und der Mensch in seinen irdischen Begrenzungen, sollte nicht richten, nicht bestimmen wollen wer recht hat.

Es liegt Wahrheit darin und ist schön, in all den Sagen, in all den Erzählungen, welche wir in den alten Schriften lesen, wie ein Engel herniederkam und mit Hiob kämpfte, oder wie etwa Gabriel niederstieg und mit Moses sprach und wie die heilige Maria die Botschaft des Engels hörte. Es liegt nichts kaltes, nichts trockenes darin, es ist schön, es ist künstlerisch. Nur müssen wir solche Sachen auf unsere eigene Art auslegen. Was in solchen Erlebnissen dem Menschen offenbart wird, ist stets ihm zugekommen, heute wie morgen, und das ist die laut gewordene innere Stimme.

Nun werdet ihr fragen, was ist eigentlich der Unterschied zwischen der inneren Stimme und der Stimme, die von aussen her kommt. Wenn die innere Stimme wirklich spricht, wieso kommt es dann, dass wir sie so oft nicht hören? Der Vorgang ist folgender: die Stimme, welche von aussen her kommt, findet ein Echo im Herzen, und dieses Echo vernehmen wir und glauben dann, es sei die innere Stimme. Was die Weisen daher von jeher getan haben, war über die innere Stimme zu meditieren, sich zu versenken, um diese innere Stimme klar und rein hören zu können. Für einige Augenblicke oder auch länger gehen sie in die Stille und dort verschliessen sie sich allen Stimmen, die von aussen kommen, so dass nur noch ihre innere Stimme ertönt. In religiöser Hinsicht ist das auf eine gewisse Art zu verstehen und von der metaphysischen Seite ist es wieder anders zu verstehen. Die religiöse Seite davon ist so erklärlich, so wie die Führung der Eltern dem Kinde in dem Maße zuteil wird, wie das Kind danach verlangt. Wenn das Kind bei jedem Geräusch zur Mutter springt, so ist selbstverständlich die ganze Aufmerksamkeit der Mutter auf das Kind konzentriert. Auch wenn das Kind dann gehen lernt, auch dann sind die Arme der Mutter immer ausgestreckt, um das Kindlein aufzuhalten, wenn es fallen sollte. Dem ist so, weil eben das Kind es bewusst erwartet, es weiss, dass die Mutter ihre Hände ausstreckt, um es vor einem Fall zu bewahren.

So ist es auch mit demjenigen, der Gott liebt, mit demjenigen, der Gott ehrt. Derjenige, welcher Gott wahrlich liebt, der weiss auch, der fühlt auch, dass allezeit die Arme Gottes ihn beschützen, ihn führen, ihn leiten. Wenn das Kind gross wird, dann geht es alleine hinaus in den Garten und die Mutter sagt sich, ja, ich lasse es, das Kind ist jetzt gross genug, sich selbst zu schützen. Und die Mutter lässt das Kind gehen, denn sie weiss, das Kind bleibt in ihrer Sehweite, und sie weiss, dass sie jeden Augenblick hinzu springen kann, ihm zu helfen. Da ist es dem Kinde nicht bewusst, dass die Mutter acht gibt, das Kind hört die Mutter, fühlt die Mutter in der Nähe, aber erst im Augenblick wo Gefahr droht, weiss das Kind, dass die Mutter hinzuspringt.

So ist es mit demjenigen, welcher Gott in Wahrheit nachstrebt, der das Gefühl hat, dass Gott immer um ihn ist, ihm immer nah ist. Für solche Menschen ist die innere Stimme immer gegenwärtig. Und diejenigen, welche wohl Gott verehren, an Gott denken, aber ihn nicht immer gegenwärtig haben, zu den Menschen kommt die innere Stimme erst im Augenblick der Not.

Nun kommen wir zum metaphysischen Standpunkt. Es gibt einen geistlichen, es gibt einen inneren Plan auf dem alles vor sich geht, bevor es auf dem physischen Plan tritt. Der ganze Vorgang jener Arbeit der geistigen Gesetze kann verfolgt werden. Die Augen des Herzens können das Arbeiten jener Gesetye sehen und die Ohren des Herzens können das Ineinandergreifen dieser Gesetze hören. Was solche Menschen sehen, das nennen sie eine 'Vision', was solche Menschen hören, das nennen sie eine 'innere Stimme'. Zu den Weisen, zu den Propheten, zu den Gottesmenschen ist es diese Stimme, die kam und ihnen vernehmbar redete.

Doch haben sie keine Gewalt über jene Stimme, sie äussert sich, ohne dass ihr Wille etwas dazu tun kann. In einer alten Geschichte wird erzählt, dass die Kinder Jakobs ihm einst einen Vorwurf machten, "Er könne jetzt nicht mehr sagen, wo sein Sohn sei, währenddem er früher aus dem Geruch der Kleider erkannt habe, dass sie Joseph gehörten." Die Antwort des Jakobs lautete, "Es war Gottes Stimme, die damals sprach." Diese Stimme lässt sich vernehmen, wenn Gott so will und nicht, wenn Gott es nicht will. Niemand kann dieser Stimme befehlen, denn Gott bleibt immer darüber Herr und Meister.

Gehen wir nun weiter in unserer Betrachtung, so kommen wir zu einem mehr logischen, mehr wissenschaftlichen Standpunkt. Des Menschen Leib ist so gebaut, dass von allen Seiten her Eindrücke von ihm empfangen werden können. In diesem Leib liegt der sichtbare Teil des Lebens, aber auch ein unsichtbarer. Der Körper besteht aus Materie und in diesem Körper gibt es Zentren, welche Sitz des Geistes genannt werden können. Und derjenige Mensch, welcher imstande ist, seinen Körper derart zu gestalten, dass er mittelst dieser inneren Stimme wahrnehmen kann, der kennt aller Weltanschauung.

Diesen Leib muss man pflegen, man muss ihm seine nötige Pflege angedeihen lassen, genau wie man es bei einem Acker tut, den man bearbeitet. Diese Kunst ist der Menschheit verloren gegangen, doch bei dem Mystiker ist sie geblieben.

Die Sufi Einweihung wird deswegen gegeben, um den Menschen instand zu setzen, am geistigen wie auch am materiellen Körper zu arbeiten, dass er fähig wird die innere Stimme wahrzunehmen. Aber nichts wird einem Jünger versprochen, denn keiner kann je die Wahrheit einem anderen einimpfen. Man kann nur die Menschen hinweisen, sie hinlenken zum Ziele, welches sie erreichen mögen. Denn Wahrheit kann nicht gelernt[3] werden; Wahrheit kann niemals gegeben werden. Wahrheit ist etwas, das

---

3. Un.tp.: "nicht gelernt" underlined for emphasis

unmittelbar aufsprudelt, aufquillt. Sie kann nur entdeckt[4] werden. Gewiss, auf dem Wege durch die Dunkelheit ist der Beistand eines Führers von grossem Wert. Daher ist für diejenigen, welche sich der Führung eines solchen Lehrers anvertrauen, die Verehrung dieses Lehrers das höchst wichtige.

Ein persischer Dichter sagt, "Selbst wenn man die Gotteserkenntnis erlangt, und man die Wahrheit entdeckt hat, so bleibt doch eines sich anzueignen, nämlich die Dankbarkeit dem Lehrer gegenüber.

---

4. Un.tp.: "entdeckt" underlined for emphasis

Angela Alt's handwriting

1 Florence, February 4th, 1925

The Awakening of the Soul [2]

The awakening of the soul is a[3] birth of the soul and unless it is born again, it will not enter into[4] the kingdom of heaven, i.e. unless it is awakened it will not enter the kingdom of[5] divine illumination. [6]You will ask, "How is it to be awakened[7]? At a certain age, or a certain[8] time, one thinks one awakens[9]?" It is no use to wake a[10] soul before the time. In the East there[11] is a custom that when a person[12] is asleep, one lets him sleep[13]. He needs it. To awaken him is a crime. Neither[14] does it help the[15] person nor[16] is it good for his[17] soul. When we think[18] relations or friends are asleep, and they must waken, then[19] we are mistaken; perhaps it is not good

---

Documents:
- Al.hw. = a handwritten text made by Angela Alt.
- Sk.tp.1 = a typescript made by Sakina Furnée, nearly identical to Al.hw.
- Sk.tp.2 = a highly edited typescript made by Sakina Furnée, possibly following editing of Murshida Sherifa Goodenough.

Notes:
1. Al.hw.: Murshida Goodenough wrote on the top of the document "incomplete report"; Sk.tp.1: "Public Lecture. Note in handwriting Murshida Goodenough: Incomplete Report." typed above the text; Sk.tp.2: "Public Lecture." added by hand, then "not in handwriting." typed above the text
2. Sk.tp.2: "THE SOUL'S AWAKENING" instead of "The Awakening of the Soul"
3. Sk.tp.2: "the" instead of "a"
4. Sk.tp.2: "into" omitted
5. Sk.tp.2: "heaven or" added
6. Sk.tp.2: "Now" added
7. Sk.tp.2: "to awaken it" instead of "is it to be awakened"
8. Al.hw.: "age" written, then crossed out and omitted in a.o.d.
9. Sk.tp.1: "awakes" instead of "awakens"; Sk.tp.2: This whole phrase "At a certain age, or a certain time one thinks one awakens" omitted
10. Sk.tp.2: "awaken the" instead of "wake a"
11. Sk.tp.2: "it" instead of "there"
12. Sk.tp.2: "to let the one who" instead of "that when a person"
13. Sk.tp.2: "go on sleeping" instead of ", one lets him sleep"
14. Sk.tp.2: "Nor" instead of "Neither"
15. Sk.tp.2: "a" instead of "the"
16. Sk.tp.2: "neither" instead of "nor"
17. Sk.tp.2: "the" instead of "his"
18. Sk.tp.2: "of our" added
19. Sk.tp.2: "and we want to waken them," instead of "or friends are asleep, and they must waken, then"

that[20] they should waken until they[21] have had enough sleep, which[22] is necessary. But again, we may be mistaken, we think that[23] one is asleep, and he[24] may be more awake than us[25]! People think they[26] are spiritual and look down on one[27] less spiritual than themselves[28], and that[29] person is more spiritual perhaps[30]!

There[31] is a story of[32] a man who was quiet and[33] never prayed and[34] his wife was sad about it. One day he found a feast prepared at home[35]. "What is it all[36] about?" he asked. She said, "My desire is[37] come true." "What desire?" "It is a secret." Then she told him[38], "Husband, you have been very[39] good and loving and have many virtues[40], but one thing made me discontented, I thought you were an unbeliever." He said,[41] "How did you find[42] I[43] am a believer[44]?" [45]"Last night," she answered,[46] "when you were asleep, I heard from your lips the name of God. You spoke it." "Did I[47]?" he said, "Alas!" And he fell down dead. In all[48] his life he had thought[49] and lived in God, in[50] every breath longing for God, his[51] whole

---

20. Sk.tp.2: "till" instead of "that"
21. Sk.tp.2: "should waken until they" omitted
22. Sk.tp.2: "for them sleep" instead of "which"
23. Sk.tp.2: "that" omitted
24. Sk.tp.1: "she" instead of "and he"
25. Sk.tp.2: "we are" instead of "us"
26. Sk.tp.2: "We may think we" instead of "People think they"
27. Sk.tp.2: "those" instead of "one"
28. Sk.tp.2: "we think" instead of "themselves"
29. Sk.tp.2: "the" instead of "that"
30. Sk.tp.2: "perhaps" omitted
31. Sk.tp.2: "Here" instead of "There"
32. Sk.tp.2: ". There was once" instead of "of"
33. Sk.tp.2: "he" added
34. Sk.tp.2: "and" omitted
35. Sk.tp.2: "the man came home and found a feast ready" instead of "he found a feast prepared at home"
36. Sk.tp.2: "all" omitted
37. Sk.tp.2: "has" instead of "is"
38. Sk.tp.2: "It was a secret. She said at last" instead of "'What desire?' 'It is as secret.' Then she told him"
39. Sk.tp.2: "so" instead of "very"
40. Sk.tp.2: "virtuous" instead of "have many virtues"
41. Sk.tp.2: "He said," omitted
42. Sk.tp.2: "out" added
43. Al.hw.: "was" written, then crossed out and omitted in a.o.d.
44. Sk.tp.2: "believe" instead of "am I a believer"
45. Sk.tp.2: "asked the husband. The wife replied," added
46. Sk.tp.2: "she answered," omitted
47. Sk.tp.2: "Did I speak it" instead of "You spoke it.' 'Did I"
48. Sk.tp.2: "For all through" instead of "In all"
49. Sk.tp.2: "of" added
50. Sk.tp.2: "in" omitted
51. Sk.tp.1: "the" instead of "his"

ideal was God. And for him to think that what was sacred to him had been[52] spoken out, it[53] became lost. And so very often we mistake[54] the human character, and[55] we misjudge those who are more spiritual than us[56]. In the depth of the soul is[57] divine spirit; we do not know what is hidden, however outwardly a person may seem irreligious[58].

And now coming to the awakening of the soul[59]. Does it depend upon a certain age? The soul may wake[60] in infancy, middle age, any time, suddenly or gradually. This awakening is not bound to a law. Of course there are cases of saints, sages, masters[61] who awakened[62] at a moment's time, and whose[63] life became different. Life is as a[64] rising from a dream, and rising he now[65] sees reality.

But you ask, "What does a person feel whose soul is awakened[66]?" He feels that he stands upon his feet[67]. When asleep he lies down. The moment the[68] soul has awoken[69] the person stands on his own feet. He has self-confidence, he trusts himself, what he believes he believes, what he knows, he knows. No experience or learning can make it different, for he sees it with open eyes.[70] There are those who because people have told him[71], others, because someone[72] preached and[73] taught[74]. Others believe because their forefathers[75] did. That belief is different. What comes after the awakening of a[76] soul, nothing can change[77].

---

52. Sk.tp.2: "was" instead of "had been"
53. Sk.tp.2: "it" omitted
54. Sk.tp.2: "misunderstand" instead of "mistake"
55. Sk.tp.2: "and" omitted
56. Al.hw.: "(we)" written above "us"; Sk.tp.1, 2: "we" instead of "us"
57. Sk.tp.2: "the" added
58. Sk.tp.2: "irreligious one may be" instead of "a person may seem irreligious"
59. Sk.tp.2: "law of awakening of souls" instead of "awakening of the soul"
60. Sk.tp.2: "awaken" instead of "wake"
61. Sk.tp.2: "masters, sages" instead of "sages, masters"
62. Sk.tp.2: "wakened" instead of "awakened"
63. Sk.tp.2: "the whole" instead of "whose"
64. Sk.tp.2: "as a" omitted
65. Sk.tp.2: "then one" instead of "rising he now"
66. Sk.tp.2: "wakened" instead of "awakened"
67. Al.hw., Sk.tp.1: Every word of this phrase is underlined
68. Sk.tp.2: "a" instead of "the"
69. Sk.tp.2: "awakened" instead of "awoken"
70. Al.hw.: a space for missing words
71. Sk.tp.2: "they have been told so" instead of "people have told him"
72. Sk.tp.2: "has" added
73. Sk.tp.2: "or" instead of "and"
74. Sk.tp.2: "them" added
75. Sk.tp.1: "forefather" instead of "forefathers"
76. Sk.tp.2: "the" instead of "a"
77. Sk.tp.2: "it" added

And what feeling is it[78]? It is a feeling of self-dependence. The awakening of the soul depends upon the keen insight[79] of a[80] soul. Once it has awakened[81], it begins to see life quite differently. What it has once[82] admired sometimes becomes unimportant;[83] things that he had striven after, upon awakening, their importance becomes less[84]. The soul begins to feel a strength, power, and independence, and stands upon[85] its feet. It may be [said][86] that is the[87] moment the soul begins to see and hear, [88]when he sees that, "That which[89] I have seen and experienced was while I was asleep[90]."

Now, what sort of life does this person lead: a religious life, an ascetic one[91]? It is[92] no matter what life he may lead[93], whether in the world or [94]the desert, it is just the same. Therefore, from [95]outward appearances you cannot judge. King, rich man, poor man, whoever he be, the[96] soul is awakened. No one can judge such[97] a soul by actions or appearances. And[98] the awakening of a[99] soul does not compel one to lead[100] an ascetic or[101] apparently religious life[102]. Neither is there heredity that can bring this awakening, nor any

78. Sk.tp.2: "does it feel like" instead of "feeling is it"
79. Sk.tp.2: "keen sight" instead of "the keen insight"
80. Sk.tp.2: "the" instead of "a"
81. Sk.tp.2: "awake" instead of "it has awakened"
82. Sk.tp.2: "he had" instead of "it has once"
83. Sk.tp.2: "important. Of" instead of "unimportant;"
84. Sk.tp.2: "the importance becomes less on awakening" instead of "upon awakening, their importance becomes less"
85. Sk.tp.2: "on" instead of "upon"
86. Al.hw.: "sad" written, then encircled and followed by a question mark; Sk.tp.1: "(said)" inserted followed by a number of dots; Sk.tp.2: "said" instead of "sad"
87. Sk.tp.2: "from that" instead of "is the"
88. Sk.tp.2: "from that moment" added
89. Sk.tp.2: "What" instead of "That which"
90. Sk.tp.2: "expressed I was asleep hitherto" instead of "experienced was while I was asleep"
91. Sk.tp.2: "Does he lead a religious, ascetic life" instead of "a religious life, an ascetic one"
92. Sk.tp.2: "It is" omitted
93. Sk.tp.2: "leads" instead of "may lead"
94. Sk.tp.2: "in" added
95. Sk.tp.2: "the" added
96. Sk.tp.2: "One may be very rich etc., yet the awakened" instead of "King, rich man, poor man, whoever he be, the"
97. Sk.tp.2: "such" omitted
98. Sk.tp.2: "And" omitted
99. Sk.tp.2: "the" instead of "a"
100. Sk.tp.2: "one to lead" omitted
101. Sk.tp.2: "life or an" instead of "or"
102. Sk.tp.2: "one" instead of "life"

study, for this is a divine heritage which[103] every soul has brought with him.

And now you ask, what is the condition of his life? The answer is that it is a life that is happiness itself. If there is sadness, it is that no one understands the language of the awakened[104] soul. It is like living in a country where one understands the others but no one understands you. Therefore, no one can sympathize. The awakened soul can naturally reach in sympathy to[105] others. The awakened soul[106] does not feel it is right to ask for sympathy from those who do not know his condition. Naturally the seers who[107] live in a crowd are[108] yet in a[109] solitude[110].

A symbolic story of India describes two dervishes wandering without regarding anyone.[111] And one day, one[112] came from one side and met the other, and[113] a feeling of respect came from the eyes of the other[114]. These dervishes are called *majzub*[115], and are not concerned with the life of others. There was a young student who wanted to know why they regarded each other and not the world. So this person went and sat near this dervish to get the answer why he regarded the other dervish. The dervish said, "I[116] put my hand on your hand[117] for a moment, for you to[118] see how the world is with my sight." And then the student saw[119] that everyone was asleep except[120] the dervishes! It becomes a living experience. The soul awakened sees others asleep. And when one sees souls asleep, one does not judge their actions, one forgives. One does not

103. Sk.tp.2: "heredity" instead of "heritage which"
104. Sk.tp.2: "awakening of the" instead of "awakened"
105. Sk.tp.2: "the" added
106. Sk.tp.2: ", but" instead of ". The awakened soul"
107. Sk.tp.2: "who" omitted
108. Sk.tp.2: "are" omitted
109. Sk.tp.2: "a" omitted
110. Sk.tp.2: ", even in the midst of a crowd" added
111. Sk.tp.2: "Here is a symbolical story from India. There were two wandered dervishes going about without regard for anyone." instead of "A symbolic story ... without regarding anyone."
112. Sk.tp.2: "dervish" added
113. Sk.tp.2: "when the two met," instead of "met the other, and"
114. Sk.tp.2: "each" instead of "the other"
115. For *majzub*, see *majdhub* in Glossary
116. Sk.tp.2: "will" added
117. Sk.tp.2: "head" instead of "hand"
118. Sk.tp.2: "so that you" instead of "for you to"
119. Sk.tp.2: "when he saw, he beheld" instead of "then the student saw"
120. Sk.tp.2: "but" instead of "except"

blame or[121] take revenge[122], nor complain[123] of faults. It is on this awakening of the soul that life's purpose depends, and as[124] long as it is not awakened, the soul will not be saved[125].

And then[126] the question, can one hasten[127] the awakening of a[128] soul? The thought of awakening[129] will help to awaken. Often before going to sleep one[130] says, "At such an hour I must wake[131]," and one awakes[132]! [133]That is the method of waking the soul. It is calling the soul to awaken[134], and it does it. The seers of all times who went[135] to the desert, they called out to the soul, and[136] in answer to the call, it awoke[137].

And now what benefit is derived from the[138] awakening? It[139] rises above anxieties, doubts, fears. It[139] finds as[140] in itself, in its[141] spirit, these[142]: indifference, independence[143], as part of its[144] being. And [145]that indifference does not signify[146], "Keep away from me." But it is this, it[147] is always inclined to serve and to[148] sympathize, but if it receives no return, it[149] is indifferent; in other

---

121. Sk.tp.2: "blame or" omitted
122. Sk.tp.2: "no blames" added
123. Sk.tp.2: "complains" instead of "complain"
124. Sk.tp.2: "so" instead of "as"
125. Sk.tp.2: "conscious" instead of "saved"
126. A.o.d.: "then" omitted
127. Sk.tp.1: "master" instead of "hasten", then corrected by hand to read "hasten"
128. Sk.tp.2: "the" instead of "a"
129. Al.hw., Sk.tp.1: "the thought of awakening" each word underlined
130. Sk.tp.2: "a person" instead of "one"
131. Sk.tp.2: "waken" instead of "wake"
132. Sk.tp.2: "he wakes" instead of "one awakes"
133. Sk.tp.2: "If this is so" added
134. Sk.tp.2: "wake" instead of "awaken"
135. Sk.tp.2: "went in" instead of "who went"
136. Sk.tp.2: "and" omitted
137. Sk.tp.2: "awakened" instead of "awoke"
138. Sk.tp.2: "the" omitted
139. Sk.tp.2: "One" instead of "It"
140. Al.hw.: "as" placed in parentheses with a question mark on top; Sk.tp.1: "as" between parentheses; Sk.tp.2: "as" omitted
141. Sk.tp.2: "oneself, in one's" instead of "itself, in its"
142. Al.hw.: "these" placed between parentheses; Sk.tp.2: omitted
143. Al.hw.: "indifference" and "independence" underlined
144. Sk.tp.2: "one's" instead of "its"
145. Sk.tp.2: "what is" added
146. Sk.tp.2: "indifference? It is not" instead of "indifference does not signify"
147. Sk.tp.2: "one" instead of "it"
148. Sk.tp.2: "to" omitted
149. Sk.tp.2: "is not returned, one" instead of "receives no return, it"

words, the awakened soul is indifferent to results [150] . Independence[151] is this, that the awakened soul finds with the growing of conscience[152], independence manifesting in itself. The reason of this[153] independence is that the awakened soul gets in touch with the spirit of all sufficiency, of[154] all that man seeks in the outer world; he finds the essence[155] in himself[156] even if it is[157] not the outward thing.

And now to what does it awaken[158]? Firstly[159], it awakes to self. The result is that he is awaken[160] to all things. And the wonder is that in[161] all this[162] conflict about, disputes of different faiths, he rises above[163], sees truth in all, yet is above all[164]. He does not dispute, as he[165] is not against; [166]he sees the one truth in all. It is never too soon to awake[167] and never too late. And the final word is, [168]great help[169] can be obtained in[170] awakening of souls by[171] the contact with awakened souls. For every soul is like a candle not yet lightened. But the candle that has qualities[172] to be lit, responds[173], and the lit candle can light others, and this is called initiation. That initiation is the confidence given by the teacher and the trust of[174] the pupil.

---

150. Al.hw.: a number of dots with a question mark followed by one or two illegible words, possibly "in action"; Sk.tp.1: "... in action (?) typed here; Sk.tp.2: "be it joy or sorrow" added
151. Al.hw.: "Independence" underlined
152. Sk.tp.2: "consciousness" instead of "conscience"
153. Sk.tp.1: "the" instead of "this"
154. Sk.tp.2: "of" omitted
155. Al.hw.: "essence" underlined; Sk.tp.2: "of it" added
156. Sk.tp.2: "the self" instead of "himself"
157. Sk.tp.2: "it is" omitted
158. Sk.tp.2: "awake" instead of "awaken"
159. Sk.tp.2: "First" instead of "Firstly"
160. Sk.tp.2: "awake" instead of "awaken"
161. Sk.tp.2: "And the wonder is that in" omitted
162. Sk.tp.1,2: "the" instead of "this"
163. Sk.tp.2: "them" added
164. Al.hw.: "above all" underlined
165. Sk.tp.2: "as he" omitted
166. Sk.tp.2: "as" added
167. Sk.tp.2: "waken" instead of "awake"
168. Sk.tp.2: "if there is a" added
169. Sk.tp.2: "that" added
170. Sk.tp.2: "by the" instead of "in"
171. Sk.tp.2: "the soul, it is" instead of "souls by"
172. Sk.tp.2: "has the quality" instead of "that has qualities"
173. Sk.tp.2: "responds" omitted
174. Sk.tp.2: "given by" instead of "of"

Angela Alt's handwriting

[1] Florence, February 5th, 1925

Revelation

Many think that a revelation comes to us. But in reality it is not so, the soul opens itself to a revelation. The whole life that we see before us, and the life not seen, it is all plain and at the same time subtle. The whole life is expressed and communicated. Plainly speaking, all beings and all things speak to us, only we cannot hear all things. In ancient beliefs we hear that first there was a word, and the word was God, and then also we hear that there was a word, a word which was lost. And when one digs into its meaning, one finds it is[2] that life was expressed[3], life was communicated, was[4], because it was believed readily[5]. Life was, is, and will[6] be always communicated. It was communicated with[7], but the communication with man was lost, and[8] it is no longer communicated. Therefore, the belief, the mystery of the lost word means that the communication that was[9], does not exist just now.

And[10] same thing in daily life. There are two friends, lovers, relations, there is a time when they understand without words and then comes the time when a wall seems to be between them. And when that communication is closed, sorrow and unhappiness come. When it was open, words were not enough[11]. For when that time

---

Documents:

Al.hw. = a handwritten document made by Angela Alt.

Sk.tp. = a typescript made by Sakina Furnée, nearly identical in wording in the type, but showing handwritten corrections.

Notes:

1. Al.hw.: "Incomplete report" written above the lecture (handwriting Murshida Goodenough; Sk.tp.: "Note Mda Goodenough: "Incomplete report." typed above the lecture, then "Public Lecture." added by hand
2. Al.hw.: "that the real meaning" written then crossed out and "it is" substituted, and "it is" in Sk.tp.
3. Al.hw.: "expressed" underlined and a question mark written in the margin
4. Al.hw.: "was" underlined, possibly indicating that Inayat Khan emphasized these words
5. Sk.tp.: "but really" instead of "readily"
6. Al.hw.: "was", "is" and "will" underlined
7. Sk.tp.: "(the help of man)" written in the margin to be inserted here
8. Al.hw.: a space for missing words; Sk.tp.: "(then)" written by hand on a number of dots
9. Al.hw., Sk.tp.: "was" underlined
10. Al.hw.: a space, missing words; Sk.tp.: "we see the" written by hand on dots
11. Sk.tp.: "enough" placed between parentheses and "needed" substituted

comes, after sweet moments of friendship, when bitterness comes, then life becomes hell without that communication. All belief[12], grief, complaints against masters, servants, friends, relations, these have one secret behind, that communication is closed. But people generally look at it blindly, blaming another, the brother, wife, sister, not seeing it is the barrier they have put between them, the want of communication.

Two friends who cannot understand one another are in worse condition than two enemies who understand. This helps us to understand that life is worth living and[13] only when we can understand; it has no value without. This understanding has its degree[14]. And mystics placed[15] in different degrees. The first degree of understanding is what we call the impression[16] of our daily life. For instance we see someone, and before he has spoken, we have an impression of him. And it is by this impression we learn whether to trust or not to trust and by it we feel we are attracted or not attracted. [Persons][17] also make an impression on us among any group of people, an impression of misery, or joy, etc. Of course these impressions differ. Some are deeply impressed, others are not to be impressed. But those who are confused in their minds are apt to have a wrong impression. Those who have an open, clear heart have correct, clear impressions. There are people who, the minute they see a person know that "with this person I can work well," or "my business will go well".

The next degree of understanding is called intuition[18]. No doubt, women are often more intuitive than men. The reason is by nature she is more respondent, and her heart is tender since in her there is put that sympathy with which to bring up children. Naturally she is respondent to intuition, and she can often tell something she has no reason for, and it is true. Often an intuitive person feels if harm or success is going to happen yet cannot give an apparent reason for this. No doubt it requires keen sight and deep feeling in order to be intuitive. A person who lives a superficial life, or who

---

12. Al.hw.: a question mark written underneath "belief"; Sk.tp.: "belief (?)" crossed out
13. Al.hw.: a space, missing words; Sk.tp.: a number of dots
14. Al.hw.: a space, missing words than "exh..." started followed by another space and "?" written in the margin; Sk.tp.: many dots
15. Al.hw.: a space, missing words; Sk.tp.: a number of dots
16. Al.hw., Sk.tp.: "impression" underlined
17. Al.hw.: a space missing words; Sk.tp.: "(persons)" written by hand over a number of dots
18. Al.hw., Sk.tp.: "intuition" underlined

deceives others, is often deceived. He who pursues truth, him truth pursues. One who deceives others is deceived by his own deceit.

The nature of life is action and reaction. Every[19] action has its reaction of some nature. You must know that if you take advantage of another, it will be taken of you, the opportunity is only waiting. Reality is the portion of the sincere[20] one by which one always sees[21] it is the sincere person who is intuitive. By learning intuition cannot be learned. It is only gained by opening the self to intuition. Intuition is an inner voice, which warns, which advises. A man without intuition, however qualified, misses much. For all that he knows of things, without intuition man [is helpless][22]. Intuition is something like a hand in the darkness; one does not know what person it is, but one has a hand, not knowing whose. It is possible that a person may be intuitive but does not render it clearly. There are two reasons for this: one is, he does not believe his own intuition; the other that his mind is too active and he does not distinguish between imagination and intuition. But as people are today, they are not inclined to believe in intuition, so it gets lost. And those whose mind goes on from one thing to another like a film picture cannot make their own picture clear. And it is the fault of the present life. When one day I asked a journalist, "There are many things mystical and philosophical to give to the world to elevate them?" and he told me, "But we are taught to use so many words in five minutes, to be a journalist." Does it not show that this life is a sort of struggle against spiritual evolution, not that each soul is unwilling to learn truth, it is the aim of every soul to get to the truth. But it is the life that we live, a life of competition and activity that we would do better without. It robs us of our spiritual happiness.

And now to the subject of revelation[23]. One degree further we come to inspiration[24]. And this comes to the contemplative who put[25] in art, writing, thinking. And what a great difference there is between inspiration and brain work. Some writers in moments of

---

19. Sk.tp.: "Even" instead of "Every"
20. Al.hw.: "successful" written, then crossed out and "sincere" substituted; Sk.tp.: "sincere"
21. Sk.tp.: "that" added by hand
22. Al.hw.: a space, missing words; Sk.tp.: a number of dots, then "(is helpless)" added by hand
23. Al.hw.: "revelation" underlined, but not in Sk.tp.
24. Al.hw., Sk.tp.: "inspiration" underlined
25. Al.hw., Sk.tp.: a number of dots, missing words

revelation[26] cannot do in five years time[27] with the brain what they did under inspiration. It is something natural and finished[28], it comes like a stream. Besides, a genius, poet, thinker, musician, writer, is never satisfied with the brain work. But when inspiration brings something, it cannot be compared with anything else in the world. When [Firdausi][29], the great Persian poet, brought his inspired work, and the courtiers discussed what gift should be given, he said, "This inspiration is greater than any gift." The[30] joy, independence, upliftment are greater than anything else.

But now you will ask a thing related to metaphysics: where does inspiration come from? Of course, if I give an answer in religious terms, it is easy: from God, from where all things come. But when according to metaphysics, it is still more interesting. That is, all the knowledge that man ever possessed in the world's history is all kept together, preserved in one mind. It is that mind, divine mind, and is thence that man draws according to the power of his desire. There is a Persian saying that your portion is according to your desire. The artist draws from the same mind and source, and the musician, the philosopher etc. But now you ask, "This inspirational work that comes in the Italian, the [French][31], the Indian etc. languages, does it come as a language? Then what is the language of inspiration?" The answer is, the mind of man is pictured as a typewriter, that has all the[32] alphabets[33] ready. And there is one who works upon the instrument, who draws upon that mind. Naturally, the language of inspiration is one and the same, but he who manifests it interprets it in his own language. There may be a poet, a master of his language, and another who is not, yet both draw inspiration. Both have the same power to draw from. But he who has the best knowledge of his language expresses it more perfectly.

And now what is it that brings inspiration? It is brought about by a perfect concentration. If the concentration is not right,

---

26. Al.hw.: "under inspiration" written then crossed out, and omitted in Sk.tp.
27. Al.hw.: "what I" written, then crossed out, and omitted in Sk.tp.
28. Al.hw.: "finished" slightly underlined and a cross written in the margin; Sk.tp.: a number of dots instead of "finished" then "finished" added by hand
29. Al.hw.: a number of dots, than "Firdausi" written above the line in another hw.; Sk.tp.: dots, "Firdausi" later added by hand. For Firdausi see List
30. Sk.tp.: "The" crossed out
31. Al.hw.: a space, missing words; Sk.tp.: "(French)" written by hand on a number of dots
32. Al.hw.: "the" repeated here; Sk.tp.: "letters of the" added
33. Sk.tp.: the "s" of "alphabets" crossed out

there is no power to draw upon the divine mind. Do the poets, writers, inventors, and the quite material not concentrate upon divine mind? There are many who do not consciously concentrate, but their work automatically obliges them to concentrate. As Edison[34] may not concentrate like a spiritual man, but the work has led him to concentrate. This shows how much we lose by our life which we live of that power which inspires our life.

There is one aspect of revelation to be considered called vision[35], an aspect mostly manifesting when man is asleep or half asleep. [The one who][36] is not in the habit of concentrating when awake so does[37] automatically when asleep. When mind is focussed in thought, that thought manifests itself in words and forms. But a most interesting thing is, in vision,[38] not the repetition of things we want to know, but the answer. And a still more interesting part of vision is that according to the evolution of the individual, the vision is either fine, or gross, or symbolical. And the symbolism of every person is in accordance with his evolution. If he found the key to his evolution, he could be the best interpreter of his own vision, because the symbolism of everyone's vision is according to his own soul.

And when we go further still in revelation, we come to actual revelation[39], and this actual revelation may be considered as a third eye open. No sooner does the glance fall upon a person than it seems that the person at once gets into communication. There is the old story that the saints and sages spoke with trees and stones. It is not only an ancient legend, today souls can[40] speak with them. The privilege of the human soul simply is the same, the same old wine which is ever new. It only wants opening to the light in order to get into communication. And now, where is the key? The key is sympathy. Sympathy with art opens the heart to art, with science to science, sympathy with a single being opens the heart to his condition, to all, opens the heart to all.

---

34. For Edison see List
35. Al.hw., Sk.tp.: "vision" underlined
36. Al.hw.: a number of dots, missing words; Sk.tp.: "(the one who)" written by hand on a number of dots
37. Sk.tp.: "so does" corrected by hand to read "does so"
38. Sk.tp.: "is, in vision," corrected to read "in vision is"
39. Al.hw.: "actual revelation" underlined; Sk.tp.: "revelation" underlined
40. Al.hw., Sk.tp.: "can" underlined

Il Serano, Rome, Saturday, February 14th
and Sunday, February 15th, 1925

Il risveglio dell'anima

Il filosofo, Inayat Khan ha parlato ieri alla Biblioteca di piazza Nicosia del risveglio dell'anima. Ogni anima, egli disse è destinata al suo risveglio, presto o tardi, ed allora soltanto incomincia la vera, vita. Allorchè essa si sveglia ha tutt'altra visione delle coso che contempla con un sentimento diverso da quello dell'anima addormentata. L'anima non si desta in un dato momento, nè vi sono segni esteriori che ne indichino il risveglio. Al riori che ne indichinó il risveglio. Allorchè si desta, allargando il proprio orizzonte, cambia il suo atteggiamentto; non vede i difetti altri, ma i proprii e diviene tollerante perchè comprende. Un'atmosfer di pace si forma intorno all'anima ridestata, ed essa si solleva al disopra di tutte le ansietà della esistenza. Mentre ognu no guarda la vita dal proprio punto di vista, l'anima illuminata la guarda da tutti i punti di vista.
L'anima risvegliata è felice della felicità trovata in sè stessa; ed è solo infelice dell'infalicita degli altri. Essa comprende il linguaggio di ogni essere, mentre il suo non è compreso. Il tempo e la distanz non contano per l'anima illuminata; per essa non esiste che la vita eterna. L'anima può affrettare il risveglio senza preoccuparsi di ciò; soltanto, allorchè sente dettarsi in sè medesima la tendenza a vedere la vita profondamente, deve imparar a contemplare e a raccogliersi nel silenzio.

E qual'è la conseguenza del risveglio dell'anima? L'adempimento del vero scopo della vita.

Angela Alt's handwriting

Rome, 4 Via di Porta Pinciana
Wednesday, 6:30, February 18th, 1925

Mureeds' Meeting

Murshid's address:

I would speak a few words this evening that a few thoughts may always remain with you. In this path of wisdom in which we have joined hands we are on our[1] journey towards the destination of life. And I am sure that it would not seem to you a new idea, for it is natural to you as far as I feel, that in this journey one takes with a spiritual guide there is a sacred link, a link which endures forever. It is not what you read that helps to the extent, nor what you meditate, this link with the guide that travels on the path with you; it is something that the people in the East have cherished all their life and found the greatest help. In the hand that is given by a guide to the pupil is a link which words cannot explain, something which one can depend upon on the earth and the hereafter. And if that was not the idea, then all the meditations and concentrations and studies would be empty, because it is that which gives to it a life, and if it has no life then it is lost.

But now, this sympathy, this link and connection, to what must it inspire you? One thing is that the pupil's actions, attitude of mind, his words must please his teacher. There is an interesting story known in the East: a pupil came to a teacher, "Would you accept such an unworthy soul as mine in your discipleship?" The teacher said, "Yes." But the pupil said, "My faults are many." The teacher said, "It does not matter." But the pupil said, "If you knew my faults you would not say it does not matter." "For instance, what faults do you mean?" the teacher asked. The pupil said, "I have taken to drink." "It does not matter" the teacher said. But he said, "There is much besides." "What?" "I like to gamble." "It does not matter" answered the teacher. "But then," he said, "sometimes I lose my temper and nothing then can control it." The teacher said, "It does not matter." He said, "I am very consoled; if you will put up with

Document:
Al.hw. = a handwritten reporting of the lecture by Angela Alt.

Notes:
1. Al.hw.: "it is our" written, then crossed out, and "we are on our" written above the line

my faults, all is well." The teacher said, "But you know one thing of course, that a certain respect is due to your teacher." "Certainly," said he. "Well, out of that respect will you accept one condition? All those things you have said are your faults, you must not do in his presence?" "Certainly," he said, "that I can manage." The teacher said, "That is all I ask[2]." And after the teacher had given him the benediction and when he went home, naturally that link grew. And one day, while going through a street, he desired to go and visit a tavern. Then he went as far as the door and returned, and so in everything he tried, he was drawn back. And when he met the teacher, he was asked, "How are you getting on?" The pupil said, "All is well[3] except that I cannot do all the things I like to do." "Why?" said the teacher. The pupil answered, "As soon as I go near things, there comes my teacher in front of me. I cannot get away from that presence to do my fault." This amusing story tells us the secret: those who think that in the path to God and in the path of truth, they can tread on the intellectual path only, it will be nothing but a mechanical effort. There is no life in it. You may study about the various planes, spheres, heavens, etc.; to what does it lead? Or that a certain feeling has a certain colour and so on. What does it all lead to? And if one thinks it is sufficient to meditate or go into the solitude and live with the all pervading, he has brought about that condition which is called death in life. But what is necessary is to continue to live, and through life to expand, for spiritual accomplishment is in expansion of the soul. There will be studies which you will read no doubt and meditations and concentrations which you will do and profit by nevertheless. You are conscious of that link by which we have come together, and it is your realization of that benediction which remains with you which will be the greatest bliss.

And in conclusion, I would say that your friendship and sympathy I feel more than I can say, and even if you have not said one word to me, no matter, for words can never express truth. And if I say anything else, it is that you can always count for ever on your Murshid's blessings.[4]

---

2. Al.hw.: "all I ask" underlined
3. Al.hw.: "but one thing" written, then crossed out
4. Al.hw.: "you can always count for ever on your Murshid's blessings" underlined for emphasis

An old typescript

Nice[1], February 22nd, 1925

The Path of Initiation

Beloved ones of God,

I will speak this evening on the path of initiation. The word initiation has its meaning in itself, for it is an initiating, it is a further step towards something to which everyone will go. Human nature is such that if the fruits of its efforts are blessed, there is no effort it will not make. You can see this in everyday life; it is not difficult to give one's whole life for an object one sees before one, it does not rise above common sense. But when a person has to step forward in pursuit of something he does not see clearly, that is the difficulty. For instance, if a person try to shoot at a target, he is pleased, he sees the point to shoot at, but if a person had to shoot in darkness, where he does not know and cannot see the mark, there a man cannot stand firm on his feet. Naturally, therefore, the path of the initiate is not the path of all; it is something taking a different direction from all else in life.

And now I would like to explain how initiations can be divided into three different classes. The first class of initiation is that which very often man receives, yet does not know it. There are times in one's life when a new consciousness arises out of a person. It may rise after a great suffering, or a great illness; it may rise after success or failure; it may rise after having lost someone near and dear; it may rise after the heart has opened to love someone. One does not know how it arrives, but it has automatic action on the self, and out of it comes a new consciousness. Often one sees in a youth a time comes in his life, a time when he looks at everything in a different way and everything is different in life. In other words, there comes a moment when a person changes, even to the extent of a snake changing its skin, and takes a new one. Of course these changes may be in a right or wrong direction, but any change that takes place resulting in the widening of consciousness, that is regarded as an initiation. Of course, this kind of initiation may be called inner

---

Document:
od.tp. = a typescript of unknown provenance.
Notes:
1. For Nice, see List

guidance, but definite guidance.

And now we come to the question of the second kind of initiation, and this initiation comes after a maturity of the soul. There comes a time in one's life whatever be one's age, when one finds everyone does not understand one's point of view, that there are problems that one looks at in a different way to those around. If one tells of his point of view, they would say it was different from common sense. That begins an appetite in the heart of man which can only be satisfied by greater light, greater life. Naturally all other appetites in life become dim and fade, but this one becomes stronger than all and man seeks he does not know what, and it is at that time that he looks for a friend to confide in and from whom to seek the answer to his soul's craving. Then comes a time in the life of the initiate when this is so much increased that nothing satisfies except a friendship, an association which can bring this knowledge. It is a trust on the part of the pupil and a confidence on the part of the teacher that is called an initiation. It is in this way that an initiation is established between *guru* and *chela*[2]. This initiation has no doubt its different degrees, and in each degree there is a trust increased and a confidence increased.

And now comes the question, what does the teacher teach on this path? He may teach nothing or a thousand things, but it is not what he teaches. If he does not teach, still it is taught, and if he teaches, still the teaching is given, because the higher knowledge is not attained by the different ways we are accustomed to attain worldly things. By studies, arguments, discussions, what does one attain but names and forms; but here we seek the nameless and the formless. Besides, the teacher giving initiation promises nothing: he promises no wonder working, there is nothing he promises on giving an initiation because it is the attainment of something you cannot make clear in words. But you will say, why is he teacher if he does not teach? The answer is that, that the teacher is an outward appearance, the real teacher is the one and only teacher. It is that inner teacher who can teach if any can. He will teach and the outer teacher's work is to help the pupil to open his heart to the truth of the real teacher. For no truth is ever taught in words; if words can explain truth then it is no more a truth. Naturally, therefore, the teacher has no words; what he can do is to help the pupil to open his

---

2. For *guru* and *chela*, see Glossary

heart gradually to that truth.

No doubt, the teacher tests and tries; he tests the patience of the pupil to the outmost whenever it is necessary. He can turn him round and round the temple of truth before taking him inside, when he realizes there is a time when he should enter and before that he should wait. Nevertheless, it rests in the heart of the teacher as a sacred responsibility to waken the pupil's heart to the object he is seeking after. If you hear or read stories of the pupil and [teacher][3], in what way the teacher helps the pupil on this path, you will be surprised to see it is a different way to those of the world. No knowledge that the pupil brings saying, "Upon this will I build." avails, for the teacher says, "Nothing you should bring to make the base of your temple; the base must be space." The pupil says, "I have so much knowledge and learning." The teacher says, "Unlearn before taking a step." There is a saying in Persian that love alone is the guide on this path and the idea of me and you, of such and such and so and so, must be forgotten ere you take a step in this path. But at the same time it must be understood that if it is most difficult, it is also the easiest, for if it is difficult it is not so in the sense in which we understand it, and if it is easy, it is not so in our general terms.

Therefore, there is no particular age entitling a person to initiation, nor is there a particular time during which everyone can accomplish his spiritual journey, because what one does in a day, another does in a year, or a lifetime. For what is to be accomplished is with oneself, not with truth and knowledge. All the work to be done is with oneself; it is like making ready a mechanism that a spark may kindle it. And therefore, if there is anything special in the life of the teacher, it is his responsibility to make this mechanism in working order, and therefore, it will be naturally understood why confidence and trust are needed. So if the pupil has no idea of that mechanism and its progress, he is not worthy to be accepted as a pupil. Naturally, in answer to that trust on the part of the pupil, the teacher's trust comes.

And now I would like to speak of the mechanism. In the first place, there is a working with the body, an outer spirit[4]. Often those spiritually inclined give little importance to the mechanism of the

3. Od.tp.: "master" written, later crossed out and "teacher" substituted by hand
4. Od.tp.: "an outer spirit" placed between parentheses and two question marks added by hand

body, but it is a mistake, for the body was made to be the temple of God, here he[5] was to be enshrined, and if this temple is not attended to then a thousand churches, synagogues or mosques avail nothing. But you may ask, what attention? Shall we feed it, take care of it? We do perhaps more than others. The idea is that there are five senses: sight, hearing, smelling, tasting, touching, so there is a sense behind them all, intuition, inspiration, revelation. There is a seat in man's body which is comprehensive, a seat in which a higher consciousness reveals itself, the seat of God[6]. It is by discovering that sense that man lives in this world a fuller life, and this is to be done by understanding the proper way of living. For a small thing I would say, how many people do not even know how to breathe naturally? That magnetism, spirit, which is attracted, absorbed by help of the breath, how can it express more knowledge, more life?

There is another thing to be considered, the mechanism of mind. How can a sailor navigate if the mechanism of his ship were out of order and the ship running alone, how dangerous it would be! Then how much more on the ocean of life when we are like boats in the sea where the mechanism is not controlled. There are many with wealth and power, but few have self-control, called the kingdom of God[7]. And this shows that man is born a prince but becomes unaware of his kingdom, and the whole work on the spiritual path is to attain to this kingdom which a simple saying hints at in the Bible, "Seek ye the kingdom of God and his righteousness...."[8] But the difficulty is that man looks for it up in heaven; he cannot see that it is in himself that he has to find it.

And now to explain what higher initiation means. This middle one I have explained is like training youth under the guardianship of his parents, but when youth has grown so that he can stand alone and look after his life, the parents say, "We have done our duty, now you must go on." Then comes a time when the pupil takes his own view on life; he is grateful to the teacher whom he has taken as master. No doubt, the unfaithful have gone on a different path, but once he has faithfully accomplished this trial, the next thing is the freedom of the soul, and now freedom of soul expands in the expansion of consciousness. It manifests itself in a keen

---

5. Od.tp.: "GOD" and "HE" written in capital letters
6. Od.tp.: "GOD" written in capital letters
7. Od.tp.: "God" written, later crossed out and "Heaven" substituted by hand
8. See Matthew 7:33

insight into nature and life, it manifests its at-one-ment with life in wider and wider horizons. It manifests in the form that life unveils itself, covers opening one by one all round. And now the question, do human beings really live in this world having arrived at this stage, because the quality of human nature has impressed us so badly that we question life, if such a thing is possible? A man asked me, "I went from America to look for fakirs, yogis and holy men about whom I had read, but I didn't find any." I answered, "You should not have taken such a long journey, for in the world of industry and commerce I often find souls worthy of respect." And what does it show? That when one's eyes open, one begins to appreciate in all people what is worthwhile, and naturally one rises above castes and creeds and divisions which keep us thinking this is right, that is wrong, this is good, that is bad. We begin to respect mankind irrespective of race and qualifications because if there is anything to respect in man, it is his humanity, which is worth everything else he possesses. As we read in the ancient scriptures, God[9] said, "I have created man in my image, that he may be the chief of all creation."[10]

---

9. Od.tp.: "GOD" written in capital letters
10. See Genesis 1:26

Kefayat LLoyd's handwriting

Geneva, E. A. Dunand
Thursday, February 24th, 1925[1]

The Madness of Life (Intoxication of Life)

Nature has manifested in such a way that every step to consciousness is a kind of intoxication. When the life is in the form of a rock it is still, when in a tree or plant it is moving, but in the plant it is more conscious, more alive. It is very interesting to study how even in the vegetable kingdom one plant is intolerant to another plant, and will not let it grow by its side, running its seed and its root to prevent it from growing near. And yet the consciousness has not opened its eyes in the plant life; it opens its eyes in the animal life. And therefore, the intoxication of life which I have called the madness of life can be fully studied in the animal life. If one watches two strange dogs meet, how they look, which is strong and which is weak, and at one moment one will show a sign of fear, and yet show that he is strong and will fight. The psychology of the two dogs is a feeling of intolerance to each other, and it is the same with lions and leopards and all herbivorous and carnivorous animals. The reason why a male will only attack a male and not a female is because in the latter case this[2] intolerance is covered by the attraction of positive and negative, but still the intoxication is there. Of course, in the case of the carnivorous animals one can say that flesh eating is the cause of it, and yet sheep, horses and other herbivorous animals also want to fight. Also between fowls, cocks and hens, there is a tendency between cocks to fight, and if one asks what is the reason, the answer is intolerance.

And what is the reason of intolerance? It is the illusion that life creates, which in Vedanta is called *maya* [3]. And the first lesson

---

Documents:
Kf.hw. = a manuscript in the handwriting of Kefayat Gladys Lloyd.
Sk.tp. = a typescript prepared by Sakina Furnée.

Notes:
1. E.A. Dunand is a building in Geneva; a note in the handwriting of Murshida Sherifa Goodenough written above the text: "Uncertain if correct report" and "(Rep. by Mrs. Reelfs)"; Sk.tp.: "Uncertain if correct report." typed above the text, and "Public Lecture." later added by hand
2. Sk.tp.: "the" instead of "this"
3. For *maya*, see Glossary

in illusion that life learns is the illusion of me and you, me a separated being, you a separated being. And in reality everything that hurts and harms in creation comes from this. Of course, this duality exists for a definite reason, but its first effect is destructive. It is a very difficult subject, metaphysical and philosophical, perhaps the essence of it is that the one who was tired of being alone and wanted someone else beside him, created this duality by his activity. But this duality he created out of himself, not like a carpenter who goes and gets wood to make a table or chair, and does not make it out of himself; the table or chair does not return to the carpenter, but the duality returns into him who made it. This is why the Prophet has said, "All came from God, and all will return to God."[4]

From this duality comes the triple aspect, called the trinity, which we also see as triangle: I, you, and he, and from this trinity comes again a duality. Three will not fight against each other. You and I against him and so again it becomes the duality.

This intoxication which rises in the consciousness of life takes a stronger development in man. It is this tendency which causes the horns of cows and buffaloes and the rhinoceros and the poisoned teeth of the serpents, and even worse things than that. For man's intolerance is much more furious and intense than that of any of these animals. And man is capable of showing his intolerance in a much more destructive way than they. He is not satisfied by hurting another person by his glance, his word, or his hand, he still invents weapons to hurt other men. With all his progress in science, he is ready and willing for some money to give cannons and weapons into the hands of the intolerant. There are many movements in the world practising vegetable diet, sobriety, and anti-vivisection, when so much preaching is necessary to save human life and teach tolerance of brother for brother.

Now as to the psychic law, I should like to say that this intolerance comes from many different causes, such as fear, passion, play, curiosity, and selfishness. Fear, a cat will play with a little piece of cloth, is afraid of its being a living thing, and yet plays with it, and wants to eat it. It is the object of the cat's fear, of its play, of its curiosity, and of its passion to destroy and eat it. Such is the condition of individuals and multitudes. If one looks at races and nations, how one wants to eat the other, or control it or destroy it

4. See Qur'an, The Cow (II.156)

from fear, or play with it, one sees that it is just like the cat with the little piece of cloth which it takes for a mouse, and the whole fury, commotion, excitement of the cat is the same with the nations and peoples[5]: activity only seems[5], but is in reality nothing.

Man cannot see more than he can see. When this disease is widely thought of it is considered health. The majority wins[6] the plume of wisdom, but a few rare ones can discern whether it is the cat's play or real activity. When people are guilty of the same fault, they try to hide each others' fault. No doubt, the moments of excitement come and go and then comes a moment of soberness, and then[7] also comes the thought of honour and no one likes to tell his faults to others. That which was begun in anger finishes in shame. And if we go still deeper in the philosophy of this madness, we find the answer, that to the stillness of the soul every motion is irritating. And this is why when one is quiet, reading, etc. in a room, it is irritating when someone comes in and makes a noise, and in reality this irritation at the calm being disturbed is at the basis of intolerance.

And when one comes to the philosophical side of it, it is the tendency of the ego, which is one, and does not want to see another beside it. And it is this tendency of the ego which makes an animal want to destroy another animal, and men and nations the same. It is this wish that, "I alone shall exist," and it is this illusion that, "I am separated from another and another is separated from me." Life is such a puzzle, and this puzzle is so interesting. Man would not like his path to be too smooth, he likes to puzzle, he likes to be fooled. If life were no puzzle, it would not be interesting. Life's errors and mistakes make it so. If man were all wise it would not have been worthwhile. Yes, it is an enjoyment [often][8], but often it [covers][9] the purpose, and this purpose is not to remain in it. The purpose is to enjoy the puzzle and at the same time to get out of it. At first there is the madness, but when man finds the way of getting out, the bitter madness is replaced by a sweet madness, and that madness is love. And therefore, in this puzzle of me and you, there are two aspects:

---

5. Kf.hw.: a space, missing words; Sk.tp.: a number of dots
6. Sk.tp.: a space instead of "wins", "waives (?)" later inserted by hand, then later crossed out and "wins" substituted
7. Sk.tp.: "there" instead of "then"
8. Kf.hw.: "after" placed between parentheses, and "often" written above the line in another handwriting; Sk.tp.: "after" corrected by hand to read "often"
9. Kf.hw.: "comes" written, then crossed out and "covers" substituted, and "covers" in Sk.tp.

the first when one cannot find the way, causes intolerance; the second is the opposite, instead of taking, it is giving, instead of hurting, it is comforting, instead of hardening, it is softening, and therefore, the same ego which was once in this puzzle a tyrant becomes a willing friend to the object he loves.

In Sufi terms the first part of the puzzle, and the first force active in it is called *jelal,* and the second is called *jemal*[10]. The former aspect is like the light of the sun, the latter like the light of the moon, which is cooling, soft to the eyes, and beautiful. And the poets of India have compared the first aspect to the male aspect and the second to the female aspect. It is the softening of the fury and the intense spirit of intolerance which gives its beauty to life. Man has five aspects or stages in his life which are: devil man, animal man, human man, angelic man, and divine man. The first aspect is when the intolerance is so intense that the person is intolerant at every existence around him and wishes to eat all around him, the vampire aspect. In old times they said there were [witches][11] and vampires; they exist now, egos who only live on the life of others. Some live for wealth, others for position, power, youth, or strength, but their whole motive is to live by taking and destroying.

The animal man[12], whose existence is only for the satisfaction of his appetites, he takes whatever he finds, and then sleeps. No doubt, he is thoughtless and does not mind what his desire does to others. He is only absorbed by his appetites. The human man[13] naturally becomes tolerant; the reason is that as he wishes another person to be tolerant to him, he has to be so first, and by this his attitude develops. The angel man[14], man attains to this condition when he walks the path of love, that love which teaches him consideration and self-sacrifice. He cannot but tolerate, because love is born in his heart, and like water spreads and falls on others. All the beauty that one sees in human nature comes from that angelic quality that man develops and which manifests in love, kindness, gratitude etc. The divine man[15] comes not only by the opening of the heart, but by the opening of the soul. The divine man is he who by

---

10. For *jelal* and *jemal*, see Glossary
11. Kf.hw.: a space, missing words; Sk.tp.: a number of dots, then "witches" inserted by hand
12. Kf.hw.: "animal man" underlined
13. Kf.hw.: "human man" underlined
14. Kf.hw.: "angel man" underlined
15. Kf.hw.: "divine man" underlined

being in tune with God is connected with all beings. No one is stranger or far from him, lower or higher. He is in all and all is in him. The world cannot know his secret, but he knows the secret of the world. His existence is the answer to all the questions in the world. It is not what man says, or how he appears, that matters; it is what he is[16].

---

16. Kf.hw.: "he is" underlined; Sk.tp.: "is" underlined

An old typescript

[1] March, 1925

Murshid's Words about Rumi

Rumi[2] was an educated man, a chief of the country and a great student of philosophy. One day Shams Tabriz[3], an ascetic, came in his house when he was working with a manuscript. The first thing Shams Tabriz did was to throw away the manuscript. Rumi looked at him. Shams Tabriz says, "Why! Is it not enough now of reading and study. Now study life instead of a book." So Rumi was wakened. To what? To the study of the life within. There is a period of studying books and there is a period when the whole nature becomes a book. Rumi respectfully listened to the words of Shams Tabriz. "All things which seem of importance, what are they the day when you depart? What is rank, what is power, what is position? A greater problem is, what will go with you, for the solution of that problem will lead you to eternity. The problems of this world, you may solve them and solve them, they are never finished. About God, about man, what have you understood? What relation have you found between man and God? If you worship God, why do you worship him? What is limitation, what perfection? And how to seek for it?" Then the ascetic went on, he would not say more. That day Rumi writes, "The God whom all my life I have worshipped today came at my door in the form of man." By his initiation Rumi's outlook is changed in a moment. He leaves all his affairs and goes heart and soul in the thought of Shams Tabriz.

Then Shams Tabriz, in a mood, goes away and Rumi is left alone to solve his own problems. For many years he lived in grief and sadness. But through his grief inspiration came and he wrote the *Masnavi*. *Masnavi* comes from grief, but what pearls he has given, living, penetrating words. They are not human, they are angelic by their depth and their simplicity.

Document:
od.tp. = an old typescript of unknown provenance.
Notes:
1. Od.tp.: "Public Lecture." written above the line
2. For Jalal-ud-Din Rumi and his *Masnavi*, see List
3. For Shams-i Tabriz, see List

Mrs. Reelfs' handwriting

1 Geneva, Salle Centrale
March 1st, 1925[2]

The Path of the Mystic

There are perhaps mystics in all peoples, and there is a mystic side to all religions. This shows that mysticism does not come from the East or from the West, it is a human inheritance and belongs to the soul. Every religion, Buddhism, Christianity, Hinduism, Judaism has a mystic aspect, and this shows that mysticism belongs to every religion, and it also shows that religion needs a mystical aspect to manifest in its fullness.

In its last stages, the world has passed through so much, so many centuries of materialism, that when one nowadays speaks of mysticism it is looked upon as something vague and incomprehensible[3]. Mysticism has always existed as a human inheritance, but the waves of materialism have effaced it. [We Sufis][4] understand the difference between religion, morality, mysticism, and philosophy.

Religion[5] is a law of beauty given to humanity by the masters of life. Morality[6] is a [series][7] of principles adopted by a

---

Documents:

Rl.hw.	=	a handwritten reporting of the lecture by Mrs. Reelfs.
Sk.tp.1	=	a document made by Sakina Furnée or under her supervision, showing some differences from the Rl.hw.
Sk.tp.2	=	another typescript made by Sakina Furnée or under her supervision.
un.tp.	=	a typescript of unknown provenance.

Notes:

1. Sk.tp.1: "Incomplete report." typed above the text; Sk.tp.2: "Incomplete" typed above the lecture, then "Public Lecture." added by hand
2. A note in the handwriting of Murshida Sherifa Goodenough written above the text: "Incomplete report"
3. Sk.tp.2, un.tp.: "uncomprehensible" instead of "incomprehensible"
4. Rl.hw.: "We S." written, then crossed out, and alternative versions written above the line: "The Sufi recognizes a difference between ... or to the understanding of the Sufi there is a difference between ..."; Sk.tp.1: first "I" typed here, then crossed out and "We should" substituted by hand; Sk.tp.2, un.tp.: "We Sufis"
5. Rl.hw., Sk.tp.1, un.tp.: "Religion" underlined
6. Rl.hw., Sk.tp.1, un.tp.: "Morality" underlined
7. Rl.hw.: a number of dots, then "law (?)" inserted in another handwriting, and "code" written above the line; Sk.tp.1: "series" written by hand above the dots; Sk.tp.2, un.tp.: "series" in type

number of persons at a given period. Philosophy[8] is a [series][9] of names, forms, conditions, and circumstances which are known by logic and knowledge. Mysticism is a way that is incomprehensible to most people because it is a way of getting to the centre of life and things which the other ways take centuries to get to[10]. The source where mystics get their knowledge from is the divine source of which Christ says, "Seek ye first the kingdom of God, and all things shall be added unto you."[11] The ordinary person cannot understand that by sitting down and closing his eyes a man can get knowledge. He also cannot see how one can get knowledge[12] without learning from exterior sources because all his life he has been used to that.

And so it is that no religious man or philosopher, however good and pure, can get at the knowledge of the mystic, because the mystic's knowledge is the greatest of all. Just as a man standing on the mountain sees more[13] than he who stands at the bottom. Or, can a man who wants to see the moon see it by looking on the ground? The words of Christ, "Seek ye first the kingdom of God" are so[14] simple, and yet understood by so few. The Christ spirit is the mystic spirit. Even before Christ mysticism has always existed: Buddha, Krishna, Moses, and Muhammad, all walked the path of the mystic. Can you tell me of Krishna going to an academy to learn? Or Christ or any other teacher learning from outer[15] sources? No, their knowledge came from the divine source.

Of course, it makes the materialist wonder, what can be the source where[16] all the knowledge of the world is accumulated? There is a very interesting story about Firdausi[17], the great Persian poet, who has written of[18] *Shah Nameh*[19]. One Shah of Persia once desired documents of the ancient history of Persia which no one could find; there was only this poet who offered to do so. Everyone wondered

---

8. Rl.hw., Sk.tp.1, un.tp.: "Philosophy" underlined
9. Rl.hw.: a number of dots, then "law (?)" inserted; Sk.tp.1: "series" written by hand above the dots; Sk.tp.2, un.tp.: "series" in type
10. Sk.tp.2: "it" instead of "to", then corrected by hand to read "to"; un.tp.: "it" instead of "to"
11. See Matthew 6:33
12. Un.tp.: "He also cannot see how one can get knowledge" omitted
13. Sk.tp.2: "as" added
14. Sk.tp.2, un.tp.: "so" omitted
15. Sk.tp.2, un.tp.: "other" instead of "outer"
16. Sk.tp.2, un.tp.: originally "when" typed, then corrected by hand to read "where"
17. Un.tp.: a space instead of "Firdausi", for Firdausi, see List
18. Sk.tp.1,2: "the" instead of "of"
19. For *Shah Nameh*, see List

how that could be done, but he said, "Wait and you will see." He went to the solitude for ten years and then he came back to the court with his book called *Shah Nama*. As he was still linked with the current of his solitary life, he was not quite himself; and when one of the knights who was very critical asked where one could find that knowledge, Firdausi called him and said, "Come and[20] sit by me, and close your eyes and see." And then that sceptical man saw all the pictures of the ancient past pass before his eyes. But a man may say, "If one is to become a mystic for the knowledge that mysticism gives, it is not worthwhile, because there is already so much knowledge in the world." But it is not only knowledge that the soul seeks, there are other things, and one is the longing for a lasting happiness which man never has. Whatever his condition or occupation, there is always something to complain of.

And this means that the home of the fish is water, and on earth, even on a tray of gold[21], it is not happy. The real home of man is the spirit of God, and elsewhere he will never be satisfied. Man cannot understand this because he gets a little substitute called pleasure. Another thing is that this pleasure is momentary, and he must always suffer to get it. There is always pain attached to pleasure and one must pay a good price for it. The true happiness is never experienced by man until he has touched that happiness that lives in his own heart. If you ask me what that happiness is like, I will tell you that it is impossible to explain to someone who has never tasted sugar, to know what sugar is like. So one cannot explain this happiness except to someone who has felt it.

There is another thing mystics experience, and this is ecstasy, and this cannot either be explained to one who has not felt it. As there are many people who profess to be mystics, the[22] real mystic keeps his experiences to himself. As now in the Western world these thoughts are coming to be known, many people make a profession of clairvoyance and spirit communication, which are a degeneration of real mysticism, which is the greatest thing. In the East these things are under the protection of religion.

Think of what loss the world has to face when mysticism degenerates into these forms, becoming commercialized and a

20. Un.tp.: "to" instead of "and"
21. Un.tp.: "of gold" omitted
22. Sk.tp.2, un.tp.: "the" omitted

sacrilege. Ecstasy is a [well][23] of light and of love which rises from the bottom of man's heart, and so high that it washes away all worries and troubles of life. On the condition of man's heart depends this divine light, as the condition of the sea depends on the cosmic light. The cosmic changes make the sea agitated or calm. In one's heart there are moments of calm so great that it charges[24] the whole atmosphere, and moments when the forces rise in man and wash away all troubles and worldly things. A poet or a gifted musician feels the same, and if you ask me why, I will say that it is that he could not create beauty unless he were an instrument of divine beauty, which is the greatest creator.

Of course a mystic who dives deep and makes his heart an instrument of the divine[25] being experiences a greater ecstasy. And as the sea responds to the cosmos more than the land, so the heart of the mystic responds to the divine light more than the heart of the average man. His heart is liquid, and that of the average man as frozen snow. Where does this freezing come from, since snow is also water? It comes from the thought of I[26], my father, my mother, my beloved, my friend, mine, and separate from yours. Whereas the first lesson of the mystic is: "Thou art, and not I." It is not only complete surrender to God, it is self-effacement. And what does the symbol of the cross explain? That, "Thou art, not me; my hands are not for me, my feet are not for me, my head is not for me[27], they are all Thine."

The Hindu saying[28], "Die before death,"[29] does not mean suicide; it means the death of the "I", the separate self. It is an error of man to call his tent his home. It is not a home, it is a tent. The body is also a tent which is temporary; he calls it "I", but it is not "I". The pleasures of life make him forget what it is in him that says "I". Think only of the helplessness, sickness and death of the body. Man never thinks of it, but acts as though[30] he should live thousands of years on this earth. There is no condition, rank or wealth that can secure man's life. What is it that makes him think he is something when he is really nothing? If he can only think of what is nothing,

---

23. Rl.hw.: an illegible word crossed out, then "well" substituted, and "well" in a.o.d.
24. Sk.tp.2, un.tp.: "changes" instead of "charges"
25. Rl.hw.: "beauty" written, then crossed out
26. Rl.hw.: "I" double underlined
27. Sk.tp.2, un.tp.: "my feet are not for me, my head is not for me" omitted
28. Sk.tp.1,2: "Hindu saying" changed by hand to read "saying of the Qur'an"
29. A *hadith* (saying) of the Prophet Muhammad
30. Sk.tp.2, un.tp.: "so as" instead of "as though"

he will realize that what was, is, and shall be, is one being: God.

Living with God is immortality. The Bible from the beginning teaches us to look for immortality within ourselves. Therefore the mystic's path is not one of study, but of meditation. In Eastern language this is called Yoga, which means connection, yoke, and this is to connect oneself with the divine spirit. And what disconnects one is the realization of one's separate entity, and what connects one is the thought of God. Sufis, as all other mystics, have had their[31] schools in all ages of this inner cult. And it must be considered a privilege that East and West are coming closer together, that the poetry and music and philosophy of East and West are becoming known to each other. And the happiness of humanity lies in friendship and harmony between East and West. And there are many ways of doing this, but there is none better than the thought of God, and love between men. It is the essential spirit, and by this all can unite.

The message of the Sufis has been given in America, France, and England, and is now being given here, and all are welcomed, because in the love and light of the path of God there is no distinction or difference[32]. No doubt, the Movement of the Sufis is working to bring about a better understanding between races and peoples, but its essential work is to open the inner eyes of man.

---

31. Rl.hw.: "methods" written, then crossed out, and omitted in a.o.d.
32. Sk.tp.2: "or difference" omitted

An old typescript

[1] München, Kunstgewerbehaus
March16th, 1925

Silence

Beloved ones of God,

I ask your indulgence to my discourse this evening on the subject of silence[2]. There is a saying that words are valuable but silence is precious. This saying will always prove true. The more we understand the meaning of it, the more we find its truth. Sufism is quietism. It is not a particular sect, a dogma, or a doctrine. It is an art, the art of silence through which beauty is produced. And before going further into this most serious subject I would like first of all to consider what is our relation with daily life. How many times we find during the day having said something which we should better not have said. How many times we disturb the peace of our surrounding without meaning it by lack of silence. How often we make our limitations, our narrowness, our smallness come out which we rather should have covered, because we did not keep silence. How very often with the desire to respect others we cannot manage to do so because of not keeping silence. And that great danger awaits man in the life of the world, the danger of confiding into a person in whom he did not wish to confide. One jumps in that danger by not keeping silence. As the great reader of life, the Persian poet Sa'di[3] says, "What value is that sense if it does not come to my rescue before I utter a word?" This shows to us, friends, that in spite of great wisdom we may have, still if there is no control over our words, we can make a mistake. And we shall find examples of this truth; those who talk much have less power than those who talk little. For a talkative person may not be able to express an idea in thousand words which those who are master of silence express in one word. Everyone can speak, but not every word has the same power. Besides, what a word says is much less compared to what

---

Documents:
od.tp. = an old typescript of unknown provenance.
Sk.tp. = a typescript made by Sakina Furnée, identical to od.tp.

Notes:
1. Sk.tp.: "Public Lecture." added
2. Sk.tp.: "silence" underlined to indicate that it is the title
3. For Sa'di, see List

silence expresses. If one asked the keynote of harmonious life, I will answer "silence".

There is a mirthful story told in India. The story tells that a woman went to a magnetizer and asked a remedy for having every day disagreement in her home. "Don't be afraid," the magnetizer said, "that is the easiest thing to cure. I shall give you some sweets, eat them, and do not speak a word while they are in the mouth. They are magnetized sweets; there will be no more inharmony in your home." And so it happened. All the days the lady had the sweets there was no disagreement. Naturally, the poor husband, nervous and rigid after the whole day's labour, found no stimulant, no bad temper, one or two words and then silence. The lady came one day to the magnetizer and asked him, "Please give me more from those sweets." The answer was, "There is no need to have more sweets; only think of them, that is enough." We can learn much from this story. In everyday life we are confronted with thousand troubles, to meet those we are unevolved. And only silence can help us. For if there is any religion, if there is any practice of religion, it is to have regard for the pleasure of God in regarding the pleasure of man. The essence of religion is to understand. And this religion we cannot live without having power over the word, without having realized the power of silence. There are so very many occasions of repenting after hurting friends which could have been avoided if there had been a control over words. Silence is the shield of the ignorant, the protection of the wise. For the ignorant does not prove his ignorance if he keeps silence. And the wise will not throw pearls before the swine if he knows the worth of silence.

Now coming to the question what gives power over words? In other words, what gives the power that can be attained by silence? The answer is, it is will power which gives the control over words; it is silence which gives one the power of silence. It is restlessness when a person speaks too much. The more words are used to express an idea, the less powerful they become. What a great pity that man so often thinks of saving pennies and never thinks of sparing words. It is like saving pebbles and throwing away pearls. An Indian poet says, "Pearl shell, what gives you your precious contents?" And the answer is, "Silence, for years my lips were closed." For a moment it is a struggle with oneself, it is controlling an impulse, but afterwards the same thing becomes a power.

And now coming to the more scientific, metaphysical explanation of silence. There is a certain amount of energy spent by words, and breath which has to bring new life in the body is hindered from its regular rhythm when all the time man speaks. Therefore, it is not that a nervous person speaks too much, but much speaking makes nervous. The great power of which you have heard attained by Yogis and fakirs, where did their power come from? It was gained by having learned and practised the art of silence. And that is the reason for which in the East at the court and in the meditative house of fakirs, there was silence. There were times in the world during different civilizations that people were taught whenever they were collected together for a feast to keep silence for a certain time. It is the greatest pity that at this time we have so neglected that question, we think so little about it. It is a question which affects health, which is related to the soul, to the spirit, to life. The more one thinks on the subject, the more one sees that we are involved in a kind of action. Where does it lead us? And what is the result of it? As far as we can see, it leads us to greater struggle, competition, disagreeableness. If we think of the result, we see that it leads us to greater care, worry, struggle in life. Like there is a saying of the Hindus, the more one seeks for happiness, the more unhappiness one finds. And the reason is that when happiness is sought in a wrong direction, it leads to unhappiness. Our experience in life is sufficient to teach us this, yet life is intoxicating, it absorbs us in action so that we never stop to think of it. This has been my own experience while travelling for some years, that it seems as if the world is wakening to spiritual ideals, and in spite of this there is more action, not only outer action, but also action of mind.

In reality mankind has shattered its nerves by the lack of silence, by action of body and mind. When the body is resting man calls it sleep, but his mind is going on the same record as during the day. Then there comes a time when man can say, "I am really restless." No doubt, life just now in the world is[4]. In this competition every man is busy hundred times more than he ever was. Naturally his life needs rest and quietude and peace more than those who live in the forest, who can call all the time their own. When action is increased and the art of silence is lost, then what can we expect?

Now coming to a metaphysical question. Where do we learn thoughtfulness? In silence. And where do we practise patience? In silence. Silence that one takes as meditation is apart, but silence that

---

4. Od.tp., Sk.tp.: a space, missing words

we should consider at every word, at every action we do, that is the first lesson to learn. If there is a meditative person, naturally he has learned to use that silence in everyday life. Who has learned silence in everyday life has already learned to meditate. Besides, a person may say, I have appointed a time when I meditate for half an hour. But when there is half an hour meditation on twelve or fifteen hours activity, the action takes away all the power of meditation. Therefore, both things must go together. A person who wishes to learn the art of silence, he must decide, however much work, to keep the thought of silence in his mind. When one does not consider this, then one will not have the full benefit out of meditation. It is just like a person who goes once to the church and the six other days keeps the thought of church as far away as possible. A Persian king was advised by his prime minister who said to this most devout king, "You are spending most of the night in meditation and all day long you do the work. How can that go on?" The Shah said that, "During the night I pursue God; during the day God follows me." If I were to say the same in connection with silence, "Who seeks silence, silence follows him." So it is with all things we wish for. When we seek after them sufficiently, they naturally follow us in time.

There are many who do not mind if they hurt anyone as long as they think they have told the truth. For them they feel so justified that if the other one cries or laughs, he says, "I don't mind." But friends, there is a difference between fact and truth. Fact is that which can be said; truth is that which cannot be put in words. The claim, "I tell the truth." falls flat when the difference is realized between fact and truth. People discuss about dogmas, beliefs, moral principles as they know it. But there comes a time in man's life when he has touched truth which he cannot speak in words. And at that time all dispute, discussion, argument finishes. It is then that man says, "If you have done wrong or if I have done wrong, it does not matter. What I want just now is to right the wrong." There comes a time when the continual question which arises in the active mind, "What is what and which is which?" finishes, for the answer rises from the soul and is received in silence.

Friends, there is an audible voice and an inaudible voice, from the living and from those who are not living, from all life. What man can say in words always expresses little. Can one say about gratefulness, about devotion, about admiration? Never one can say it if there is profound devotion, admiration, or gratefulness, never one can say it. There is a lack of words. Every feeling, every deep feeling has its own voice; it cannot be expressed in outer words. This voice is coming from every soul; every soul is only audible to the heart. And how the heart is prepared? Through silence.

We need not be surprised to think that they[5] have sought the mountains and the forest and preferred the wilderness to the comforts of worldly life. They sought something valuable. They have given something of their experience gained by their sacrifice. But it is not necessary to follow them to the forest or to the cave of the mountain. One can learn that art of silence, through the busy life, one can maintain silence. It is in order to make a facility for those who are seeking after truth that the Sufi Movement exists in different countries, that seekers may come to this.

Thank you for your sympathetic response. God bless you.

---

5. Od.tp., Sk.tp.: "we" written then crossed out by hand, "they" substituted

An old typescript

[1] München, Herschelstrasse 11 at house of Frau Wasner
Afternoon, March 17th, 1925

Relation of Murshid and Mureeds

My *mureeds*[2] and friends,

It is not a lecture I wish to give, but a talk. In the first place I would like to say something about the relation the *Murshid*[3] is to his mureeds. This is like a relation between father and child or mother and child. In Murshid you have both. Since my mureeds were struggling here alone and the group was not yet standing on its feet owing to the infancy of the Movement, I thought it better to come here. But you must know, whether I am here or not, I am always eager to answer the call of my mureeds. When I can come, nothing can keep me back from coming and seeing them. These lectures before the public are outer work which is necessary but not essential. What is essential is the work with my mureeds. For what I say to the public is what I can say to all. But what I say to individual mureeds is to every particular soul. So you must be able to distinguish, the lectures, which is one thing, and the personal training, which is another thing.

No doubt, although it is the infancy of the Movement in Germany, we have every reason to be hopeful. There are some only, but [they][4] are sincere. We hope that their service to humanity and the cause will develop in Munich. If only the mureeds realized that it is not only the personal development, but that it is working in unison with one another which will bring the desired result. It must be understood also that the initiation which is given to the mureeds is not a thing for which a service in return is expected. Those who offer willingly their service to the cause are such mureeds who sympathize with Murshid and carry on their shoulders some of the

---

Documents:
od.tp. = an old typescript of unknown provenance.
Sk.tp. = a typescript made by Sakina Furnée, nearly identical to Od.tp.

Notes:
1. Sk.tp.: "Private Lecture." added by hand
2. Sufis use the word *mureed* for an initiate, see Glossary
3. The word *murshid* designates a spiritual teacher, see Glossary
4. Od.tp.: "there" typed; Sk.tp.: "there" typed, then crossed out and "they" substituted

burden that weighs on the shoulders of Murshid. I regard gratefully any service from my mureeds but do not expect a service in return for what they receive. Although thanks need not be given in words, for once the mureed is in at-one-ment with Murshid, Murshid and mureed becomes one.

When we think what can[5] be done in Germany, what must[6] be done, our resources and assistance is very little. But I am not discontented or discouraged trusting that if ever there is a success, it only belongs to truth. It is only a matter of time. Success gained by untruth is false success and has no relation with real success, which is truth. As there is a saying in Sanskrit language, "Truth alone will succeed in the end." It is in that faith that we trust that with a little number of labourers we shall have great results.

And now I will tell you what are the things expected of a mureed. The first thing is that the exercises given as esoteric instructions are done regularly. Without those exercises, if the mureed wishes to work for the cause he may work, but he is as a soldier without munition. The benefit is not only in the practice but in the faith in the practice. Practice apart, even if one has no faith in the medicine of the doctor, it diminishes its value. The hopeful attitude of the mureed pushes him forward. It is the doubting attitude which holds him back. A doubting mureed is better not a mureed. For there is a saying of a Brahmin who was asked, "O Brahmin, you worship this God of stone who will never answer your prayer!" The Brahmin answered that, "If I have faith, even this God of stone will answer me. If you have not that faith, even your God of heaven will not answer you." Then one might ask, "If there are no such dogmas, doctrines, or beliefs which can be called Sufi dogmas, doctrines or beliefs, then what is the belief of Sufism?" The simple answer is, "Attitude, outlook on life we learn." It is with that attitude and outlook that we see life differently. We cannot speak it in words; it is an experience one must make for oneself. We do not dispute, we agree with all things once this outlook is opened. Once we have taken this attitude in life, the same life seems in a different way. If I call it simple, it certainly is[7] simple. If I call it subtle, there is nothing more subtle than this. It is what it is, it cannot be said in words. Therefore, in the path of Sufi initiation there is something to be

---

5. Od.tp., Sk.tp.: "can" underlined for emphasis
6. Od.tp., Sk.tp.: "must" underlined for emphasis
7. Od.tp., Sk.tp.: "is" underlined for emphasis

learned, but little to be learned. Something has to be learned and unlearned. What is necessary is to come to that consciousness where the outlook on life is changed. We do not mind in what manner a person arrives to that outlook, through what religion, belief, or sect. What we know is either, "You know" or "You do not know." We never question how, we only see whether he knows or knows not. Sufi initiation is given in order to give that which is not to be said in words. It is a great thing, but when you show it, it is as small as possible. For our policy is, "If you want to do great things, show them then as small as you can; if you want to do little things, show them as big as you can."

An old typescript

München, at Baronin Eleonore von Rommel's
Afternoon, March 18th,1925

Talk around the Table[1]

Mureeds and[2] friends,

This evening I am not giving an address but a talk around the table. We are very happy today to see among us the leader of the group here, Mrs. Hoeber[3]. I as well as you who have responded to her and helped her, thank her for the service she has rendered to the cause. The other happiness is that we have among us today Dr. Steindamm[4], a *mureed*[5], a friend and worker from Berlin. His presence promises a link established between the group in Munich and Berlin. For the cooperation of the mureeds in Munich and Berlin we have in Dr. Steindamm a most valuable helper. I hope that a cooperation between the two groups will be established by the enthusiastic and earnest efforts of our friends.

And now I would like to say a few words about our work. When one looks at the seed of a tree, neither one sees flowers nor fruits, but once it has become a tree one sees fruits and flowers. This is the condition of our work just now in Germany. It is in the form of a seed, it has neither leaves nor fruits nor flowers. As the seed promises seeds, so this Movement promises what is going to come. But does it promise because we are a large number? We have only a small number. Therefore what the promise is in, is sincerity. For it is sincerity which alone is the test of human nature. It is a privilege in life when one can say, "I have one sincere friend."

Now I would like to say a few words which you already know, yet never too often these words may be spoken, that is that at

---

Documents:

od.tp. = an old typescript of unknown provenance.

Sk.tp. = a typescript made by Sakina Furnée, nearly identical to od.tp.

Notes:

1. Sk.tp.: "Private Lecture." written by hand above the text
2. Sk.tp.: "and" omitted
3. for Mrs. Hoeber, see List
4. for Dr. Steindamm, see List
5. Sufis use the word *mureed* for an initiate; see Glossary

the present what is most necessary is to establish a mechanism of the work. If you ask me how to do it, by doing three things: the first is that you will keep the circle of study going; the second is to continue the Universal Worship[6], the blessing of which is the protection for our infant movement; and the third is to continue the brotherhood activity even if you could not call it brotherhood. This is in order to keep you together and friends even if they are not initiated. This activity will produce in your heart inspiration of the ways and means by which you can be more serviceable to your fellow men.

Now I wish to repeat that what we believe is to understand the belief; what we do is the proof of our belief; and what we think is according to our outlook on life. Since you, my mureeds, are privileged to be pioneers of the Movement in Germany, you will have difficulties. You will have the difficulty of people's antagonism, of those who do not understand. For mankind is so ready to [belittle][7] things which do not appear grand at once. It is just like an architect making a building. Before the building is prepared, people criticize. The best thing is to become conscious of your responsibility, firm on your feet, maintaining that belief that success in the end belongs to truth.

I wish I could come more often than I could come. But to bring this wish to practise is difficult. Nevertheless, when I am away, I am still more near to my friends. Space does not divide souls. The light of the divine truth in which we are bound together is a bond which cannot break. As the hours will pass, and the days and the months, this bond will be stronger and stronger. And by the strength of this bond we shall do our humble service to humanity.

---

6. for Universal Worship, see List
7. Od.tp., Sk.tp.: "lighter" written, then underlined with dots, and "belittle (?)" written in the margin

An old typescript

[1] München, at the home of the painter Staeger
Evening, March 18th, 1925

Mysticism

Friends,

Now I would like to say a few words on what we call mysticism[2]. Mysticism is a means to an end. Mysticism is not the goal, but through it one arrives at the goal. If you ask me, "What is Sufism? Is it a philosophy, is it mysticism?" the answer is, "It is both." This evening I would like to speak a few words on the mystic side of Sufism. The mystic side of Sufism may be recognized as seeing and as hearing. To see further than one sees, to hear keener than one hears. In other words, to see what the eyes cannot see, to hear what the ears cannot hear. This experience brings to realization, to see without eyes, to hear without ears. No doubt, for the mystic seeing and hearing, these two words, have different meaning. When we say seeing, we mean what we see through the eyes. When we say hearing, we mean what we hear through the ears. But for the mystic seeing is not only through the eyes, but even without eyes. Hearing for the mystic is not only through the ears, but without ears.

There happens to exist a word in English language, seer. It means someone who with eyes and without eyes can see. Now the question comes, if there is such a seeing and hearing, every soul would be most happy to attain to it, for it would be just like having wings to fly. Who would not? Everyone will. And if there is this possibility to see and hear, why is not everybody seeking after it? The reason is that not everybody believes it, that [which][3] can only be attained by belief, never without it. Therefore, it is that something every soul seeks after, every soul doubts about. And if a soul believes, the question is if he has patience enough to go through it. For it is patience which is required in this way because a certain

---

Documents:
- od.tp. = an old typescript of unknown provenance.
- Sk.tp. = a typescript made by Sakina Furnée, showing a few handwritten corrections.

Notes:
1. Sk.tp.: "Private Lecture." written by hand above the text
2. Sk.tp.: "mysticism" underlined for emphasis
3. Od.tp.: "what" typed; Sk.tp.: "what" typed, then corrected by hand to read "which"

preparation is necessary to hear and see. For everyone would like to see and hear, but if he were open to it, would he be strong enough to endure the disadvantages? For an instance, mankind, as ready as it is to criticize its fellow men, if it could see faults still more, what will you do? A man who is absorbed in life's interests, if he sees a terrible thing coming upon himself, upon his dear ones, will he be able to endure? A person who is ready to give the secret of one to another, if he knew by this power the secrets of his fellow men, what a terrible thing he would do. A person who is affectionate, afraid of any harm or hurt touching his dear ones, if he saw it coming, his nerves would be shattered to pieces.

Therefore, we see that[4] there is a possibility of seeing and hearing in every soul and every soul would be too delighted to attain to this power. Yet not every soul is ready to have it nor would it be good for every soul to have[5]. Naturally, for that reason it is called mysticism. If there is any secret in it, that is the only secret. Before a person has developed his outlook, he must not hear, he must not see. Therefore, not in order to make one see and hear, but to change the outlook, the teacher gives initiation. But when the pupil says, "I come to see and hear," the teacher says, "You wait." For I will tell you my own experience. Before looking for my teacher I began to have the faculty of seeing developed. It is that which gives the desire to seek for a teacher, for the teacher can give the explanation of life. I did not tell my teacher about this faculty for I was too impressed, too respectful to say what I could see and hear. But one day, after association with my teacher, I ventured to speak about it. And what was his answer? "I am sorry." I was expecting a word of encouragement. Following to it, he said, "It is not seeing or hearing, it is to acknowledge it, what hinders one's progress."

When there is this hearing, they call it clairaudience, this seeing, clairvoyance. How badly today these words are used. Anyone who is troubled in his mind, who wants to know about the future and speaks about it, is called a clairvoyant. How surprising it is to hear a person say, "I am clairvoyant." In reality this gift of seeing and hearing is a gift from the divine being. Someone who has this power is trusted with the secret of life; the more he claims, the more he attracts people, the more he sins against the law of divine nature. It must be understood, when this seeing and hearing begins,

---

4. Sk.tp.: "though" added by hand
5. Sk.tp.: "it" added by hand

from that time an initiation is given and man becomes responsible for the secrets revealed to him. Besides, if man was not prepared, if he had not reached a certain point, what is the benefit? As once I was amused to hear from a man, "The condition of our country? We have so much freedom that we do not know what to do with it." The same thing with the person who can see and hear; he finds so much to see that he does not know what to do. The Sufi, therefore, is grateful for what he sees and hears and grateful for what he does not see and hear. He learns resignation in the path of the divine voyage.

Now one might ask what kind of preparation? The answer will be, "It is a moral preparation." But not in the sense as we understand in everyday life the word moral. What we understand is selfish because we judge another with our law instead of considering him with his law. The moral according to the Sufi idea, in this preparation specially, is another thing; it is consideration of the law of friendship, of the relation to one's elder or superior or younger or inferior. Although it is a simple thing to consider friendship, it is most difficult to practise. If one knows the principle of friendship, one does not need the moral of the world. When instead of his own profit and laws[6], man considers the profit and laws of another, then he begins to see his soul. As long as he sees the other as a separate being different from himself, he will see him wrongly.

Therefore, friends, what Sufism offers, is a facility of becoming acquainted with these ideas. After this acquaintance naturally the soul unfolds. And as a natural consequence of the soul's unfoldment, one gradually hears more and more.

- - - - - - - - - - - - - - - - - - - -

Now I shall be glad to answer if there are any questions.

Q.: May one seek for this power?
A.: Food is for the hungry. If you are hungry, you must seek for food. If you wish, you will naturally see more. But if you do not wish it, it does not matter. It is according to the appetite. If there is appetite, there must be food. If it is a sin to see more, it is also a sin to see with the eyes. The eyes are given to see, the soul to see further. Nevertheless, to seek for extraordinary powers, for

---

6. Although here and in the following instance both typescripts have "laws", it seems likely that Inayat Khan said "loss", which sounds very similar

phenomena, is going backwards instead of forwards. If one goes in the path of beneficence, all that is to be given, will be given. But as I say, if we live a life of friendliness, there is nothing better we can live for.

Q.: [7]
A.: The idea is this, as long as one understands the principle of friendship, one will find what is necessary and what not. If a Sufi has relations who belong to the Catholic church, who would be too delighted if he went to the church also, if he considers the law of friendship, he will go to the church but will not let it take away Sufism. All the ceremony of those who love it, he does not disturb.[8] Why should he? Wisdom is not to separate, it is to unite. I will tell you a little story. When I was travelling in the ship from a French port to New York, three services were given. I attended to all those three services. Nobody expected me to be there; I went there not to please anyone but to please myself. Not in one service I felt worshipping God less. I felt in all three services the worship of the same God. But suppose a person did not go to the service and only went to the dance after dinner, would he be less Sufi therefore? He would also have done a worship, as much as in the service.

---

7. Od.tp.: the question is missing, "(missed)" typed instead; Sk.tp.: a question mark
8. Sk.tp.: "All the ceremony of those who love it, he does not disturb." crossed out and "He does not disturb the ceremony of those who love it." substituted by hand

An old typescript

[1] München, at the home of Dr. Ludwig
Evening, March 19th, 1925

Sufism

Beloved ones of God,

It is my great pleasure to address this meeting in the home of my friend Dr. Ludwig. This evening I would like to speak on the subject of Sufism. Sufism can be divided into three parts: firstly, as it existed in the past, historical Sufism; secondly, Sufism in essence; and thirdly, Sufism as it is being given to the world just now.

When we come to the word Sufi, it at once explains what it means, *sophos* means wisdom. If one asks, "When did Sufism come in the world?" the answer is, "At the same time as wisdom came to the world." If one says, "Who brought it?" The one who brought wisdom. No one can say when wisdom came or who first brought wisdom. So one cannot say when Sufism came and who was the first who brought it. As far as history knows, Sufi traditions are to be found in the schools of the East as far as the time of Abraham. Even today there exist schools in the East directly from the time of Abraham. However, Sufism has little to do with history, with tradition. Sufism is directed by the soul, not by the ears. It belongs neither to the East nor to the West. It is a message of the soul, the spirit. In all periods of history such schools existed, but it is a school which never had a mission or a sect. People had to work and earn to deserve to be admitted in it.

There is a little story told of a Sufi of Bukhara. To him someone came who had abandoned his kingdom, a king who wanted admission in this school of contemplation. The first command was that he had to begin as everybody else, to look after the house of the *mureeds*[2]. Of course the mureeds did not feel comfortable that one who was a king was going through this process. Besides, a personality who had abandoned his kingdom in order to enter the

---

Documents:
od.tp. = an old typescript of unknown provenance.
Sk.tp. = a typescript made by Sakina Furnée, nearly identical to od.tp.

Notes:
1. Sk.tp.: "Private Lecture" written by hand above the text
2. Sufis use the word *mureed* to indicate an initiate; see Glossary

kingdom of thought, the mureeds found it too much. When a few weeks had passed, the mureeds begged the teacher to give this person admission, initiation in the path. The teacher said, "The time has not yet come." They still requested, "We all feel he may be released of such a duty." The teacher said, "Well, we shall see. One must go when he is working with the basket of garbage and push it." So one of them did it. When the basket fell, the king looked at him and said, "I would have shown you if I was what I was; alas, I am not that." When the news [was][3] brought to the teacher, he said, "Did I not tell you the time has not yet come?" The next time they tried in the same way. He said nothing, he looked only. When the news was brought to the teacher, he said, "The time has not yet come." The third time, he did not even look, he took the scraps in his basket and went away. When then they told the teacher, he knew it was time to receive him in the school of wisdom which leads man towards the light.

By telling you this what I mean is to make you understand that Sufism has never been a mission or a religion. It is a school of seekers after truth. Those who are initiated in this school are most trusted by the teacher. No doubt, these schools existed in different races and therefore, they developed under different influences. Among the Chaldeans, the contemplation side, the ecstatic side was developed; among the Arabs the intellectual side, among the Persians the literary side. The great poets of Persia, Sa'di, Hafiz, Rumi[4] won a great fame by the delicacy of their poetry. The modern world will appreciate these treasures of beauty in which truth is explored. Then there comes a phase of Sufi development in India. This phase is greater than any other phase of Sufism. In India, where fakirs, Yogis, and ascetics made mystical experiences, Sufism had an opportunity of developing. The proof of this can be found today. There is not one village where there is not either a Sufi's tomb or cottage where everyone comes with the desire to be friendly, be it Hindu or Muslim or Christian, where all rejoice in one brotherhood.

And now coming to the essence of Sufism, what is it? If one calls it religion, it is certainly not a[5] religion, it is the essence, it is all religions. If you call it a philosophy, it has no fixed theories or

---

3. Od.tp., Sk.tp.: "were" written, then crossed out by hand, and "was" written above the line
4. For Sa'di, Hafiz, Rumi, see List
5. Od.tp., Sk.tp.: "a" underlined for emphasis

dogmas or conceptions. Then what is it? If one calls it mysticism, it is not altogether mysticism. If one plainly explains it, it is an outlook on life. From beginning to end the teaching of Sufism is leading to a new outlook on life, which cannot be spoken in words. If you ask what the Sufi teaches, what *Murshid*[6] [teaches][7] to the mureed: what Murshid teaches is the attitude by which this outlook may be attained in life. And how is it attained? It is by learning continually and by continually unlearning. The difficulty generally is that by indigestion a person does not know how to unlearn. I myself have seen a man who had read hundred books and had written perhaps fifty books and did not know what is what.

This attitude is, to analyse and to synthesize at the same time; the study is analysing life and the best subject to analyse is oneself. It is by self-analysis that one develops analysing others and conditions. But it must be understood that if one were only analysing and not synthesizing, one would develop an unbalanced condition. Therefore, study is analysing, practice is synthesizing. For an instance, there is one man who says, "This is right and that is wrong." He has been tempted with analysis. The Sufi has analysed in the same way, but by synthesis he sees in this wrong the right and in this right the wrong. Naturally, in the worst person he sees the good, in the best person the wrong. This synthesis brings one above the fixed ideas of life which every person fixes. The Sufi sees right and wrong at the same time, the good and bad side of each thing. By this analysis he begins to understand. He finds out his mistakes and errors which generally man covers from his own eyes and sees in others. For the Sufi says, "No one would call another wicked if wickedness were not in himself."

There is a story of Jesus, that a person came to Jesus and said, "Who is Jesus?" Jesus said, "What you think of Jesus." In other words, "You think of him as man, angel, friend or foe, Jesus is that." No doubt, the subtle idea of the Sufi is difficult to understand. But no reasoning, thinking person can go against it. He can only say, "It is unusual," perhaps, or "strange". But consciously or unconsciously we are often before strange things.

Now coming to the simple idea of the Sufis, leaving aside the subtle thoughts. Never it is the desire of a Sufi to acquire great

---

6. Sufis use the word *murshid* for a spiritual teacher; see Glossary
7. Od.tp.: "teached" written; Sk.tp.: "teached" written, then corrected by hand to read "teaches"

powers, to perform wonders, or to attain a reputation of great goodness. He thinks, "If there is[8] goodness, it must be natural. If it is learned, it is nothing. If there is a wonder, it must be a natural wonder." To seek power in order to come to the wonder is beneath him. The Sufi is not delighted in doctrines, theories, or dogmas, nor is he opposed to them. There is no such doctrine as can be called a Sufi doctrine. The Sufi gives freedom to everyone to think and express himself as he happens to do. For an instance, he thinks if he says "seven heavens", "why you also say seven". It may be right when you say "ten".

The Sufi instead of separating, unites, not politely, but rightly. The Sufi thinks that if it were for materiality, it would not be necessary that man existed. For animals eat and drink and make merry and for them it is enough. If man was born it is to realize the spirit. Nevertheless, there are angels enough to sing the song of praise to God. Therefore, for the Sufi it is nor materialism nor spirituality; it is nobility which is to be deserved by tracing the aristocratic heritage which is the divine heritage of man. Every man is born with a heritage which is divine heritage. To become conscious of it, in this is nobility. Man is as large as is his ideal, as small as his need. When man is absorbed in the thought of his needs, he is conscious of his earthly heritage. But when he is conscious of his ideal, then naturally he is large. By learning music one begins to learn which is the false note, which is the right note. So it is by trying to develop in us the consciousness of ideal that we learn to see when we strike the right and when the false note.

It is not only that the Sufi does concentration and meditation for one or two hours a day. From morning till evening the Sufi realizes where he acts beneath his dignity, when he comes up to his dignity, from morning till evening he asks himself, "Which is my dignity?" The Sufi begins to watch at each step how small he is or how large. By watching this continually, he naturally tries to become larger and larger. And his life's purpose is fulfilled in the expansion of his consciousness.

The fruits of Sufism, the tree perhaps sown for numberless years, are now to be taken by humanity. To give a facility to

---

8. Od.tp., Sk.tp.: "is" underlined for emphasis

different people, to seekers after truth, Sufism is given in a group such as exists here in Munich that many may attain this Message.

God bless you.

An old typescript

[1] München, Kunstgewerbehaus
March 20th, 1925

Concentration

Beloved ones of God,

I ask your indulgence of the discourse of this evening on the subject of concentration[2]. Concentration is a subject which is interesting to every thoughtful person. But to have the knowledge of concentration requires study not only, but also balance.

Before touching this subject, I would like to first explain what motive we have behind concentration. There are two aspects of life, the audible life and the silent life. By audible life I mean all experiences, all sensations we experience through our five senses, namely sight, hearing, smelling, taste and touch. All that we experience through these senses is sensation. This is divided from the life which I call silent life.

Now the question is what benefit one derives from getting in touch with the silent life? In answer to this one can say that the benefit is as abstract as is the silent life. The life of sensation is clear; its benefit is clear. And yet as limited as is the life of sensation, so limited is its benefit. Therefore, in the end of the examination we find all our experiences of little value. Their importance is so long as we experience them, but after the experience the importance of the sensational life is finished. But the value of silent life is independent. Naturally we consider that a value which considers our outer life. By touching silent life we cannot touch a certain benefit, but a general benefit. In other words, if there is a certain hurt on the skin, a little wound on the body, an external application of medicine can cure it. But there are medications which can cure the general condition and this is better than the outer cure. The latter cure is not so much noticed, not so noticed as the former.

Documents:
od.tp. = an old typescript of unknown provenance.
Sk.tp. = a typescript made by Sakina Furnée, identical with od.tp.

Notes:
1. Sk.tp.: "Public Lecture." typed above the text
2. Od.tp.: "concentration" underlined

Naturally, one cannot exactly say what profit is gained by concentration. But really speaking, every profit is to be attained in all directions through concentration.

Now I will divide the idea of concentration into two parts: firstly automatic concentration, secondly, intentional concentration.

Automatic concentration is found in many people who do not know that they concentrate and yet they do. They concentrate automatically, some to their disadvantage, some to their advantage. Those who concentrate to their advantage are the ones whose mind is fixed on business, on any occupation they do. And they are the ones who can be most concentrated and can work more successfully, be it a composer, a writer, a musician, according to his power of concentration he will have a success. The man may not know but his power of concentration may be great. For an instance, I had the pleasure of hearing Paderewski[3] in his house. He began gently on his piano. Every note took him to a deeper and deeper ocean of music. Any meditative person could see clearly that he was so concentrated in what he did that he knew not where he was. Great composers who left such works which will always live, which win the hearts of men, from where do they come? From concentration. So it is with a poet, so it is with an artist, that it is concentration which brings colour and line, which makes the picture. Naturally, be it an artist or a writer, a musician or a poet, somebody who is in business or industry, by the absence of concentration he can never succeed.

Now coming to the concentration which works to the disadvantage. There are some who get to think that, "I am unlucky, everything I do goes wrong," some who think that everybody dislikes them, that everybody hates them. Then some begin to think that, "I am unable to do anything, I am incapable, useless." Some out of self-pity think that they are ill. In that way, if they are not ill, they create illness. Some by concentration cherish illness, always think of it. No physician could be successful with them. As an old physician has said, "There are many diseases, but there are many more patients." Once a person has become a patient through concentration, he is difficult to be cured. Never think for a moment that there are few such cases. There are many cases of automatic concentration to the disadvantage of man.

And now we come to intentional concentration. This no

3. For Paderewski, see List

doubt is taught by thinkers, philosophers, meditative people. The whole mysticism, esotericism is based upon the idea of concentration. This mystical concentration can be divided into four different grades. The first is concentration, the next contemplation, the next meditation, the fourth realization.

The definition of the first grade is to fix one's thought upon one object. No doubt, the question arises, "Which object?" A person need not concentrate upon any object that comes along because what you concentrate upon has effect upon you. When you concentrate on a dead object, it has the effect of deadening the soul. If you concentrate on a living object, it naturally has a living effect. In this the secret is to be found of the teachings of all prophets and mystics. This concentration is made in three different ways. The first way is by action. One does a certain movement or action which helps the mind to concentrate on a certain object. The other way is by the help of words. By the repetition of certain words one learns to think automatically on a certain object. The third way is made by the help of memory. Memory is like a storehouse of an architect. From this the architect takes everything he likes, tiles, pillars, bricks, whatever he wants. To give a picture, for the play of children they have made toys to build houses. The same thing the man who makes this concentration does. He gets things, composes objects in order to concentrate on the wished object.

Now coming to the subject of contemplation. When a person is advanced enough, then alone he can contemplate, because contemplation is not on one object, it is on one idea. No doubt, man thinks he is ready to do anything, that after concentration he can contemplate. The nature of the mind is such that it slips off of your hands the moment you try to hold it. Therefore, before one has thought, the mind has thrown off the object of concentration like a restive horse. Mind is not so unruly always. It proves to be unruly when it wants to rule. It is like the body. You may feel restful sitting naturally, but as soon as you keep it still for five minutes, it begins to feel restless. It is still more difficult to make the mind obey. Yes, automatically it will, but when one wishes, it will not. Mystics, therefore, find a rope to tie the mind in a certain place where it cannot move. What is that rope? That rope is breath. It is by that rope that they bind it and make mind stand where they wish it to stand. It is like the bird which puts out its saliva to make its nest. So it is with the mystic who out of breath creates atmosphere, creates light and magnetism in which to live.

Now before speaking on the third subject, the third grade, I should first like to say what quality mind has. These two characteristics of mind must be understood, it is like the gramophone record, whatever is impressed upon it, it is able to produce. So is our mind. All it takes upon itself it repeats. If it is a pleasing impression, a happy impression, it gives happiness. If it is an ugly, depressing impression, it produces unhappiness. How few there are who think about this. How more ready one is to see the bad side than the good side of things. The other characteristic of mind is that it is not only a gramophone record, but it creates what is impressed upon it. If ugliness is recorded, it will produce disagreement, inharmony. Learning of concentration clears the record, makes it produce what we like, not what comes automatically. In this world one is so open to impressions. One goes about with eyes and ears open. But it is not only the eyes, not only the ears which are open, the lips are open to give them out. That is the dangerous part. Suppose one goes on in life like that? Where does it end? It would end into nothing.

Now coming to the third part of concentration, which is meditation. In this grade one becomes communicative, one communicates with silent life and naturally a communication becomes open with the outer life also. It is then that man begins to realize that all the outer and inner life, all is communicative. Then man begins to learn what can never be learned by study, or from books, that silent life is the greatest teacher who knows all things. It does not only teach, but gives that peace, that joy, power and harmony which makes life beautiful. No one can claim to be meditative, for a meditative person need not say it with the lips. His atmosphere says it. One can say that it is true or that it is false, but atmosphere alone can say if it is true or false. Once I asked my spiritual teacher what was the sign of knowing God. He said, "Not those who call out the name of God, but those whose silence says it." Many go about looking, searching for something worthwhile, something wonderful. But there is nothing more wonderful than the soul of man.

Realization is the result of the three other grades. This fourth kind of experience is that in the third kind of experience man pursued meditation, but in this meditation pursues man. If I may say it in other words, it is that no longer the singer sings the song, but the song sings the singer. This fourth grade is a kind of expansion of consciousness. It is the enfoldment of the soul. It is diving deep within oneself; it is communicating with each atom of life existing in the whole world; it is realizing the real I in which is the fulfilment of life's purpose.

God bless you.

Sakina Furnée's shorthand reporting

Sorbonne, March 23rd, 1925

The Law of Action[1]

[2]I ask your indulgence to my subject[3] of this evening on the law of action. To say that results are similar to deeds sounds simple, for mostly everyone knows it. But it is not always that everyone follows[4] it. And the reason is that knowing of a law does not enable man to observe the law. Besides, the nature of life is so intoxicating, that one, absorbed in the activity of life, mostly forgets this rule. It is natural that the most simple thing is most difficult to practise. And the very reason that it is simple, man neglects to think seriously about it.

In order to prove this theory that the results of deed are similar to the deed, one [need][5] not go far. One can see in one's own life and in the life of others numberless examples. For it is like an echo: what one does has an echo, and in that echo is the result.

And now [we][6] come to the saying of Zarathushtra[7] who says that actions may be divided into three kinds: a deed, speech and [thought][8]. One may not do wrong, but one may say wrong; one may not say wrong but think wrong, and the wrong is done just the same. And how many make an excuse that, "I said it, but I[9] did not do it." But a person can bring that excuse even to himself that, "I did not say it. I only thought it." According to the idea [of the][10] mystic, the[11] world in which we make our life they call *akasha*[12], and akasha[13]

Documents:
Sk.sh. = Sakina Furnée's shorthand reporting of the lecture, newly transcribed by B.v.d.B.
Sk.tp. = a typescript prepared by Sakina Furnée.

Notes:
1. Sk.sh.: "The Law of Action" added in lh.
2. Sk.tp.: "Beloved ones of God," added
3. Sk.sh.: "of me" written ("of" retraced to read "to"), then crossed out
4. Sk.sh.: "follows" indistinctly written
5. Sk.sh.: "heed" retraced to read "need"; Sk.tp.: "need"
6. Sk.sh.: "they" retraced to read "we"; Sk.tp.: "we"
7. For Zarathushtra, see List
8. Sk.sh.: "act" written, crossed out, "thought" inserted; Sk.tp.: "thought"
9. Sk.sh. "had" written but crossed out
10. Sk.sh.: "of" retraced to read "of the"; Sk.tp.: "of the"
11. Sk.sh.: "word" written, then crossed out
12. For *akasha,* see Glossary
13. Sk.sh.: "A." abbr. for "akasha"

means capacity. It is pictured by them as a dome, and then whatever is spoken in it has its re-echo, and therefore no one can do, say, or think once for a moment that it[14] will become non-existent. It is recorded, and the record of this is creative. It is not only that what one does, what one says, what[15] [one][16] thinks is only recorded on the memory or in the spheres[17], but this record of the[18] every moment creates, that every line and the letter[19] of this record becomes the seed or the germ that produces the similar effect.

I had heard a sculptor[20] say, and truly he said, that every man is the sculptor[21] of his own image[22]. But I would add to it that [it is][23] not only this, but every man is the creator of his own conditions, favourable or the adverse[24], disfavourable[25]. The difficulty is that man never has patience to wait till he sees the result, for the result takes some time, and before that he has contrary effects. For instance, a person who had just robbed another person and when he was coming home, he met with ever[26] good luck, and that was that he found in the street a purse full of gold coins. Naturally he happened to think that, "What a good result[27] after a good work! Now that is the good work; I must continue it. They are simple ones who say things[28] against it. It is a for[29] profit, it is a ready money. [But][30] what they say is a saying, but I have seen experience." And life is so intoxicating that it gives man no time to think that the result is perhaps waiting; this is the result of something else.[31] [32]

When we consider the law of action, it can be divided into five different aspects. One aspect of the law of action is the law of

---

14. Sk.tp.: "it" omitted
15. Sk.sh.: "of" written, but omitted in Sk.tp.
16. Sk.sh.: "one" in sh. inserted
17. Sk.tp.: "sphere" instead of "spheres"
18. Sk.tp.: "that record at" instead of "this record of the"
19. Sk.sh.: "letter" alternately reads "latter"
20. Sk.sh.: actually "sculpture" written in lh.
21. Sk.sh.: "sc. re." in lh.; Sk.tp.: "sculptor"
22. Sk.sh.: "image" repeated in lh.
23. Sk.sh.: "it" retraced to read "it is"; Sk.tp.: "it is"
24. Sk.sh.: "the adverse," crossed out, then only "adverse" reinstated
25. Sk.tp.: "unfavorable" instead of "the adverse, disfavorable"
26. Sk.tp.: "a" instead of "ever"
27. Sk.sh.: a blank
28. Sk.tp.: "things" omitted
29. Sk.sh.: a blank or a pause; Sk.tp.: "for" omitted, a number of dots, missing words
30. Sk.sh.: "For" retraced to read "But"
31. Sk.sh.: a blank
32. Sk.sh.: "this saying will always prove through that present is the reflection of the past and future will be the echo of the present" written, then crossed out

the community. A law that suits one community[33] may not suit another community, for it depends upon the particular development of that community. This law is made for the comfort and convenience of the members of that community.

And the other aspect of this law is to be called the law of the state, a law by which different classes of people and different communities are governed in one whole. No doubt, as limited is[34] the mind of man, so limited these aspects of law are. Naturally, therefore, many laws are rejected, and many new-made laws are brought to practise. And as time will go, so people will see that the members of the community of[35] the state will always wish for different changes to be made in the law. This has always been and will [always][36] be[37].

And now we come to the third aspect of the law. And that is the law of a church, a law which perhaps comes from tradition, and a law that people take not only because it is a law that governs, but because it is a law that is concerned with their faith, with their belief which is sacred to them. It is this law that makes a conscience more than any other aspect of the law.

But then there is another aspect of the law, and that law is that which is brought by the prophets from time to time. And what this law is? This law comes as an interpretation of the hidden law that a[38] prophet could see. But at the same time, a law that is given by a prophet has its relation with the period in which the prophet has come, has its relation with the people of that period to whom they[39] came and their particular evolution. And when we study the different religions given by different prophets to different people in this world in different periods of the world's history, we shall find that the truth which is behind the religions is the same. And if the teaching differs, it only differs in the law that they have given. And people have always disputed in vain to this difference of law that the different teachers have given to their people, not knowing that the law had[40] so much to do with the people to whom it was given and with the time when the law was given.

---

33. Sk.sh.: "C." abbr. for "community"
34. Sk.tp.: "as" instead of "is"
35. Sk.tp.: "or" instead of "of"
36. Sk.sh.: "already" appears to be written; Sk.tp.: "always"
37. Sk.sh.: "be" indistinctly written
38. Sk.tp.: "the" instead of "a"
39. Sk.tp.: "he" instead of "they"
40. Sk.sh.: a dotted underlining of "had"

But these four laws which I have just now separated[41]: the law of community, of state, of church, of the prophet, they have the limitations. But there is one law, and[42] it is that law which leads man towards the unlimited, and it is this law that never can be taught and that never can be explained. [43]At the same time, it is this law which is rooted in the nature of man. And there is no person, however unjust and wicked he may seem, who [has not][44] this faculty in the innermost being. And this may we call a faculty, a faculty of knowing proper and improper, a property of discerning whether it is right or whether it is wrong.

But now we come to this question, that what determines a thing to be called right or wrong. It is four things: the motive behind action, the result of the action, the time and the place. Wrong action with the right motive may be right. And a [right][45] action with a wrong motive may be wrong. We are always ready to judge an action, and we hardly[46] think of the motive. Therefore, we readily accuse a person for his wrong, and excuse readily ourselves[47] for our wrong because we know our motive best.

We perhaps could excuse another person as we excuse ourselves if we tried to know the motive behind his action also. A thought, a word, an action in its wrong[48] place turns wrong even if it be right. A thought, word or action at a wrong time may be wrong even if it maybe seems[49] right. And when we analyse this more, we shall say, as a Hindu poet has said, "There is no use feeling bad about a wrong deed of another person. We must content ourselves knowing that he could not do better."

And now there is another side to look at it. Things seem to us as we look at them. To a wrong person everything looks wrong, and perhaps to a right person everything looks right. Because right person turns[50] wrong also into the right, and [a][51] wrong person turns[52] right into wrong. The sin of the virtuous is a virtue, and the

41. Sk.sh.: "sep." abbr. for "separated"; Sk.tp.: "said"
42. Sk.sh.: "this" written, then crossed out
43. Sk.tp.: "And" added
44. Sk.sh.: "has not" retraced through a now illegible sh. symbol
45. Sk.sh.: "wrong" written, then crossed out, then "right" substituted; Sk.tp.: "right"
46. Sk.sh.: actually "heartly" written here, inadvertently
47. Sk.sh.: "ourselves" indistinctly written
48. Sk.sh.: "in its wrong" encircled
49. Sk.tp.: "may seem" instead of "maybe seems"
50. Sk.sh.: "for" written, but omitted in Sk.tp.
51. Sk.sh.: an illegible sh. symbol; Sk.tp.: "a"
52. Sk.sh.: "not" written, but omitted in Sk.tp.

virtue of a sinner is a sin. Things very much depend[53] upon our interpretation, as on no action, on no word, on no thought, there is a seal which decides it to be wrong or right.

And now there is another side of it to look at: how much our favour and disfavour play[54] its role in discerning right and wrong. In someone whom we love and like and admire, everything wrong we wish to see it in a right light. Our reason readily comes to the rescue of the loved one. It always brings an argument which is right and which stands for his wrong. And how readily the person whom we disfavour[55], we see his faults and his errors. [56]He easily does wrong before us, for we easily see it.

And it is a difficult thing for us to find a fault, even if we wanted to find a fault in someone whom we love. Therefore, if in the life of Christ we read having forgiven[57] those who were accused of great faults, great sins, we now ought[58] see it naturally, that the one who was the lover of mankind could not see a fault, only what he could see was forgiveness. [59]We see that a stupid person, a simple person is ready to see the wrong in a person and ready to form his opinion and ready to judge. And a wise person you will find always diffident[60] in expressing his opinion of others, always trying to tolerate and always trying still more to forgive.[61]

The Sufis of Persia have classed evolution of personality into five different grades. The first category is the person who [errs][62] at every step in his life and who finds fault with others at every moment of his life. The picture of this is like this, that a person who is likely to fall,[63] or who once[64] on the point of tumbling down[65] ; the same picture with the one who falls.[66] He, while falling at once, catches

---

53. Sk.sh.: "even" written, then crossed out
54. Sk.tp.: "plays" instead of "play"
55. Sk.sh.: "disfavour" encircled
56. Sk.sh.: "He is" written, then crossed out and omitted in Sk.tp.
57. Sk.sh.: "en" in lh. added to read "forgiven"
58. Sk.tp.: "can" instead of "ought"
59. Sk.sh.: a single bracket is placed in front of "We"
60. Sk.sh.: "defident" added in lh.
61. Sk.sh.: an editorial marker (star) is placed here; Sk.tp.: "This saying will always prove true that, 'Present is the reflection of the past, and future will be the echo of the present.'" added
62. Sk.sh.: "ears" in lh. crossed out, "errs" in lh. substituted, then "ears" re-emphasized by way of a broken underlining; Sk.tp.: "who errs"
63. Sk.sh.: "tum." abbr. for "tumble", "or to tumble" then crossed out, omitted in Sk.tp.
64. Sk.tp.: "is" instead of "once"
65. Sk.sh.: missing words; Sk.tp.: dots
66. Sk.sh.: lost word or words

another person[67]. And it is not a rare case to be found. It is generally to be found if we studied[68] the psychology of man. The one who finds fault with the other[69] very often is the one who has most of the faults in him. The thing is that the right person first finds fault with himself, and the wrong person last finds fault with himself; after having found fault with the whole world, he finds fault with himself. And then everything is wrong; the whole world is wrong.

And the next grade of personality is of the one who begins to see the wrong in himself and the right in the other. Naturally, he has the opportunity in his life to correct himself, because then he has all the time to find all his own faults. The one who finds fault with the others, he has no time to find fault with himself. Besides, one cannot be judged[70]. The faculty of justices[71] cannot be wakened unless one began to practise that justice by finding fault with oneself.

And the third person is that person who says, "What does it matter if you did wrong, as[72] if I did wrong. What is needed is to right the wrong." He naturally develops himself and helps his fellowmen also to develop.

And there is the fourth man; he never can see what they call good without the possibility of being bad, and he can never[73] see what they[74] called[75] bad without the same[76] possibility of turning [what they call bad][77] into good. The best person in the world cannot hide his fault before him, and the worst person in the world will show his merit to his eyes.

But when one has risen to the fifth category of people, then these opposite words, right or wrong, good or bad[78], these seem to be the two ends of one line. It is that time that he can say little about it, for people will not believe him. He is the one who can judge rightly, and he is the one who will judge the last.

---

67. Sk.sh.: more than half the line is left blank; Sk.tp.: dots for missing words
68. Sk.tp.: "study" instead of "studied"
69. Sk.sh.: "and" written, but omitted in Sk.tp.
70. Sk.tp.: "just" instead of "judged"
71. Sk.sh.: the plural "s" of "justices" is crossed out, then "justice" in lh added; Sk.tp.: "justice"
72. Sk.tp.: "or" instead of "as"
73. Sk.tp.: "never can" instead of "can never"
74. Sk.sh.: "can say" written, then crossed out
75. Sk.tp.: "call" instead of "called"
76. Sk.tp.: "same" omitted
77. Sk.sh.: "what they call bad" inserted
78. Sk.sh.: "bad" retraced for clarity

There are three different ways that men adopt[79] in order to progress towards human perfection. And a person who is not evolved oneself to adopt the third way or the second way, he may not be forced to adopt. If he was forced, it would be that a manner was taught to him at a wrong[80] time. For these three ways of which I am going to speak to you now are like three steps[81] towards human perfection.

The first degree is the law of reciprocity. It is in this degree that one learns the meaning of justice. The law of reciprocity[82] is to give and to take sympathy, and all that sympathy can give and take. It is according to this law that the religion's law[83] is made, the law of the state is made, the law of the community is made. The idea of this law is that you may not take from me more than you could give me. I will not give you more than I could take from you. It is a fair business that you love me and I love you; you [hate][84] me, I can hate you. And if a person has not learned the just measure of give-and-take, he has not practised justice. He may be innocent, he may be loving, but he has no common sense, he is not practical. And the danger in this law is that a person might[85] esteem more what he does, and may decrease the value of the thing done by another. But the one who gives more than he takes, he is progressing towards the next grade.

It is easy for us to say that this is a very hard and fast law. But at the same time, it is the most difficult thing to live in this world and to get out of it. One must ask a practical man, a man with common sense, how impossible it is to live in this world and to be regardless of this law of give-and-take. And if the people of this world were no better this[86] keeping this law properly, there would be much less trouble in this world. There is no use thinking that people will become saints or sages or great beings. If they became just, it would be something.

And now we come to a step[87] further. That law is the law of

79. Sk.sh.: "adopt" added in lh.; Sk.tp.: "man adopts"
80. Sk.tp.: "wrong" omitted
81. Sk.sh.: "to" written, then crossed out
82. Sk.sh.: "R." abbr. for "reciprocity"
83. Sk.sh.: "law" alternately reads "also"; Sk.tp.: "religion also" instead of "religion's law"
84. Sk.sh.: actually "rate" written for "hate"; Sk.tp.: "hate"
85. Sk.tp.: "may" instead of "might"
86. Sk.tp.: "than" instead of "this"
87. Sk.sh.: "step" indistinctly written

beneficence. And that law is to be disconcerned[88] what comes from the other person to us in answer to what we do to the person in love and in sympathy. What one is concerned is with this, that what he can do for the other person. It does not matter[89] if a favour is not appreciated. But even if the favour[90] absolutely ignored, even then the satisfaction that the beneficent man gets is out of what he has done, not out of what the other has expressed who has received it. When this sense is born in man, from that day he begins to live in the world. For his pleasure does not depend upon what he receives from others, but his pleasure depends upon what he does for others. And, therefore, if I said that his happiness is not independent, his happiness is undependent[91], he [becomes][92] the creator of his happiness. His happiness is in doing, not in taking.

But now what do I mean by giving? We give and take every moment of the day. Every word we speak, every action we do, every thought and feeling we have for one another, this is all giving, this is all taking. And it is this man who will forget his sorrow. It is this person who will forget his miseries. It is this person who will rise above[93] pains and miseries of this world.

And a step further comes another law, the third law. And that law is the law for renunciation. When one observes this law, for him giving means nothing. For [them][94] he is not even conscious that he gives; he gives automatically. He does not mean then, nor he thinks about it, that "I give". He thinks that it is "being given". This is a person who may be pictured as of someone walking on the water. For it is this person who will rise absolutely before disappointments, and distresses, and pains of life, which are so numberless. Besides, renunciation[95] means independence and indifference. Indifference to all things and yet not by the absence of sympathy, an independence to all things and yet not independent in the crude sense of the word.

Renunciation, therefore, may be called the final victory. And one among millions can come up to this ideal, and the one who has come to this ideal, it is he who may be called elevated, liberated.

---

88. Sk.sh.: "disconcerned" clearly written in lh., also in Sk.tp. but "with" added
89. Sk.sh.: inadvertently "math" written here
90. Sk.tp.: "were" added
91. Sk.sh.: "undependent" clearly written here; Sk.tp.: "independent"
92. Sk.sh.: "begon" retraced to read "becomes"; Sk.tp.: "becomes"
93. Sk.tp.: "the" added
94. Sk.sh.: "they know" written, then retraced to read "them"; omitted in Sk.tp.
95. Sk.sh.: "R." abbr. for "renunciation"

Sakina Furnée's shorthand reporting

Sorbonne, Paris, March 24th, 1925

The Power of Thought[1]

There are some who by life's experience have learned [that][2] thought has some power, and there are others who wonder sometimes if thought really has some power. But there are many who listen to this subject with a preconceived idea that if ever[3] thought had a power, it has its limits. But if I were to give my candid opinion on the subject, I would consider that it is no exaggeration if I said that the thought has a power which is unimaginable[4]. And in order to find proof of this idea we do not have to go very far. All that we see in this world is but a phenomena[5] of thought. We live in it and we see it morning till evening, and the very thing we doubt if it is so. This shows that this outer dutiful[6] from morning till evening gives us a pride and vanity that we understand things better[7]. The less a person believes [in][8] the power of thought, the more positive he thinks he stands on the earth. Nevertheless, he, consciously or unconsciously, is feeling his limitation, and he is[9] searching for something that will give him a strength in his belief in thought.

Thought can be divided into five different aspects:

Documents:

Sk.sh.= Sakina Furnée's shorthand reporting of the lecture, newly transcribed by B.v.d.B.
Sk.tp. = a typescript prepared by Sakina Furnée, showing editorial changes.
Hq.st. = a stencil prepared at Headquarters, Geneva, for distribution to Sufi Centres, showing many editorial changes.
Hq.tp. = a typescript prepared at Headquarters, Geneva, only mentioned where it differs from Hq.st.

Notes:

1. Sk.sh.: "The Power of Thought" in lh. added above the sh. title; Sk.tp.: "Public Lecture." added; Hq.st.: "SOCIAL GATHEKA." and "Number 34" followed by the Sufi Invocation added above the title
2. Sk.sh.: "their" retraced to read "that"; a.o.d.: "that"
3. Sk.tp.: "every" instead of "ever"
4. Sk.sh.: "un" in lh. written separately, then "imaginable" in sh., then "unimaginable" added in lh. again
5. Sk.sh.: "phenomena" in sh., Inayat Khan characteristically uses the plural form only (not further noted); Sk.tp., Hq.st.: "phenomenon"
6. Sk.sh.: a blank, then "all" inserted, then crossed out, then "trompe" added in lh.; Sk.tp.: "our beautiful" followed by a number of dots instead of "outer dutiful"
7. Sk.sh.: "that we understand things better" underlined; Hq.st.: this whole fragmented sentence omitted
8. Sk.sh.: "at" appears to be written; a.o.d.: "in"
9. Sk.sh.: "reaching" written, then crossed out

imagination, thought, dream, vision and materialization. Imagination is that action of mind which is automatic. From morning till evening, either a person is working or if he is resting, his mind is working just the same on imagination. It is the automatic thinking;[10] what it produces is called imagination. And then we come to the word thought. Thought is that thinking which is thought with a willpower behind it. And in this way we distinguish between the imaginative and the thoughtful. And therefore these two persons cannot be confused, for one is imaginative, which means a powerless thinking, automatic[11] thinking; the other is thoughtful, whose thinking is powerful.

And then this automatic action which takes place in the state of sleep, it is that which is called dream. No doubt, this is[12] distinct and different from imagination, because while a person is imagining, his senses are open to this objective world and therefore his imagination does not take a concrete form. But when in the dream it is the same automatic action of mind, when it goes on, there is no objective world to compare it with. Therefore, the dream brings[13] more imagination than in a wakeful state.[14] Therefore, to see the condition of mind the mystic always finds it by hearing the dream of the person, by knowing about how a person dreams. Because in the dream the automatic working of the person's mind is[15] much more concrete than in his imagination. There are some who tell perhaps character[16], who know how to read the character, and there are some who can read what they call their[17] future by knowing what the person imagines. They always ask a person, "Give [me][18] a name of a flower, of a fruit, of something you love, you like," that they can find the stream of imagination, where it goes[19]. And[20] from that stream of imagination[21] they find out something about the character of that person and about his life. And it is not necessary that a person must be a character reader, or a fortune teller in order to know that

---

10. Sk.sh.: "which" written, then crossed out
11. Sk.sh.: "automatic" indistinctly written
12. Sk.sh.: an indecipherable symbol crossed out
13. Sk.tp.: dots instead of "brings"
14. Hq.st.: this sentence omitted
15. Sk.sh.: "more" written, then crossed out
16. Sk.sh.: "therefore" written, then crossed out
17. A.o.d.: "the" instead of "their"
18. Sk.sh.: "his" retraced to read "me"; a.o.d.: "me"
19. Sk.sh.: "it" written, then crossed out
20. Hq.st.: "And" omitted
21. Sk.sh.: "I." abbr. for "imagination"

any wise and thoughtful person can understand by the way a person dresses[22] or by the way his environments[23] or ...[24]. A thoughtful person can understand what way his thoughts go, what are his imaginations. Since the state of dream gives mind that possibility to express itself more concrete, therefore dream is the best thing to understand from what state the mind [of][25] a person is. And when once that is understood there is little reason left to doubt if dream has not any effect upon a person's life and upon a person's future. For I would repeat the same thing again which I have said at[26] the commencement of my lecture, that man does not know, man cannot imagine to what extent thought works upon life.

And now coming to the question of what we call vision. In order to make it simple, I would explain vision, that state of dream which one experiences in their[27] wakeful state. A person who is imaginative or a person who is capable to imagine is capable of making a thought. And when this thought which he has created becomes his, an object upon which his mind is focussed, then all else becomes hidden to him, only that particular imagination that stands before him as a picture. No doubt, the effect of this vision is greater than the effect of dream. [The][28] reason is that this imagination which can stand before one's mind in one's wakeful state is naturally more strong than the imagination which was working in one's state of sleep.

But then the fifth aspect is materialization of thought, and it is[29] in the study of this subject that we find the greatest secret of life. No doubt you can make a person convinced by telling him that, is it not architectural[30] imagination that the beautiful building is[31] built[32]? Is it not [33]the gardener's imagination that a beautiful garden is made? But when it comes to nature[34] and all things [that][35] spring

---

22. Sk.sh.: "dresses" indistinctly written
23. A.o.d.: "are" added
24. Sk.sh., Sk.tp.: missing words indicated by dots; Hq.st.: "or ..." omitted
25. A.o.d.: "of" added
26. A.o.d.: "in" instead of "at"
27. A.o.d.: "the" instead of "their"
28. Sk.sh.: "Their" appears to be written; a.o.d.: "The" instead of "Their"
29. Sk.sh.: "in this" written, then crossed out
30. Sk.tp.: "the architect's"; Hq.st.: "by the architects" instead of "architectural"
31. Sk.sh.: a blank
32. Sk.sh.: a blank
33. Hq.st.: "by" added
34. Sk.sh.: "in all" written, then crossed out; a.o.d.: "matter" instead of "nature"
35. Sk.sh.: "this" retraced to read "that"; a.o.d.: "that"

from nature[36], then man begins to wonder how far imagination or thought has a power upon it. Nowadays, as psychology is beginning to spread throughout the Western world, people would at least patiently listen to what it is. But[37] otherwise there are many who would with a great belief take a medicine, but if they are told that a thought can cure you, they will smile at it. And this shows that with all the progress that humanity seems to have made it has gone back in one direction, and that direction is the higher thought, the elevated thought. For man today generally disbelieves in thought and still less believes in what he calls emotion. And in the point of[38] fact, if there is a soul to be found in the thought, that soul is the feeling which is at the back of it. For the reason is that souls become confused when there are only words and there is no feeling behind it. What convinces a thought is the power behind it, and that power consists of feeling. The general tendency is to wave off what is called imagination. "That person imagines" means "that person amuses himself." When a person says, "Oh,[39] you think it, but it does not exist in reality, you think it." But in reality when one has imagined, that imagination is created and what is once created exists. And what is thought, that exists, and that lives longer because thought is more powerful than imagination. And what man calls today sentimentality, which means nothing, in this way he ignores that power which is the only power and the greatest power that exists. It is with this power that the heroes have conquered battles. And it is with this power that if anyone has accomplished a great thing in the world, it is with this[40] power of heart that he has accomplished it, and[41] not with the power of brain. The music of the most wonderful[42] composers and the poetry of the great poets of the world, it has come from the bottom of their heart; it has not come from their brain. And if we close doors for sentimentality, for imagination and for thought, that only means that we close the doors for life to come in.

And now coming to the fancies of[43] fantasies. Perhaps, if not all, some of you have read[44] the stories of fakirs and dervishes in the

---

36. A.o.d.: "matter" instead of "nature"
37. Sk.sh.: "But" indistinctly written
38. Sk.sh.: "p.o." abbr. for "point of"
39. Sk.sh.: "for" written, but omitted in a.o.d.
40. Sk.tp.: "the" instead of "this"
41. A.o.d.: "and" omitted
42. Hq.tp.: "beautiful" instead of "wonderful"
43. A.o.d.: "and" instead of "of"
44. Sk.sh.: "this" written, then crossed out

East. Perhaps you have read them as a novel, or perhaps they have been exaggerated in some way in order to make the book more beautiful. Nevertheless, it asks your attention to study the matter a little more and to understand something of a race, a nation who has for so many thousands of years devoted itself at the sacrifice of the whole life for thought.

There exists perhaps in every little district, in every little village a man who is called the healer of the scorpion sting. And in the heat, as it is in India[45], in the[46] house a scorpion[47] is found, especially in the time of summer. And it is not seldom that a child or a grown-up person is stung by a scorpion, and the sting is something very poisonous and very painful. [48]But in spite of all that there are healers and several of them. And sometimes there is a healer who says, "You are cured; it is gone." And immediately the person is well. And then we come to the sting of the snake bites. That the poison of the serpent is such that hardly[49] a person lives after a serpent[50] bite. There are some who have by the passing of their hands cured it. There are some by [saying][51], "It is cured," they have cured.

And then I will tell you my own experience once, that there was a dervish to whom a person came and said, "There is a case going to be in the court next week." And he said that, "I am so poor that I cannot even have a lawyer to speak for me. And the other person, being rich, he will use every influence and I am without it." And that dervish said, "Tell me what is the condition." And after hearing it all he said, "[As][52] you are not found[53] guilty in this, I dismiss this case." He told him to go simply, "All will be well." [When][54] the man went to the court and he was asked by the judge [everything][55]; at the end the judge wrote[56] exactly the same words

45. Sk.sh.: "Indi." written for "India"
46. A.o.d.: "every" instead of "the"
47. Sk.sh.: "S." abbr. for "scorpion"
48. Sk.sh.: "for" clearly written, but omitted in a.o.d.
49. Sk.sh.: "heartly" inadvertently written for "hardly"
50. Sk.sh.: "serp." abbr. for "serpent"
51. Sk.sh.: "saying" retraced through a now illegible sh. symbol
52. Sk.sh.: "You are, I have found you that" written, then crossed out, then "As" inserted after the cross out; a.o.d. have "As"
53. Sk.sh.: "called" written, then crossed out
54. Sk.sh.: "Then" retraced to read "When", and "When" in a.o.d.
55. Sk.sh.: "everything" traced through an illegible sh. symbol; a.o.d. have "everything"
56. Sk.tp.: "said" instead of "wrote"

that the dervish had said. If I were to give any explanation, words fail to speak about it. Only this can be said, that the heart [of the][57] judge for this dervish[58] [59]was just like a receptive machine of the wireless telegraphy. The great seer and mystic of Persia, Jelal-ud-Din Rumi[60], he says that, "Fire, water, earth[61] and ether[62] are dead[63] things to those who see in them no person. But before the creator they all are live beings; they are his obedient servants." And the great thinker of the Hindus says in Sanskrit[64] language that this whole creation is the dream of Brahma, means the creator.

And now I come to Sufism, what Sufi thinks of the idea of the creator and the[65] creation. Sufi sees both, the creator and the creation, both in man. The limited part of man's being is the creation and the innermost part of his being is the creator. And if that is true, then man is limited and man is unlimited both. If he wished to be limited, he can be more and more limited. If he wished to be unlimited, he can be more and more unlimited. If he cultivates[66] in himself the illusion of being a creation he can be more and more that. But if he cultivates[66] in himself[67] the knowledge of the creator he can be more and more that. Every kind of weakness, [68]every kind of[69] illness, every kind of[69] misery, the more one gives in to it, the more it comes[70] upon one's back. And one goes into it, even to such an extent sometimes that the whole world falls on his back and he is buried under it. And there is another person who gets out of it. It may be difficult, but at the same time it is possible, little by little, gradually but with courage and patience he can get out of it and stand upon the same world which would have otherwise crushed him with[71] it.

---

57. Sk.sh.: "is" retraced to read "of the"; a.o.d.: "of the"
58. Sk.sh.: "D." abbr. for "dervish"
59. Sk.sh.: a blank
60. For Jelal-ud-Din Rumi, see List
61. Sk.sh.: "earth" indistinctly written
62. Sk.tp.: "air" instead of "ether"
63. Sk.sh.: "dead" retraced to read "bad"
64. Sk.sh.: actually "Sanscrit" written in lh.
65. Sk.tp.: "the" omitted
66. Hq.st.: "cultivated" instead of "cultivates"
67. Sk.sh.: "if he cultivates in himself" repeated from the previous sentence by way of dittos
68. Sk.sh.: "every" written, then crossed out
69. Sk.sh.: "every kind of" repeated from the beginning of the sentence by way of dittos
70. Sk.sh.: "above" written, then crossed out
71. A.o.d.: "under" instead of "with"

The former thing is going down, the latter thing is coming up. Both things depend upon the attitude of our mind and it is to change this attitude that is the principal thing in life from a material point of view or from a spiritual point of view[72]. All that is taught in the Sufi esoteric studies and practices is to gain that mastery little by little, gradually, in order to arrive at that fulfilment which is called mastery. But, you will say, it is a great struggle. But I will answer, the struggle is in both ways; in coming down and in going up, in both ways there is a struggle. It is just as well to struggle and come up instead of struggling and going down. And whenever a person goes down, it only means that he is feeble in his thought. And why he is feeble in his thought, because he is weak in his feeling. If feeling[73] protects thought and if thought stands firm, whatever be the difficulty in the life of man, it will be surmounted[74].[75]

---

72. Sk.sh.: "p.o.v." abbr. for "point of view"
73. Sk.sh.: a blank
74. Sk.sh.: "surmount" apparently spoken in the present tense; the "ed" symbol for the past tense is missing; a.o.d.: "surmounted"
75. Sk.tp.: "God bless you." added; Hq.st.: "To be read at the Meetings of the World Brotherhood." added

Sakina Furnée's shorthand reporting

Sorbonne, Paris, March 25th, 1925

Magnetism

The subject of magnetism[1], [as][2] interesting it is from a scientific point of view[3], so interesting, or still more interesting it is from a mystical point of view. For in the first place[4] magnet[5] and something which is attracted to the magnet have a relation. [6]Magnet represents the essence, the[7] part of which that object[8] which is attracted holds[9]. Very often one does not find the trace of that essence in the object that [10]magnet attracts. But at the same time, the essence is there and that is the logical reason that[11] it is attracted, because its essence is there. And what they used to call among the old ancient[12] people a[13] blood-relationship and[14] [is][15] an influence of that recognized by them. In the East this blood-relationship was always signified [by][16] the [magnetism][17] which exists between two

Documents:

Sk.sh. = Sakina Furnée's shorthand reporting of the lecture, newly transcribed by B.v.d.B.

Gd.tp. = a typed version of the lecture with extensive editing by Murshida Sherifa Goodenough to prepare it for publication.

Km.tp. = a typescript prepared by Kismet Stam, mostly following the editorial changes in Gd.tp.

Sk.tp. = a typescript by Sakina Furnée, also showing the editorial changes in Gd.tp.

Notes:

1. Sk.sh.: "M." abbr. for "magnetism"
2. Sk.sh.: "is" retraced to read "as"; a.o.d.: "as"
3. Sk.sh.: "p.o.v." abbr. for "point of view"
4. A.o.d.: "a" added
5. Sk.sh.: "magnet" written in lh.
6. A.o.d.: "The" added
7. A.o.d.: "a" instead of "the"
8. Sk.sh.: "that" written, then crossed out and omitted in a.o.d.
9. Sk.sh.: "it" appears to be written; a.o.d.: "it" omitted
10. A.o.d.: "the" added
11. A.o.d.: "why" instead of "that"
12. A.o.d.: "ancient" omitted; in Sk.tp., "old" later crossed out (but then restored) and "ancient" added by hand
13. A.o.d.: "a" omitted
14. Gd.tp., Km.tp., Sk.tp.: "and" omitted
15. Sk.sh.: "a kind of" written, then crossed out; a.o.d.: "is" added
16. Sk.sh.: "with" appears to be written; a.o.d.: "by" instead of "with"
17. Sk.sh.: a symbol written showing "r-e-s-s" and "im" (retraced), then "magnetism" added in lh.; a.o.d.: "magnetism"

persons who have the same blood. And the[18] deep[19] study of this fact will certainly prove that there is an unknown attraction between two people having a blood-relationship[20]. Lately, I had an experience of the same thing, a friend was telling me in Stockholm. This friend[21] was visiting London where he thought that[22] he had no relations, and[23] if there were any relations, they were perhaps of[24] a century ago. And while walking in a part of London, he met someone who called him by his name. When he turned back, this person excused[25], saying, "I am sorry, I have [made a][26] mistake." But this man asked, "How did you know my name; the same name[27] is mine?" And when they spoke together, they found that they were cousins. But cousins only if they studied genealogy. We do not give attention to this subject, but the more we give attention to this subject[28], the more proof we can find of this element which is drawn to its similar element. And Sa'di[29], the great poet of Persia, he[30] says that[31], "Element attracts element as eagle is attracted to eagle, and a dove attracts to a dove[32]." But do we not find the same thing in life every day? A gambler, when he goes to another country, by the help of providence—one does not[33] know how—[34] attracts another gambler very soon. A person who does not know what a[35] thief means, he[36] perhaps[37] does not know of [him][38], but a person who is a thief, it[39]

---

18. A.o.d.: "a" instead of "the"
19. Sk.tp.: "deep" corr. in hw. to read "deeper"
20. A.o.d.: "between them" added
21. A.o.d.: "An incident that occurred lately was an experience of it. A person from Stockholm" instead of "Lately, I had an experience ... in Stockholm. This friend"
22. A.o.d.: "that" omitted
23. A.o.d.: "or that" instead of "and"
24. A.o.d.: "of" omitted
25. A.o.d.: "himself" added
26. A.o.d.: "made a" added
27. A.o.d.: "name you said" instead of "same name"
28. A.o.d.: "it" instead of "this subject"
29. For Sa'di, see List
30. A.o.d.: "he" omitted
31. A.o.d.: "that" omitted
32. Gd.tp.: "an eagle is attracted to an eagle, and as a dove is attracted to a dove"; Km.tp., Sk.tp.: "a dove is attracted to a dove and an eagle is attracted to an eagle" instead of "eagle is attracted ... to a dove"
33. Sk.sh.: "does not" retraced for clarity
34. Sk.sh.: "for that he" written, a.o.d.: omitted
35. A.o.d.: "the term" instead of "a"
36. A.o.d.: "he" omitted
37. Sk.sh.: "will" written, then crossed out
38. Sk.sh.: "a" retraced to read "him"; a.o.d.: "a thief" instead of "him"
39. A.o.d.: "it" omitted, but added in hw. in Sk.tp.

will not take him[40] any time to find another thief in a country where he arrives. It is not only that when two persons of the similar element see one another that[41] they are attracted to one another, but even conditions, the[42] life itself brings about their meeting, which[43] life itself draws them together. And therefore, it is natural that a person who is very sad naturally[44] attracts a miserable one to join him together[45]. The one with joy, the one[46] with happiness, naturally attracts happiness. And in this way the[47] magnetism[48] is working throughout the whole creation, and in all aspects you will see the phenomena of magnetism, in the physical world as well as in the mental spheres.

No doubt that[49] one cannot always say that it is the[50] element which attracts [51]element, but also the element attracts what [it is][52] lacking, what is opposite to it. And when we think of friendship, that to[53] some we feel inclined to be friends, and with[54] others we feel inclined to keep away[55]. And the most interesting part is that those whom we feel uninclined to be friend[56] with, they have also some who are drawn towards them in friendship. And[57] this takes us to find the truth which lies in musical harmony, how two notes have a relation with one another, and the[58] combination brings about a harmony.

And[59] now coming to the question of the practical use of magnetism. Whether you are in business or in[60] industry, whether

---

40. A.o.d.: "him" omitted, but added in hw. in Sk.tp.
41. A.o.d.: "that" omitted
42. A.o.d.: "the" omitted
43. A.o.d.: "which" omitted
44. A.o.d.: "naturally" omitted, but added by hand in Sk.tp.
45. A.o.d.: "together with him" instead of "him together"
46. A.o.d.: "the one" omitted
47. A.o.d.: "the" omitted
48. Sk.sh.: "m." abbr. for "magnetism"
49. A.o.d.: "that" omitted
50. A.o.d.: "an" instead of "the"
51. A.o.d.: "the same" added
52. Sk.sh.: "it" retraced to read "is"; a.o.d.: "it is"
53. A.o.d.: "we see that with" instead of "that to"
54. A.o.d.: "with" omitted
55. A.o.d.: "from" added
56. A.o.d.: "disinclined to be friends" instead of "uninclined to be friend"
57. A.o.d.: "And" omitted
58. A.o.d.: "their" instead of "the"
59. A.o.d.: "And" omitted
60. Sk.sh.: "if" written, then crossed out

you are in a[61] domestic work or in[62] political work of the state, in whatever condition you will always find that magnetism is the secret of your progress in life. And you will find at the same time that the[63] qualification to which we give such a great importance, we shall[64] find [65]numberless people most qualified[66] do not[67] make a way through life because of the lack of magnetism. Very often a person most qualified[68], but before he speaks to[69] his qualification, the person to whom he has gone has[70] enough of him. And[71] personality takes such an important place in life that even the absence of qualification is tolerated when [72]personality[73] has magnetism, especially in these times, when materialism is on such an increase that personality is given much less importance in the[74] society. And at such times[75] when heroism has no place in life, automatically magnetism works and proves to be the most essential thing even now, and it will always prove it[76]. Only when[77] comes the question of magnetism, a person does not [come][78] different[79] into the subject, and he only recognizes a personal magnetism by the attraction that he feels.

But when we think of the personal magnetism, we divide[80] into four different classes. [The][81] one kind of[82] the ordinary kind of magnetism is what is concerned with the physical plane. And this magnetism has to do with nourishment, with hygiene, with regular living, and with right breathing. Also this magnetism depends upon the regularity of action and repose. Besides, this magnetism works

---

61. A.o.d.: "a" omitted
62. A.o.d.: "the" added
63. A.o.d.: "as to" instead of "you will find at the same time that the"
64. A.o.d.: "you will" instead of "we shall"
65. A.o.d.: "that" added
66. A.o.d.: "most qualified" moved before "numberless people"
67. Sk.sh.: "after" written, then crossed out
68. A.o.d.: "there may be a most qualified man" instead of "a person most qualified"
69. A.o.d.: "of" instead of "to"
70. A.o.d.: "had" added, but in Sk.tp. crossed out
71. A.o.d.: "And" omitted, but added by hand in Sk.tp.
72. A.o.d.: "the" added
73. Sk.sh.: "who" written, then retraced to read "has", then crossed out
74. A.o.d.: "the" omitted
75. A.o.d.: "a time" instead of "times"
76. Sk.tp.: "it" corrected in hw. to read "to be so"
77. A.o.d.: "there" added
78. Sk.sh.: "know" retraced to read "come"; a.o.d.: "go"
79. A.o.d.: "deeper" instead of "different"
80. Sk.tp.: "it" added in hw.
81. Sk.sh.: "There" appears to be written; a.o.d.: "The"
82. A.o.d.: a comma instead of "of"

with the age as the ascending [and][83] descending of [notes][84] in an octave. This magnetism may be likened to[85] the season of the[86] spring which comes and which goes. And at the same time this magnetism is dependent upon all things of this physical world, since this is a physical magnetism.

And[87] now we come to the magnetism which is called mental. Naturally, a person with a sparkling intelligence becomes the centre of[88] his society. The man who perceives well, the man[89] who conceives well, it is that man who is liked by everyone. For[90] the person who has a[91] wit, a person[92] who can express freely, the person[93] who can understand quickly, that is the person who always attracts others around him. The person who has knowledge of human nature, the person[94] who knows of things and conditions, it is that person who[95] naturally draws persons[96] towards him. And in reality this is the[97] qualification, if there is any qualification[98]. And without this qualification, no other qualification can be of very great use. But this sparkling condition of intelligence is born with a person. It is this person who becomes a genius, and it is this person who accomplishes something, if ever he[99] accomplishes. And it is this person who helps others to accomplish something, for on his mind others depend. It is this person who can guide himself and direct others. And with all our thought of equality in which we are so much absorbed, we shall find that it is this person who will win the battle in life. [100]And it is this person who stands above the masses, and it is this person who leads, and without this person[101] many are lost.

---

83. Sk.sh.: "in" attempted to retrace, but remains "in" visibly; a.o.d.: "and"
84. Sk.sh.: "note" appears to be written; a.o.d.: "notes"
85. Sk.sh.: "a spring" written, with "spr." in lh. added, then crossed out
86. Gd.tp.: "seasons of the spring" altered to read "season of spring"; Km.tp., Sk.tp.: "the" omitted
87. A.o.d.: "And" omitted
88. Sk.sh.: an illegible retracement added
89. A.o.d.: "the man" omitted
90. A.o.d.: "For" omitted
91. A.o.d.: "a" omitted
92. A.o.d.: "a person" omitted
93. A.o.d.: "the person" omitted
94. A.o.d.: "the person" omitted
95. A.o.d.: "it is that person who" omitted, but added by hand in Sk.tp.
96. A.o.d.: "people" instead of "persons"
97. A.o.d.: "the" omitted
98. Sk.sh.: "Q." abbr. for "qualification"
99. A.o.d.: "anyone" instead of "he"
100. Sk.sh.: "It" written, but omitted in a.o.d.
101. A.o.d.: "him" instead of "this person"

And[102] now, coming to a[103] question: How can this magnetism be developed? This magnetism is developed by study, by concentration,[104] by a keen observation of life, and by the knowledge of repose. And[105] very many intelligent persons, without knowing how to concentrate and how to take repose in their lives, in time they blunt[106] their intelligence, because there is a certain[107] fund of energy which is reserved and which is limited, and when there is too much pressure put upon that limited energy, in the end what happens? A person becomes less and less intelligent, and his power of mind becomes [littler][108] every day. And whenever you will find a most intelligent man being[109] every day more dull, that always proves that the amount of energy that has been there has been spent. And[110] it is therefore, when one knows how to reserve one's energies by repose, and when one knows how to concentrate and sharpen[111] one's[112] intellect, then[113] that[114] magnetism remains in a right condition. What generally happens [is][115] that it is the intelligent person on whom a great responsibility falls. Much more is asked of him than of the[116] others who lack intelligence. If he does not give a rest to his mind by knowing the manner of repose, and if he does not concentrate and by it sharpens[117] his intellect, naturally, just like a knife which is always used, it will become blunted; naturally, the continual use of intellect will make him short of funds[118].

And[119] now coming to the third aspect of magnetism. Perhaps this aspect of magnetism may be called [higher][120] a high[121] kind

---

102. A.o.d.: "And" omitted
103. Sk.tp.: "the" instead of "a"
104. Sk.sh.: "by observation of life" written, then crossed out
105. A.o.d.: "And" omitted
106. Sk.sh.: "blunt" written in lh.
107. Sk.sh.: "amount" written, then crossed out
108. Sk.sh.: "less" crossed out, then "littler" substituted; a.o.d.: "littler"
109. A.o.d.: "becoming" instead of "being"
110. A.o.d.: "And" omitted
111. Sk.sh.: "sharpen" indistinctly written
112. Sk.sh.: "intelligence" written, then crossed out
113. A.o.d.: "then" omitted
114. A.o.d.: "this" added
115. Sk.sh.: "the" retraced to read "is"; a.o.d. "is"
116. A.o.d.: "the" omitted
117. Sk.tp., Gd.tp.: "sharpen" instead of "sharpens"
118. A.o.d.: "words" instead of "funds", but Sk.tp. later crossed out "words" and wrote "funds" instead
119. A.o.d.: "And" omitted
120. Sk.sh.: "of" written, but omitted in a.o.d.
121. Sk.sh..: "high" written, but "higher" in a.o.d.

than the two which I have[122] explained to you[123] before. For this magnetism is more profound, and it touches another person deeper[124]. And this magnetism is[125] of love, of sympathy, of friendliness: a person who by nature is [sympathetic][126], a person who tolerates, who forgets, who forgives, a person who does not keep bitterness in his mind, [127]malice [128]in his mind against anyone; a person who admires beauty, who appreciates beauty, who loves it, who loves it in art, in nature, in all its forms and who goes out to his friend and foe, to the acquaintance, to the stranger, to all. The person who can endure and who can suffer and who has the power to have patience through all conditions of life, who feels the pain of another in his heart and who is always willing to become a friend, it is that person whose magnetism is greater than all different magnetisms that we know of. We do not need to go far to see this. Only if we were to[129] look for good things in persons, we shall find this. For[130] among our surroundings we can find many people in whom we can appreciate that quality.

One day a man who had travelled very much saw me[131] and[132] said, "We heard so much and we have read so much about the saints and sages and mahatmas [and][133] masters that lived[134] in India[135], but after having gone there, I found no one." And I[136] told him, "You need not have gone so far. The souls who are worthwhile, the souls who love one another, they[137] are to be found[138] everywhere. [139]What do we seek saints and sages for? It is for that

---

122. A.o.d.: "have been" instead of "I have"
123. A.o.d.: "to you" omitted
124. A.o.d.: "more deeply" instead of "deeper"
125. A.o.d.: "This is the magnetism" instead of "And this magnetism is"
126. Sk.sh.: "sympatic" clearly written; in French "sympathique"; a.o.d.: "sympathetic"
127. A.o.d.: "nor" added
128. Sk.sh.: "against" written, then crossed out
129. A.o.d.: "If only we" instead of "Only if we were to"
130. A.o.d.: "For" omitted
131. A.o.d.: "an Indian mystic" instead of "me", Sk.tp. restores "me" but then goes back to "an Indian mystic"
132. A.o.d.: "he" added
133. Sk.sh.: "over" appears to be written; a.o.d.: "and" instead of "over"
134. Sk.tp.: "d" crossed out to read "live"
135. Sk.sh.: "Indi." abbr. for "India"
136. A.o.d.: "the mystic" instead of "I", Sk.tp. restores "I" but then goes back to "the mystic"
137. Km.tp.: ", they" omitted
138. Sk.sh.: "everyone" written, then crossed out
139. Sk.sh.: "Why" written, then crossed out

that we seek[140]; they are to be found everywhere." I[141] said, "I am here, away from home, all for that[142] time. Do I not find them? I find them everywhere." If we can appreciate, we can find them. But if we cannot appreciate[143], if an angel came we cannot[144] find these qualities in him. Nevertheless, call it[145] a saint or a sage, [call][146] it[147] a prophet, or a mahatma; if there is anything that draws man towards man, it is their[148] love element that he pours out.

And[149] now the question is how can one develop this quality? And my[150] answer will be by one thing: by studying, by knowing, by practising and by living the life of a friend. By contemplating this thought from morning till evening that[151], "To[152] everyone I meet, [153]those who love me and those who hate me, do I practise in my life that thought of friendliness, that outgoing, that pouring out of sympathy and [love][154]? If I do it, that is quite enough." And besides this, apart from[155] magnetism that one gets from it, when we consider life as it is, with all its limitations, with all the pain and troubles and responsibilities as[156] it gives us, if there seems to be anything worthwhile, it is only one[157]. And that [is the][158] thought and impression that we have done our best to be gentle, to be tender to those whom we meet in our everyday life. If there is any prayer, if there is any worship, if there is any religion, it is this. For no one is[159] there to please. If there is anyone to be pleased and whose pleasure it is worthwhile to earn[160], it is here, it

---

140. Sk.sh.: "for that that we seek" is ed. underlined; a.o.d.: "It is for that that we seek" omitted
141. A.o.d.: "This Indian mystic" instead of "I"
142. A.o.d.: "this" instead of "for that"
143. Sk.sh.: "we can not even" written, then crossed out, including an illegible sh. symbol after "even"
144. A.o.d.: "could not" instead of "cannot"
145. A.o.d.: "him" instead of "it"
146. Sk.sh.: "or" retraced to read "call"; a.o.d.: "call"
147. A.o.d.: "him"
148. A.o.d.: "the" instead of "their"
149. A.o.d.: "And" omitted
150. A.o.d.: "the" instead of "my"
151. A.o.d.: "that" omitted
152. A.o.d.: "Toward" instead of "To"
153. A.o.d.: "toward" added
154. Sk.sh.: "all-love" written, then the "all" section of "all-love" crossed out
155. A.o.d.: "the" added
156. A.o.d.: "that" instead of "as"
157. A.o.d.: "thing" added
158. Sk.sh.: "a" appears to be written, but "is the" in a.o.d.
159. A.o.d.: "there is no one" instead of "no one is"
160. Sk.sh.: "earn" indistinctly written

is man; and it is in the pleasure of man that[161] if one understands[162], that there is the pleasure of God.

And now we come to the fourth aspect of magnetism. And this aspect is magnetism itself. The lack of magnetism is when[163] this aspect is hidden. And that magnetism is the soul of man. And if I were[164] to define what[165] soul is, I would say[166] soul is the self of man. But if you asked[167] which self, I will say[168] that self of which he does not know. As there is a humorous story of India[169] that some peasants were travelling, but it was the first time in their life that they went to travel. And being worried about one another, they thought that next morning they must count if all the[170] peasants were there. And[171] they were very disappointed after having counted; [172]they counted nineteen[173]. And it was understood that twenty[174] peasants had left home. And so each peasant counted, and each said that it is[175] nineteen; and[176] they could not find who was missing, for everyone was there. At[177] the end they found that the one who counts[178] forgot to count himself. That is the condition of the soul. It sees all selves, but it does not see itself. And the day when the soul realizes itself, that day begins a new life, a new birth. And[179] it is the self-realized soul which grows, which expands. So long as the soul has not realized itself, it does not develop, it does not grow. Therefore, [180]the moment[181] the soul begins to realize itself, it is[182] at that moment[183] that man really begins to live in the world. But it

---

161. A.o.d.: "that" omitted
162. A.o.d.: "it" added
163. A.o.d.: "means that" instead of "is when"
164. A.o.d.: "And if I were" omitted
165. A.o.d.: "the" added
166. A.o.d.: "it may be said, the" instead of "I would say"
167. A.o.d.: "if you asked" omitted
168. A.o.d.: "I wil say" omitted
169. A.o.d.: "Indian story" instead of "story of India"
170. Sk.sh.: an ed. marker is placed after "the"
171. A.o.d.: "And" omitted
172. A.o.d.: "for" added
173. Sk.sh.: the number "1" of "19" is ed. doubly underscored
174. Sk.sh.: "20" is doubly underscored
175. A.o.d.: "there are" instead of "that it is"
176. Sk.sh.: "that" written, then crossed out
177. A.o.d.: "In" instead of "At"
178. A.o.d.: "counted" instead of "counts"
179. A.o.d.: "And" omitted
180. A.o.d.: "it is at" added
181. A.o.d.: "when" added
182. Sk.sh.: "there" written, then crossed out
183. A.o.d.: "it is at that moment" omitted

must be understood that the magnetism of the self-realized soul is greater than any magnetism one could ever imagine. It is power, it is [wisdom][184], it is peace, it is intelligence, it is all. It is this magnetism that heals, heals bodies and heals minds. And it is this magnetism [that][185] raises those fallen into difficulties, in pains and sorrows. It is this magnetism that takes out those in confusion, in darkness. It is by this magnetism that the illuminated souls spread out their love, attracting thereby all beings. It is for[186] this magnetism that Christ said to the fishermen, "Come hither, for[187] I will make you fishers of man."[188] It is with [this][189] magnetism that the great ones, such as Buddha, [such][190] as Moses, Muhammad, Christ came and who [attracted][191] humanity, and humanity for ages has not forgotten. It is [that][192] magnetism that after[193] having them[194] gone to the other side, have held million[195] and millions of people in one bond of brotherhood, of [sympathy, of][196] friendship. The immense power that the soul magnetism gives represents a divine magnetism. It is a proof of something behind the seen world.[197]

---

184. Sk.sh.: an indecipherable sh. symbol retraced to read "wisdom"; "wisdom" in a.o.d.
185. A.o.d.: "that" added
186. A.o.d.: "of" instead of "for"
187. A.o.d.: "for" omitted
188. See Mark 1:17, and other gospels
189. Sk.sh.: "which" retraced to read "this"; a.o.d.: "this"
190. Sk.sh.: "so" inserted after "Buddha"; a.o.d. have "such"
191. Sk.sh.: the "-ed" for the past tense is absent; a.o.d.: "attracted"
192. Sk.sh.: "this" retraced to read "that"; a.o.d.: "that"
193. A.o.d.: "their" added
194. A.o.d.: "them" omitted
195. A.o.d.: "has held millions" instead of "have held million"
196. Sk.sh.: a pause; a.o.d.: "sympathy, of"
197. Sk.tp.: "God bless you." added, but crossed out in Gd.tp.

Sakina Furnée's shorthand reporting

Baronne d'Eichthal, March 28th, 1925

The Certitude of the Life in the Hereafter[1]

[2]I would like to speak a few words on the questions of the certitude[3] of the life in the hereafter. This is a question which occupies every mind. Sooner or later[4] in life a person begins to think if there is such a thing as a continuity of life. There are many who by their pessimistic idea think that there seems to be nothing afterward. And there are others who, owing to their optimistic idea, they think[5] whether there is something or whether there is not something, it is just as well to think that there is something. Nevertheless, this thought is most painful when a person thinks that there will be nothing after death. And how many reasons he has[6] at the support in his belief, that belief itself is worse[7] than death. There are some who [through][8] different phenomena[9] wish to get the proof of the life in the hereafter. But they meet with ninety-nine disappointments and perhaps one reality. And when we come to the idea of the Sufi, his idea is that life lives[10], death dies. In other words, to life there is no death, and to death there is no life. But his way of attaining to the certitude of life is not only an intellectual one. Because a person may study all the philosophies, all the metaphysics all through his life which may in every way prove by reasons that there is the continuity of life. Still this realization gained by the effort of mind will not give that feeling of certitude which one wishes to have. The Sufi, therefore, practises that process through which he is able to touch

---

Documents:
Sk.sh. = Sakina Furnée's shorthand reporting of the lecture, newly transcribed by B.v.d.B.
Sk.tp. = a typescript prepared by Sakina Furnée.

Notes:
1. The title is from Sk.tp.
2. Sk.tp.: "Beloved ones of God," added
3. Sk.sh.: "certitude" written in lh., then "of the life in the hereafter" inserted in lh.
4. Sk.sh.: "for" written, but omitted in Sk.tp.
5. Sk.sh.: "yet" written, then crossed out
6. Sk.tp.: "may have" instead of "has"
7. Sk.sh.: actually "worser" written, then the "er" ending crossed out
8. Sk.sh.: "of" retraced to read "through"; Sk.tp.: "through"
9. Sk.sh.: the plural "s" is clearly written here, It seems Inayat Khan used "phenomenas" for plural instead of "phenomena" Sk.tp.: "phenomena"
10. Sk.sh.: "a-lives" written, then the "a-" crossed out

that part of life in himself which is not subject to death. And by finding that part of life, he naturally gets the feeling [of][11] certitude of life. It makes him more certain of life than of anything in the world because he sees in all things changeability and limitation. For everything that is constructed, [all][12] is subject to being destroyed. Everything that is composed is subject to be decomposed. Every[thing][13] born[14] is subject to death. But he finds in finding that life, that that was his self, and that was the real life, and all else that he knows about life, that begins to lose its importance.

And now you will say, in what way does he discover that life in him which was never born and will never [die][15]? By self-analysis, but according to what mystics know of self-analysis. To understand what this vehicle, what we call[16] body is to us, what relation we have to it, and by understanding what this mind which we call mind consists of. And then by knowing that am I then, am I this body, am I this mind, there comes a time when he begins to see that he himself is the knower of the body and of the mind. But to this realization he only arrives when the body and mind he can hold in his hands, [as][17] his objects which he uses for his purpose in life. Once he has done this, then the body and mind, these two things become as the two corks[18] which the person puts on himself in order to swim in the water, and there is no danger of drowning. The same body and mind which cause man mortality, at least in his thought, the very body and mind then become the means of his safety of being drowned in the water of mortality.

In reality, mortality is our conception; immortality is reality. We make a conception of mortality because we do not know the real life. By the realization of the real life, the comparison between real life and mortality makes one know that mortality is non-existent. Therefore, it would not be an exaggeration if I said that the work of a Sufi is an unlearning. What he is accustomed to call or recognize as life, he then begins to recognize as death. And what he is

11. Sk.sh.: "over" appears to be written; Sk.tp.: "of"
12. Sk.sh.: "for" retraced to read "all"; Sk.tp.: omitted
13. Sk.sh.: "Every" clearly written, "--thing" is missing; Sk.tp.: "Everything"
14. Sk.sh.: "for" written, but omitted in Sk.tp.
15. Sk.sh.: "tie" retraced to read "die"; Sk.tp.: "die"
16. Sk.tp.: "the" added
17. Sk.sh.: "in" appears to be written; Sk.tp.: "as"
18. Sk.sh.: "cords" added in lh., then "?ballon" added in lh.; Sk.tp.: "cords"

accustomed to [call][19] as[20] death he then begins to recognize [as][21] life. And, therefore, life and death both are not for him conditions to which he is subject, but are conditions which he brings about upon himself. A great Persian Sufi, Bedil[22], he says, "By myself I become captive, and by myself I become free." If I were to interpret it in a simple language, I would say that, "By myself I die, and by myself I live." But why does a Sufi say this? Why does everyone not say it? Because for a Sufi, it is a condition which he brings about. For another person, it is a condition in which he is helpless.

And now you will ask me, in what way this realization is to be brought[23] about? The first thing is that one must learn in every little thing in life the way of unlearning. For the difficulty in one's[24] own work I find greatly when a person comes to me and says, "Now, so far I have learned, will you add to my knowledge more?" And in my heart I say, "The more you have learned, the worse it is for me; and if I would like to add to it, it would not be adding, it would be taking away from it in order that I may[25] unburden you from all you have learned, that you may be able to unlearn first and that through this unlearning what will come will be the true learning." But one might say, "Then is it all useless for us to learn what we learn in life?" And the answer is, "No, it is all useful, but for what? [26] For that object for which one has learned; for it is not all learned for that object [which][27] you are searching after." When you wish to search after the secret of life, the learning which one calls learning, that is the first thing to unlearn. No doubt, it is something which is a difficult thing for everyone to understand. And yet when we read the life of Rumi, a great teacher, and his teacher, Shams Tabriz[28], the first lesson he gives to Rumi[29] was that, "Unlearn all that you have learned." And now you may ask me, "Is this unlearning all[30] forgetting all that one learns?" Not at all. It is not necessary. This unlearning is to be able to say with reason, with logic, the contrary

---

19. Sk.sh.: "recognize" written, then crossed out; "call" substituted; Sk.tp.: "call"
20. Sk.tp.: "as" omitted
21. Sk.tp.: "as" added
22. For Bedil, see List
23. Sk.sh.: "for" written, but omitted in Sk.tp.
24. Sk.tp.: "my" instead of "one's"
25. Sk.sh.: "after" written, then crossed out
26. Sk.sh.: an illegible sh. symbol
27. Sk.sh.: "for" retraced to read "which"; Sk.tp.: "which"
28. For Rumi and Shams Tabriz, see List
29. Sk.sh.: "R." abbr. for "Rumi"
30. Sk.tp.: "all" omitted

to what one knows. When you are accustomed to say, "This is wrong, this is right; this is good and this is bad; this is great and this is small; and this is higher and this is lower; this is spiritual and this is material; this is up and[31] down; and this is before and this is behind[32]." If you can use the opposite words for each with reason and with logic, naturally you have unlearned them[33], what you have once learned. It is after this that the realization of truth begins. Because[34] then the mind is not fixed. And it is then that one has become alive, for his soul has become born. It is then that one will become tolerant, and it is then that one will forgive, for he will understand his friend and foe both. He never then has one point of view[35]; he has all points of view. You might say, "Is it not dangerous to have all points of view, then I have not my point of view?" It is not necessary[36]. You may have one room in the house or you may have ten rooms in the house. You may use each as you like. As many points of view[37] as one can see, so large is his point of view.

But all this is attained by meditative process: by tuning oneself, by bringing oneself to a proper rhythm, by concentration, contemplation, and by meditation, and by realization, by dying and living both at the same time. In order to rise above death, one must die first. In order to get above mortality, one must know what it is. But this is certain, that if there is the greatest and most important thing that one wishes to accomplish in life, it is one, and that one thing[38] is to rise above the conception of death.

- - - - - - - - - - - - - - - - - - - -

Q.: How can you rise above the conception of death?
A.: As I have already said, that the most necessary thing is to play death and to know what death is. And it is a great learning how to play death. For what we do is a very false thing, and that is we play life when we are subject to death. If we played death, it would be a real thing; it would not be a hypocrisy. And it is out of that that we

---

31. Sk.tp.: "this is" added
32. Sk.tp.: "beneath" instead of "behind"
33. Sk.sh.: "them" indistinctly written, omitted in Sk.tp.
34. Sk.sh.: "Because" indistinctly written
35. Sk.sh.: "p.o.v." abbr. for "point of view"
36. Sk.sh.: "over" written, then crossed out
37. Sk.sh.: "so" written, but omitted in Sk.tp.
38. Sk.sh.: "for" clearly written, but omitted in Sk.tp.

shall discover life. [39]We experience death by playing in[40] life, and we experience life by playing death. [41]What we call death is a death of this body. But if we attach ourselves to this body as ourselves, then it is death. [42]A simple man asked a person, "How can I know that I am dead?" "Well," the man said, "it is very easy. When your coat has [become][43] rotten and torn and worn out, then it is a death[44]." Of course, when the coat was worn out and torn, then this man was thinking that he was dead, and he was weeping bitterly. And some [thoughtful][45] person came and told him, "It is your coat that is torn. But[46] how can you cry, you are still alive." It is actually[47] the condition of the mystical idea. For the mystic, the body is a garment. But it is no use realizing it intellectually. Because if one says intellectually, "Body is my garment, but then what [am][48] I, and where am I?" And as I have said, by the meditative process one finds where one is, [and][49] what one is. And, therefore, this does not remain as a belief; it becomes a faith; even greater than faith, it becomes conviction.

Q.: In what way can we play death? How can we do it?
A.: There was a king who thought that he would give up his kingdom and he would become a mureed. That is to say[50] to become a disciple of a teacher, and that[51] to give up all the worldly things and just go in the spiritual thought. And when he went to Bukhara, under the guidance of a teacher, the teacher gave him the probationer's work. And that work was to sweep and clean the whole house where all the pupils lived[52], and everyone[53], and to take the garbage, and to take it out of the village. Of course, the pupils

39. Sk.tp.: "For" added
40. Sk.tp.: "in" omitted
41. Sk.sh.: a single bracket is placed before "What"
42. Sk.sh.: "It is like saying, but if disease is too strong then if a person told a simple man" written, but omitted in Sk.tp.; it seems to represent a sentence started but not completed by Inayat Khan
43. Sk.sh.: an indistinctly written sh. symbol, possibly "went" or "between"; Sk.tp.: "become"
44. Sk.sh.: "for" written, but omitted in Sk.tp.
45. Sk.sh.: "thoughtfully" retraced to read "thoughtful"; Sk.tp.: "thoughtful"
46. Sk.sh.: "it is" written, then crossed out and omitted in Sk.tp.
47. Sk.tp.: "exactly" instead of "actually"
48. Sk.sh.: "manner" seems to be written, but "am" in Sk.tp.
49. Sk.sh.: "on" appears to be written; Sk.tp. "and"
50. Sk.sh.: "for" written, but omitted in Sk.tp.
51. Sk.tp.: "that" omitted
52. Sk.sh.: "a-lived" clearly written; Sk.tp.: "lived"
53. Sk.sh.: "over" written, then crossed out and omitted in Sk.tp.

were very much in sympathy with this man, and they were very shocked that this man, who used to sit on the throne and be a king, this is [once][54] a thing which he was never accustomed to do; it must be a terrible thing for him! No doubt, [55]teacher, knowing the object that he had before him, he could not do otherwise, [56]said, "He must do it, for he is not yet ready." Once all the[57] disciples went, and they said, "Teacher, we are all in sympathy with this man, and we think he is so fine and so nice and so cultured, and we would so much like if you would relieve him[58] of this duty." And then they said to the teacher, "It is a long time, now he must be relieved of it." The teacher said, "We shall have a test." He,[59] [one][60] day when he was taking his garbage pail outside of the town, somebody knocked against him and all was spilled on the ground. He looked back and said, "Well, it is not the days of the past, what can I tell you?" And when the report was brought to the teacher, he said, "Did I not say that the time has not yet come?" And next time a test was made again, after a little time. And when the same thing was done, this man looked at him and said nothing. The teacher said, "Did I not say that the time has not yet arrived?" And[61] third time when he was tested, he did not even look at the man who spilled his basket; he took all that was there[62] in the basket and carried[63] along. The teacher said, "Now is the time, now he can play death." All the teachings that Christ has taught, that if[64] one will[65] [66]strike you [on][67] one side of the face, give the other side; if one will ask you to go one mile, go still further; if one asks you for your overcoat, give your cape also[68] — when we think of it all, what is it? Is it not the teaching to play death? Therefore, at any time if the teachers of truth have prescribed to their pupils any process of behaviour with their fellowmen, that process can be called nothing else but playing death.

---

54. Sk.sh.: "which" retraced to read "once"; Sk.tp.: omitted
55. Sk.tp.: "the" added
56. Sk.tp.: "he" added
57. Sk.sh.: "all" written again, but omitted in Sk.tp.
58. Sk.sh.: "him" indistinctly written
59. Sk.tp.: "He," omitted
60. Sk.sh.: "one" inserted
61. Sk.tp.: "the" added
62. Sk.sh.: "on" written, then crossed out
63. Sk.tp.: "it" added
64. Sk.sh.: "you will" written, then crossed out
65. Sk.sh.: "will" indistinctly written
66. Sk.sh.: "give" written, then crossed out
67. Sk.sh.: actually "not" written; Sk.tp.: "on"
68. See Matthew 5:39-41

But one might think that it is very hard; it is very cruel on the part of the teacher. But the instructor had to go through the same cruelty once at a certain period of his life. But sometime[69] the greatest cruelty is the greatest kindness. It is hard, but[70] [71]the hardest path can be conquered by this. And if I were to speak about it in simple words, it is this way: How many times we take to heart unnecessary things? How many times we cause or we take interest in inharmony[72] which could just as well have been avoided? How often we resist evil, which could have been[73] just as well not resisted? This is all playing life. And what I have said before is playing death. When we play death, we arrive at life[74]. When we play life, we arrive at death.

[Q.:][75] Is it not [sometimes][76] [77]others[78] to become insensible at the pain of others to just look at them and not share with them?
[A.:] What[79] I have said, playing with death is rising above sensible and unsensible[80], because sensible and unsensible[81] has a certain stage. One can rise above that [stage][82], then all is sensible. Besides[83] you can always find among those who play death or who have played death, they have been the most sympathetic and the most open to the pain of others. Because when they are playing [death][84] [automatically][85] they are playing life too. And, therefore, although they are as death from all the wrong things[86] come to me[87], but they

69. Sk.tp.: "sometimes"
70. Sk.sh.: "it is" written, then crossed out and omitted in Sk.tp.
71. Sk.sh.: "for" written but omitted in Sk.tp.
72. Sk.sh.: "inharmony" added in lh.
73. Sk.tp.: "been" omitted
74. Sk.sh.: "for" written, but omitted in Sk.tp.
75. Sk.sh.: the "Q.:" for "question" is missing, so also is the "A.:" for "answer"; both are in Sk.tp.
76. Sk.sh.: "sometimes" is retraced through a now illegible sh. symbol
77. Sk.sh.: "to look at" written, then crossed out
78. Sk.tp.: "others" omitted
79. Sk.tp.: "But" instead of "What"
80. Sk.tp.: "insensible" instead of "unsensible"
81. Sk.sh.: "S." (in lh.) abbr. for "sensible"; "uns." (in lh.) abbr. for "unsensible"; Sk.tp.: "insensible"
82. Sk.sh.: an indecipherable sh. symbol; Sk.tp.: "stage"
83. Sk.sh.: "you have always" written, then crossed out
84. Sk.sh.: "by" appears to be written; Sk.tp.: "death" instead of "by"
85. Sk.sh.: "the automatical" written; Sk.tp.: "automatically" instead of "the automatical"
86. Sk.tp.: "that" added
87. Sk.tp.: "them" instead of "me"

are alive to everything that can happen from them to the others. [88] [89]

Q.: May I ask in what consists that state, where at certain days and at certain hours, one no longer feels one's body and all the thought is alive and awake?
A.: It is a condition. As I say, any condition that automatically comes is not a normal thing, even if it be a high condition. But if it automatically comes, it is not normal. The normal thing is to be able to experience any condition one wishes to. To be able to experience death, to be able to experience life, that is the right thing. The one who already[90] experiences death and does not experience life, that is abnormal too.

Q.: [91]How[92] to have a balance?
A.: To have[93] balance one must do everything from morning to evening that is balanced.

88,. Sk.sh.: "p.t.o." abbr. for "please turn over" has been added and refers to two qa.s inserted in the next page
89. Sk.sh.: "end Q. + A. after lecture The Certitude of the Life in the Hereafter" is noted above this qa. section
90. Sk.tp.: "always" instead of "already"
91. Sk.sh.: "For" written, but omitted in Sk.tp.
92. Sk.sh.: "who are" sh. symbols overlap each other, thereby forming an approximation of "How"; Sk.tp.: "How"
93. Sk.tp.: "a" added

Headquarters' typescript

May 23rd, 1925[1]

[2]

The Fourth[3] Aspect of the Nature which leads to the Path of Wisdom

When the lips are closed, then the heart begins to speak; when the heart is silent, then the soul blazes up, raising its flame, which illuminates the whole life. It is this idea which shows to the mystic the great importance of silence, which is gained by repose. It is so little known to the generality what repose means because every person who experiences repose feels that he needs it after being tired, but if one were not tired he would never see the necessity of repose. Repose has many aspects. There is one repose, when a person retires from the action of everyday life and finds himself alone in his room. He breathes a breath of thankfulness, which means, after all interesting or uninteresting experiences, "I am just alone by myself." It is not an ordinary feeling; there is a far deeper feeling behind it. The meaning is the certainty there is nothing to attract his mind and nothing which demands his action. At that moment his soul has a glimpse of relief, the pleasure of which is inexpressible. But the intoxication of life from which every man suffers is such that he cannot very well appreciate that moment of relief which every person expects in the time of retirement after the actions of his daily life, rich or poor, tired or not.

Does this not teach us that there is a great mystery in repose, a mystery which a person very often is ignorant of? Besides this, we always find a thoughtful person reposeful by nature and a reposeful one thoughtful by nature. It is repose which makes one more thoughtful, and it is a continual action which takes away even that thoughtfulness from a sensible person. People working in the telephone or telegraph or post office, upon whose mind there is a continual demand, in time develop impertinence, insolence, lack of

---

Documents:
Hq.tp. = a typescript prepared at Headquarters with a handwritten correction by Sakina Furnée.
Hq.st. = a stencil prepared at headquarters, nearly identical to Hq.st..
Notes:
1. Hq.st., Hq.tp.: "Number 12." instead of the date
2. Hq.st., Hq.tp.: "GATHEKA." followed by the Sufi Invocation written above the text Then follows "SUFI MYSTICISM IV."
3. Hq.st.: "Fifth" instead of "Fourth"

patience. They do not become less sensible; it only means that lack of repose, which weakens their sense of control, makes them give in to such things. This shows that repose is not only necessary for a person who walks through the spiritual path, but for every soul living on the earth, whatever be his grade of evolution, whatever be his standard in life. This is the one thing which must be developed in nature. And not only in grown-up people, this is something which should be taught from childhood. Education nowadays thinks so much about the different intellectual things the child will want in life, so little about the repose which is for the child the greatest necessity. Sometimes cats and dogs prove more intuitive than mankind. Are animals capable of more things than man? No, man is more capable. But man does not give himself time to become more intuitive, he does not give enough time to it. It often amused me to see in New York, where one easily becomes exhausted by the noises of trains and trams and elevators and factories, that at that time where a person has a little time to sit in train or tube, he is looking at the newspapers. All that action is not enough. If not in the body, then there must be action in the brain. What is it? It is nervousness, a common disease which has almost become normal health. If everybody suffers from the same disease, then this disease may be called normal. What is called self-control, self-discipline, only comes from the practice of repose, which is helpful not only in the spiritual path, but also in one's practical life, in being helpful, considerate.

The mystic, therefore, takes this method of repose, and by this he tries to prepare himself to tread the spiritual path. The spiritual path is, as I have said, not an outward path, it is an inward path one has to tread, and therefore, the laws and journeying through the spiritual path are quite contrary to the laws and journey through the outer path. To explain in plain words what the spiritual path is, I should say, "It begins by living in communication with oneself." Because it is the innermost self of man in which is to be found the life of God. This does not mean that the voice of the inner self does not come to everyone. It always comes, but every person does not hear it. Therefore, to begin one's effort in this path, the Sufi begins to communicate with, to address his self within. And when once he has addressed the soul, then from the soul comes a kind of reproduction, as the singer could hear of his song on a disc which has been produced from his voice.

Having done this, he has taken a first step in the direction within, when he has listened to what this process reproduces and this process has wakened a kind of echo in his being, either peace or happiness, light or form, whatever he has wished to produce, it is produced as soon as he has begun to communicate with himself. Now you can compare the man who says, "I cannot help being active, being sad, being worried, as it is the condition of my mind and soul," with him the worker, who communes with himself, and it is not long before the self begins to realize the value of it.

This is what the Sufis have taught for thousands of years. The path of the Sufi is not to commune with fairies and ghosts[4], it is to commune with one's deepest, innermost self, as if one blows one's inner spark to divine fire. But he does not stop there, he goes still further. He then remains in a state of repose and that repose could be brought about by a certain way of sitting and breathing, and by a certain attitude of mind. Then he begins to become conscious of some part of his being which is not the physical body but which is above it. The more he becomes conscious of this, the more he begins to realize the truth, which is a sure truth of the life hereafter. Then there are no longer his imaginations, nor his belief; it is his actual realization of the experience which is independent of physical life. And it is in this state that one is capable of experiencing the phenomena of life. The Sufi, therefore, does not dabble with different wonder-workings and phenomena. Once he realizes this, the whole life is a phenomena. Every moment, every experience brings to him a realization of that life he has found in his meditation.[5]

The being of man is a mechanism of body and mind. When this mechanism is in order there is happiness, fullness of life; when anything is wrong with the mechanism, the body is ill and peace is gone. And this mechanism depends upon winding. Just as a clock is wound and it then goes on for twenty four hours, so also in meditation, when a person sits in a reposeful attitude and puts the mind in a condition of repose and regulates the work of this mechanism by the process of meditation, it is like winding. Its effect is felt all the time, because the mechanism is put in order.

It is therefore that the belief of a mystic is not an outward belief in a deity he has not seen; the mystic's worship is not only an

---

4. Hq.tp.: "ghosts" typed, then placed between parentheses and "jinnies" inserted by hand; Hq.st.: "God" instead of "ghosts"
5. In the typescript and the stencil Gatheka 12 ends here, and Gatheka 13 begins

outer form, that by saying prayers his worship is finished. He makes the best use of the outer things, but at the same time his pursuit is logical, scientific, and he will, if possible, unite them with the mystical conception. But mysticism is the scientific explanation, also the realization of things taught by religion, things which otherwise would have no meaning to an ordinary person. When an ordinary person reads about the kingdom of God and heaven, he reads these names but he does not know where heaven is; he feels there is a God, but there is no evidence. And therefore, a large number of intellectual people who really are seeking the truth, are going away from the outer religion, because they cannot find the explanation, and consequently then become materialistic. The mystic says the explanation of the whole religion is investigation of self. The more one explores oneself, the more one will understand all religions in the fullest light and all will become clear. Sufism is only a light thrown upon your own religion like a light brought in a room where all things you want are. The one thing needed was light.

Yes, the mystic is not always ready to give his answer to every person. Can parents always answer every question of their infant children? No. There are questions which can be answered, and some there are for which we should wait until that person shall come to that point, until he understand[6]. I used to be fond of a poem which I did not understand, and yet I could not find a satisfactory explanation. After ten years, all of a sudden, in one second's time a light was thrown upon it, and I understood. There was no end to my joy. Does it not show that everything has its time? When people become impatient and ask for an answer, something can be answered, something cannot be answered; and the answer will come in its time. One has to wait. Has anyone in the world been able to say what is God to the full, with all scriptures and prophets? God is an ideal too high and great for words to explain. Can anyone explain such a word as love, say what is truth?

Very often people ask, "What is truth?" I often felt as if I should write the word truth on a brick in charcoal and put it into their hands and say, "There, hold this, then you can hold truth!" If truth is to be attained, it is only attained when truth itself has begun to speak, which comes about in revelation. Truth reveals itself; therefore, the Persian word for truth is *khuda*[7], which means self-

---

6. Hq.tp.: "understands" instead of "understand"
7. For *khuda*, see Glossary

revealing, for this word unites God with truth. So God is truth. Neither can one explain the first, nor the second word. The only help the mystic can give is how to arrive at this revelation. No one can teach or learn this, he has to learn himself. The teacher is only there to guide him to this revelation. There is only one teacher, who is God, and the great masters of the world, they were the greatest pupils, they knew how to become a pupil.

How is it all taught or brought to the consciousness of those who tread the path of truth? By *bayat*[8], by initiation. It is a trust from someone who guides to someone who is treading the path. The treader of the path must be willing to risk the difficulties of the path, to be sincere, faithful, truthful, undoubting, not pessimistic nor sceptical, else his efforts will not reach his aim. He must come wholeheartedly, or else not come. Halfheartedness has no value. And then what is necessary is some intellectual understanding of the metaphysical aspect of life, which some have, but not all. What is necessary besides are the qualities of the heart, love as a first principle, which is known to be divine. Then action, such action as will not hinder in the path of truth, such action as creates greater and greater harmony, and then repose, that which is learned by the study of one year is learned by the silence of one day. If one only knows the real way of silence.

[9]

---

8. For *bayat*, see Glossary
9. Hq.st.: "To be circulated among the Candidates for Initiation in the Sufi Order." typed underneath the lecture; Hq.tp.: "To be read before Candidates for Initiation in the Sufi Order" typed underneath the lecture

Headquarters' stencil

May 24th, 1925[1]

The Way Reached by Action[2]

Very often man is apt to think that it is study and meditation and prayer which alone can bring man to the way leading to the goal. But it must be understood that there is a great deal to be done by action. Few indeed know what power every action has upon one's life, what power a right act can give, and what effect a wrong action can have. What man is concerned with is that he is only on the lookout what others think of his actions, instead of thinking what God thinks of them. If man knew what effect an act produces upon himself, he would understand that if a murderer has escaped the hands of the policeman, he has not escaped from the fault he has done. For he cannot escape his self; the greatest judge is sitting in his own heart. He cannot hide his acts from himself. No doubt, it is difficult, almost impossible for a man to judge the acts of another person, for man knows not what is the condition of another. But man can best judge himself. Man, however wicked, is not pleased himself with his wrong actions, and if he is pleased for a moment, this pleasure will not continue.

But one might ask, "What is right and what is wrong?" No one can stamp any deed as right or wrong. But there is a natural sense in man which distinguishes between right and wrong, just or unjust, a sense which is even in the child. He also sees the line and colour in art or decoration; he sees if the tablecloth is not laid straight on the table, when a line that should be straight is not straight. Even a child knows when things should be harmonious in line and colour. A child normally loves harmony in line and colour. There is a natural tendency in the heart of man, the natural instrument that the masons use for building the house.

Different religions have taught different morals and it was

Documents:

Hq.st. = a stencil prepared at Headquarters, Geneva the provenance is unknown.

Hq.tp. = a typescript prepared at Headquarters, Geneva nearly identical to Hq.st.

Notes:

1. Hq.st., Hq.tp.: "Number 14." instead of the date
2. Hq.st., Hq.tp.: "GATHEKA." written above the text, followed by the Sufi Invocation, then "SUFI MYSTICISM VI." follows

right for the multitude for that time. No doubt, the law of the masses must be respected, but the real conception of right and wrong lies in one's deepest self. The soul is not pleased with that which is not right. The soul's satisfaction is always in something which gives it an entire happiness. The whole method is based on the practice not only of thought, but of action. All religions have been based not only on the truth, but on action. Things either material or spiritual have been accomplished by action. For the mystic, therefore, action is a most important thing. During my travelling from place to place, having come in contact with different people, having had the opportunity of staying with them, I have met some who, perhaps, have never in their lives read a book of theology or studied mysticism, their whole life having been spent in their work, their business and industry, and yet I have felt that spiritual advancement made naturally by their right action in life. They had come to a state of purity which perhaps another might find by the way of study or meditation.

Coming to the subject of action, one might ask what is the best way, the best road to take in everyday life, that might lead one to the ideal of life? The best way of action is to consider harmony as the first principle to be observed, that in all circumstances and situations and conditions to try and harmonize with one's fellow creatures. It is easy to say, but most difficult to live. It is not always easy to harmonize. But if we question ourselves why is it so difficult, the answer is that it is not always that people are difficult and not pliable. It is we ourselves, we cannot bend. The palm tree that grows straight up and the stem of which is so straight and strong with all its strength and goodness cannot harmonize with the other trees. There are many good people, but they are not harmonious. There are many true people, but their truth is not always comforting. They may tell the truth which is like a slap given to a person. They are just like the palm tree, straight and righteous, and at the same time inharmonious. A harmonious person can bend, is pliable, he can meet with another. No doubt, in order to harmonize one has to make sacrifice, one has to bend to people one does not want to bend to. One has to be more pliable than one is by nature, one has to be more clever than one really is. And all these efforts will not succeed unless one make an effort, unless one realize that harmony is the most essential thing in life.

Why does a mystic give such great importance to harmony? Because for a mystic his whole life is one continuous symphony, a playing of music, each soul contributing to the symphony his particular part in this music. The success, therefore, depends upon the ideal of harmony the person has. Very few people in the world give attention to harmony. They do not know that without this there is no chance of being happy. It is only the harmonious ones who can make happy and partake of that happiness. Otherwise it is hard to find happiness in the world. The fighter has no peace. Battle will be ever increasing. It is the peacemaker who is blessed. No doubt, in order to make peace, he will have to fight with himself and so will be able to make peace with others. Whatever a person's education or position in life, he may possess all he wants, but if there is one thing lacking in his life and heart, nothing can bring him peace. Think of what value it would be if one knew what a thing it is to create harmony, what the main thing[3] is in life, in everything one thinks and does.[4]

Now coming to action. There are certain actions as eating, drinking, sitting, walking which are not different from those of the animals. Therefore, if man in his actions does not show something which is not to be found in animals, then he has not awakened to human nature who cannot show something of the characteristics of a human being. One might ask, "What are these?"

The very same actions, such as eating, drinking, sitting, sleeping have at the back of them a light to guide, the very same action can become characteristic of human nature. For instance, if a man thinks he must not push another back when he is walking and says, "I am sorry," he shows a tendency different from an animal for they must rub against one another and man shows he will not do so. Animals will pass before one another and instead of bowing to one another show their horns and their greetings will be a howl. Man will be different. What is the special characteristic of man is consideration, refinement, patience, thoughtfulness. And once he has practised these, it leads to another action, that leads to the practice of self-sacrifice, which leads to divine action. When man sacrifices his time, his advantage in life for the sake of another he loves, he respects, he adores, this sacrifice raises him higher than the standard of ordinary human beings, which is the divine nature, which is not human. Because the human being begins to think as God thinks, and

---

3. Hq.st.: "it is to create harmony, what the main thing ..." actually written by hand in the margin to be inserted
4. In the typescript and the stencil Gatheka 14 ends here, and Gatheka 15 begins

because his actions become more and more divine, and become the actions of God. That person is greater than the person who merely believes in God, for his own actions have become the actions of God.

The one of awakened soul, he sees all the doings of grown-up people as the doings of children of one father. He looks upon them as the father would look upon all human beings on the earth without thinking that they are Germans or Englishmen or Frenchmen. They are equally dear to him. He looks at all full of forgiveness not only on those who deserve it, but also on the others. For to awakened souls not only who deserves it but also those who do not deserve it, he understands, for he understands the reason behind all. By seeing good in everybody and everything, he begins to develop that divine light, which expands itself, throwing[5] itself upon the greater part of life, making the whole life as a scene of the divine sublimity. What the mystic develops in life is a wider outlook, and this wider outlook changes his action. He develops in himself a point of view which may be called a divine point of view. You cannot help calling this the divine point of view. When a person rises to a state when all that is done to him, he feels that it is from God, and when he feels that when he does right or wrong, he feels that he does the wrong to God. Once arrived at this, this is true religion. There can be no better religion than that, the religion of God on earth. This is the point of view which makes a person as God, divine. He is resigned when badly treated. But he will take himself to task if he happens to find a shortcoming in his own action, for that is the action to God. Then the conception of the mystic of the deity is not only of a king or a judge or a creator. The mystical conception of God is the beloved, the only beloved there is. To him all the love of this world is like little girls playing with their dolls, loving them. In that way, they learn the lesson they have to realize later in their life of taking care of the home. The mystic learns the same lesson by proving sincere and devoted to all sorts of creatures, and he must devote and make himself devoted to waken himself to the beloved, the only beloved there is and to whom all love is due. [6]

---

5. Hq.tp.: "(projecting)" added by hand
6. Hq.st.: "To be circulated among the Candidates for Initiation in the Sufi Order." typed underneath the text; Hq.tp.: "To be read before Candidates for Initiation in the Sufi Order." typed underneath the text

Preface for Plays

From the extensive account of Inayat Khan's childhood in the *Biography*[1], we know that from an early age he had a penchant for imaginative play. Consider the following:

> Frequently Inayat would play at circus. Assembling as many children as he could, he made each represent some animal, which was to jump high or low, walk, trot, run or stand still, as occasion required. Whip in hand he would stand in the midst and direct the movement of each child most accurately by the dexterous use of his whip. (*Biography*, 38)

It seems he was always the director in these childhood games, making up the story and then assigning roles to his friends and managing their performances. It would be possible to see an analogy to the role he was to take in the lives of his followers later in life, except that instead of using a whip he used kind words and gentle persuasion.

He sometimes created dramatic situations, but was very aware that this was make-believe:

> He was always pleased to buckle on a boy-sword and to drill a group of boys. When once someone asked: "Whose head are you going to cut off with this sword ?" "No one's," he said, "rather than cutting off another person's head, I would cut off my own." (*Biography*, 38)

He apparently also liked playing doctor, sometime with more than play-like results:

> Inayat often took the part of a doctor. He would get a few glasses and any kind of white powder and mix a dose and then invite the sick of the household to come and be cured. And often it happened that some of the simple maids and servants in the house were cured instantly. (*Biography*, 38)

---

1. *Biography of Pir-o-Murshid Inayat Khan* (East West, London and The Hague, 1979)

This tendency received a strong escalation when he saw his first stage play. The Parsees, Zoroastrians relocated in India, especially around Bombay (Mumbai), launched a programme intended to give them cultural credibility in their new land which consisted of staging plays based on the ancient literature of India. They travelled the region presenting these plays, and sometimes ventured as far afield as Gujerat, including Baroda (Vadodara). Here Inayat saw his first stage presentation, a dramatization of the story of King Harish Chandra, an earthly ruler responsive to the spiritual hierarchy.

> The first drama that Inayat saw in his life was a most ancient play of India: Harish Chandra, the drama of renunciation, which brings out the moral of keeping one's honour. It made such an impression on young Inayat that for years he craved to see the drama. He saw it three times, but it was never enough; then, he enacted it himself at home. (*Biography*, 40)

It was not only that this was the first play he saw that intrigued him, but also the theme of the play itself, the unshakable, quite unreasonable sense of honour with which the king kept his word to the *rishi*s who were directing the drama invisibly. There was a fanatical side to Inayat's personality, not about doctrines or beliefs, but about personal honour and especially keeping one's word. He acknowledged that this was his own high sense, and emphasized that he would never ask his followers to adopt such uncompromising standards. The story of Harish Chandra was one that continued to appeal to him throughout his life, and he retold the story often to his followers in the West. The surprising thing is that he did not himself write a play about it.

He did also after that make up plays and recruit his playmates to act them out, remaining firmly in control:

> Many times Inayat would make up a play and get the other children to act it. To each child he would give a part and teach him how to perform it. When the time came for giving the play, the children would forget; but as often as one forgot and could not think how to act, Inayat would stand

behind, speak the words and tell the player how to act. So in reality the whole play was performed by himself. (*Biography*, 41)

Once he had relocated to the West, the idea of writing and presenting plays which would expose Western audiences to the Indian background of which they were largely ignorant appealed to him. The remnants in our archive of his early work are largely undated, but we do have three plays he worked on in the early days in a fragmentary form. The first was a musical presentation he conceived based on the *Rubaiyat* of Omar Khayyam in Edward FitzGerald's recreation. This was the only Sufi poetry already well-known in the West, and Inayat Khan evidently had the idea to present it on stage in an arrangement of the poetry designed to create some dramatic plot, and with a rich use of Indian music to be provided by his brothers and himself. The manuscript of the play seems mostly complete, and there are even some musical numbers sketched out. Unfortunately, other matters seem to have distracted him and his brothers from ever staging the drama, which might indeed have drawn attention to Sufi literature.

Another drama he conceived was a presentation of the story of Rama from the *Ramayan*, one of the two great epic poems of ancient India. For this play we have only a very extensive outline of the intended play, with a small amount of dialogue, and the work never seems to have progressed beyong that stage.

The third instance of early work is a play about Tansen, the renowned musician in the court of the Emperor Akbar. Inayat Khan's own musical career was crowned by being named Tansen of India by the Nizam of Hyderabad around 1903, after which he found his teacher and devoted himself to Sufi studies (though he always continued his music). The play recounts a well-known incident in the Emperor's quest for spiritual advancement. So far as is known, it has never been produced.

For several years, as he was travelling extensively and building up his Sufi organization, Inayat Khan's interest in stage drama seems to have waned. However, when he was returning to Europe aboard a steamship after his first return there in 1923, the spark was reignited. Having a number of days with no possible engagements, he set to work and produced the beginnings of a play to be presented later at the Summer School in Suresnes. With this he could accomplish two things: he would provide an entertainment for the followers gathered in Suresnes for the nearly three months of the Summer School, and he could once again exercise his creative casting in giving parts to his followers. He did not direct the plays himself, but he did cast them, and he seems to have taken special delight in giving some of his followers roles quite opposite to their positions in real life. Sometimes, however, the casting was straightforward. The lead role of Una in the play of the same name was written specifically for Bakhti Eggink, the lovely young woman who accompanied his 1923 tour of the United States. She was with him when he began writing the play, and assisted throughout the process. Inayat Khan's lively sense of humour, perhaps not always readily apparent, took special delight in anti-type-casting, and he is said to have often burst out laughing watching his followers struggle with playing someone so different from themselves.

The play *Una* was elaborately staged, with full costumes, at the end of the 1923 Summer School. It seemed to everyone a great success, a kind of lightening of the atmosphere from the very serious teachings, and Inayat Khan evidently decided he liked it so well that he subsequently produced one new play for each Summer School: in 1924, *Ameen, the Faithful Trustee*; in 1925, *The Bogeyman*; and finally, in 1926, *The Living Dead.*

When Munira van Voorst van Beest and Sharif Graham were working on the book 1923 I, the second to be presented in this series, in the middle 80s, Munira asked Sharif, because of his literary, scholarly background, to take charge of the presentation of the very complicated manuscripts on *Una*, which he did. Therefore, that play is not included in the present volume. When work was nearly finished on the volume 1924 II, it was discovered that the book had grown to enormous length, and just the lectures took nearly a thousand pages. It was therefore decided not to include, for the moment, the play *Ameen, the Faithful Trustee*, which rightfully belongs there. However, the period in 1925 before the Summer School contains relatively few lectures, and that presented an opportunity to include all the plays (except *Una*) in one place together without creating a huge volume, so that is what has been done. This does not follow the strict chronological presentation of the *Complete Works*, but that is perhaps much more important with the lectures than with the plays.

The play *Una* centres around an idealistic artist who struggles in a superficial world. The next play, *Ameen, the Faithful Trustee*, presents the story of the Prophet Muhammad without naming him. Amin (or Ameen), meaning trustworthy, was indeed the name by which Muhammad was known in his youth and represents his reputation in his early years. The play does not adhere strictly to the facts known about Muhammad. For example, Ali is presented as a contemporary of Muhammad, whereas in actuality he was much younger, a kind of adopted son of the Prophet and later his son-in-law. But Inayat Khan was never a stickler for facts, which he considered far from truth. He had long wished to promote understanding of Islam, his native religion, in the West, where he saw much prejudice and misunderstanding, and this play was undoubtedly part of that quiet project. A note tells us that: "The play was beautifully staged by Baroness van Tuyll and the management was in the hands of Murshida Green." The cast included 17 speaking parts, and many non-speaking parts, as part of the intention was to give everyone an opportunity to play something.

The play for 1925, *The Bogeyman*, has as its main character a person not unlike Inayat Khan himself, and in fact many of the lines spoken by the Sage, the character's only name in the play, are quite similar to Inayat Khan's own sayings. The other characters deftly represent the various reactions to his person and teaching Inayat Khan had encountered in the West. It is certainly the most autobiographical of his plays. There are 16 speaking parts, and the direction was again taken by Baroness von Tuyll, along with Mr Eggink, who had played Ameen, and who also painted the scenery.

The final play, *The Living Dead*, had an ever larger cast, 26, plus 4 children, played of course by Inayat Khan's own 4 children, of whom we have a precious photograph in costume. It concerns a prince, Puran, who is falsely accused of wrongdoing (the story resembles the story of Joseph in Genesis), ordered executed, but then sent away by his designated executioners into exile, and then returns years later unconsciously bestowing blessings, forgives everyone, and heads to "another country". In a way it is an appropriate farewell from Inayat Khan, who shortly after the performance set off for India and never returned, due to his unanticipated death at 44. But the evidence does not suggest he had any hint of that at the time he wrote the play.

There is a delightful account by Murshida Ratan Witteveen, who was a child at the performance: "None of the players, chosen by Murshid among his mureeds, is professional, which makes this dramatic story from time to time very funny. Here is the flash, unforgettable, during one of the presentations in the Hall in Suresnes. Murshid has taken place in the middle of the first row and his family is sitting on his left and right side. All children, except for Murshid's, are sitting on the second row, me just behind Murshid's broad back, so I cannot see or understand anything of the play on the podium. All of a sudden I see at close range in front of me Murshid's shoulders and head starting to move up and down in a slowly increasing speed—Murshid is laughing, laughing abundantly at the appearance of the two Kazaks who have been ordered to kill the prince in the name of his father, the Maharaja, the king. Especially the abundance, the intensity of Murshid's laughing with his whole body, the immense fun he has seeing the two tall, aristocratic Dutchmen—in daily life very important people, VIPs—trying to be rough Kazaks. They struggle with their swords, their guilt, their fear, their awful reluctance and disgust to do the job after having heard Prince Puran's moving, innocent prayer to God. Finally they let him go, 'Go far, far away.'" [2] From another source we know that the two Dutchmen in question were Baron Sirdar van Tuyll and Sirkar van Stolk; the part of Puran was played "very successfully" by another Dutch aristocrat, Baron Huzurnawaz van Pallandt, who later edited the 12 Sufi Message Volumes.

The plays were for Inayat Khan something between an entertainment and an indirect teaching. From the standpoint of literature, they are not remarkable. However, they have been produced from time to time since the Summer Schools for which they were created, and, depending on the production, have proven quite entertaining still, at least to followers of Inayat Khan's tradition.

---

2. *Sufi Mysticism into the West: Life and Leadership of Hazrat Inayat Khan's Brothers 1927-1967* , appendix, "80 Years of Sufism: Remembrances." Ratan Witteveen-De Vries Feyens.

OMAR KHAYYAM

Play written by Pir-o-Murshid Inayat Khan in his youth.[3]

CHARACTERS

Omar Khayyam, a young tent-mender
Sultan Mahmud
Zalim Pasha, his nephew, Commander of the Army[4]
Qazi[5])
Mufti) Religious officials
Mullah)
Omar Khayyam's father, a tent-mender
Khizr[6], a guiding spirit that is supposed to guide when guidance is needed
Potter
Huzuriah, Ushers of the Court
Jemadar, Captain of Zalim Pasha's forces
Policeman
Sultana, wife of Sultan Mahmud
Dayah, Nurse in the Royal Household
Khidmat) Attendants upon Husana'ara
Jurat)
Omar Khayyam's mother
Omar Khayyam's sister
Husna'ara, daughter of Sultan Mahmud
Maidens, Courtiers, Dancers, Female guards, Soldiers, Streetboys, Street sellers, Crowd

---

3. Ls.tp.: "Play written by Pir-o-Murshid Inayat Khan in his youth" omitted
4. St.tp.: "Commander of the Army" omitted
5. For *Qazi, Mufti* and *Mullah,* see Glossary
6. For Khizr, see List

ACT I

SCENE I

Scene: Jungle, Nishapur. Tent-mender's cottage.Omar Khayyam asleep. Apparition of Khizr in his vision is singing, with dancing angels.

<u>Song 1</u>

Awake, for morning in the bowl of night,
Has flung the stone that puts the stars to flight.
And lo, the hunter of the East has caught,
The sultan's turret in a noose of light.[7]

Awake, my little ones and fill the cup
Before life's liquor in its cup be dry,[8]
You know how little time[9] we have to stay,
And once departed may return no more. [10]

(The vision disappears. Omar Khayyam awakes and looks round wonderingly)

Omar Khayyam — Oh, what a surprise! I have never seen a man like this. Was he a man, or was he an angel? My soul heard him say that he was Khizr, who comes and awakens the slumbering souls from their fast sleep. Our four days on earth certainly is not for sorrow nor is it for sleep. Sleep, perhaps we slept before we opened our eyes on earth, and shall sleep for ever in the graveyard. This little time is for us to see all that life shows, with the praise of beauty and with the intoxication of love.

(Omar Khayyam's father comes in a great hustle)

---

7. Quatrain I.
8. Last two lines of Quatrain II
9. EF.: "while" instead of "time"
10. First two lines of Quatrain III

Father — What are you fussing with all this time? Here we need a thousand things in the house. You have not mended the tent for weeks. Are you possessed by a spirit or losing your mind? I cannot understand.

Omar Khayyam — Yes, father, you are right.

(Omar Khayyam's mother comes and soothes the father. Turning to Omar Khayyam)

Mother — I do not know, child, something is the matter with you. I don't know what it is, but you do not seem to mind your work and we have not seen for months the face of a diram[11].

(Omar Khayyam looks down. His sister comes meanwhile)

Sister — *(turning to her mother)* Mother, I want some silver spangles for my peshwaj[12] and father has promised me for the last three years to get me bracelets.

Mother: Tell your brother who is sitting there like a log, not doing anything to make a few dirams even for our daily bread.

(*Omar Khayyam sadly looks down)*

Mother — If you don't like your own work, child, go and find something else to do in the town.

Omar Khayyam — Yes, mother. Perhaps that would suit me better. I will go at once.

Mother — *(rising from her seat)* Come, my dear child. I will give you something to eat before you go.

(Sister singing while at work)

---

11. For *diram*, see Glossary
12. For *peshwaj*, see *pishwa* in Glossary

Song II

Oh, where is my lover?
Here my body remains
But he has my heart,
Would I could meet him with one little dove,
Then I would send him a message of love.
Oh, my own dear lover, would at this sweet moment
I could send thee my thoughts.
As there is no dove, I just think of love.

(Omar Khayyam coming out of his room and going out, bidding them good-bye)

ACT II

SCENE II

Scene: Market. A Persian bazaar. People buying and selling eatables, carpets and draperies. A potter working in his workshop.

Omar Khayyam wanders about and halts at the potter's workshop and looks with interest at the potter busy at his work.

Potter — Why are you standing there? Go your way. Mind your business.

Omar Khayyam — I have become interested in your work. I would like to make these beautiful pots such as you make.

Potter — Mind your business, man. What is your interest in my work to me? Do you want to carry off some of my pots from here? Begone! Begone!

Omar Khayyam — Would you engage me in your work?

Potter — *(astonished)* I cannot teach a dunce. Yes, if you knead the clay, I can engage you.

Omar Khayyam — Yes, I will knead the clay.

Potter — Then come along and work, my boy. I will give you three dirams at sunset.

(Omar Khayyam takes charge of the clay, and dreams the time away looking at different pots)

Potter — Go on, go on with your work. Why are you playing the fool here?

(Omar Khayyam engages himself in his work, then forgets it again)

Potter — I'll teach you how to knead clay.

(Omar Khayyam again forgets his work. Potter wants to knock his head off with the pot)

Omar Khayyam — I am sorry. *(Goes on again with his work)*

Potter — Now I am going, and mind you have finished kneading that clay by the time I come back. *(Goes away, leaving Omar Khayyam some more clay to knead)*

Omar Khayyam — *(Kneads the clay for a little while, then looks at the pots and becomes more and more interested, so that in the end he forgets the work)* Oh, from there I hear music. It sounds to my mind's ear as if the pots were singing. Oh, what lovely tones! What a beautiful thought it says! *(Sings)*

Song III in four[13] divisions

13. Both ls.tp. and st.tp have four but in fact there are six

I [14]My substance from the common earth was taken
That he who subtly wrought me into shape
Should stamp me back to common earth again.
Surely my life is not in vain[15]

Omar Khayyam Another says: *(sings)*

II Why ne'er a peevish boy would break the bowl from which he drank in joy.
Shall he that made[16] the vessel in pure love and fancy[17] an after-rage destroy?[18]

Omar Khayyam None answers this, but this vessel of ungainly make says[19] *(sings)*

III They sneer at me for leaning all awry.
What, did the hand then of the potter shake?[20]

Omar Khayyam What does he say? *(sings)*

IV [21]Folks of a surly tapster tell
And daub his visage with the smoke of hell.
They talk of some strict testing of us (pish!)
He's a good fellow and 't will all be well.[22]

Omar Khayyam Now he cries, with a long drawn sigh. *(sings)*

---

14. First line: Then said another - "Surely not in vain" omitted
15. Quatrain LXI
16. EF.. : "made" in italics
17. EF.: "fansy" instead of "fancy"
18. Quatrain LXII
19. EF.: "None answered this; but after Silence spake A vessel of a more ungainly make:" instead of "None answers this, but this vessel of ungainly make says:"
20. Quatrain LXIII
21. EF.: *"Said one -"* added
22. Quatrain LXIV

V [23]My clay with long oblivion is gone dry,
But fill me with the old familiar juice,
Methinks I might recover by and [24]by.[25]

Omar Khayyam — Oh, they jog each other and say: *(sings)*

VI Brother, brother, hark to the potter's shoulder knot a-creaking.[26]

(During the last imagination the potter has already come and is standing, seeing him so absorbed with his imaginations, shaking his fist at him, full of wrath. On the word "creaking" he hits him on the shoulder and repeats)

Potter — Creaking! Are your shoulders creaking now? Why have you wasted all this time so crazily, neglecting all the work given to you? Get out of my shop this minute. I am not going to pay you a single diram, my boy.

(Omar Khayyam silently looks down. The potter thrusts him out by the shoulders, repeating)

Potter — Creaking! Creaking.

(Omar Khayyam taken up by the boys in the market who hoot at him and tease him as a crazy man)

<u>Chorus I</u> — Boo, get along with you,
You're a fine fellow you are,
I'll show you
We don't want the likes of you here
Out of it, you silly idiot!
Ah, ah, ah, ah, ah, ah,
Come out of it.

---

23. EF.: "Then said another with a long-drawn sigh:" added
24. EF.: "bye" instead of "by"
25. Quatrain LXV
26. EF.: last line of Quatrain LXVI

	I'll show you what for. I'll give it to you.
Policeman	Well, what's all the row about? Come now, move on What the dickens are you standing here for? Move on, move on, move on.

ACT I

SCENE III

Scene: Road before the palace.

Omar Khayyam walking, looking at the beauty of the Royal Palace. He sits down on a stone coping. Qazi, Mufti and Mullah speaking among themselves.

Qazi	O, this is the man we need. He seems to be off in the clouds. Such are the people among whom we can find someone who can interpret our Sultan's visions.
Mufti	Let him alone. He seems to be a crank. Just see how he looks up and down.
Qazi	I tell you it is such as these who know the things of mystery, and if we cannot find anyone to interpret his vision, do you know what will happen?
Mullah	What?
Mufti	The Sultan will make us shave our moustaches and beards and will send us out of the city riding on donkeys, our faces tarred. How terrible! Let us go then, and you ask him, won't you?
Qazi	Yes, what matters it? I will ask.

(Mufti and Mullah stand aside, while Qazi goes forward)

Qazi — Assalaam aleika[27].

(Omar Khayyam looks the other way)

Qazi — (*then goes to the other side*) Assalaam aleika. *(He goes back to the same side as first)*

(Omar Khayyam looks up into the sky)

Qazi — *(near his ears)* Assalaam aleika.

Mufti — Shake him, shake him.

(Instead of shaking him [Omar Khayyam] Qazi takes him by the shoulders and stares into his eyes, holding him by the shoulders, bringing his face close)

Qazi — Where are you?

Omar Khayyam — *(looks at him in astonishment)* What do you want from me?

Mullah — *(comes)* Assalaam aleika.

Qazi — Our Sultan has seen a vision, and he is curious to know its cause and effect, and who can tell it except someone like you lost in the space?

Omar Khayyam — Oh, let me alone. What have I to do with you or your sultan? I am happy wandering about.

Mufti — You are happy, but we are not happy, hearing that we shall be sent away, leaving our home and children, if within forty days we do not tell the

---

27. For *Assalaam aleika*, see *as-salām 'alaika/'alaikum* in Glossary

interpretation of his vision or procure someone who can tell it. We shall all be turned away from the city and great distress will come upon our children. Even if you do not care for the sultan pray be kind to us, for the sake of Allah who is most merciful and compassionate.

Omar Khayyam — *(at once consents)* I am ready to come if I can do anything to save you.

ACT II

SCENE I

Scene: Durbar[28] *in Shahi Mahal. Courtiers ranged according to rank.*

<u>Song of Salutation</u> *(sung by all)*

<u>Chorus II</u>

True King and Ruler, thee we always love to praise.
Power and gain are thine as in former days.
Thou art life's sustainer and our judge while we live.
Thou has the power to punish, thou rewards[29] canst give.
Thee we pray to guide our wandering feet,
Direct them in the paths thou in wisdom perfect deemest meet.
Beauty rare shineth in thy heavenly face,
Never being was so blest with such perfect grace.
None can rival thee, ever take thy place.
Thine we always are, thou canst make or mar.

---

28. For *Durbar,* see Glossary
29. St.tp.: "reward" instead of "rewards"

Shield us with thine arm, rule with kingly charm.
One and all agree we shall always see
Paradise in thee.

(Entry of Huzuriah)

Huzuriah	Khudawand[30], Qazi Sahib has come with a stranger who, they say, is the knower of mysteries. We await your majesty's command.

(Enter Qazi, Mufti and Mullah with Omar Khayyam. All three bow, bend down and salute the king. Omar Khayyam does so also)

Sultan	Be seated. Who is this young man with you?
Qazi	Forgive our faults, O King. This young man is the knower of mysteries, and I am sure, will be able to answer your Majesty's question.
Sultan	Can he interpret my vision?
Mufti	Oh, refuge of our lives, to interpret the vision is simple. He can even tell the vision that your majesty had, I am sure.
Qazi	*(turning to Omar Khayyam)* Say yourself young man, to the Protector of Lives, what you can do.
Omar Khayyam	What shall I say? There is nothing to tell about.
Sultan	Young man, tell me if you can see into things mysterious.
Omar Khayyam	Everything is a mystery when it is not known.
All	*(one to another)* How true!

30. For *Khudawand*, see Glossary

Sultan Yes.

Omar Khayyam *(continuing)* But to him who sees it is no more a mystery.

Sultan You are right, I am sure of it.

(Qazi, Mufti, Mullah looking at each other, moving their heads as if they understood)

Sultan You are the man who should tell me of my vision.

Omar Khayyam Your Majesty has seen himself eating sweets from a gold plate and a black dog eating from the same at the same time, staring strongly and growling at you.

(Qazi, Mufti, Mullah looking down)

Sultan Wonderful! The same was my vision without slightest doubt. *(turning to attendants)* Bring for this young man the Khilat[31] and from this day he is appointed Sirdar[32] of our court.

(They immediately bring the Khilat on a gold tray. Qazi takes the tray for the king to touch and then awards the Khilat to Omar Khayyam in the presence of all. Omar Khayyam bows and makes salaams)

Music and Court dancers, dancing the Durbar dance.

Dance I

Song: This supreme durbar, O Sultan, is like Paradise,
To us, thy merry dancing girls,
And we pray that God may prosper this

31. For *Khilat*, see Glossary
32. For *Sirdar*, see Glossary

Thy land for evermore, thy noble, sunny land
May the nations proclaim thee as ruler
May they bless thee and praise thee, obey thee,
Adore thy name for ever,
Their love increasing always toward thee,
Thy consort, thy lovely sweet daughter.

(All courtiers and dancers go and Omar Khayyam and Qazi, Mufti and Mullah remain before the King. Sultan rises from his seat.)

Sultan — What do you think the vision means?

Omar Khayyam — The planet Zohra[33] leaves its protection upon your head and you are going under the influence of Mushtari[34], the effect of which will be fateful. Someone from among your favourites will prove faithless to his salt and will bring disaster upon you on the first day the chance avails him.

(Qazi, Mufti and Mullah look startled.)

Sultan — O, Allah, by thy mercy protect me from all danger.

Qazi — O, Protector of the world, he has told you the vision aright, but no one save Allah can know what fate has in store.

Mullah — But if Your Majesty desires that the ill effect of this dream be warded off, it is our great Qazi Sahib who can do it.

Qazi — *(nods his head)* Yes, it is charity that lightens all burdens.

Mufti — Yes, Khudawand, Qazi Sahib is right. There is no better safety from calamity than this. Our Qazi

---

33. For *Zohra*, see Glossary
34. For *Mushtari*, see Glossary

Sahib knows all the ways of proper charity.

Sultan — *(startled with coming fear, commands the treasurer)* Bring one lak of dirams[35] to Qazi Sahib for charity and let him see to it.

Qazi, Mufti, Mullah — May our liberal Protector live long! No danger will ever touch him.

(Durbar dismissed.)

ACT II

SCENE II

Scene: Road opposite the palace.

Dayah — *(meets Omar Khayyam in the road opposite the palace, before he comes to the palace the next time)* Oh, young man, can you read a letter written in Pahlavi[36]?

Omar Khayyam — Yes, I can.

Dayah — Then please come with me, you are wanted.

(Omar Khayyam follows her to the courtyard of the Zenana[37]. On arriving there)

Dayah — Now wait here. The one who has desired you to be here will soon come.

---

35. For *lak of dirams*, see Glossary
36. For *Pahlavi*, see Glossary
37. For *Zenana*, see Glossary

Omar Khayyam — *(half startled, fully confused)* The one who has desired will soon be here? What is all this she said, and hurriedly went away? I cannot understand what it is all about, whose courtyard this is, why I am wanted and who has desired me to come here.

Husna'ara — *(coming from behind)* It is I who gave you the trouble of coming and I hope you won't mind.

Omar Khayyam — *(turning back and looking at her, dazzled by her beauty, to himself)*
Is this a Peri[38] from fairyland, or a Hur[39] of Jennat[40]? Is this a Fereshta[41] from the angelic world or the Padamy[42] on earth whom the Creator has created in the daylight? *(To Husna'ara)* I am here at your service, but know not why I was called. Command, O rival of the moon, if there is any order that I can carry out.

Husna'ara — Command? It is thy command which has brought me here. Order? It is thy order that has called me here.

Omar Khayyam — *(to himself)* It sounds something that I have never known of. My command? My order? How can that be?

Husna'ara — My heart has responded to the call of thy soul, that is the command. Thy soul has kindled the flame in my heart, that is the order. What more could be said?

---

38. For *Peri,* see Glossary
39. For *Hur,* see Glossary
40. For *Jennat,* see Glossary
41. For *Fereshta,* see *farīshta* in Glossary
42. For *Padamy,* see *padmani* in Glossary

Omar Khayyam — Thy loving heart is as a precious gem, though all the earth gems are naught to me. But where am I and where are you? The difference of heaven and earth. How dare I claim a love for thee? But pray remember that from the moment of thy love's call my heart beats with thine.

(Husna'ara gives him her hand. Omar Khayyam kisses it and presses it to his breast, and while they are whispering the tale of love Dayah comes running.)

Dayah — Bibi, your playmates have all come.

(They part from each other with heavy heart.)

ACT II

SCENE III

Scene: Parlour of Zenana.

Dances II, III, IV:

(Maidens playing with water in the fountain and singing the song of spring and dancing to it.)

Dance with song of maidens:

Welcome to thee, our monarch's sweet daughter,
Bring us delight which always belongs to thee.
Thy face outshines the silvery moonbeams,
Giving thy father's soul sweet peace,
Filling thy mother's heart with rapture.

(Husna'ara sitting quiet, not taking any part in the play. When all disperse.)

Khidmat — *(takes Jurat aside)* What is the matter with Husna'ara this evening? She seems so self-absorbed and spoke to no one. Do you think she is ill?

Jurat — It is no wonder these birds of the gold cages fall ill. Any little thing can make them so. They are one minute cheerful and the other minute indisposed. Since when do you think she is like this?

Khidmat — She has been like this since she went to the galleries when the durbar was held. I am afraid she has been exposed to an evil eye. May God protect her from all evil! She is so sweet.

Jurat — No, God forbid. Never an evil eye can fall on her moonlight face. But I am afraid her eye has fallen on some object of the light and has retained the image in the pupil.

Khidmat — *(in surprise)* What do you say? Do you really mean this? I think our innocent Shahzadi is so young and remote that the thought of man cannot even touch her.

Jurat — O, my simple girl, be quiet! You consider everyone like yourself? These birds of gold cages can grow to know in one hour what we cannot even think in the whole day.

Khidmat — Yes, you are right. They read a thousand books, they look at a thousand things, and so they are much more grown up in months than we are in years. If it is true I am sure she must be in love with Zalim Pasha, and why should she not be? He is the only young man in our royal family who can match her in rank.

Jurat — No, my dear girl, no. You are as ignorant about her as an outsider? She hates the very name of Zalim Pasha, although he has left no stone unturned to induce our Sultan and Sultana to give

Husna'ara to him in marriage and he has given lots of bribes to the household of our palace, to Qazi, Mufti and Mullah, and has done all he could to win the affection of Husna'ara. But do you think she listens? No, not at all. If he comes from the south, she turns to the north.

Khidmat — Be quiet, there is someone coming.

(They are quiet. Sultan comes into the parlour. Husna'ara absorbed in her thoughts, not noticing his arrival.)

Sultan — *(to Khidmat and Jura)* Why is it so quiet here today? Quite unusual. There is always singing, dancing or playing going on. Today it seems dull and cheerless.

Khidmat — Khudawand, Shahzadi's enemies are unwell it seems.

Sultan — What is the matter with her? May Allah keep her!

Jurat — Huzoor, all today Shazadi has not taken any food nor has she taken part in any parlour games which we have been having here. Seeing her like this, all the maidens left the palace today sooner than usual.

Sultan — *(turning to his daughter)* What, Husna'ara, my dear child, are you not feeling well today?

Husna'ara — *(still more self-conscious and looking down, softly whispers)* No, father dear.

Sultan — But what is the matter? Do your brows ache?

(Husna'ara leans still more to one side and says nothing.)

Sultan — *(to Khidmat)* Go and call her mother. Tell her that Husna'ara is not feeling well.

(Khidmat runs to call the Sultana.)

Sultan — Do you bring the attardan[43]? Perhaps some fragrance will make her feel better. *(sprinkles rose-water on her handkerchief. In the meantime the Sultana comes in)*

Sultan — Do you know that Husna'ara is indisposed?

Sultana — May my life be sacrificed on my dear pet! What is the matter with her? Are her enemies ill today? *(She sits on the marble couch and takes the head of Husna'ara on her lap)*

(Husna'ara shows still more fainting.)

Jurat — Khudawand, all the ministers are ready to submit their works before your Majesty.

Sultan — Yes, tell them we are coming in one moment's time. *(To the Sultana)* I am going now, well-favoured. I hope you will see to Husna'ara. I will come soon.

Sultana — Allah be your protection!

(Sultan goes out.)

Sultana — *(to Khidmat)* Since how long has Husna'ara been like this? And why did you not tell me?

Jurat — *(answers instead of Khidmat)* Shazadi has not felt well all day today, but it gradually increased. Before Huzoor came it was not so bad.

---

43. For *attardan*, see *'attārdann* in Glossary

Sultana	I don't know what can have caused this.
Jurat	Bibi, it is nothing, It is quite natural.
Sultana	What do you say? Can illness be natural?
Jurat	Yes, pardon. It is natural. It is the change of season.
Sultana	The season in our land has not yet changed.
Jurat	Yes, but here in the palace it is changed.
Sultana	*(makes grimaces to herself and keeps quiet)* I cannot understand your crazy explanation.
Jurat	Bibi, I beg your pardon.

(Husna'ara seems to be fast asleep.)

Sultana	Is there a cushion here?

(Khidmat takes a cushion and gives it to the sultana. She places the cushion under Husna'ara's head and comes forward and takes Jurat and Khidmat on one side.)

Sultana	Jurat, from your conversation I surmise that it has a leaning towards something else. Now tell me if I understood you right, for you both are her favourite maids. Without you she is never happy. She tells you everything, and you should know her every thought and every move she makes. Do you think that she has anyone in mind?
Jurat	Yes, Bibi, it is natural. Now she is of age and the child of the palace, she has nothing but love and happiness all around her, and it is quite likely, although I am afraid to say so, that she may have taken a fancy to someone.
Sultana	But I am in a puzzle to whom she could have

	taken a fancy. Among the young men from royalty here there is no one expect Zalim Pasha, whom she hates like poison. We, of course, cannot think of finding a match among people, can we?
Jurat	No, Bibi, surely you cannot. But love is blind.
Sultana	*(heaves a deep sigh)* Do you know to whom she may have taken a liking? Have you the slightest idea?
Jurat	Pardon, O Bibi. How dare I utter a word in this respect?[44]
Sultana	Say, I desire you to.
Jurat	Pardon, Bibi. I cannot say for certain, but it is since the day that the new young man who was rewarded with a Khilat and was sitting at court seems to have attracted Husna'ara's attention so much, that all that time she did not speak to us, so completely absorbed was she in looking at him. We never saw her like this before. She did not seem to be on earth but as if she were somewhere else. Since then we have seen a great change in her.
Khidmat	Yes, yes, it must be true. It is since the same day, I know, that she is not inclined to eat nor does she sleep well, and in speaking she has answered yes in place of no and no in the place of yes. I stay up in the night and continue to fan her sometimes until the[45] midst of the night. She is turning about from left to right, from right to left, as if the bed were made of thorns, and I have never heard her sigh before but since that[46] day, as Jurat says, you can see from the dryness of her rosebud lips and

44. St.tp.: exclamation mark instead of question mark.
45. St.tp.: "the" omitted
46. St.tp.: "this" instead of "that"

the fadedness of her champak[47] face.

Sultan — *(arrives anxiously)* How is the well-favoured, my darling child Husna'ara?

Sultana — Thanks be to God! May her sickness go to her enemies! But, O father of Husna'ara, I come to know that there is something hidden under her indisposition.

Sultan — May Allah keep me in his mercy! What is the matter? What do you mean?

Sultana — It seems that she has a liking[48] to some young man whom you have newly appointed as a Sirdar of your court. Imagine for the girl of kingly blood, that it should ever cross her mind to consider anyone from the people, and when she has already a suitor from the imperial descent and since long he has asked for her hand, and she has always ignored him! Oh, I don't know why the girls of the present generation are so thoughtless and independent!

Sultan — I think she is not wrong in considering this new young man, for, although he is not from royalty, yet he has at least humanity in him, and it would be a great sin on our part to forbid her to make her own choice.

Sultana — But do you not know what influence her suitor Zalim Pasha commands in our country? And if he is disappointed he will upset the whole country, and first of all your own courtiers will not agree to the idea of Husna'ara's wedding a stranger, a two day's acquaintance.

Sultan — I would rather make Husna'ara's life happy by

---

47. For champak, see Glossary
48. St.tp.: "has taken a liking" instead of "she has a liking"

allowing her to have her own choice than take into account what people will have to say.

Jurat — *(comes)* Khudawand, the durbar is ready,waiting[49] for your Majesty's gracious presence.

Sultan — Yes, we come. *(to Sultana)* Will you also accompany me to the durbar this evening? I shall try to move the question in the durbar and see what everybody has to say.

ACT II

SCENE IV

Scene: Sultan with Sultana in Jharoka in Shahi Mahal. Qazi, Mufti and Mullah present, with female guards and attendants.

Qazi — I wonder what makes Huzoor so absorbed in thought. I have been watching this lately.

Sultan — O Qazi Sahib, you know as well as we know the responsibilities of life, and now —may Allah grant her all good!—our Husna'ara is of age and there are a thousand things for us to think of.

Qazi — O protector of lives, Allah has blest you will all things, enormous wealth, power and possessions. Your command everyone obeys. There is nothing much to think about in this matter. Whomever your Majesty will choose from among the youths of the royal family to grant this privilege, he will deem it an honour beyond imagination. I apologize a thousand times before mentioning this before you, our support, yet Zalim Pasha is the most shining youth in our land to-day.

(Expressions of the Sultan and Sultana change.)

---

49. St.tp.: "awaiting" instead of "waiting"

Mufti — Yes, Huzoor, Qazi Sahib rightly says. We have not his like here in our land in birth and rank both.

Mullah — Of course, his father was Nawab[50] Zul Kadr Jang, the greatest warrior of his time.

Mufti — And his grandfather was Hissam-ul-Mulk.

Qazi — His uncle lived before me, Vikar Umrah Bahadur.

Mufti — But his great grandfather was the only man of his time, Haushid Jah, the lord of the armies.

Sultana — You are right, Qazi Sahib.

Mufti, Mullah — Yes, Huzoor, that is so.

Sultana — And it is a pity that there is no one else in our land who can be compared with him. But alas, she turns to ice if his name is mentioned before her.

(Expressions of Mullahs change.)

Qazi — Our Sultana of high merits, Shazadi Husna'ara is but a child. She does not know life's spring and fall.

Mufti — Of course, the child who has never stepped out of the palace cannot be expected to know about the dryness and coldness of the world.

Qazi, Mufti, Mullah — But, may Allah keep our Sultan and Sultana as the blessed canopy over her head. They will not do what is not becoming to the royal blood.

Mufti, Mullah — True, true.

---

50. For *nawab*, see Glossary

Sultan	*(heaves a deep sigh)* Oh, what is high birth and greatness of rank? To me it seems as empty-handed we came so we go.
Mullahs	*(with discouraged expressions)* Yes, yes, Huzoor such is life.
Sultan	I do not believe in forcing the child who has her own life to lead; and our blessed Prophet - may peace be on him, - said, "Ye are all equal in the sight of Allah." Therefore I am of opinion that the child must be given her own choice in the matter.
Sultana [51]	Yes, but if she chooses to give her hand to him who was nobody, such as now she has taken a fancy to this new man Omar Khayyam, whom you have admitted to the Court, now what may be done in this case?

(Qazi, Mufti and Mullah look at each other in great bewilderment.)

Qazi	But, world's protection, how cannot it be possible? What relation can earth have with the heavens?
Mufti, Mullah	True, true.
Sultan	But in Islam we are all brothers and everyone has equal right? Don't you think so, Qazi Sahib?
Qazi	*(hums and haws)* Yes, Huzoor it is right. But in the case of our new young man, Omar Khayyam, I doubt if he is a Mussulman[52].
Sultan	*(in astonishment)* What makes you doubt, Qazi Sahib?

---

51. St.tp.: "Yes ... this case?" inserted
52. For Mussulman, see Glossary

Qazi — I think, Huzoor, that his thoughts are extravagant.

Mufti — Yes, true. His head seems to be whirling all the time.

Mullah — Of course, his eyes whirl too.

(A royal coach arrives. Husna'ara followed by her maidens. All the courtiers bow to her and she sits down beside the Sultan.)

Sultan — With what have you been busy this day, my beloved child?

Husna'ara — Nothing, father dear, I was just whiling away the time in the Kutubkhanah of our palace.

Sultana — Where had all your maidens gone, my darling pet? Did they not entertain you?

Jurat — Bibi, we have induced the Shazadi in every way to come and play near the fountain, but Shazadi did not come, and all other maidens came and went away, for Shazadi was busy with her books in Kutubkhanah[53].

Sultan — What books was Shazadi busy with?

Jurat — I think some new manuscript of poetry, your Majesty.

Sultan — Poetry?

Jurat — Yes, Huzoor. The manuscripts written by Omar Khayyam, our new courtier, engaged the mind of Shazadi very much.

Sultan — *(to himself)* Of course, she has always shown interest in poetry. Did you like any verses of

---

53. For *Kutubkhanah*, see Glossary

	Omar Khayyam, my dear child?
Husna'ara	Yes father, I like them immensely.
Jurat	Yes, Huzoor, perhaps our dear Shazadi has learnt them by heart.
Sultana	Has she?
Sultan	Of course. By the gift of Allah her memory is such that if once read she knows it by heart.
Jurat	Yes, Huzoor, that is right, if she is at all interested.
Qazi	Does Omar Khayyam write poetry?
Mufti	I wonder.
Mullah	I have my doubts, Qazi Sahib, whether the verses that our intelligent Shazadi has admired are his own.
Husna'ara	I don't know why they should not be his verses.
Sultan	Why not recite a few verses, child, that we may also hear.
Husna'ara	*(recites)*

Come, fill the cup and in the fire of spring,
The winter garment of repentance fling;
The bird of time has but a little way
To fly - and lo! The bird is on the wing.[54]

Oh, come with old Khayyam, and leave the wise
To talk; one thing is certain, that life flies;
One thing is certain and the rest is lies;

---

54. Quatrain VII

The flower that once has blown for ever dies.[55]

Ah, fill the cup, - what boots it to repeat?
How time is slipping underneath our feet;
Unborn to-morrow[56], and dead yesterday[57],
Why fret about them if to-day[58] be sweet[59]!

One moment in annihilation's waste,
One moment of the well of life to taste -
The stars are setting and the caravan
Starts for the dawn of nothing - Oh, make haste![60]

How long, how long, in infinite pursuit
Of this and that endeavour and dispute?
Better be merry with the fruitful grape
Then sadden after none, or bitter fruit.[61]

But leave the wise to wrangle and with me
The quarrel of the universe let be:
And, in some corner of the hubbub coucht,
Make game of that which makes as much of thee.[62]

For in and out, above, about, below,
't is nothing but a magic shadow-show,
Played in a box whose candle is the sun
Round which we phantom figures come and go.[63]

And if the wine you drink, the lips you press,
End in the nothing all things end in - yes -
Then fancy while thou art, thou art but what
Thou shalt be - nothing - thou shalt not be less.[64]

---

55. Quatrain XXVI
56. EF.: "TO-MORROW" capitalised
57. EF.: "YESTERDAY" capitalised
58. EF.: "TO-DAY" capitalised
59. Quatrain XXXVII
60. Quatrain XXXVIII
61. Quatrain XXXIX
62. Quatrain XLV
63. Quatrain XLVI
64. Quatrain XLVII

While the rose blows along the river brink
With old Khayyam the ruby vintage drink:
And when the angel with his darker draught
Draws up to thee - take that, and do not shrink.[65]

Gatekeeper	Huzoor, Omar Khayyam is here to pay respects to your Majesty.
Sultan	Yes, let him come.

(Mullahs looking at each other. Omar Khayyam enters, pays his respects.)

Sultan	Be seated. We understand that you write poetry.
Omar Khayyam	Nothing, Huzoor. It is making black marks on the white paper.

(Qazi, Mufti and Mullah wink at each other.)

Qazi	*(to Omar Khayyam)* Is it since receiving His Majesty's bounty that you have taken to drink, for it seems there is nothing else than praise of wine in your verses?
Mufti, Mullah	La houla Allah huvat. *(Words of contempt.)*
Omar Khayyam	Pardon, O Qazi Sahib. Since the Saki with his own hand has offered me the glass I have taken to drink.
Qazi	Were you a born Muslim?
Omar Khayyam	Yes, Qazi Sahib. No one is born anything else. It is afterwards that they are turned to this or that by

65. Quatrain XLVIII

their parents.

Qazi — No one is ever born Mussulman. Afterwards we make him.

Mufti, Mullah — True, true.

Omar Khayyam — No, that Mussulman I am not.

Qazi — Then you are liable to be called kafir[66].

Mufti — What doubt is there?

Mullah — His every verse is an evidence of it.

Sultan — Oh, of what use is disputing before knowing what it is about? *(to Omar Khayyam)* Will you let us hear some of your verses, young man?

(Expression of face of Husna'ara changes.)

Omar Khayyam — They are not worth reciting before Huzoor, but I think it would be insolence on my part if I did not obey the command of your Majesty.

Myself when young did eagerly frequent
Doctor and saint and heard great argument
About it and about, but evermore
Came out by the same door as in I went.[67]

With them the seed of wisdom I did[68] sow,
And with my own hand laboured it to grow;
And this was all the harvest that I reap'd -

---

66. For *kafir*, see Glossary
67. Quatrain XXVII
68. EF.: "did I" instead of "I did"

"I came like water and like wind I go."[69]

Into this universe, and *why* not knowing,
Nor *whence,* like water willy-nilly flowing:
And out of it, as wind along the waste,
I know not *whither*, willy-nilly blowing.[70]

What, without asking, hither hurried *whence*?
And without asking, *whither* hurried hence!
Another and another cup to drown
The memory of this impertinence![71]

Up from earth's centre through the seventh gate
I rose, and on the throne of Saturn sate,
And many knots unravel'd by the road;
But not the knot of human death and fate.[72]

There was a door to which I found no key:
There was a veil past which I could not see:
Some little talk awhile of me and thee[73]
There seemed - and then no more of [74]thee and me.[75]

Then to the rolling Heav'n itself I cried,
Asking "What lamp has destiny to guide
Her little children stumbling in the dark?"
And "a blind understanding!" Heav'n replied.[76]

Then to this[77] earthen bowl did I adjourn
My lip the secret well of life to learn:
And lip to lip it murmur'd - "While you live

---

69. Quatrain XXVIII
70. Quatrain XXIX
71. Quatrain XXX
72. Quatrain XXXI
73. EF.: *"ME and THEE"* capitalised
74. EF.: *"THEE and ME"* capitalised
75. Quatrain XXXII
76. Quatrain XXXIII
77. EF.: "the" instead of "this"

Drink! - for once dead you never shall return."[78]

Qazi (*to Sultan*) Now it is for the wise protector of our lives to see how much kafir is expressed in all his verses, and under the reign of your Majesty, the support of religion, every kafir must have his recompense.

Mufti Yes, Huzoor, from what is written in the red book his penalty would be death.

Mullah No, a kafir should be flayed alive.

(Husna'ara in tears.)

Sultan (*to Qazi, Mufti and Mullah*) Your pronouncement is rather too early. You must wait for my decision. His wine to me is the ray of life, the wine of Kousar[79], the heavenly wine, and your piety before it is as the darkness of night before day.

Qazi Huzoor, you have the power to say or do whatever you like, but I am not responsible for the results.

Mufti True, Qazi Sahib. It is the reign of religion and when its law is not strictly observed by the crown I am afraid the whole nation will shake.

Mullah There is no doubt about it. Danger always awakes the errors of sultans.

Sultan How dare you say that?

Qazi We dare say it, Huzoor, for we are honest.

Husna'ara What honesty may there be in wanting to ruin the

---

78. Quatrain XXXIV
79. For *Kousar*, see Glossary

same man who saved your life, I cannot understand.

(Sultan gives the orders to dismiss the Durbar and all go their ways.)

ACT III

SCENE I

Scene: Jungle. Zalim Pasha's camp. Tents.

Qazi — *(to Zalim Pasha)* We have done our best, Huzoor. Allah is our witness, besides these two pious souls.

Mufti, Mullah — *(move their heads)* But alas, alas, our Sultan has somehow or other lost his senses. Who on earth can be so fitting a suitor for Husna'ara as Your Highness.

Zalim Pasha — No, there is no other way left for me than violence. How while I am living on this earth shall Husna'ara be destined for someone else? *(in a rage)* Oh, I would sit on the breast of the Sultan and drink the blood coming out of his veins before I would let him give Husna'ara in marriage to anyone else.

Qazi — Husna'ara, our beautiful princess, always loves to see your face, Huzoor. Your name spoken before her fills her with delight.

Mufti — Of course, she knows that no one equals our lord Zalim Pasha in birth and rank both.

Mullah — Well, she has been impressed from her childhood by the praise of your lordship that our Qazi Sahib has always spoken.

Zalim Pasha	I know, I know. All the fault is of the cursed Sultan. *(in fury)* I will shave my moustache if I will not cut the Sultan's head off with my sword. *(He calls Jemadar. The head of Zalim Pasha's armed gang comes and bows)*
Jemadar	Huzoor's command?
Zalim Pasha	Command your Sipahis[80] to be under arms at once.
Qazi	May Huzoor's right shoulder be victorious and may your flag fly over our land.

ACT III

SCENE II

Scene: the royal road before the palace. Men and women running hither and thither, frightened. Shops looted. Policemen beaten. Sentries arrested. Zalim Pasha marching with his gang into the palace. Loud cries of men and women from the palace; the Sultan is murdered. Proclamation of Zalim Pasha made in the bazaar:

Hail, Zalim Pasha, our good sultan!
The world has only one Zalim and he is our good King!
Let us sing the praise of mighty Zalim!

Qazi, Mufti and Mullah present. All the military and ministers sing his national anthem:

<u>Chorus III:</u>

May thy reign be blest by Allah
Sultan mighty conqueror,

80. For *Sipahis,* see Glossary

Giver of courage and of valour,
May good fortune attend thee forever,
May it grow from day to day,
Until thy glory shall extend
Throughout thy land from end to end.
May thy foes respect thy majesty,
Yield the homage due to thee.
Here before thee now we stand
On the desert soil, our native land,
And lo, we bend before our sultan
Praying for him and for motherland.

ACT III

SCENE III

Scene: Omar Khayyam's study. Omar Khayyam busy writing verses.

Song, Khizr:

Think, in this battered caravanserai
Whose doorways are alternate night and day,
How Sultan after Sultan with his pomp
Abode his hour or two and went his way.[81]

They say the lion and the lizard keep
The courts where Jamsshyd[82] gloried and drank deep
And Bahram[83], the[84] great hunter, the wild ass
Stamps o'er his head and he lies fast asleep[85].

81. Quatrain XVI
82. For Jamsshyd see List. EF.: *Jamshyd*
83. For Bahram, see List
84. EF.: "that" instead of "the"
85. Quatrain XVII

Omar Khayyam — *(in bewilderment)* Oh, what voice is that? *(setting his pen and paper down)* Oh, how appealing! *(looking here and there)* But who may this be, I wonder? *(looking up)* Oh, I think it is the voice of Khizr! *(in a worshipful mood)* No doubt it is you, my inspirer! It is your voice, I am sure. Oh manifest before me. Oh, let me see thy vision once again.

(The voice comes nearer. Omar Khayyam heaves a deep sigh and falls into a trance.)

Husna'ara — *(opens door and comes in. Calls him)* Omar, Omar!

Omar Khayyam — Khizr! Oh, what a revelation!

(Husna'ara hurriedly shakes him.)

Omar Khayyam — *(opens his eyes and looks surprised)* O Husna'ara, what brought you here? What a surprise!

Husna'ara — Father is murdered, my beloved Omar, and most unfortunately on my account.

Omar Khayyam — Alas, but how wonderful! I just had the same vision that my inspirer, Khizr, told me. Sad! Sad!

Husna'ara — Now there is no time for dreams. Wake up, my beloved Omar. Zalim thinks that now he will accomplish his wicked object, but he must wait till the day of Kayamat[86]. It is not the kingdom that his

86. For *Kayamat*, see *qiyāma*, in Glossary

sword can win, it is a woman's heart. Husna'ara's heart is no longer her own. It is given to Omar and it will be his forever. Now may the protection of Allah be with you. I must leave at once for the Sahrah[87] before the search for me begins. The camel is waiting outside. And you take the first opportunity of coming.

Omar Khayyam — Oh take me with you, my life's flame. We shall lose each other.

Husna'ara — No, it will not be wise for us both. If we are seen together we shall surely be traced. No, my heart's life, the flame of love which is kindled in our hearts will surely unite us. No earth, no water, no fire, no air can ever disunite two hearts that have become one.

(They embrace each other. Omar Khayyam overwhelmed with the pain of parting. Husna'ara hurries and leaves for the Sahrah. Omar Khayyam falls on one side in despair.)

Symphony 2

ACT III

SCENE IV

Scene: Courtyard. Qazi, Mufti and Mullah with Zalim Pasha.

Qazi — It is the glorious fate of Khudawand that has brought victory to your Majesty's sword.

---

87. Believed to be phonetic Arabic pronunciation of Sahara

Zalim Pasha	It is your help and thought too.
Mufti	Of course, Qazi Sahib has made every possible effort to bring about this glorious day.
Zalim Pasha	But now one thing remains. That ought to be done soon.
Qazi	Yes, Huzoor, I understand.
Mufti	We all understand Khudawand your Majesty's wish.
Mullah	But now it should no more be called a wish. It is Huzoor's command.
Zalim	Yes. The palace is in my possession now, but the one on whose account I have done all this must be brought before me not as a captive but as the Princess.
Qazi	Of course, she will be our Sultana now.
Mufti	Our Qazi Sahib has always had great influence with her.
Mullah	Yes, yes. Qazi Sahib's word is a voice from the skies to our future Sultana. Anything he says to her will be done.
Zalim	My eager heart cannot wait any longer.
Qazi	Your Majesty, there is no reason to wait. As the whole capital is now in Your Majesty's possession, Husna'ara is not excepted.
Mufti	Then why wait, Qazi Sahib? Let the wedding ceremony take place to-morrow.

Zalim	Without asking Husna'ara?
Mullah	How dare Husna'ara refuse Huzoor's command, who has all the this time so loved and admired your Majesty?
Zalim	Then let us have the wedding to-morrow, at the palace. I can have patience no longer. *(To Qazi)* Make all the necessary preparations, Qazi Sahib. Let it not be delayed any longer.
Mufti	Yes, tomorrow is the lucky day, as written in the Red Book.
Mullah	Yes, Huzoor, tomorrow is full moon also.
Qazi	Wonderful, how nature reaches out a helping hand in the prosperity of our great Sultan!
Zalim	Go immediately then and make all necessary preparations in the Zenana, and spend from this money all that is necessary. *(hands him two purses of gold)*
Qazi	The bride will be ready in her wedding attire, and all necessary preparations will be made to anticipate your Majesty's wishes.

(All three begin to[88] *bow and say, "May our life's protector prosper")*

88. St.tp.: "go" added

ACT III

SCENE V

Scene: Parlour in the Zenana.

(Dayah weeping and Jurat and Khidmat mourning with her. Qazi enters with Mufti and Mullah. They cease speaking when they see these men coming.)

Qazi Salaam Aleikum[89].

(Dayah begins to weep still more.)

Qazi *(holds her hands)* What is the matter?

(Dayah throws her arms round Qazi and Qazi holds her and she embraces him and cries. Seeing this, both the other girls cry too, and Mufti and Mullah hold each, keeping them from weeping.)

Qazi But what has happened?

(Dayah says nothing, but cries.)

Qazi I know dear, that you love me, but I have also loved you always. Why do you cry?

Dayah My bad fate has no end. In this prison of the palace I have always been as a captive, and have never breathed the air outside.

Qazi But I have watched you always with great love. You have won me at every move you made, whenever you came to give me some message of the late Sultan.

---

89. For *Salaam Aleikum*, see *as-salām 'alaika/'alaikum* in Glossary

Dayah — But you seem never to have cared for me.

Qazi — I did not care? I have always admired you as the rose of the garden of Eden, but how could I ever have plucked you when it was watched by the gardener?

(Dayah has another spell of weeping.)

Qazi — Why?

Dayah — *(clings to his neck still faster)* Oh, the days of the past!

Qazi — Why cry about the days of the past when the present is pleasant? If you wish I will take you home and you will be my queen. But I wish to ask of you one thing which is absolutely in your power.

Dayah — *(wiping her eyes)* I am ready. What is it?

(All listen.)

Qazi — If you can make Husna'ara consent cheerfully to marry her well-suited suitor, our Sultan, Zalim Pasha, under whose reign we are all. She will have to marry anyhow, for his is the kingdom and his is the command. And Zalim Pasha, I am sure, will set you free to come to my house and we shall be smothered with gold.

Dayah — Yes, but where is she?

(Qazi at once lets go his hold of her, most startled, and the same thing Mufti and Mullah do too, looking at each other in fear and amazement)

Qazi	*(to Dayah, in extreme amazement)* What do you say?
Dayah	I speak the truth.
Qazi	Has she run away? *(to Jurat)* When did she?
Jurat	We have not seen her since the funeral of the Sultan and the Sultana was taken away. Oh, she was sweet! *(she cries and falls in his hold. He holds her and yet is frightened.)*
Mullah	*(to Qazi)* O Qazi, Sahib, but what will become of us? You know the anger of Zalim Pasha. He will cut us all in pieces and give them to the vultures.
Khidmat	*(crying)* Oh, will he? *(clings to Mullah's neck)*
Qazi	*(to Mullah and Mufti)* No use wasting any time, we must at once decide what to do. It has come upon our lives. We must take to our heels.
Mufti	There is no way but this.
Dayah	But what will become of us?
Khidmat	Oh, but will you leave us here to die? *(she clings to the neck of Mullah)*
Jurat	*(to Mufti)* But what about me? If Zalim Pasha finds us here he will grind us in the oil-press. And what about all these jewels?

(On hearing the word "jewels" the expression of every man changes.)

Qazi	Why? Did she not take the jewels away with her?

Dayah	*(weeps)* Oh, no. My darling pet went away without a single ornament on her. *(clings to the neck of Qazi)*
Mufti	*(to the women)* We must take you too.
Mullah	But you must pack up all the jewellery and precious things in bundles very nicely that nothing may be left behind. No use being sad any more now. We shall all enjoy the money we have, and besides all these jewels, and it will last with us for twenty generations to come.
Qazi	But what have you thought about being able to enter?
Dayah	The difficulty will be to go from this back door of the Zenana. The doorkeepers will never allow any man to enter this door after sunset. And how can we carry the tons of jewels collected and preserved by our royal family for ages?
Mullah	We are able to carry them all. Our Qazi Sahib alone can carry fifty bundles if they are of jewels.
Dayah	Oh, I suppose that will not be very difficult.
Jurat	If you all came disguised as women, no one will stop you at the gate, and you can take a ladder in the back yard of the Zenana and we will first lower all the packets of jewels to you, and if you help us to climb down the ladder we shall make a safe escape.
Mufti	That is the wisest thing to do.
Mullah	That is the only way it can be done. We shall be most glad to come and take you and the bundles.

Qazi *(to Mufti and Mullah)* Let us go then and prepare our camels for the journey.

Mufti *(to Jurat and the others)* Will you then pack up all things that are worth taking and be ready when we come.

Mullah Look here, do not leave one thing that is of some value.

Khidmat Yes.

(They embrace and part, kissing each other. When Qazi, Mufti and Mullah are gone.)

Jurat This faithless Qazi has been the curse of our royal family.

Khidmat Surely he has caused all this disaster.

Dayah And these two Satan's children at his right and left hand.

Jurat Such are the insects who by their greed eat up the most fruitful plants of nations.

Khidmat Yes, such are the germs which bring decay to the fruits of desires.

Jurat If we had not managed them so skilfully they would have caused all the wrath of Zalim to fall on us, and we should have fallen victims to their doom.

Dayah Oh, let us not trouble about them. Now they have already been given poison in lumps of sugar. Their neck will be caught in their own noose. We must be gone from here soon to save our lives, and if it will be our good fortune we shall meet some day our long loved Shazadi.

(They all change their expression and sadly depart from there.)

ACT III

SCENE VI

Scene: Durbar Hall. Shahi Mahal.

(Procession. Courtiers entering in their gorgeous costumes, singing the wedding song.)

Song.

Let us gaze on our wonderful lord
On the way to the great and glorious Palace.
On his wedding day.
May to-day be the best of all days vouchsafed to Zalim.
The happiest day on earth for his lovely bride.

(Women entering, carrying presents and singing the "Good Luck" song.)

Song:

Good luck to thee, our regal bridegroom brave.
Good luck to thy lovely bride.
Oh, may long life be given you,
May pleasure be ever at thy side.
This world has never known a royal pair
So blest with virtues rare.

(Zalim enters in bridegroom's garments coming with a canopy over his head and taking his seat on a wedding seat specially made for that occasion)

Zalim *(To his courtiers)* Where is the Qazi Sahib, Mufti

	and Mullah? They should have been present here[90] long before.
Courtiers	They are not present here, Your Majesty.
Zalim	Why is there nobody here to receive and welcome the wedding procession?
Courtiers	We don't know, refuge of our lives, perhaps they are busy adorning the bride.
Zalim	Go and enquire what delay there is.
Courtiers	*(run and bring answer)* No one answers from the Zenana. It seems as if no one were there.
Zalim	No one is there? How can it be possible? *(to the female attendants)* Will you go and look in the Zenana and first get the answer why there was nobody at the door to receive me.
Ladies	*(go and bring answer)* No one is in the Zenana. It seems that Shazadi has disappeared.

(The face of Zalim Pasha becomes flushed with rage.)

Zalim	There is no one there to answer?
Ladies	No one, our life's protection.
Zalim	Ah, fate! What a blow thou hast given upon my heart! Where are those Mullahs, the mischief-makers? *(to Courtiers)* Send at once men all around and order them to bring the fugitive at once. Until she is brought before me and I have given her a fitting penalty my heart will never be at

90. St.tp.: "here" omitted

rest.

Courtier *(coming in great excitement)* Found! Found! Found!

(Noise from the other streets)

Courtier *(bows)* They say the fugitive is found with her companions.

Zalim Bring them. I am athirst for their blood.

(Three women arrested, hiding their faces under their saris are brought.)

Those holding them up *(panting)* O, support of the poor, grant us a liberal reward! We caught them getting out of the courtyard by a backdoor, by a ladder, but their strength is so great that we three men could not manage to hold one woman. It was with great difficulty that we held them and did not let them go out of our hands.

Zalim Certainly, you have done well. *(to the women)* O, shameless ones, what mischief have you played with me! You wanted to run away from my hold. It would have been as to run away beyond the canopy of the sky. I had thought of making you my queen, but now you will be a slave of my slaves. Shameless one, why hide your blackened face? Show its disgrace to all present here.

(He asks the attendant ladies to unveil their faces. They hide still more. With great difficulty the coverings are taken off their heads, and they appear as Qazi, Mufti and Mullah. All present surprised.)

Zalim Oh, you liars! O, children of Satan! Where were

	you lost and how do you happen to be in this deceitful guise? You are the mischief-makers. Now tell me what you have to say?
Qazi	I can say nothing, your Majesty. We are doomed! We are doomed! The household of the Zenana has fled, and we are wrapped up in saris by force.
Zalim	I do not wish to see your blackened face anymore. And I do not wish to hear one word from you, for you are the mischief-makers who led me to this end. *(to the chief of the gang)* Paint their faces black, tie them alive to the feet of the mad elephant.

(They cry for forgiveness. The soldiers hush them up. Zalim Pasha in a rage, clenching his fists, and gnashing his teeth, goes out.)

ACT III

SCENE VII

Scene: Wilderness. Clouds gathered and darkness all around. Omar Khayyam sitting with Husna'ara on a rock. Omar Khayyam sings.

<u>Song:</u> Oh, my beloved, fill the cup that clears,
To-day[91] of past regrets and future fears.
To-morrow,[92] why to-morrow I may be
Myself with yesterday's sev'n thousand years.[93]

Lo, some we loved, the loveliest and[94] best,
That time and fate of all their vintage pressed.[95]

---

91. EF.: "TO-DAY" capitalised
92. EF.: "To-morrow?" question mark added
93. Quatrain XX
94. EF.: "the" added
95. EF.: "prest" instead of "pressed"

Have drunk their cup a round or two before,
And one by one crept silently to rest.[96]

(Husna'ara sings and pours wine into his glass)

Song: And we that now make merry in the room
They left, and summer dresses in new bloom
Ourselves must we beneath the couch of earth
Descend, ourselves to make a couch for whom[97]?

Oh[98], make the most of what we yet may spend
Before we too into the dust descend.
Dust into dust, and under dust to lie,
Sans wine, sans song, sans singer and sans end![99]

(As they sing this, it becomes darker still. Thunder and lightning.)

Husna'ara Oh, how frightened! What will happen? Is the jealous spirit around us, who always revolts at seeing lovers happily united?

Omar Khayyam No, perhaps insolence on my part to the supreme ideal of man's worship before whom constantly the angels bow.

Husna'ara Does this lightning show the wrath of God?

Omar Khayyam It is not wrath, but it is the reminder to the individual soul who when born said: "Lord", to God, the Soul of Souls.

Husna'ara *(looking up)* Oh, God, Lord of the Universe, we

96. Quatrain XXI
97. Quatrain XXII
98. EF.: "Ah" instead of "Oh"
99. Quatrain XXIII

bow to Thee. *(Taking the hand of Omar Khayyam and bowing with him)* Have mercy upon us. *(They sing a duet)*

<u>Song:</u> Here with a loaf of bread beneath the bough,
A flask of wine, a book of verse and thou
Singing beside me[100] in the wilderness
And wilderness is Paradise enow[101].

"How sweet is mortal sovereignty[102]!"
Think some[103]; others: - "How blessed the Paradise to come."
Ah, take the cash in hand and waive the rest;
Oh, the brave music of a distant drum[104]!

Oh, thou who did'st with pitfalls and with gin
Beset the road I was to wander in,
Thou wilt not with predestination round
Enmesh me, and impute my fall to sin?[105]

Oh thou who man of baser earth did'st make,
And who with Eden did'st devise the snake,
For all the sin wherewith the face of man
Is blackened, man's forgiveness give - and take[106]!

(As they sing, it becomes clearer. At the end of their singing a procession seems to be descending from the heavens. Procession of heavenly beings and a heavenly throne on which Khizr is seated. Music of procession. Procession dances. Throne stands still.)

<u>Song:</u> Great Allah has sent me from Heaven above
To crown you with glory and everlasting love.

---

100. EF.: "Beside me singing" instead of "Singing beside me"
101. Quatrain XI
102. EF.: "Sovranty!" instead of "sovereignty"
103. EF.: "- think some" comes after "sovereignty" instead of starting new line
104. Quatrain XII
105. Quatrain LVII
106. Quatrain LVIII

On these and they loved one, good Omar Khayyam
He sends perfect peace and his everlasting calm.

Thy words will be sung in the worlds evermore
And thee all the people on earth will adore.

The falseness of both mortal worlds thou hast seen,
By mercy of Allah thy sight is now[107] keen.
Jehovah thou seest in nature sublime.
Thy drinking of this wine can never be a crime.
Thy outlook on life's joy and sadness is vast.
The wine hath now washed all thy sins of the past.

(Omar Khayyam and Husna'ara amazed. Omar Khayyam recognises Khizr. Both bow their heads, while Khizr crowns them with the heavenly crown of love's glory. Ballet of the Fairies. Khizr sings, blessing them.)

---

107. St.tp.: "now is" instead of "is now"

RAMA[1]

Play by Pir-O-Murshid Inayat Khan,
written in Murshid's early years.

CHARACTERS

Janaka, father of Sita
Dasharatha, father of Rama and his brothers
Ravana, King of Ceylon
Karana, a rajah and suitor for the hand of Sita
Chief Priest at the Court of Janaka.
Vashishta, a holy man, tutor of Rama and Lakshman[2]
Rama) brothers, and sons of Dasharatha
Lakshman)
Bharat[3]) stepbrothers to Rama and sons of Dasharatha
Shatragan)
Hanuman, King of the Wild Men of the woods
Kumbhakarna, brother of Ravana
Ranee, Queen of Dasharatha, mother of Bharat[4] and Shatragan
A Lady in waiting to the Ranee
Sita, daughter of Janaka
Shabari, a wild woman of the woods
Maidens, holy men, rajahs and suitors, wedding guests, wild men of the woods, subjects of Hanuman

Scenes:
Scene 1 - Cottage of Vashishta, in a lonely and secluded place
Scene 2 - Great hall in the palace of Janaka

Documents:
Sk.tp. = a typescript made by Sakina Furnée.
Notes:
1. Sk.tp.: Added by hand
2. Sk.tp.: "Lakshuman" but then with u crossed out through majority of text, therefore Lakshman used throughout
3. Sk.tp.: "Bharata" with last "a" crossed out
4. Sk.tp.: "Bharata" but "Bharat" throughout rest of typescript

Scene 3 - Palace of Dasharatha, the queen's room
Scene 4 - Palace of Dasharatha, anteroom to the banqueting hall
Scene 5 - The forest
Scene 6 - The garden of Lanka, palace of Ravana in Ceylon
Scene 7 - Rama's camp before Lanka

SCENE I
Cottage of Vashishta on a hillside at the edge of a wood.

1. Vashishta alone; he has returned after a journey of some days. He speaks of the character of Rama, showing that he foresees his great career. He speaks also of the gentle character of Lakshman; describing also the training that he has given the two boys, which has all been with the definite aim of preparing Rama for the great future which he believes will be his.

2. After the soliloquy of Vashishta the two boys enter, they have been getting wood in the forest. They welcome Vashishta and show by their recital of what they have been doing the contrast in their characters.

3. Vashishta tells them that they will all three set out to the Court of Janaka to witness the betrothal ceremony of Sita within a few days. He tells them that the time has come when they must leave him to take their part in the world to which they belong. He describes to them Padmini, the ideal woman, which they will see in the form of Sita.

SCENE II
The great hall at the court of Janaka.
1. The king Janaka is discovered on his throne, surrounded by his holy men. Facing the throne is a gallery, where the maidens of Sita are chanting a bridal song, preparatory to the approach of Sita. Under the gallery are grouped the suitors in gorgeous array. In the centre of the room is the ancient bow.

2. Bridal song of the maidens which heralds Sita who enters and takes her place in the gallery. After she is seated, the chief priest welcomes the guests of Janaka, and invites the suitors to test their

strength by lifting the bow.

3. Karana steps forward, he replies to the priest, thanking Janaka in the name of all the guests for their presence at this great festival. He stoops to lift the bow, but is unable to move it. He calls on Ravana to make a trial.

4. Ravana, with a flourish of music, is beginning to greet the King. Dramatic interruption: Vashishta enters with the two boys, who cross the stage and take their place between the group of suitors and the wise men. Their simple and unassuming dress arouses the astonishment and contempt of the suitors, who laugh and do not conceal their scornful amusement. Ravana begins his interrupted greeting again. He stoops to lift the bow but is unable to.

5. Vashishta's song, he introduces the boys to the King and to the court. Sita leans over the balcony, listening attentively. Rama in silence steps out, lifts the bow, braces it, aims and hits the target.

6. As no other suitors come forward, Janaka announces that Sita may now make her choice. Sita descends from the balcony down into the middle of the room, and hangs the garland on Rama's neck.

7. The priest blesses the union, and all present join into the chorus, except Ravana who with great haughtiness withdraws.

SCENE III

Queen's room in the palace of Dasharatha.

The queen speaking to her confidante of the coming betrothal in honour of her stepson Rama and of Sita. She is consumed with jealousy and fear for her own sons, Bharat and Shatragan, now that Rama is married to the daughter of so powerful a king. The confidante urges her to remind Dasharatha of his vow made at the birth of Rama to God and to insist that it shall be carried out literally. The queen does not welcome the suggestion. At this point Dasharatha enters, describing to the queen the arrangements for the marriage feast, and the reception of Sita and Rama.

N.B. The vow made by the king at the birth of Rama, his eldest son, was that the boy should be dedicated to Heaven and should make a pilgrimage of 12 years duration on reaching manhood, and before ascending the throne.

SCENE IV

The anteroom to the banqueting hall. Sita and Rama are standing in mundapa under a canopy of flowers. The guests pass through to the feast, presenting gifts of all kinds to them. Lakshman stands near to Rama.

1. The king, Dasharatha, enters with the queen, full of joy at the sight of Rama and the beauty of Sita, he impulsively pours out blessings upon them and thanks to Heaven. The queen, stung by his words which seem to overlook and slight her own two sons who are beside her and are unnoticed by Dasharatha, reminds him suddenly of his vow; saying that if he keeps the words that he uttered at Rama's birth, that Rama should not be allowed to rest even one night in his palace.

2. There is a sudden silence. Rama has listened attentively, then turning to Sita he asks her permission to speak. She gently gives assent, and then he tells his father that he is ready to set out at once on his pilgrimage. He insists that he must go, it would be impossible for him to stay now in his palace.

3. Dasharatha in a broken way says that he will guard Sita with all a father's love in the palace. But Sita for the first time speaks, saying she will not be parted from Rama.

4. Lakshman steps up to his brother saying he will never forsake him. And the two stepbrothers join in, saying they will share Rama's exile.

5. The queen overcome with emotion, faints.

6. Dasharatha's lament of farewell. He speaks of the consolation and responsibility of children, of his despair at not being able to go instead of Rama on the journey, of his love of Rama.

SCENE V

Sita alone in the forest.

She sings, describing their journeyings and the tenderness to her of Rama. She speaks to fate, asking why fate is so changeable and uncertain. She prays heaven to be merciful to Rama. She plays with a little lizard on the rock. She calls to the birds, who listen as she speaks.

A Shabari, or woman of the woods, enters, with a quantity of fruit that she has gathered. She sees how weary Sita is and offers her the fruit. Sita gladly accepts, but refuses to eat, saying she must keep this fruit for Rama and his brothers who are away looking for a spring of water, and who will shortly return, doubtless footsore and weary. She gives the Shabari a necklace from her neck.

Then comes a pedlar who, seeing the fruit, asks Sita for it, saying he is hungry. She, a king's daughter, has never refused a gift to the poor and hungry, and gives though she would gladly have kept the fruit for Rama. As she hands the fruit, Ravana seizes her and lifts her away.

The evening approaches. Lakshman enters, he is surprised not to find Sita, sees the fruit, but though hungry does not eat. Bharat and Shatragan come in, they eat of the fruit. Night falls. Last enters Rama with Hanuman, laughing and full of joy. Hanuman knows the ways of the forest, where fruits grow and where springs of water are. Lakshman speaks gently to Rama of Sita. He hints that she may have been devoured by some wild beast. Bharat and Shatragan say they think she may have been too faint and weary to endure and that she may have returned to the village they passed the day before in order to try to return to her father's court. Hanuman says no beast can have touched her for there is no trail, but he sees the trail of a man. Rama shouts at once that it is Ravana who has taken her by force, and that it will be at his palace of Lanka that she will be found.
The Shabari comes in bringing more fruit for Sita and speaks to them of the lady whom she had seen, and of the fruits she had kept for Rama.

Rama breaks into lamentation. Hanuman promises to see if she is at

Lanka, and says he and his subjects will not rest till they can give Rama news of her. Everywhere where trees and gardens are, is the kingdom of Hanuman, who knowing all animals knows the secret ways to approach.

SCENE VI

Garden of Lanka.

A little summerhouse where Sita is. Ravana enters and sings to Sita; she makes no reply. He relates how quiet she was when he seized her and took her away, as if she were frozen and incapable of speech, so that he could not find it in his heart to treat her in any other way than with gentleness. He asks her to tell him if he has ever been other than gentle to her since she came to Lanka? She does not speak. He begs of her to speak and promises to lay everything at her feet if she will only show friendship to him. But she continues to be silent.

Ravana calls his brother Kumbhakarna (a fat and jolly person, fond of a pipe, and fond of a joke, a simple, good-natured fellow) and tells him to wander in the garden, and to keep guard over Sita, who he believes will soon be weary of her silence, and will change, and will respond to kindness and friendliness.

After Ravana is gone, Kumbhakarna waddles over to Sita, and speaks to her of the beauty of the golden palace of Lanka. He tries to be friendly and amusing; he cracks a joke or two; he shows her a precious jewel on his finger; he offers her a particular fine fruit from the garden. But she remains mute and despairing. He shrugs his shoulders, and waddles off, asking who could understand woman? Or who could understand his brother making so great to do about a woman; marvel of marvels, he thinks. He takes out his pipe, and settles down to a nap in the shade.

Hanuman enters stealthily, he comes close to Kumbhakarna, and sees that he is fast asleep. He imitates him, then he creeps close to the summerhouse, he swings himself up into a tree, and from there drops a note into Sita's lap. She reads the note, looks up, and sees Hanuman who whispers down to her. He climbs down and speaks to her of Rama. She hastily writes a note on a leaf, which she gives

Hanuman. As Hanuman rustles off Kumbhakarna awakes. He looks up to see if Sita is there, all is well, and he falls asleep again.

SCENE VII
Rama's camp before Lanka.
Rama, a general surrounded by his brothers. They have returned from the battle. Ravana is killed. The palace is surrounded and also the garden of Lanka. A number of wild men enter bearing Sita on a chair.

Hanuman enters with the general of Ravana's forces who surrenders to Rama, acknowledging him lord of Lanka.

Rama asks all honour to be paid to the body of Ravana.

They all disperse, and Rama relates to Sita how he set forth with Hanuman against Ravana.

SCENE I
Vashishta's cottage, in a lonely and sheltered spot, by a wood.

Vashistha enters. He has returned from a journey. He comes up to the cottage, and looking in, finds no one there.

Vashishta — Home again, and all empty within. *(he calls)* Rama! Lakshman! Rama! Rama! Alas I am too old for these journeys. One more I have to take, and that will be the last. *(he sits down)* But thanks be to Thee, my God, for the great task Thou gavest me - for the greater the responsibility the greater is the reward - Valmiki wrote of Rama - foretelling his great and glorious life - but to me, to me destiny gave the part of moulding this ideal, of guiding the boyhood of a hero who shall raise humanity! Thanks and thanks, and unending thanks to the omnipresent and omnipotent, who gave the teachable spirit and mind that is found in Rama. His is a heavenly spirit - and in his veins flows the blood of princes, children of the sun, the blood of Rughu Kula. Rama, he is the ideal, in him divinity shapes the hero; and Lakshman, as are the two eyes that make the sight, so are these two brothers, so harmonious, so loving. The braveness and courage of Rama, the gentleness and faithfulness of Lakshman, so blend and unite that a nucleus of human brotherhood is found in these two together. Rama, the first to see beauty, adventure, delight - the keenest to see, the first to do - poet and leader, fire and heart equally tempered in him.

I have taught them to swim, and how beautifully they do it; swordplay and to fence - and what skill they show in it; wrestling - whereby they have learned the place and function of sinews, muscles and bones and thus much of the art of healing; shooting with bow and arrow, they are practised in, and in riding, all princely sports. But with this the other side of life has not been forgotten, and grammar, poetry, law, philosophy and moral, in all we have studied deeply.

How often I am lost in clouds of amazement to see these youths, who in childhood swung in the ivory cradles of the palace of Dasharatha, where with every move a dozen attendants sprang to their bidding - so happy and content here in the forest - learning with ardour, patient in their fastings, and in these long vigils by night in the mountain which have given control of the body, poise of mind. What respect and affection they show me. I, a hermit sage, far removed from life's attachments, am won every moment by their affection and gentleness.

No task has it been, but a new life I have lived in their young lives since they were brought to me; and each day has been a fresh urge to me to do my part.[5]

(Enter Rama and Lakshman, carrying fishing rods)

Rama — Vandan Guru. When did you come? How good that you are back again.

(Vashishta puts both his hands on the shoulders of each in turn, pressing their shoulders in salutation)

Lakshman — It seemed a long time Guru, and lately we were expecting you every minute.

Vashishta — Yes, child, I was long in returning for I was detained by the rishis who are preparing the swamwar of Sita.

Rama — Swamwar, what is that Guru? And who is Sita? I seem to remember this name.

Vashishta — Swamwar, that ancient custom of the kings of our land, the festival that celebrates the day when a princess makes her choice of a mate. And now once more in India, kings and princes are coming to the palace of the great Janaka, so that Sita, his daughter, may honour the one she wishes to honour. Every king will come eager that the choice may fall on him. But that one for whom destiny has prepared this happiness will be crowned. The honour will be great, not only because Raja Janaka is great, his fame is great, his city is great, but Sita is the rare jewel of our land.

Lakshman — It will be a gathering worth seeing.

---

5. Sk.tp.: "Rama ...." added by hand

Vashishta	Yes child. A gathering of a king that takes place perhaps once in a 1000 years. It is a privilege even to be present at it. And I too have been asked to come, and will take you my sons with me.
Rama	What rareness, did you mean, in Sita, Guru?
Vashishta	Child, jewels are precious, but among even jewels are some that are rare. And so woman is fair, and fine and beautiful, but yet among women there is an ideal that is rare to find. All things are difficult to attain, power is difficult, fame difficult, name difficult. And still more difficult, is it to attain a queen among women. For woman completes man's life, makes it ideal.
Lakshman	Guru, what call you ideal in woman?
Vashishta	Children, this side of life's philosophy I have not as yet touched upon, for I waited for this moment. Woman in Vedanta is called ardhangi, that is one half of the whole man, completes in man what he lacks. Through her his life is coloured with grace and beauty. She raises his life from earth to heaven, she gives to his mortality immortality, that is if she be a padmini.
Rama	Padmini, what is she?
Vashishta	A beauty within and without. You may know her by gentle manner, her low sweet voice, her tender heart, her modest glance, her kind expression, her serene and peaceful ways. But most of all by her devotion. Fearless and true. There is for her but one ideal in life, which once seen by her, she never forgets, and with desperate sincerity she follows her chosen path. No thought of self, no fear of duty, her duty is her joy, the very essence

of her life, as she (adorns) as her chosen way, with beauty. That rarest treasure of all, a queen among women. *(Rama seems lost in thought)*

Lakshman — And when is this festival?

Vashishta — In three days time, and distant almost three days travelling. No time to lose my children. Tomorrow at dawn, before the sun has risen we must start. Early to bed my sons, and I to my prayer and meditation by the spring, where you, coming in the morning for your early plunge, may find me, and call me to a light repast, which you may prepare overnight.

(They pick up their fishing rods and go into the cottage. Vashishta stands watching them, then turns and goes slowly towards the wood)

TANSEN[1]

Written and produced by Inayat Khan

CHARACTERS

Akbar, Mogal Emperor of India
Birbal. Prime Minster
Tansen, a Singer
Ustad, Gous, a Sufi (Tansen's teacher)
Mira, maiden of Rajputana
Hira, her Maid
Navratan, the nine chief courtiers of Akbar

Document:
SM. = *The Sufi*, a Quarterly Magazine, I.2 April, 1916, 18-23.
Notes:
1. For Tansen, see List

ACT I

Scene: Akbar's durbar. Male and female singers are displaying their skill. Tansen, a peasant lad, enters amid the sneers and jeers of the royal assembly; he is presented to Akbar by the Birbal, and is commanded to sing. He immediately obeys, and the whole assembly are held spellbound on hearing his marvellous voice.

Akbar *(Looking from one to the other of the assembled courtiers)* How doth this singer please thee?

(Courtiers in chorus praise him in high words. Akbar then descends from his throne and approaches Tansen, giving him the "Khilat" of the Chief Singer, electing him as one of his Navratan)

Akbar *(addressing Tansen)* Who is thy Ustad, O gifted one? If thy singing be so wonderful, how much more miraculous must be that of thy Ustad?

Tansen Huzoor, my Ustad, is a Sufi who dwelleth in a cave of the Himalaya; he careth not for the world, and I become speechless when I try to describe the wonder of his voice, and how uplifting is his song.

Akbar Will he not come here and enchant me with his music?

Tansen Oh Khudawand, that would be impossible, my Ustad is too great to obey the command of a King.

Akbar What if I go to him?

Tansen Even then I am doubtful, Huzoor, his ascetic pride might revolt at the sight of a King.

Akbar Cannot I go to him disguised as your slave?

Tansen Banda Nawaz, this suggestion covereth me with confusion, but, indeed, this seemeth to be the only way.

(On the dismissal of the Court, Akbar takes Tansen with him to prepare for his journey to the Himalaya)

ACT II

Scene: A cave situated amidst the springs of the Himalaya. Akbar arrives at the cave, disguised as Tansen's servant leading his horse. They both bow low at the feet of the Ustad, who with outstretched hands blesses them. Tansen, with bent head and folded hands, humbly pours out the yearning of his heart, and touching the feet of Ustad, begs to be again blessed by hearing his most inspiring voice.

Ustad *(looking earnestly at Akbar)* I am aware of the presence of Akbar. Had he come before me in any other guise than that of a servant, my supreme ego would have refused to entertain him, but his humility melteth my heart and moveth me to satisfy his hunger.

(A profound silence reigns; presently an exalted sound like unto humming becomes audible. Then the voice of Ustad is heard singing Malkaus, upon which the mountain rills cease to flow, the blowing wind turns into a gentle breeze, the song of the birds is hushed, the animals of the jungle are spellbound, while Akbar and Tansen are lost in ecstasy. Towards the close of the song, Ustad levitates, and gradually becomes invisible to the human eye. On awakening from their ecstasy, Akbar and Tansen find that Ustad has vanished. They leave the cave in rapture and bewilderment. Akbar mounts his horse, and Tansen as his servant, leads it)

ACT III

Scene: Akbar's Zenana. Akbar is seen revelling in his Zenana. He is admiring the dance of the Nautch girls, and presently sends for Tansen, who immediately obeys his command, and arrives accompanied by his band of musicians.

Akbar *(addressing Tansen)* Sing us, O Tansen, some such song as did thy great Ustad.

(Tansen at once complies with his request. He sings to the great joy

of all present. Akbar alone remains unmoved)

Akbar Why canst thou not produce the same rapture as did thy Ustad?

Tansen *(embarrassed)* Huzoor, it is because I sing to thee, but my Ustad singeth to God.

Akbar Sing for us, O Tansen, Dipuc.

Tansen It has fire in it, therefore I beg thee have me excused.

Akbar Nay, show what miracle thy song can perform.

Tansen Takhsir, it ends in destruction.

Akbar Nevertheless, I would hear it.

(Tansen, invoking the name of his Ustad, "ya yons", commences to sing Dipuc. All the lamps hanging around are gradually ignited, and on the cheeks of the fair ones the light is reflected. The fire then is kindled in the heart of Tansen, and flames burst out from his body. He leaves the Zenana in flames saying)

Tansen Is this the assembly of the fair, or a feast prepared for the moth?

ACT IV

Scene: Udipur Marwar. A well situated at a short distance from the river bank. Tansen, in flames, arrives on the outskirts of Udipur. Women, bearing pitchers on their heads, are coming from the city to bathe in the river and to draw water from the well. Mira approaches with her maid. They first bathe, and then come to draw water. The maid fills the pitcher of Mira first. Tansen draws near to the well, and begs for some water. Mira takes pity on him, and pours some into his outstretched palms for him to drink. The maid, startled at seeing the flames coming out from his body, tries to draw her mistress away. Tansen beholds the beautiful Mira in silent wonder, and Mira seems as if she understands, and responds to his appeal.

Maid *(speaking hurriedly)* Madame, why dost thou tarry here, why doth this man burn, whence come these flames?

Mira *(with pity in her voice)* Alas! Poor man, he seemeth to be burnt by Dipuc.

Maid Canst thou not heal him with thy song of Malhar?

Mira He shineth like the sun; what can I, a poor maiden, do?

Maid Nevertheless, O Mira, if he shineth like the sun, thou beamest as the moon.

(Mira, embarassed, looks at Tansen, who seems to be lost in rapture at her vision. She at length consents to sing. Sitting down on the steps of the well, her arms encircling the neck of the maid, she sings Malhar. Tansen is won by her song, and listens in rapt attention. Then a miracle happens. Clouds gather, thunder crashes, and lightning flashes, and the rain commences to fall, and all the flames gradually become extinct. Tansen approaches near and gratefully addresses Mira)

Tansen Thou has saved my life; I have nothing to give, but my devoted heart is thine forever.

(Mira bashfully lowers her eyes, but at the same time seems to yield)

Maid *(approaches indignantly)* How dares he so address thee?

(Tansen approaches still nearer, and bends down to humbly touch her feet. Mira modestly prevents him. He then, holding her hands, kisses them and presses them to his breast. Mira, overcome with shyness, turns her face away. The maid, on seeing this, is startled, and moves away, calling for help.

In the meantime the citizens arrive, and see a stranger holding the hands of Mira, who is considered so remote and sacred by them all)

All those of her caste in turn say

What disgrace hast thou brought upon us all; it were better hadst thou died at thy birth than be so touched by an outcast.

(She covers her face with her arm, her maid holds her with one hand, and with the other indignantly points at Tansen. They all surround and threaten him. He defends himself. In the meantime others come with pikes to kill him. Mira, on seeing this, faints, and falls into the arms of her maid. At the same time the people sent by Akbar in pursuit of Tansen arrive. They rescue him, and repulse the would-be murderers. He is taken away, and Mira regains consciousness and is led away by her maid. All the people follow and deride her until she is lost to view)

ACT V

Scene: Dwarka. The Temple of Krishna. Mira is praying in the Temple of Krishna, having taken the vow of sanyas (the retired life of the Hindu). Tansen goes in search of her. He by chance approaches the Temple and finds there a sanyasini praying. He implores her for the love of God to show him by the aid of her mystic powers where he can find Mira.

Mira *(recognizing Tansen, closes her eyes for a moment, then speaks in a low toned voice)* Mira is dead!

Tansen *(heaving a deep sigh)* Life without Mira is as dross to me; I prefer therefore to die.

Mira How would thy death avail thee? Why not devote thy life to the service of thy originator to whom it belongs?

Tansen *(ponders over these words in silence, then again speaks)* What meanest thou by these words, O sanyasini?

Mira I would tell thee, O Tansen, that this life belongeth not to thee. By what right callest thou this self thine? Didst thou possess it before birth, and will it be thine when thou are no more?

Tansen Tell me then, O holy one, to whom this self belongeth, and for what purpose was I born.

Mira He to whom thou belongest possesses all things, and to fulfil His purpose wast thou born.

Tansen Was not I born for mine own satisfaction?

Mira Nay! If thou hadst been born for thine own satisfaction, then would Mira have been thine. But where thy will moveth an inch his moveth a mile.

Tansen *(deeply moved)* Guide me, O sanyasini, that I may fulfil His purpose, for henceforth will I no more live for myself!

Mira *(handing him the robe of an ascetic)* Come and adorn this garb of humility, may the rich ones of the world envy thy poverty, may life's grandeur kiss the feet of thy simplicity. Live for God, and live for ever. *(Tansen bows his head and Mira puts on him the robe and the rudraksha-mala, placing her hand on his shoulder in blessing)* Now art thou dead to the unrealities of life, but alive until the real and lasting. Mira is not far from thee, neither art thou separated from her. Raise thine eyes and behold, lo, here is Mira. The living dead thou could'st not have found hadst thou not been dead to mortal life.

(They greet each other after the manner of sages. In the meantime Akbar himself arrives; and Mira's relatives, hearing of her saintly life, come also to see her. A sacred celebration takes place; Mira sings Bhajan in which all present devoutly join)

AMEEN – THE FAITHFUL TRUSTEE[1]

by Inayat Khan

Foreign Expressions:

Sari — veil in which Eastern women are dressed
Bibi — title of a distinguished lady
Kouri — a weight
Diram)
Vazan) — money values
Dinar)
Kuskus — a children's game
To crack the hands against the cheeks — an Eastern way of greeting

---

Documents

Sk.tp =	a typescript made by Sakina Furnée, probably in preparation for publication
Tp.1 =	a typescript of unknown provenance on long paper, representing the final version of the play.
Tp.2 =	another typescript of unknown provenance, very similar to Tp.1
Fm.tp.=	a typescript prepared by Murshida Fazal Mai Egeling, with handwritten corrections and changes, some by Inayat Khan himself. Although probably earlier than Tp.1, it appears to have been a working copy, not a final version, marked for use in performance.

Notes:
1. Some earlier versions of the play have "Trusty", now considered archaic (or humourous)

CHARACTERS

Ameen, a boy of nine years in the first scene, twelve years in the second scene, twenty five years in the second act
Three boys, companions of Ameen
Halima, Ameen's foster-mother
Talib, Ameen's uncle
Mutal, Ameen's grandfather
Karima, Ameen's aunt, Talib's wife
Ali, Ameen's cousin, a little older than Ameen
Teja, a wealthy and distinguished lady, older than Ameen, whose business-manager he becomes; afterwards she marries Ameen
Johla, Teja's maid
Humadan, Teja's uncle, an old man
A Constable
The Chief
A Colleague
Four Companions of Ameen
Twelve Travellers
Two Inhabitants
A Shawl-seller
A Customer
A Swindler
A Fruit seller woman
A Boy
A Rich Man
A Slave-seller
Three Slave Girls
A Dancing Girl
Two Accompanists
A Medium
A Young Man
A Woman in Mourning
A Palmist
A Young Man
A Beggar
A Man
A Young Woman
A Wayfarer

Two Priests
A Police Officer
A Soldier
A Maid of One of Teja's Relatives
A Woman Artist
Two Men with Gifts
Dancing Girls
Musicians
An Envoy from Hijas
A Crowd
The Sheriff of Mecca
Four Authorities

ACT I

SCENE I

Scene: Peasant-house[2] in a village of Arabia. Ameen looking after the farm, petting and stroking[3] his lamb.

Ameen — My little fellow, you feel drowsy today, don't you? I will give you a bath in the little pool of water, and then[4] I must take you in the sun, so that you will feel cheerful.

(Enter several boys)

1st Boy — What are you doing, Ameen? Always busy with the home and farm, isn't he? We have come to play a game today; now what shall we play?

2nd Boy — Yes, let us play kuskus.

---

2. Fm.tp.: "House of a peasant" instead of "Peasant-house"
3. Fm.tp.: "and stroking" missing
4. Fm.tp.: "I will give you a bath in the little pool of water, and then" missing

(Boys play, Ameen leading. One boy pushes another, he falls down. The other hits him back. Ameen comes and brings about reconciliation between them. They continue the game. After the play is finished they rest, sitting on blocks of wood)

3rd Boy — Do you know, Ameen, what[5] great fun we had on our way while coming here? There was a camel loaded with dates. We made a hole in the sack and took out a lot of dates. See, we all have our pockets full. Would you like to have some?

(Ameen smiles)

1st Boy — I'm sure you would, take some!

Ameen — No, I will not take any.

2nd Boy — Why, don't you like them?

Ameen — Yes, I like dates, but I do not like this way of taking them. It is not fair.

2nd Boy — Fair! Ha! Ha! Ha! Ha![6] *(all the boys laugh)* What is fair and unfair in these few dates? You are a funny fellow, Ameen.

3rd Boy — Do you know, Ameen, we have planned to go to the town today to have a jolly good time.

Ameen — I am sorry, I cannot come with you today. Halima has been out since morning, and she has left me the care of the farm. So you see I cannot come.

1st Boy — Why must you be tied at home because Halima said so? My mother this morning would not let me go, but do you think I could be detained by her? I simply

---

5. Fm.tp.: "a" instead of "what"
6. Fm.tp.: "ah! ah! ah!" instead of "Ha! Ha! Ha! Ha!"

told her, I must go. She grumbled a while, and then quieted down by herself. Why can't you do the same? Halima is not your mother.

Ameen — Halima is my foster-mother, and I must listen to her as I would[7] to my own mother. Besides, I am entrusted with the home; therefore I will not leave my charge.

2nd Boy — Well, then we are going, that's all; please yourself! *(Exit boys)*

(Ameen engages himself with domestic duties. Enter Halima)

Halima — My darling sweetheart, what have you been doing?[8] I am so sorry I was detained in [9]town, Ameen; there was such a crowd today at the market; I tried to hurry, but I could not get back soon. Look what I have brought. *(Showing, taking out her basket tomatoes, pineapple and sugar-canes)*[10] You did not go with your playmates[11] today?

Ameen — They had come to fetch me, but I could not go as you had asked me to look after the farm.[12]

(Halima kisses his forehead)

Halima — My darling, it is so sweet of you to think of your Halima[13]. *(Halima sighs deeply, raising her head,*

---

7. Tp. 1: "listen" added
8. Fm.tp.: "are you still looking after the farm—I had thought so!" instead of "what have you been doing?"
9. Fm.tp.: "the" added
10. Fm.tp.: "Look what I have bought. (Showing, taking out her basket tomatoes, pineapple and sugar-canes.)" missing
11. Fm.tp.: "playmate" instead of "playmates"
12. Fm.tp.: "I refused to leave home, left in my care, to go with them." instead of "but I could not go as you had asked me to look after the farm."
13. Fm.tp.: "so" added

then looking down) Bless his mother.[14]

Ameen — *(speaks in a broken voice)* Halima, where has my mother gone? Shall I see her again? *(Halima is silent for a moment)* Do they ever[15] come here again, who have passed away, or do they never return? What is death, Halima? It always puzzles me. Why do people die? Because they are ill, or because they are called away? Are they always lost to the world? Can anyone see them? I would so much like to see mother!

Halima — *(in tears)* Your father was called away first, my darling, even before you were born. It was afterwards that your mother followed him to heaven, peace be on her! How delighted would your father have been to see you now, if he were alive; and how much your mother would have rejoiced to watch you grow, sweetheart; it tears my heart to think of it.

Ameen — *(sad, looking down)* But what can one do to find those one has lost, Halima? Is there any way of meeting them?

Halima — They say, those we love are never away, even if they have gone to the other side of life. Those who really love must some day meet again, even if it be after death. Life is a mystery, my darling child, one cannot say much about these matters. You are yet too young to think of such things. You will know when the time comes.

Ameen — When will that time come, Halima? I would so much like to know all these things.

Halima — It won't be long, my child. When one thinks how

---

14. Fm.tp.: "Bless his mother." missing
15. Fm.tp.: "never" instead of "ever"

quickly the days pass, years slip by before we look at them. One day you will be grown up, and will think out things as every thoughtful man does[16]. It is only a matter of time. Now go and take a round in the farm; see if everything is in order.

(Ameen goes, Halima sits down[17])

Halima — What a privilege it is for me to bring up this orphan. What trust his mother, peace be upon her, gave me. But it is a responsibility, a great responsibility, to bring up this child who is unlike to anyone.[18]

(Talib enters)

Talib — Here I am, Halima. Did you send for me?

Halima — Yes, Talib, come in, sit comfortably.

Talib — It is long indeed since I saw you last. How are you getting on? Nicely, Halima?

Halima — No woman on earth could be as[19] privileged as I am, having charge of this darling child. No boy have I ever seen or known like Ameen, your nephew, bless him! He is so affectionate and tender, so thoughtful and considerate, that never a cross word have I heard from him. At moments I have been impatient with him, but he never talked back to me. He is most affectionate to the children of his age, gentle with all who come here; he has [20]regard for the elders. Young as he is, he thinks like a person advanced in age. Indeed he is an old soul. His feelings are deep and yet he is so innocent that I most often notice in

16. Fm.tp.: "thinks" instead of "does"
17. Fm.tp.: "sets [sic] in despair" instead of "sits down"
18. Fm.tp.: this speech missing
19. Fm.tp.: "so" instead of "as"
20. Fm.tp.: "a" added

him something of his babyhood. I cannot always understand him. Most of the time he is nearer to me than my own heart, and at times he seems to be so far away in the cloud, that I cannot reach him. He is always a mystery to me. Yet he has an acute sense of humour, he is quick to see the funny side of things. He is often energetic and lively. To have him in the home is the greatest joy to me. He helps me to forget life's woes, making my life's burden easy for me to bear.

Talib — Where is Ameen? Please call him.[21]

(Halima leads Ameen to his uncle)

Halima — Do you know who this is, my darling? This is Talib, your uncle. Your mother's last wish was that you should be given into[22] his care. *(to Talib)* This is the treasure that was entrusted to me. Now I give him into[23] your arms, as it was his mother's wish that he should be brought up under your parental care. *(crying)* I don't know what will become of me when he is gone!

(Talib holds Ameen's hands and looks at him)

Talib — Well son, are you willing to come with me? [24]Your aunt is eagerly waiting for you at home, and your grandfather has longed to see you ever since you were born. And then, there is your cousin, who will be so happy to have you as his playmate.[24]

(Halima embraces the child and cries. Talib takes his hands)[25]

---

21. Fm.tp.: this speech omitted
22. Fm.tp.: "under" instead of "into"
23. Fm.tp.: "in" instead of "into"
24. Fm.tp.: "I am sure you will find a good playmate in your cousin at home." instead of "Your aunt is eagerly ... to have you as his playmate."
25. Fm.tp.: this stage instruction omitted

Halima I give this trust to you. *(Turning to Ameen)*[26] God be your protection, my darling child[27].

ACT I

SCENE II

Scene: House of Talib. Talib's wife is[28] *sewing. Mutal*[29]*, his father*[30]*, smoking a water-pipe*

Mutal Ameen is so quiet that it does not seem that another boy has come[31] to live in the house. His influence seems to make even Ali quieter[32].

Karima Though he is so quiet, it seems he has brought [33]sunshine into[34] our home. In spite of his quietness there is something lively in him, which makes Ali more bright than he has ever been. No wonder his mother had many wonderful dreams previous to the time he was born, giving good tidings. Now that I see him, I begin to see the meaning of her visions, significant in his unfoldment.

Mutal His father, peace be[35] on him, he was simple and yet so intelligent that he was a glow of which Ameen is a blaze. How do they get on? Do the boys get on well together?

Karima Father, since Ameen has come, Ali has become

---

26. Fm.tp.: this stage instruction omitted
27. Fm.tp.: ", my darling child" omitted
28. Sk.tp., Fm.tp.: "is" omitted
29. Fm.tp.: here and sometimes later in the scene, "Sharif" instead of "Mutal"
30. Fm.tp.: "grandfather" instead of "father"
31. Fm.tp.: "there has come another boy" instead of "another boy has come"
32. Fm.tp.: "quiet" instead of "quieter"
33. Fm.tp.: "a" added
34. Fm.tp.: "in" instead of "into"
35. Fm.tp.: "be peace" instead of "peace be"

	quite different. Ali follows every turn that Ameen takes. Ali seems to be so much more thoughtful and happy since the coming of Ameen. They seem to blend with one another as sugar and milk.
Mutal	Ameen with all his gentleness is steady and firm, and so Ali, however energetic, responds to his influence.
Karima	Father, it is interesting to watch them both grow fond of one another, every day more and more.

(Ali enters with a lot of leaves[36])

Ali	*(to Karima[37])* I have found these leaves after all, I had to go far in the forest to fetch them, but I wouldn't have come without having got them!
Karima	Child, you must no go far into the woods. Very often one meets there with [38]wild animals[39].
Ali	I am not afraid of wild animals. I would fight if I met any.

(Mutal laughs. Ali occupies himself with the leaves. Ameen enters)

Karima	Where have you been, Ameen?
Ameen	I was learning. I have learned many words today. I like very much to learn to speak better. *(to Ali)* What are you doing, Ali?
Ali	I am preparing wreaths for the gods of Ka'ba, for

36. Fm.tp.: "and says" added
37. Fm.tp.: here and sometimes later in the scene, "Hasina" instead of "Karima"
38. Fm.tp.: "the" added
39. Fm.tp.: the typescript is marked to move "there" to the end of the sentence, and eliminate "with", but these changes do not appear in later typescripts

there are very few days left before we shall have the annual celebration of our gods.

Ameen — I do not like to call these idols of stone gods, Ali. I don't know why I have never liked all they make of stone gods. I cannot enjoy the feasts. It all seems to me foolish.

Ali — You must not say so, Ameen. If Father hears it, he will not like it. Grandfather many times told[40] me that we must regard with reverence the gods of Ka'ba.

Ameen — I don't know, Ali, why I feel like this, but I can never feel sympathetic towards these hideous gods, and I get a kind of revolt against all that is made of them. I sometimes feel like breaking them into pieces. I cannot understand why people go crazy about them by hundreds and thousands.

Ali — I cannot understand either, Ameen, but it[41] is our religion, we must not say anything against it.

Ameen — I tell you, Ali, I cannot follow such a religion; it only amuses me, it is all so funny. *(Ali laughs)*

Mutal — What's the joke, boys?

Ali — Ameen is wondering about the religious festivities; they amuse him.

Ameen — Yes, I don't feel interested in all they make of the stone gods; it all seems to me so childish. People could as well choose to do something else. I should think there is much to be done.

---

40. Fm.tp.: "often said to" instead of "many times told"
41. Fm.tp.: "that" instead of "it"

Mutal It is a custom, child, our people have observed for ages.

Ameen Has this custom always been among [42]people, grandfather?

Mutal No doubt, in the beginning the stone of Kaaba was set there by our ancestor Abraham, when he was returning from Egypt, after his initiation into the ancient mysteries. He has set here[43] this stone as a token of his initiation, making it a centre of pilgrimage for the children of Beni Israel. The line of our family, son, is traced back to Ishmael. Neither Abraham nor his son Ishmael worshipped the idols of many gods. It was afterwards, I suppose, in order to draw more people to Ka'ba, that these idols were placed there. However, since a long time this has become the religion of our people; they expect to see in Ka'ba the gods of their families. If it were not for these festivities, there would be left[44] no interest in our religion.

Ameen What is meant by religion, grandfather? Is it not a faith rather than a form?

Mutal It is a most difficult question to answer, my son. Besides, you are yet too young to think about these subjects. There is so little one can say in these matters, and the less said, the better it is.

(Talib enters)

Talib *(to Ali)* Please, Ali, go and tell the man to make the camel ready or me to start on my journey.

---

42. Fm.tp., tp.1, Sk.tp.: "our" added
43. Fm.tp.: "here" appears after "this stone"
44. Fm.tp.: the tp. is marked to move "left" to after "no interest", but this change does not appear in later versions

(Ali goes)

Talib — *(to Ameen, resting his hand on his shoulder)* I am going on a long journey to Syria, on business, Ameen [45].

Ameen — I will come with you[46].

Talib — I would not think for a moment of taking you with me, my son, for it is a long journey; miles of land in the desert to be crossed, all sorts of hardships one goes through, and one meets with many dangers on the way.

Ameen — *(embracing his uncle)* Uncle, dear, please take me with you on your journey. I do wish to travel. I do not mind what difficulties I may have to experience on the way.

Talib — *(looks at Ameen's eager face for a moment)* I will take you, my child, go and get ready. *(Karima takes Ameen to prepare and brings him back. Ameen and Talib bid goodbye to all present, and depart[47])*

---

45. Fm.tp.: "Now you will stay here." added
46. Fm.tp.: "to Syria" added
47. Fm.tp.: "while Talib promises to take Ali on the next journey" added

ACT I

SCENE III

Scene : [48]*A bazaar at Jerusalem. A shawl-seller bargaining with his customer. A swindler putting his hand into the pocket of the man who is busy purchasing. Customer examines the structure of the cloth in his hands.*

Seller — It is four dirams a yard. *(customer throws the cloth at him and goes away. The seller follows him, pulling his robe)* Two dirams, two dirams a yard.

Customer — No, no. No, no.

Seller — All right, one diram, take it.

Customer — *(takes the cloth, puts his hand in his pocket)* Someone has taken my money. Police, police!

(An old fruit seller woman walking with a basketful of fruit under her arm)

A Boy — *(to fruit seller woman)* How much for a kouri ?

Woman — One vazan.

Boy — Too dear, too dear! Are these sweet cherries?

Woman — Sweet as sugar.

---

48. Fm.tp.: most of this scene is indicated only by the following stage direction: ""A bazaar at Jerusalem. Shops of all kinds. Pedlars moving around to sell their goods. Woman dancers in the street, players of instruments accompanying them. Spiritualists promising to get rewards for the dead. Fortune-tellers carrying on business. Swindlers at work. Lighthearted young men busy making merry. Poverty stricken ragged people walking through the bazaar. Rich persons buying slaves. Evil in religious [places added in hw.]. Officers oppressing, no notice taken of the oppressed. Bribery going on. Ameen with Talib passing through the bazaar, halting at every step, observing keenly the degenerate condition of the place."

(Boy puts his hand into the basket, takes one and puts it in his mouth. Woman looking at him with disgust. The boy puts his hand again into the basket. The woman pushes his hand off. The boy upsets the basket, and all the fruit falls on the ground. Other street boys come and seize upon them. A dancing girl comes, scantily dressed, with accompanists. The crowd follows her and gathers around. Her violinist pushes the crowd back with his bow, making space for the dance. One fighting with him, not willing to be pushed back. The violinist showing as if he would strike him with his violin. The man lifting a stone to throw at him. Many clapping their hands to the rhythm of the dance. The accompanist singing, people merrymaking. At the finish of the dance many throw kisses to the girl. A medium standing in concentration with closed eyes by the side of a mosque)

A Woman — I beg you, I pray you, will you communicate with my daughter, and tell her that from the moment she has died food and drink have become as poison to me. I weep all day and I am sleepless at night. I would like to know how she is over there. Is she happy?

Medium — *(moves his head round and round, raising the pupils of his eyes upwards)* I see, I see, I see your daughter. O, she is happy, more happy than she has ever been.

Woman — Do you see? I am so glad. Please ask her, is there anything she is in need of?

Medium — She has everything she wants there. But she is attached to all the beautiful clothes and jewelry she had here, and she wants all that over there.

Woman — O, I would be willing to give anything, anything, if I only knew how to send it there.

Medium — I will take things for you if you want me to, when I go there at night; you have only to bring them to me. *(the woman goes)*

(A young man enters)

Young man *(to medium)* I had a dream that my father who has recently died, is not happy in heaven.

Medium Wait, I will write a letter to the keeper of the heavens.

Young man Please.

Medium *(writing a letter. Then reads)* "Brother Israel, the father of this young man, Faruk ibn Kalil, died on the 5th of Ramadan, and is now in your world. Give him two trees of plums and one tree of pears, a tank of honey, and a fountain of milk, with ample bread and meat." *(to young man)* Now what will you pay?

Young man Five dinar.

Medium No, that is not enough for all this I have asked in my letter.

Young man I have only ten dinar.

Medium Well, then I will take off two trees from this letter.

(The young man gives the dinars. The medium seals the letter with his thumb, licking it and pressing it on the paper, winking one eye when sealing it. The woman returns with a box of jewellery and a sack of beautiful clothes. Hands them over to the medium)

Woman I have brought in this, not only my daughter's jewels and clothes, but all I had, that you will take them from me to my daughter. I want her to be happy. I am so thankful to you for all you will do for me.

(A palmist sitting with his astrological chart spread over his lap)

Palmist *(to young man)* Come here. *(the young man comes near)* Sit down. Show me your hand. *(pointing with his finger in his palm)* Very distinct long line of fortune, but you will not get it yet. And here. *(points on thumb)* A beautiful wife, but there will always be a quarrel in the house. *(looks in centre)* Some relative will leave great wealth for you. But you will have a hard time in getting it.

Young man But tell me, shall I have good luck in the business I am going to start today?

Palmist Put here five diram. *(the young man does it)* There are some planetary influences standing in opposition to your work, but I will make things right for you.

(A young woman moving about through the crowd, covering her face from a gay wayfarer, looking at him from the corner of her eyes)

Wayfarer *(pulling away the sari from her face)* One, just make it one. *(she looks annoyed. He kisses her and walks away. A beggar, scantily dresses, with patched sleeves, with a tin pot in his hands)* Please one penny; be ye well.

A man Go further!

(A woman selling three slave-girls. A man richly dressed, with his conpanion. Examines the slaves)

Man How much?

Woman *(shows "ten" on her fingers. He shows "five")* Ten, ten. *(he gives ten dinar, takes the slave-girl along with him)*

(Two drunken priests enter)

1st Priest How many prayers did you say this morning?

2nd Priest I said only one prayer, because he did not bring me more than one bottle of liquor. I say only one prayer each bottle.

1st Priest That is why you are always drunken.

2nd Priest You are crazy.

1st Priest You are mad. *(they fight with fists. Police officer takes them both. The 1st priest gives the police officer a purse)* Let me go, let me go!

Police Officer *(changes his attitude, bows to the priest who gave him the money)* High priest! *(goes away with the other one)*

(Ameen with Talib passing through the bazaar, halting at every step, observing keenly the degenerate condition of the place)

[49]Ameen Uncle, does no one tell these people to act differently? Have they always been like this? This life does not interest me; there is something in it which does not seem to me to be right. Have they never been told to do better?

Talib Child, in this world one cannot expect things to be better than they are. People have been taught the way of righteousness by the great souls who have come time after time to guide the children of the earth. But when some years pass, and the real way is forgotten, then a period of disintegration comes, and people become degenerate. It is sad to think that human beings should fall beneath the level of[50]

49. Fm.tp.: the text of this scene begins here
50. Sk.tp.: "the" added

animals; and yet there is nothing to be surprised at[51], for man can rise higher than an angel and fall lower than a[52] devil. As it is said[53], "When a glimpse of Our Image is caught in man, when Heaven and earth are sought in man, then what is there in the world that is not in man? If one only explores him, there is a lot in man."[54]

Ameen — But what is this that one dislikes in them, is an evil? Then what[55] does it differ from good.

Talib — Good and evil are relative terms, my son. Evil is nothing but the[56] lack of good. Nevertheless, good is real and evil is its shadow. When one believes this, and tries to bring out in another the good there is in him, one finds that no soul, however wicked, is void of goodness. To understand all is to forgive all.[57]

(Ameen[58] deeply impressed by all he sees at the bazaar and by all his uncle says)

---

51. Fm.tp.: "there is nothing to be surprised at" crossed out, and "it is not surprising" written by hand, but this change is not reflected in later versions
52. Fm.tp., tp.1, Sk.tp.: "the" instead of "a"
53. Fm.tp.: "A poet says" instead of "As it is said"
54. The quotation is from Inayat Khan's own book of sayings, *Gayan*, where it is the first saying. See *Complete Works of Pir-o-Murshid Hazrat Inayat Khan*, Sayings I (1982, 1989), p. 1.
55. Fm.tp., tp.1: "where" instead of "what"
56. Fm.tp.: "a" instead of "the"
57. The usual rendering into English of Mme de Staël's "Tout comprendre rend très-indulgent" from *Corinne*
58. Fm.tp.: "is" added

ACT II

SCENE I

Scene : Drawing room of Teja's house

Johla — Bibi[1], I beg your pardon, tell me why for some time I have noticed you don't seem to be altogether here. You seem to be somewhere else. You don't mind me asking this; but as I feel sad with you, I would like to know what is the matter. Excuse me for asking you.

Teja — Yes, you are right, Johla. My mind has been in such a condition, I am sorry to say, that I could not very well manage to conceal my feelings. I am not surprised that you have observed the change. There is nothing in my life to make me sad. As you know, I have been blessed by providence, I am thankful to say, yet I have had a feeling of loneliness, particularly of late. I had[2] tried to get over this feeling, but I cannot always manage it. Knowing how false human nature is, I preferred to live alone, and the independence I experienced in life has taken the place of a companion. Only since I have seen this young nephew of Talib, who has just returned from Syria, I am in a sort of maze, I don't know where I am. He strikes me as a most promising young man, and he inspires one with trust, for his appearance says that he is honest. He seems to be so tender-hearted, and has such a refined way that one cannot but love him.

---

1. Fm.tp.: throughout this tp, "Bébé" instead of "Bibi"
2. Tp.1: "had" altered to "have" by hand

Johla [3]Now I remember Bibi; it is[4] since the time he came you've been like this. If any man would make me so miserable, I would give him a good shaking! I would not allow anyone in the world to make my life wretched!

Teja Don't talk nonsense! You must learn to keep your lips closed. Listen. I have engaged him to attend to my business affairs. But oh! It is not business that I care for. It is he.

(Teja moves restlessly)

Johla Bibi, do you know, the neighbours' cook was drunk last night, and he fought with his wife until she put him out of the house. Ha! ha! ha! ha![5] He was lying there in the street swearing at her all night long. He! he! he! he![6]

Teja I don't feel like hearing your funny stories, silly!

Johla Bibi, if you have a fortune, every man will bow his head before you. [7]Do not be sad over nothing!

Teja No fortune can be compared to a truly worthy man!

Johla May I bring you the cat for you to amuse yourself with? Last night it played and played with me until it tore my apron. Where is my darling pet? *(stands looking around the room)* Puss, puss, puss, puss![8]

Teja Please Johla, leave me alone! Go and play with your kitten! *(holds her head in her hand. Johla retires,*

3. Fm.tp.: "Oh" added by hand
4. Fm.tp.: "ever" added by hand
5. Fm.tp.: "ah! ah! ah!" instead of "Ha! ha! ha! ha!"
6. Fm.tp.: "eh! eh! eh!" instead of "He! he! he! he!"
7. Fm.tp.: "So" added by hand
8. Fm.tp.: "puss" repeated three times instead of four

muttering)

Johla I would not let any man cause me a headache! Puss, puss, puss, where has he[9] gone?

(Exit Johla)

Teja *(goes to the window, looks out)* I wonder what day it is today. *(walks restlessly about the room)* Is this the last of the month? *(looks from the window again)* Lo, it's[10] the new moon! Will Heaven grant me my star, I wonder! *(comes back from the window)* I don't know if he has the slightest thought of the feeling I have for him. He seems[11] so shy and reserved that all the time he sat before me, his eyes were cast down, and there was an innocent expression on his face, showing that he was not at all conscious of a woman's presence.

(Knock heard at the door. Johla comes in, running)

Johla Bibi! Bibi! The young man [12]about whom you have been talking to me has come. Shall I tell him, Bibi is busy just now, to come some other time? *(winks)*

Teja No! No! Bring him in after a moment. I will soon be ready.

(Exit Johla. Teja throws a[13] veil over her face. Enter Ameen. Bows)

Teja I was just wondering if you had arrived here[14].

---

9. Fm.tp.: "it" typed instead of "he", then changed by hand to "that cat"
10. Fm.tp.: "it is" instead of "it's"
11. Fm.tp.: "seemed" instead of "seems"
12. Fm.tp.: "The young man has come. Teja." " Which ['one' added by hand]?" Johla. "The same young man about whom you have been talking to me." instead of "about whom you have been talking to me has come."
13. Fm.tp.: "her" instead of "a", crossed out by hand
14. Fm.tp.: "this day" added

Somehow or other I felt that you must be coming today. I hope all went well with you in your journey?

Ameen Yes, Bibi. It seemed as though every person and every condition was favourable to me; all went well with our business. I have carried out the affair according to your instructions, and at the same time to the mutual advantage of all. Therefore the other party is pleased also.

Teja I am sure[15], everything you undertake[16] must succeed.

Ameen Bibi, I should think everyone would succeed in business, if they knew the key of the secret. That key is fairness in dealing[17].

Teja I have no doubt about it. And you are in the most honest person I have ever had to carry out my business.

Ameen Bibi, I will try to come up to your expectations. Please do not think too well of me yet, for you don't know me and my work. I only hope I shall not disappoint you.

Teja No, I cannot think for a moment that you could be other than I know you to be. No soul in the world have I ever seen who has won my confidence to the extent that you have. I cannot doubt even if I wanted to. Besides, you will[18] not disappoint me, even if you did not carry out the business profitably, for I do not give more importance to the qualifications

---

15. Fm.tp.: "had no doubt about it" instead of "am sure"
16. Fm.tp.: "I am sure" added
17. Tp.1, Sk.tp.: "dealings" instead of "dealing"
18. Fm.tp., Sk.tp.: "will" changed by hand to "would"

than to the person. In you I see the person who is more precious than the wealth of this earth.

Ameen — Bibi, I have no words to express my gratitude[19] to you for so kind an appreciation of me. I'm not yet at all worthy of it.

Teja — Please take a seat, Ameen, and be comfortable. You must be tired after your journey. I must not[20] keep my face veiled before you, for you seem no longer a stranger.

(Ameen takes a seat close to Teja)

Teja — I am thankful, Ameen, that you were brought to me. *(puts her hand on the arm of his chair)*

Ameen — Pardon, Bibi, would you allow me to make clear to you the details of the affair which I have attended to for you?

Teja — No, Ameen, you do not need to. I'm quite satisfied as you know it[21]. I would like to hear something of your personal[22] life.

Ameen — My personal[22] life? There's not much about it. I was the only son of my father, who passed away before I was born, and my mother followed him after giving me birth. I was left with Halima, my foster-mother, who then gave me in charge of my uncle. I never allowed myself to feel [23]an orphan, for I always had a natural[24] leaning on the maker of this world, in

---

19. Fm.tp.: "joy" instead of "gratitude", later crossed out and "gratitude" written by hand
20. Tp.1: "not" missing, added by hand
21. Sk.tp., Fm.tp.: "it" omitted
22. Fm.tp. tp.1: "personal" omitted
23. Fm.tp.: "as" added, later crossed out by hand
24. Tp.1: "naturally" typed, but "-ly" crossed out

whom I saw my mother and father both. The first journey I made was to Syria. I accompanied there[25] my uncle in his business. That was a great privilege to me to become acquainted with the various aspects of life in the world. Though I am most thankful to have seen it all, yet it has left on[26] my mind an impression[27] of sadness, which I cannot easily[28] forget.

Teja — What did you see that made you sad, Ameen?

Ameen — It was[29] the falseness of human nature, playing its different roles under many and varied conditions. By this I do not mean to say I am exempt from it, but it only brought to my sight my own infirmities.

Teja — *(touches Ameen's hand)* No, I do not see in you any infirmities. You seem to be far, far away from them. If all men were like you, the world would be quite different. But when you said, "It left on me an impression[28] of sadness," what I thought was, a tender spot on your heart being kept alive by the continual memory of someone perhaps[30] you loved there[31].

Ameen — No, I never as yet allowed my mind to dwell on that subject.

Teja — Do you mean to say you have determined[32] to keep

---

25. Fm.tp.: "there" marked to move to after "my uncle", but this change is not reflected in later versions
26. Tp.1: "on" added by hand
27. Fm.tp.: "a mark" instead of "an impression", later changed by hand to "an impression"
28. Fm.tp.: "always" changed by hand to "easily"
29. Sk.tp.: "is" instead of "was"
30. Tp.1: "perhaps" omitted
31. Fm.tp.: typescript marked to move "there" to after "alive" and to reverse order of "perhaps you" to "you perhaps", although these changes are not reflected in later versions
32. Fm.tp.: "detained" changed by hand to "determined"

your heart free from the love of a woman?

Ameen — No, Bibi, I only meant that I have not so far allowed myself to think on the subject.

Teja — Why did you not think on the subject? Do you consider it a sin?

Ameen — In the first place, I began life as an orphan, and then felt the weight of every act of kindness done to me[33]; and it continually kept me engaged in[34] thinking how I could return my obligations to those relatives and friends, to those near and dear to me, who have[35] done acts of kindness to me[36]. This thought has continually occupied my mind and has never allowed me to think on any other subject. Besides, the poverty of the people in this country takes away every possibility of doing anything for oneself. Frankly speaking, my state is as the saying goes, "Qazi, why are you so thin?" The Qazi said, "The anxiety about my citizens." Yet I am not without hope, it is only a matter of time.

Teja — Ameen, you are dear; the more you speak to me, the more I feel I am won by you. For every word you say goes through my heart. I think it is because you are so sincere. My engaging you to attend to my business was the first step; now I feel as if you are engaged to my soul.

(Teja gives him her hand, he kisses it and holds it next to his heart, his eyes cast down in modesty. Knock heard. Enter Johla. She looks surprised. Teja and Ameen separate)

---

33. Fm.tp.: "by anybody" added, changed by hand to "by others"
34. Fm.tp.: "engaged in" crossed out by hand
35. Fm.tp.: "had" instead of "have"
36. Fm.tp.: "done acts of kindness to me" changed by hand to "been kind to me", but this changes does not appear in later versions

Johla I beg you pardon for having entered without knocking. Why am I so forgetful! Bibi, there is a young soldier who wishes to see [37]Ameen

Ameen May I take your leave and see what he wants[38]?

Teja Call him[39] here; I will go in[40] my room for a moment.

(Exit Teja and Johla. Enter soldier)

Soldier I have come to tell you from the Ministry of War[41] that there is a sudden call to arms. The young men of the country are expected to defend their land against the[42] invasion of a mighty enemy, who is already approaching with his troops the gate of our town[43]. It is the wish of many in charge of affairs that you should take the lead of the army for the defence[44] of our country.

Ameen Please thank them all. I feel most privileged to take charge of our troops, and nothing would please me more than to render this service to my country, even if it were at the cost of my life.

(The soldier salutes, and departs. Enter Teja, who appears nervous)

Teja What did the soldier come to tell you?

Ameen Bibi, our country is being invaded by a mighty

---

37. Fm.tp.: "immediately" added
38. Fm.tp.: "says" instead of "wants"
39. Fm.tp.: "in" added by hand
40. Fm.tp.: "in" replaced by hand with "away", and "my room" missing
41. Fm.tp.: "War Office" written by hand as an alternative to "Ministry of War"
42. Fm.tp.: "an" instead of "the"
43. Fm.tp.: "town" altered by hand to "city"
44. Tp.1: "defend" instead of "defense", apparently an error

	[45]enemy, who is quite near our door. So all the country is called to arms. The authorities wish me to lead the first troop going for[46] the defence of our country. I consider it the greatest privilege to fight for my land.
Teja	My darling sweetheart! You are too precious to be sent in the[47] battle. Your life is too valuable to be sacrificed in this way! O, I don't know what will become of me when[48] you are gone!
Ameen	I beg your pardon, Bibi, I must hurry now. I am sure your thoughts will be with me, so all will be well.
Teja	*(crying)* Know that I shall not feel I am living while you are away. It is you who will make me alive when you will return safe from there.
Ameen	Be sure that no harm will come to me, and soon we shall meet[49].

(Ameen kisses her hands, she lays her head upon his shoulder. They embrace each other)

Teja	*(still weeping)* God be with you!

45. Fm.tp.: "army" crossed out
46. Fm.tp.: "for" changed by hand to "to"
47. Fm.tp.: "a" instead of "the"
48. Fm.tp.: "what will become of me when" altered by hand to "how will I be able to live while"
49. Fm.tp.: "again" added by hand

ACT II

SCENE II

Scene: Teja's home. Teja ill, lying in armchair[50], *Johla moving the fan.*

Teja Give me some[51] cold water, my throat is dried up. It seems as if flames arise out of my body, oh! ah![52]

(Johla runs and fetches rose[53] *water, sprinkles it over Teja)*

Johla Bibi, Bibi.

(She gets no answer)

Teja *(suddenly waking from her swoon)* Yes.

Johla Are you here, Bibi?

Teja No, Johla, I was not here, I was at the front, where the battle is taking place, going through the agonies, sharing the experience of my beloved.

Johla Here is [54]water, Bibi, you wanted, I have fetched it.

Teja Thank you, Johla. *(Teja drinks)* Now I feel cooled. I feel ease through my breath. Something seems to tell me that all is well with him. A feeling comes to me as if I were reading his letter, that he is coming back.

Johla Will you eat something, Bibi? It is several days

---

50. Fm.tp.: "(on couch)" substituted by hand for "in armchair"
51. Fm.tp.: "soon" instead of "some"
52. Sk.tp.: "oh!" instead of "ah!"
53. Fm.tp.: "sprinkled" between "rose" and "water", and "sprinkles it over Teja" omitted, "and calls" added
54. Fm.tp.: "the" added

since you have had practically anything[55] to sustain your body. If not for yourself, then for his sake, to give him [56]pleasure. You must take care of yourself, you must feel[57] well.

Teja — No, don't mention food to me. I have no mind for it. I shrink even from looking at food.

Johla — Bibi, you must make yourself strong.

Teja — Will you help me, Johla, to get up.

(Johla lifts her up. She walks, her head on the shoulder of Johla. Johla holding her. Teja looks out from the window, Johla looks with her)

Johla — I don't see him yet.

Teja — *(resting her hand over Johla's shoulder, cries)* I see him! I see him! [58]He is coming back!

Johla — Don't act like a delirious person! You must not stand here, you have no strength. Come and sit[59] down in this chair.

(Johla puts her into the chair[60] and fans her)

Teja — *(Still slightly crying)* I see him, I see him come!

(Knock at the door. Johla runs out to see who knocks. Teja opens her eyes and sits up)

Teja — I wonder!

---

55. Fm.tp., Sk.tp.: "nothing"; Tp.1: "no thing" instead of "anything"
56. Fm.tp.: "the" added
57. Fm.tp.: "feel" changed by hand to "get"
58. Fm.tp.: "He's coming." added
59. Fm.tp.: "be", changed by hand to "sit"
60. Fm.tp.: "Into the chair" changed by hand to "on the couch"

(Johla enters hurriedly)

Johla Bibi, you will be pleased to know that a soldier has come on horseback with a message from Ameen.

Teja Show him in.

(Soldier salutes and presents the letter to Teja. She opens it and reads aloud)

"By the Grace of God, the Most Merciful and Compassionate, the battle is won, and the enemy admitted his defeat. The final arrangements are already completed, I am now preparing to come back. I kiss your dear hand, the hand which I always felt next to my heart."

(Teja wiping her tears of joy, gives gold coins to the soldier)

Teja Has all gone well?

Soldier Yes, lady. Ameen showed [61]great bravery; he most courageously fought[62], and wisely[63] made peace. He has won both the love of his friends and the admiration of his foes. He is the young man of the day; we are all proud of him for his proving so worthy of our trust. *(salutes)* I take my[64] leave, lady.

(Teja wiping her tears of joy. As soldier approaches the door, Johla meets him. Johla as if frightened. He as if amazed to see her. Both as if just missed bumping into each other)

---

61. Fm.tp.: "a" added
62. Fm.tp.: "fought" marked to move to before "most courageously", though this change does not appear in later versions
63. Fm.tp.: "wisely" marked to move to after "made peace", though this change is not made in later versions
64. Fm.tp.: "your" instead of "my"

Soldier — Hullo, queen of [65]kitchen!

Johla — Hullo, king of spades!

(They wink at one another, throw a kiss. The soldier goes out)

Johla — Now I am sure you are happy, Bibi, are you not? Now I shall bring [66]you some food, shall I? I am sure you must be hungry.

Teja — The news is nourishing to my soul, I don't need any food. But prepare some food, if you like. Ameen may come any moment.

Johla — If I had such [67]good news, Bibi, I would have eaten for[68] dinner twice as much as usual[69]! I wouldn't have waited for anyone! You think I am crazy, don't you? But I tell you, I would rather die than starve.

Teja — *(smiles)* You[70] go and eat your dinner[71]; don't wait. You need not starve waiting for me, Johla.

Johla — Thank you, Bibi.

(Exit Johla. Knock at the door heard)

Johla — *(quickly returns, exclaiming)* Ameen is there!

Teja — Call him in. *(Teja gets up from her seat. Ameen enters. Teja runs to meet Ameen, and falls fainting into his arms)*

---

65. Fm.tp.: "the" added by hand; Tp.1, Sk.tp.: "the"
66. Fm.tp.: "for" added, and "for you" marked to be moved to after "food", although this changes is not made in later versions
67. Fm.tp.: "a" added
68. Fm.tp.: "my" instead of "for"
69. Fm.tp.: "dinner twice as much as usual" reordered by hand to "twice as much dinner as usual"
70. Fm.tp.: "The" altered by hand to "You"
71. Fm.tp.: "yourself" instead of "your dinner", altered by hand to "your dinner"

Ameen, kissing her forehead, makes her sit in the chair[72]*, and sits by her side*

Teja — Now tell me, Ameen, all that happened. You must have had a terrible time!

Ameen — To tell you all since I left here and came back! From where shall I begin the story, and where shall I end it! All's well that ends well! It was a dream, a dream of one night, a nightmare rather. It's finished with the breaking of the day, and now there is sunshine everywhere.

Teja — I heard that you fought very bravely; they all admire you courage so much. You did not only make [73]war bravely, but you made peace so wisely.

Ameen — I tried to do my duty, Bibi; that is all one can do. Success and failure both are in his hands, without whose will nothing moves in the universe. Nevertheless, this experience on the battlefield has been quite an experience for me. I no more[74] will look for war, and will try to bring peace, not after, but before, if I can[75]. Did war have a hardening effect upon my heart? No, it made it much more tender than I have ever known it to be. I had[76] known to be affectionate to my friends, but it was[77] this war which has taught me to even love my enemies. I hitherto loved you, but it is during this war that a longing for you was produced in my heart. It had its disadvantages, yet one cannot ignore the advantages it has[78]. I am glad my people won

---

72. Fm.tp.: "in the chair" altered by hand to "on the couch"
73. Fm.tp.: "a" added
74. Fm.tp.: "no more" marked to move to after "will look", but this change not made in later versions
75. Fm.tp.: "could", changed by hand to "can"
76. Fm.tp.: "was" instead of "had"
77. Fm.tp.: "was" changed by hand to "is"
78. Fm.tp.: "it had" crossed out

victory over the enemy; but this has enlarged my view so that I cannot only consider[79] my countryman as my people, I am beginning to consider all[80] men in the world my people.

Teja — But you did not tell me the pains you have gone through, which I have felt all along through this war.

Ameen — It is both pain and pleasure which make life complete. If there was[81] no pain, one would not enjoy pleasure. I do not wish to recall to my memory the disagreeable past. [82]Only pleasant memories I allow my mind to hold, which were with you[82].

Teja — Now the pain has passed, and pleasure is in store for us. Next week our wedding takes place. My people are busy preparing for it. God has heard our prayer, Ameen, at last.

(They embrace)[83]

ACT II

SCENE III[84]

Scene: Ameen and Teja in their new home. Teja arranging cushions on the sofa. Ameen fixing his arrow and bow. People bringing wedding gifts. A lady brings flowers, gives them to Teja

Teja — O, how beautiful they are. Who has sent them?

---

79. Fm.tp.: "only consider" marked to reverse to "consider only", but this change not made in later versions
80. Fm.tp.: "all" added by hand
81. Fm.tp.: "was" changed by hand to "were"
82. Fm.tp.: "Only pleasant memories I allow my mind to hold, which were with you" altered by hand to read "I only allow my mind to hold pleasant memories which are of you"
83. Fm.tp.: this scene continues with the last two speeches in the following scene
84. Fm.tp.: this scene, except for the last two speeches, omitted

Lady Bibi, you father's sister's cousin's daughter, Salima, who is married to Omar Abdullah Hujuri. *(she leaves)*

(Teja brings the flowers to Ameen, kisses him and shows him)

Teja How beautiful they are, my darling sweetheart.

Ameen They were more beautiful on the stem, beloved; are these not plucked in vain? *(Teja looks with surprise. He kisses her forehead and laughs)* Don't you think so too? All beautiful things are in their greatest glory when they are in their own place. Arrange them, my sweetest wife. Now that they are brought to us, we may just as well turn our room into a garden.

(Another woman comes, greets Teja, cracking her hands against her cheeks)

Woman I have made this picture of Ameen, Bibi, you will be glad to see it.

Teja O, wonderful; he looked like this when he returned from the battlefield. Thank you. I am very glad to have it.

(Woman[85] cracks her hands and leaves)

Teja *(takes picture, shows it to Ameen)* Do you see, Ameen, who it is; do you know this man?

Ameen I don't know him, who is he?

Teja Is it not your beloved image? How nicely the artist has made it. Now what shall I do with it? Shall I

---

85. Sk.tp.: "again" added

frame it and put it on the wall, or shall I place on the sandal bracket above the divan? I think that is the proper place for it, do you not think so?

Ameen — Place its front against the wall, showing its back outside, beloved, if you ask my earnest advice about it.

Teja — *(looking at him surprised, as if asking: why do you say so?)* How could I destroy your picture?

Ameen — This is not my picture. The artist who has made it, has not seen me, beloved.

Teja — He has not seen you? You mean to say, he did not see you?

Ameen — Yes, I mean it, beloved.

Teja — Then perhaps I have not seen you also?

Ameen — I do not think so. To tell you the truth, I do not want anyone to make my picture; I do not wish my picture to be placed on a pedestal, I do not want my picture to represent me after I have gone. This mortal form itself is a shadow; and what is a picture? The shadow of a shadow.

(Knock at the door. Two men enter, the body of a lamb hanging on a stick over their shoulders)

Man — This is a wedding gift they send to you.

Teja — From where?

Man — From the community house.

Teja — How nice. Please give them our thanks and loving greetings.

(The two men take their leave)

Teja — *(to Ameen)* Here we have something really nice to make a three days' continual feast.

Ameen — Yes, the poor lamb must be asked first how it is to be sacrificed for our feast!

(Enter dancing girls, accompanied by musicians, who perform the dance of wedding wrapped in several veils, lifting one after the other as they dance)

Teja — *(engaged in seeing the performance, takes Ameen's arm, brings him to the room where the dancers are, while he is hesitating)* Beloved, it is wonderful; these are the best dancers we have in the country. Everyone speaks of their talent. They have trained every muscle, making it supple to twist and turn as they want to, and they so swiftly move to the rhythm of the drum, that their graceful movements make a living picture of music.

Ameen — May I request these talented dancers not to remove their veils any more?

Teja — But is is their dance, beloved, it is their way; how skilfully they unveil themselves.

Ameen — But what do they unveil? The earth; not heaven.

Teja — *(gives the musicians a purse)* Thank you, take no more trouble.

(Musicians greet and depart)

Ameen — Do you mind if I ask you something, beloved?

[86]*(shy, looking down)* [87]Ever since I have been in the open space and have observed wide horizons in the war, the wilderness attracts me. I long to walk in the desert, and to dwell in the mountains. If you will permit me Bibi, I will take a trip through the desert, that I may unload my mind from the disturbing impressions of the war.

Teja — Yes, my darling, you may go to the mountains whenever you desire, if it is not for a long time! While you are away I shall think of you with every breath[88].

(Ameen[89] kisses Teja's hand. They embrace[90])

ACT III

SCENE I

Scene: Hera, a rocky mountain in the desert. Ameen wandering alone there, looking at the wide space

Ameen — Home is a world; the life outside[91] home is the underworld, but this wilderness is my paradise. I feel myself only when I am by myself. It is then that I look at the whole world as an onlooker. There must be some reason why I am attracted to this spot. There are many reasons, but how many can be explained?[92] The heavy responsibility of home life[93] and the continual struggle with the outside world; the smallness of human character, the ever-changing

86. Fm.tp.: these two speeches complete the previous scene
87. Fm.tp.: "Yes!" added
88. Fm.tp.: "I can go to see my kinsfolk. Now you must be tired, it is late already" instead of "I shall think of you with every breath"
89. Fm.tp.: "asks her leave, he" added
90. Fm.tp.: "Ameen departs." added
91. Fm.tp.: "of" added
92. Fm.tp.: "but how many can be explained?" omitted
93. Fm.tp.: "life" omitted

nature of life, the falsehood that exists in the life of the[94] generality, the absence of justice and the lack of wisdom, all these and many other things make life unbearable for me[95]. Besides, the ever jarring influences coming from all around[96] work upon my sensitive heart and make me feel lost sometimes. It is only here, away from the continual turmoil of life in the world that I find some rest. And yet I wonder if my heart is really at rest[97]. No, my heart[98] cannot be really rested. If I am[99] here away from the world and my fellow men are in the midst of the turmoil, it cannot give me the peace[100] I want; it keeps my mind uneasy[101]. What could I do to make the condition of my people better? Shall I work and be rich and help them with my riches? But how far will those riches go to provide for their endless needs? Shall I be powerful and control them and rule them? What will that do? It will only turn them from servants to slaves. Shall I teach them goodness? But where does goodness belong? It belongs to God. I must seek God[102] myself first before I speak of goodness to my fellowmen. And where shall I find[103] him? If he is to be found anywhere it is here in the solitude where my soul feels free. I become attuned to[104] nature. I could sit silent here for days, looking at this wide space of endless horizon, where not even a bird makes a sound by the fluttering of its[105] wings. I need not try to be silent here; silence

---

94. Fm.tp.: "the" added by hand
95. Fm.tp.: "to live" instead of "for me"
96. Fm.tp.: "which" added
97. Fm.tp.: "I am really rested" instead of "my heart is really at rest"
98. Fm.tp.: "I" instead of "my heart"
99. Fm.tp.: "rest" instead of "am"
100. Fm.tp.: "rest tha" instead of "peace"
101. Fm.tp.: "busy" instead of "uneasy"
102. Fm.tp.: "Him" instead of "God"
103. Fm.tp.: "seek" instead of "find"
104. Fm.tp.: "the" added
105. Fm.tp.: "its", later changed by hand to "his"

reigns here, the spheres are silence[106] itself. O thou, longed for beloved, if thou art[107] anywhere to be found, it is here. I do not speak, I will not speak; I only listen, I will listen. Speak to me!

(He sits silent. A voice comes to him)

Voice Cry in the name of thy Lord! Cry in the name of thy Lord! Cry in the name of thy Lord![108]

(He invokes the sacred name of God, and again sits silent)

Ameen Through the whispering of the breeze, through the cooling of the wind, through the rippling of the water, through the cracking of the thunder, through the fluttering of the leaves, I hear thy gentle whisper in answer to my heart's cry. Beloved God, where art thou not present! Thou art everywhere. O thou, who wert[109] the ideal of my belief hitherto, now art a reality to me! In the flood that is caused by thy manifestation, my little self has become drowned. I am lost to my own view. Thou alone art now before me, O pearl of my heart!

(Ameen falls in a sort of swoon)

Voice Thou art the man! Arise, and wake[110] thy fellow men from the sleep of ignorance!

Ameen O what[111] task, what responsibility thou givest me. My Lord, my King, I tremble. I cannot dare look at myself. Let me cover myself from my own eyes! I

---

106. Tp.1: "silent", apparently an error
107. Fm.tp.: "are" instead of "art"
108. Fm.tp.: "etc., etc." instead of "Cry in the name of thy Lord! Cry in the name of thy Lord!"
109. Fm.tp.: "were" instead of "wert"
110. Fm.tp.: "waken" instead of "wake"
111. Fm.tp.: "a" added by hand

cannot look at the vastness of the mission thou givest me with this, my limited[112] being.

(Again goes in a swoon)

Voice — Thou art the man! Arise, and wake[113] thy fellow men from the sleep of ignorance!

Ameen — Yes, I obey, I rise[114]. I march to the rhythm of the music of thy call.

ACT III

SCENE II

Scene: Teja's house. Ameen sitting on a cushion in an ecstatic condition[115]. Teja, one hand on his shoulder, sympathizing with him.

Teja — What is it, my darling sweetheart, why are you acting so strangely? You seem to be frightened of something, as if you had a nightmare. It seems as if something frightful has been impressed upon your mind. What is the matter, my beloved? I am most anxious about you.

Ameen — Bibi, I have had an experience which is indescribable. I did not wish ever to tell[116] anyone about it.

Teja — Not even to me? I thought there would be nothing you would keep hidden from me.

---

112. Fm.tp.: "the littleness of my" instead of "this, my limited"
113. Fm.tp.: "awaken" instead of "wake"
114. Fm.tp.: "arise" instead of "rise"
115. Fm.tp., tp.1: "in an ecstatic condition" omitted
116. Fm.tp.: "you" crossed out

Ameen — Well, beloved, not even to[117] you. For it is something which I cannot even[118] explain to myself. And yet, when I think of it, it seems as if my soul has always known it, although my mind is quite unable to grasp it. It is something so big that I cannot look at it[119] and at the same time look at my little self. For there is no comparison between this experience of mine and what I know myself to be. The difference is as there is[120] between the[121] heaven and the[121] earth. If I try to say it, my lips tremble and my throat chokes. I feel like covering myself from my own view when that wonderful influence comes over[122] me.

Teja — I feel very eager, Ameen, to hear. Will you not tell me a little more about it?

Ameen — It was to quiet my mind, upset by the turmoil caused[123] by the life in the world, that I sought[124] my refuge under the clear sky during the rising moon, in the wilderness. I called upon that God, whom people seek, some in the idols of rock, some in the spirit of their ancestors, some in the animals, some in birds, some in the trees of long tradition, some in heroes, some in the bright sun. He answered me during my quietude through[125] nature, whose voice I heard, which was[126] louder than the thunderbolts. I was taught to cry[127] the name of God. And his answer came to me as a re-echo of my cry. The spot where I

---

117. Fm.tp.: "to" added by hand
118. Tp.1: "even" moved to after "explain"
119. Fm.tp.: "it" added by hand
120. Fm.tp.: "that" instead of "there is"
121. Fm.tp.: "the" crossed out
122. Fm.tp.: "big thing comes upon" instead of "wonderful influence comes over"
123. Fm.tp.: "caused" added
124. Fm.tp.: "sort" corrected to "sought" by hand
125. Fm.tp.: "the" crossed out by hand
126. Fm.tp.: "which was" crossed out by hand
127. Tp.2: "in" crossed out

sat in the desert far away from the world and its noise, produced for me a sublime vision of the immanence of God. The speechless rocks, it seemed, received a tongue to answer my call. God, who is the belief of an average being, then became for me a living identity, and myself for[128] that moment was lost to my own[129] view. How can words explain the splendour of that moment, the glory of God, which was in its full bloom at that time. It seemed as though the spheres played music and nature danced. The heaven of which they talk, I saw come on earth!

Teja How wonderful! And then what happened?

Ameen I cannot very well say it to you, my dearly loved wife. It came to me as a command telling me to rise and try to better the condition of my fellowmen.

Teja In what way?

Ameen In every way.

Teja But how?

Ameen To warn people of the coming disasters, to waken them to the light of truth, to help in bettering their[130] condition in their life in the world. To serve them in their need, to give them a hand as they climb to the top of the spiritual ideal. And to remove thorns[131] from their way. I cannot, I cannot understand this. Why I should be called for this great task? A trust, the weight of which mountains could not sustain, trees could not bear. And yet, though my soul has heard, I cannot make my mind believe it. Is it my

---

128. Fm.tp.: "at" instead of "for"
129. Fm.tp.: "own" added by hand
130. Fm.tp.: "the" instead of "their"
131. Fm.tp.: "storms" changed by hand to "thorns"

delusion, Teja, do you think I have become possessed of a spirit? What is it?

Teja — My precious one, if you ask me, I will repeat the same: thou art the man. I have seen it all along and I have felt it, though I could not give full expression of[132] my thought.

Ameen — How can I believe this to be true, Teja, in spite[133] of all this experience I have had, when I think of my shortcomings and my limitations.

Teja — You are the man, Ameen, who is born to serve his fellow men, to better their conditions. You do not know how good[134] you have been to all; most attentive in your duties, persevering in your labours, honest in your business dealings, a brave soldier at the battlefield and[135] wise peacemaker[136]. Have you not been an ideal husband to me, and a father so kind and loving! Your respect for the aged, your affection for those who depend upon you, and your consideration to those to whom it is due. Besides, your generous spirit covered under your modesty, all these things give me a sufficient proof to believe[137] without a doubt that you are the man. And if there was not one person in the whole world to support my belief, I still will believe so. For my belief in you is my conviction.

(Ameen, moved to tears, kisses her hand and presses it to his heart)

---

132. Fm.tp., Sk.tp.: "to" instead of "of"
133. Fm.tp.: "spite" crossed out and "the fall" written by hand, then crossed out and "spite" restored
134. Fm.tp.: "good" added by hand
135. Fm.tp.: ", a" instead of "and"
136. Fm.tp.: "as a statesman" added
137. Fm.tp.: "it" added, later crossed out

Ameen You are my inspiration[138], Teja, you are my strength[139].

(A moment silence)

Ameen Now I must leave, well-beloved, and see what can be done. It is difficult, being[140] alone, to begin the[141] work. Still, the one who has inspired me to work will be my guide.

(They rise. Ameen about to depart. Johla enters)

Johla Bibi, your uncle[142] has come to see you.

Teja Show him in.

(Teja goes forward to meet him. Ameen salutes and shakes hands with him)

Teja Uncle dear, you have come at a[143] time when[144] you are badly needed.

Uncle I am[145] needed! I am surprised! I thought nobody in the world needed someone[146] who is now looking at life as the past, and seeing before him his end[147].

Teja Uncle, you must not say that. The more one lives, the more precious one becomes; for life deepens a soul. We can always profit by your counsel, your

---

138. Fm.tp.: ", my strength" crossed out
139. Fm.tp.: "backbone", then crossed out and "life" written by hand, then that too crossed out and "strength" written by hand
140. Fm.tp.: "just" instead of "being"
141. Fm.tp.: "now to set to" instead of "to begin the"
142. Fm.tp.: "There is your uncle, Bébé", later changed by hand to "Bébé, your uncle"
143. Fm.tp.: "the proper" instead of "a"
144. Fm.tp.: "when" added by hand
145. Fm.tp.: "was" instead of "am"
146. Fm.tp.: "needs" instead of "needed, and "some-" of "someone" crossed out by hand
147. Fm.tp.: "death" instead of "his end", with "his" added by hand

word of advice, dear Uncle. Ameen is lately having some strange experience. He feels as if he[148] heard a voice calling him to serve his fellow men. This has come to him since he has taken to retire in[149] the solitude; sometimes [150]hours and sometimes days [151]he spends in the wilderness.

Uncle Good tidings! This has been the experience of all those who have ever been called to serve humanity in a special way[152]. He is a reformer, even greater than a reformer, for he is a prophet. *(turning to Ameen)* There is a great task before you, my son! I am afraid you will have a hard time. Man is the worst enemy of his best friend, he always has proved to be so. It's the same old wine, put in a new bottle. But the world before drinking the wine, will examine the label on the bottle; and if it is not the same label that they are used to, they will call it a different wine. I would not be surprised, Ameen, if your most loving[153] friends will not turn into your bitterest[154] enemies as soon as[155] you have commenced your work. The people here in this land are very[156] backward; they are in a hopeless state. There is everywhere[157] idol worship. Religious places have turned into money counters. Gaiety and merriment are[158] the occupation of the young, and the old indulge in superstitions[159]. Who could,

---

148. Fm.tp.: "he" added by hand
149. Fm.tp. "to" added by hand
150. Fm.tp.: "for" added
151. Fm.tp.: "which" added by hand
152. Fm.tp.: "path", changed to "way" by hand
153. Fm.tp.: "best" instead of "most loving"
154. Fm.tp.: "worst" instead of "bitterest"
155. Fm.tp.: "no sooner than" instead of "as soon as"; Tp.1: "no sooner" instead of "as soon as"
156. Fm.tp.: "much" instead of "very"
157. Fm.tp.: "everywhere" marked to move to after "idol worship", though this change was not made in later versions
158. Fm.tp.: "is" instead of "are"
159. Tp.1: "superstition" instead of "superstitions"

Ameen, if you could not be the man?[160] You are the man, I am sure. I wish I were young, to have shared some of your troubles. But I am too old now to venture. You are fortunate, Ameen, to have your devoted[161] wife[162]. God be with you both, my children! Goodbye!

(Teja embraces her uncle. He puts his hand[163] on their shoulders. Ameen embraces Teja and leaves)

ACT III

SCENE III

Scene: Ameen standing on the highway[164], speaking to the passers-by. Travellers coming and going.

1st Traveller I have heard you talk here to the travellers; tell me to what church you belong.

Ameen My church is the globe, the earth is[165] its ground, the sky[165] its dome.

2nd Traveller But which is your God?

Ameen The same God who is the God of all.

3rd Traveller But you don't worship the God of our[166] tribe, do you?

Ameen I worship the God of all tribes.

---

160. Fm.tp.: sentence marked by hand to be reordered to read: "Who, Ameen, could be the man, if you could not?", though this change was not made in later versions
161. Fm.tp.: "devoted" added by hand
162. Fm.tp.: "as your first follower, who is [altered by hand to "and"] your backbone and support"
163. Fm.tp., tp.1, Sk.tp.: "hands" instead of "hand"
164. Fm.tp.: "in the woods" instead of "on the highway"
165. Fm.tp.: "is" added by hand
166. Fm.tp.: "you" corrected by hand to "our"

3rd Traveller	But every tribe has its own God.
Ameen	Yes, but the[167] God of all tribes is my God.
4th Traveller	But what religion do you teach?
Ameen	The same one[168] religion which has always been taught to humanity.
1st Traveller	You don't mean to say that you preach the religion of our sect, for you are not our priest.
Ameen	It is not the religion of one sect, it is the religion of all sects. It is the religion which was revealed before; the same[169] is being revealed now.
5th Traveller	But it is not the religion of our ancestors which you teach.
Ameen	It is the same one religion of truth. It is the same religion of "peace on earth and goodwill to men", now given to you as a reminder.
5th Traveller	What are your teachings?
Ameen	Quit all laziness, earn money by labour, live an honest life, a life harmonious and peaceful. Respect your elder[170] people, giving a[171] loving care to the younger people. Be charitable to the poor, give a part of what you earn in charity. Worship one God, who is the Lord of all people. Know that you will have to give an account of your deeds.[172] Know that purity is the first lesson of piety. Do not shirk your

167. Fm.tp.: "the" added by hand
168. Tp.1: "one" omitted
169. Fm.tp.: "as it" instead of "; the same"
170. Fm.tp.: "elder" changed to "older" by hand
171. Fm.tp.: "give" instead of "giving a"
172. Tp.1: this sentence omitted, probably inadvertently

duties. Travel even to the other end of the world if it was for learning. Forget not your obligations, practise honesty in business. Know that all things in earth and heaven are made for you to make the[173] best use of them. In[174] man's cause is the world created, and man is the master therein.

6th Traveller What nonsense[175]! What does he know of heaven! Has he been there? [176]If he has ever been there, why then is he still lingering here on earth?

7th Traveller He is born on earth as everyone else. What right has he to teach others, when he's only a man? He's not a God!

1st Companion What he says is touching. I don't see what wrong he has[177] said. He does not[178] need to be other than a man to guide man[179] on the right path. It's absurd when one expects a guide to drop directly from heaven. It is the son of man who understands the difficulties of man, and who can sympathize with him. Therefore it is[180] man who is needed to guide man[181], not an angel!

8th Traveller I have known him for[182] a long time. Is he not the same one who used to work at the farm?

9th Traveller I think I have seen him working as a business agent, if I do not make a mistake.

---

173. Fm.tp.: "the" added by hand
174. Fm.tp.: "On" instead of "In"
175. Fm.tp.: "rubbish", later changed by hand to "nonsense"
176. Fm.tp.: the word "Another:" appears to indicate another speaker
177. Fm.tp., tp.1: "has" omitted
178. Fm.tp.: "don't" altered by hand to "doesn't"
179. Fm.tp., tp.1: "men" instead of "man"
180. Fm.tp.: "Therefore it is" omitted
181. Fm.tp.: "him" changed by hand to "man"
182. Fm.tp.: "since" instead of "for"

10th Traveller — Is he not the same one I knew at the battlefield during the last war? And now he is coming to tell us of kindness!

11th Traveller — But who made him a priest to give us long sermons? Has he got nothing to do at home? He has a home with wife and children, he is not a hermit!

12th Traveller — Nay! I cannot believe all this talking. If he be real, he would show a miracle. Can he give a tongue to the dumb? Can he give hearing to the deaf? Can he give sight to the blind, or can he raise the dead from their graves?

2nd Companion — He need not perform wonders in order to serve God and his fellow men. If he can inspire the ignorant to speak words of wisdom, it is better than if he gave tongue to the dumb. If he opened the heart of a person to hear the inner voice, it is greater than giving ears to the deaf. If he opens the eyes of the seeking soul to reality, it is better than giving sight to the blind. If he wakens a mortal soul to immortality, it is greater than raising the dead.

(Ameen, sitting on a rock, resting his head on his hand, hearing all this silently. Many more persons enter)

Some persons — Here he is! Here he is!

1st Inhabitant — You have commenced to work against the religion of our forefathers; you wish to believe in another God rather than the gods of our tribes. You are influencing our young men to give up the worship of our idols. Leave this moment the soil of our country! If not, the state will take you to task.

(They fight with fists with the four companions who try to protect Ameen Some try to take Ameen away from the danger)

Ameen — Was it for this day that thou hast commanded me to warn these people!

(Ameen is taken away from the crowd by his companions)

2nd Inhabitant — *(holding his arms)* If you at all care for your life, never step on this soil again!

(Many persons rejoicing. Some sorrowing. A few women weeping)

ACT IV

SCENE I

Scene: At Yaman. Companions[183] *of Ameen presented at the court, as having trespassed upon*[184] *the land. The policeman*[185] *bringing Ameen's four companions before the Chief.*

Policeman — Sir, these men have trespassed in our country without permission, and they come with the excuse that they are exiles from their own land.

Chief — Yes. We have received a letter from the authorities of their country, saying that they must not be allowed to enter here. *(turning to one of the four companions)* What have you to say about this?

---

183. Fm.tp.: "Friends" altered to "Companions"
184. Fm.tp.: "upon" omitted
185. Fm.tp.: "constable" changed to "policeman"

1st Companion — We beg to be excused[186] for having entered your soil, but it was inevitable. We were persecuted as heretics by our people, and were thrown out of our country.

Chief — What is the reason of this persecution? What have you done against your people's religion?

1st Companion — We have done nothing against the existing religion of our people.[187] Our blessed leader has been speaking for some time to those who cared to listen, of the ways to better their condition in life, individually and collectively. And those among them who wish to keep the simple people of our land under their sway, oppose the message of God[188].

Chief — Where is your leader? Send for him. I would like to see him.

1st Companion — Yes, sir, I'll go and fetch him. I am sure he will be able to explain to you better all you wish to know.

(The companion leaves the court. A policeman follows)

Chief — What is the name of your leader? What is he? Does he work wonders? Has he anything extraordinary in him which made you follow him?

2nd Companion — We shall follow him, sir, to the end of the world,

---

186. Fm.tp.: "apologize to you" instead of "be excused"
187. Fm.tp.: this sentence crossed out by hand
188. Fm.tp.: "the message of God" crossed out and "our movement" substituted by hand

whether he takes us to heaven or hell. We trust him too much to ever doubt him. He is to us a messenger of God, though he for himself is most unpretentious. He does not perform miracles, he does not claim to have any extraordinary powers. He says, "I am a human being as anyone else, subject to pleasure and pain, birth and death." The only privilege he has is in the service[189] for which he has been called.

(Ameen enters with the companion, followed by the policeman. Ameen greets Chief.[190])

Chief What have you to say? What do you teach?

Ameen I warn my people of the coming of that day when man will no longer hold his position, his rank, however high or great. Those near and dear to him will remove him from their midst[191] the moment that the breath leaves the body. If life on earth is a few days only, there is a time to come to answer for every grain one has eaten from this earth, and to pay for every drop of water one has drunk there. This world, I say, is not a stage set for man to amuse himself, it is a school for him to learn his lesson. I tell them that if you will[192] trust anyone, trust in God; if you will[192] depend on anyone, depend on God; if you will confide in anyone, confide in God; if you will revere anyone, worship God. Death is not the end of this life, death is the bridge that unites friend with friend[193]. Therefore, when[194] doing his duties honestly in this world, man must think of that

189. Fm.tp.: "of mankind" added by hand
190. Fm.tp.: "nods" added by hand
191. Fm.tp.: "them" instead of "their midst"
192. Fm.tp.: "wish to" instead of "will"
193. Fm.tp.: "stepping stone to that life which continues, in that life in the hereafter" instead of "bridge that unites friend with friend"
194. Fm.tp., Sk.tp.: "while" instead of "when"

life also, which is to come.

Chief — It is quite clear to me all you say[195]. I do not think any of us here would make[196] objections to[197] your teaching. On the other hand, we would be only too glad to have among us a man like you, who brings to us the knowledge which is the need of every soul. Truly they say that, "A prophet is not recognized[198] in his own country."[199] I do not see why they must have gone so far as to exile you from your country[200]. If one door is closed behind you, another door is opened[201] before you. You are welcome here. I am quite[202] sure my colleague workers, who are the principal authorities of our state, think the same as I do.

Colleague — Yes, certainly we do.

Chief — We shall give you every facility for you to stay here among us, to give the advantage of your teaching to our people, who, I am sure, will be immensely benefited by them. Besides, your inspiring guidance we shall seek in the reconstruction of our commonwealth, considering your coming now at the moment of our social and political crisis as the hand of providence.

Ameen — Nothing better I would wish for than to be of some service to you, sir, and to your people to whom I feel indebted for having allowed me to live among

---

195. Fm.tp.: "teach" changed by hand to "say"
196. Fm.tp.: "make" changed by hand to "raise"
197. Fm.tp.: "of" changed by hand to "to"
198. Fm.tp.: "a prophet" instead of "recognized"
199. See Mark 6:4
200. Fm.tp.: "exile you from your country" changed by hand to "treat you so disgracefully", but this change does not appear in later versions
201. Fm.tp.: "open" instead of "opened"
202. Fm.tp.: "very" changed by hand to "quite"

you. I sought refuge with you[203], and you have confided to[204] me the affairs of your homeland. I will try my best to prove worthy of your trust.

(Ameen leaves with companions.)

ACT IV

SCENE II

Scene: Ameen sitting in the seat of honour. Colleague and Chief sitting to his right and left. Four companions sitting behind him. Coffee served.

Chief *(to all)* Here we have among us[205] Ameen, who has won our hearts, who has illuminated our souls. Our trust in him is eternal, no time however long can develop that confidence in our hearts, which he has kindled in us in a moment[206]. We see before us in our social and political activities a promise, as no problem there is that remains unsolved, once Ameen throws his light upon it. Things which seemed difficult, he makes them easy for us; things subtle become[207] simple in his presence. Nothing new he tells us; all he says to us appears as if we have always known, and yet we were not conscious of it. Ameen is our light, not only in life's dark corners, but he is the torch that illuminates our path.

Colleague True it is, all you have said, Chief, we must value and appreciate Ameen's presence among us by trying to understand him better, and by trying to

---

203. Fm.tp., Tp.1, Sk.tp.: "under your shelter" instead of "with you"
204. Fm.tp.: "in" instead of "to"
205. Fm.tp.: "in the seat of honour" added
206. Fm.tp.: "instantly" instead of "in a moment"
207. Tp.1: "them easy for us; things subtle become" omitted, probably inadvertently

follow all he teaches us, more closely.

(Policeman enters)

Policeman *(to Chief)* There is an envoy from our neighbouring country, who wishes to see you, sir.

Chief Yes, send him in.

(Envoy enters and greets the Chief)

Colleague Please take a seat.

Chief What has brought you here?

Envoy I am sent by the authorities of my state, sir, with a summons. We ask you, sir, to give us our criminals, who have fled from our country.

Chief What crime have they committed?

Envoy They are accused of every crime, sir. All crimes put together make one crime, and that crime is the one for which they are accused.

Chief But what crime?

Envoy A crime beyond words.

Chief But I want to know what crime[208].

Envoy The crime is beyond comprehension, sir.

Colleague Do you know before whom you are standing? This is Ameen, now the head of our commonwealth, to whom you have brought a summons.

---

208. Fm.tp.: "it is" added by hand

(Envoy frightened, with startling[209] *eyes, trembling like a leaf, turning his head right and left)*

Chief Go and tell the authorities of your state that your accusations are unfounded. Ameen is now the leader of our people in their worldly and their spiritual strife.

Envoy Then I will go, sir, and tell my people all you have said. Thank you very much, goodbye.

(Envoy goes out hastily. He tumbles down on the way; pulls the leg of the policeman[210]*)*

Envoy *(to policeman)* Come along.

Policeman *(with his hand on his neck)* Go.

(Ameen sad looking)

4th Companion Our master, I feel your sadness over the stupidity of our people. I[211] cannot help feeling, since our hearts are focussed to yours.

Ameen Yes, you are right, but it is a passing cloud; it will pass away in time. All balances up in the end, cruelty on their part and kindness on yours. What I feel deeply and very often is that the call for service came to me on the Hera, and it was meant that my people there should be enlightened and helped. And in spite of all the good work which is being done here, I continually feel that something is remained[212] undone. And so long as that work will not be

209. Fm.tp.: "starting" instead of "startling"
210. Fm.tp.: "saying" added
211. Fm.tp.: "We" instead of "I"
212. Fm.tp.: "remaining" instead of "remained"

attended, I shall not consider my task accomplished, I will always feel a sore spot in my heart.

Chief — We shall spare no effort, out teacher! Our means, our energy, even our lives we shall place at your call, if we can assist you in accomplishing your task.

4th Companion — We are ready to answer your call, master, even if it be at our life's sacrifice. Command any of us to go and spread your ideas among those who do not understand them[213].

Ameen — No, I will not risk your lives; you[214] are too precious to[215] me. I only ask of you to let me go to deliver his message to my people.

Chief — No, Ameen, that cannot be; if you go, we shall be your bodyguard; if harm comes to you, we shall be your shields. For death in a holy cause will be our liberation.

(Ameen deeply touched by their readiness to serve)

Ameen — Let us all go, for it is meant that we should share one another's joys and sorrows.

Chief — *(to Ameen)* We are most happy that you have granted our request. *(to colleagues)* Prepare and be ready to start on the journey to guard our leader, and to defend our cause. *(all stand and say, waving hands)* Ameen victorious!

(Happy and enthusiastic they leave)

---

213. Fm.tp.: "preach gospel to your adversary" instead of "spread your ideas ... do not understand them"
214. Fm.tp.: "they" changed by hand to "you"
215. Fm.tp.: "for" instead of "to"

ACT IV

SCENE III

Scene: Commotion at the town hall. People rushing hither and thither restlessly. Sheriff of Mecca entering. Authorities receive him.

Sheriff — I just heard the[216] news that we are threatened with invasion by our neighbouring state.[217] From one source I have the news that they are already on the way. And we are not in the least ready to defend our land[218]. Alas, we have not among our young men another Ameen "One man with the spirit is greater than an army." How we miss Ameen at this time of our need.

1st Authority — Yes, if only he had not become so crazy over his religious fad.

Sheriff — Now what can we do? Have we any means of defence?

1st Authority — We are not prepared! We did not know of it until this morning. Nothing can be done!

Sheriff — But what can we do to maintain the pride of our people?

2nd Authority — Pride! If we have nothing to be proud of, what is it to us?

---

216. Fm.tp.: "this" typed, changed by hand to "a"
217. Fm.tp.: "Crowd: Oh!" added by hand
218. Fm.tp.: "our land" crossed out by hand

Sheriff (*Sad)* These last few years we have gone from bad to worse!

3rd Authority Worse[219]! We cannot fall any lower!

(A soldier enters)

Soldier Sir, a large band of armed men have almost approached the gate of [220]Mecca.

Sheriff Now what do you think we shall do?

4th Authority Surrender without hesitation!

(Women enter in a state of alarm. Soldier enters)

Soldier They are entering our gate, the town hall is surrounded!

(Ameen enters in general's uniform, his bodyguard following him. Sheriff with the[221] authorities greet him)

Sheriff We surrender, sir, being not prepared for your sudden invasion.

Chief At the head of our army is Ameen, the one who was an exile from your land, whom you threw out of your country with insults, and made him homeless. His companions were caused all manner of injury by you, and those who sided with him were wounded and some killed.

Sheriff We are sorry for all that was done by our people to

---

219. Fm.tp.: "Worst" instead of "Worse"
220. Fm.tp.: "our town" added "Mecca", but then crossed out
221. Tp.1: "the" omitted

Ameen. We are willing to pay you the sum of money you demand.

Chief — Before you pay us any money, I ask that you submit to[222] us all Ameen's adversaries, who have shown Ameen hostility in the past.

(Criminals brought. Some come with agitation, some trembling, some with stern faces[223], some repentant)

Chief — *(to Ameen)* Here are the ones who have tortured your life and that of those near and dear to you. Command the sentence that must be given to them.

(The criminals attentively listen, looking at Ameen to hear what he will say)

Ameen — I have forgotten all they have done[224]. I forgive, and ask the Lord to forgive them.

(All surprised. Authorities touched. Sheriff moved to tears. They bring before Ameen sacks of gold coins to pay the indemnity of the war[225])

Ameen — *(turning[226] to Chief)* Have we come here to take from them money? Do you wish for any material gain from these people?

Chief — No, our prophet! We have accompanied you to be with you. If only we have you, our master! No money or territory is our object in coming here; it is to serve you!

Sheriff — *(to Ameen)* You are the pride of our people, and

---

222. Fm.tp.: "before" instead of "to"
223. Fm.tp.: "face" instead of "faces"
224. Fm.tp.: "to me. All." added
225. Fm.tp.: this last sentence omitted
226. Fm.tp.: "Turning" omitted

your absence from here was the cause of our decline. Nothing would please us more than if you took this whole territory of Hijas, and we shall feel most honoured to proclaim you king.

[227]*(The authorities bring a crown and a sceptre, and the Sheriff holds them before Ameen)*

Sheriff — Here is crown and sceptre for you, Ameen.[227]

Ameen — As much as I appreciate your asking me to become king, I will not do so. It is not for the kingdom I have come here, it is to serve you, my people, whose welfare is my heart's deep desire. I have come to deliver to you God's message.

Authority — I beg your pardon, sir, where can we find someone as[228] inspired as you to govern our people, to control our affairs. You appeared as an enemy and prove[229] to be our[230] friend.

Sheriff — What message do you wish to give us? We are ready to accept it from someone so selfless as you, Ameen!

Ameen — Believe in one God. Remove the gods of Ka'ba, which are but idols of rock. Consider love greater than law.[231] Know that all men are equal before God; perform your prayers, therefore, all standing before his divine majesty, rich or poor, saint or sinner, all on one level. Tell your sorrows to your Lord, if you are sad; bring your repentance to your God, if you are repentant. Disgrace not your soul by prostrating before idols, for even man is limited. To

227. Fm.tp.: the stage instruction and the speech of Sheriff do not appear
228. Fm.tp.: "so" instead of "as"
229. Fm.tp.: "proved" instead of "prove"
230. Fm.tp.: "any" changed by hand to "our"
231. Fm.tp.: "Consider love greater than law." omitted

God alone all praise is due.

Sheriff We accept your message, Prophet, from the bottom of our hearts, which we shall hand down to posterity. We witness that there is one God, and that you, Prophet, are[232] his messenger. [233]It is not your sword which has won victory over our hearts, it is your noble spirit[234]. Therefore, though you have given us our freedom by refusing to rule us, we shall maintain your reign forever[235] over our souls[233 236].

Ameen I am a man, one like any of you, subject to pain and death. Remember that you will not make of me an ideal which you will not be able to uphold long. Raise me not beyond my limit, that you may have to throw me down one day through disappointment[237]. Consider me your brother, an honour which I value[238] most. I leave my word with you, for you to guard the message against all opposition[239]. I leave this[240] sacred manuscript with you, for you to hand over to the coming generation, uncorrupted. My success is not in earthly gain; renunciation is my real[241] victory. *(to the Chief)* I bless them all, but I will come with you, who have been my friends in need.

Chief Hail to[242] Ameen, our faithful trustee!

---

232. Fm.tp.: "are" added by hand
233. Fm.tp.: this whole passage added later by hand, it also appears written out on a separate small piece of paper with "forever" added at end
234. Fm.tp.: in the handwriting, "and your personality" crossed out
235. Fm.tp.: "forever" omitted
236. Fm.tp.: "till the sun will shine on the earth" crossed out, and "forever and ever more" added with "and ever more" crossed out
237. Fm.tp.: "through disappointment" added by hand
238. Fm.tp.: "deem" changed by hand to "value"
239. Fm.tp.: "uphold for your liberty" instead of "guard...opposition"
240. Fm.tp.: "the" changed by hand to "this"
241. Fm.tp.: "final" changed by hand to "real"
242. Fm.tp.: "Hail to" added by hand

THE BOGEYMAN

by Inayat Khan

CHARACTERS

The bogeyman
Queen
Prince
Noblemen (two)
Brahmins (two)
Governors
Guardian
Eight chelas
Candidate
Speculator
Modernist
Lover
Lady
Policemen (two)
A crowd (twelve people)
A man who has lost the control over his nerves
A woman who is obsessed
A bad tempered woman

ACT I

SCENE I

Scene: Sarai[1].

Modernist sitting on a stool reading a newspaper. Speculator enters, gets close to the modernist.

Speculator — What is the rate of exchange today?

Modernist — *(looks at him and then looks down at his newspaper again)* I have not come to it yet.

Speculator — Then what did you read? That is the first thing one must read. Yesterday money had gone down and I have made a profit. The other day I bought some shares which I sold and got four times the amount.

Modernist — I am not at all interested in speculations; I am looking for what papers say about the new cabinet that is to be formed. I am wondering who are to be elected to work in Parliament. If the Labour-Party gets the upper hand, the state of affairs will change, conditions will improve.

Speculator — It does not matter a bit to me which party comes up and which goes down. "God save our bread." What I am concerned about is if money rises or falls. What difference does it make if one party goes and another comes? It is always like this with the government.

Documents:
od.tp. = typescript (which includes only Acts 1-3) used for performance, Summer School, 1938.
bk. = *Three Plays*, Deventer, Holland, 1939, for Acts 4-7.
Notes:
1. Bk.: resting place for travellers

(Enter Lover)

Lover — O, o, she never did care for me, she never did love me. I now realize how she has treated me. I never thought she could be so heartless. Day after day I have followed and night after night I dreamt of her. I thought of her at every moment of the day. It is of her that I have spoken, if ever I have spoken. Woman, woman, I wish I could die.

Speculator — *(rushes at him)* What is the matter with you?

Lover — O, it is she, it is she who is the cause of all. Now I am good for nothing, why should I live any longer?

Speculator — Silly man, think of something else. If you get money, you have everything you want in the world.

Lover — I have failed, I have failed in life.

Speculator — Have you lost your money? Have you been bankrupt? How have you failed?

Lover — No. My only love has disappointed me.

Speculator — Make money and the world will be yours. It is no use dying because a woman turns away from you.

Lover — My love, my love!

Speculator — Love money; the only worthy object of love.

Lover — I have never thought of money in my life. I only lived for love.

Speculator — Silly you are. If you have not yet learned how to make headway in the world, you have wasted your life. Time is money. If you have money, everybody is drawn to you. If you are poor, no one cares for you. *(goes to Modernist)*

Modernist — What is the matter with that fellow? Is he love sick? Hi-hi-hi-hi-hi.

Speculator — He has got inflammation of the heart. Ha-ha-ha-ha.

Modernist — Science has proved today that love is a convulsion of the brain.

(Enter Lady, chicly dressed)

Lady — *(speaking to herself)* I hate, I hate the sight of a woman, I do not mind men.

(Speculator looks at her with surprise)

Lady — Turn away your evil eye, ugly creature!

Speculator — What did you say?

Lady — Why did you look at me? How dare you look at me? *(to Modernist.)* Why are you hanging your head? Why do you not look at me? You offer me an insult. Am I not dressed in the up-to-date fashion?

(Modernist looks up and then looks down)

Lady — Disgusting! *(sits down on a seat)*

Modernist — *(looks at her out of the corners of his eyes; then looks down, whispering)* Silly!

(Enter Sage, simply clad. He looks at no one, sits there for a rest. The others look at him astonished)

Speculator O, who is this?

Modernist A freak.

Speculator What did you say?

Modernist A freak. Someone who wanders about having nothing to do. Fools his time away.

Lady *(laughs, looking at him)* Bogeyman.

Speculator *(to Modernist)* I think there is something in this man. You don't know. Sometimes such men can tell you your fortune.

Modernist Nonsense.

Speculator Well, I will go and speak with him and see what he says. *(he goes to the right side and greets. The sage being absorbed in his thoughts does not see him. Goes to the other side, winking at the modernist, and greets him. The sage still absorbed in his thoughts. Then he goes before him and greets him. Sage responds by nodding)*

Speculator *(sits down)* Excuse me asking you, but I think men like you can tell many things. What do you think, will money rise or fall?

Sage What will rise must fall and what will fall must rise. Rise and fall are natural to life. No rise is permanent, nor fall everlasting. It is reality behind it all which is steady and dependable.

Speculator *(closes one eye, scratches his head)* Well, can you tell me if I will make some profit next week?

Sage There is only one profit which is worth striving

after. That profit is to gain what no one can take away from you.

Speculator *(points with his finger to his forehead)* Thank you. *(goes away laughing)*

Speculator *(goes to the lady who is seated there)* Where did you get that precious necklace? *(touching necklace)*

Lady *(strikes him on his shoulder)* Away, don't touch my necklace with your awkward hands. I have many rings and necklaces. I am a high-class woman. How dare you touch my necklace? Can't you talk from a distance? Keep to where you belong!

(Speculator moves his eyes, goes away, rubbing where she has struck him)

Modernist What did he say?

Speculator Who? That funny lady?

Modernist No, no, that strange looking man.

Speculator *(laughs)* He told me much, but I did not understand one word. He is not all there; he seems to be flying in the air. When I talk to him about the south, he tells me about the north.

Modernist Let me go and see what he says. (*goes near the sage, greets him and sits there)* Excuse my asking you some questions.

(Sage looks at him)

Modernist I suppose you do not interest yourself in the present political situation. But I should like to know what you think. Do you think the Labour-Party will win at the present election?

Sage — Whichever party comes to power, it certainly fulfills the law from above. The various parties seem different to our eyes, but there is his will that is done, and his will that will be done. When we show preference to one party over the other, it is our limitation. Men group themselves into parties; when we see behind all different parties, there is one perfect whole, working out its destiny towards the fulfilment of the purpose of life.

Modernist — What do you think of the great wrong being done towards the people by those at present in power?

Sage — Those who wish the better conditions by fighting against all that is wrong, often do a greater wrong. The more parties there are, the greater the inharmony. It is dividing one into many. It is by unity that the purpose of life is achieved.

Modernist — But what do you think of the people who have held wealth and high position for generations while depriving others of the same?

Sage — You are right. Every man must have his chance of attaining all that is good and worth attaining. But there are two ways of attaining. One way is to rob, and the other way is to earn. One earns by deserving it, one robs, without deserving it. There must be a mutual goodwill on the part of those who possess something and those who do not possess. Those who do not possess must deserve and own it. Those who possess must make all sacrifices possible in order that every man in the world may have his chance of prospering and rising in life. The undeserving one by robbing will never be able to enjoy and use his possession fully. For to possess something and to enjoy something one must earn it and one must deserve it.

Modernist Do you think a sense of mutual goodwill can be aroused among the people in high positions without any strong measures?

Sage Every hurt and harm caused to another rebounds. Any little destruction results in a greater destruction. Man is born with a sense of justice in the innermost of his being. And if a proposition of justice is brought before him, sooner or later he must respond to it. Harmlessness is the principal thing in religion. Inharmony causes greater inharmony, it is harmony that results in peace.

Modernist Thank you, I will reflect upon it. *(gets up and goes)*

Speculator What did the fellow tell you?

Modernist He does not speak my language. While we are thinking of struggle, he is thinking of peace.

Speculator Now I'll have some fun… I'll take this lady before that man and see what he says. *(he goes to the lady, puts his arm in hers)* Come along, old dame, if you want your fortune to be told.

Lady *(strikes him on his arm and pushes him away)* Why do you touch me, naughty man? Can you not keep at a respectful distance? Will he tell me my fortune?

Speculator Yes, he will.

Lady I'll come.

Speculator	*(brings her to the Sage)* This grand lady wants to talk to you.
Lady	Will you read my hand and tell me my fortune?
Sage	No lady, I do not tell fortunes.
Lady	No? They all say you can tell fortunes. Won't you tell me; I'm an unhappy woman.
Sage	Why are you unhappy, lady?
Lady	The troubles at home. The servants these days have become so neglectful, so independent and rude that you cannot expect them to do one thing properly.
Sage	Lady, this is the phenomenon of the time. It is the weather of the season. The best thing is to take everyone as he is and to know that he cannot be any better. Appreciate all that he can do and overlook all that he does not do. It is with kindness that you must treat those who depend upon you, it is kindness alone that can move rocks.
Lady	*(wiping her eyes)* Servants apart, even my friends have turned away from me. One day I think I can have trust and confidence in a friend. Next day the same person makes a breach of trust. I am so disappointed in people that now I cannot say whom I can call my friend.
Sage	Lady, do not expect much from friends. Why must they be as you want them to be? They are not made by you. They are as they are. You must try to be for them what they expect you to be. It matters little if your friend proves to you to be a friend. What matters is, if you prove to be a

friend.

Lady — No, I don't want even to look at friends who have once turned away from me. Even my husband is unsympathetic to me.

Sage — What do you do about it?

Lady — I have told him so very often.

Sage — There you are. Instead of kindling the fire of his heart by blowing, you pour water on it.

Lady — Now my heart is closed.

Sage — Is not your heart yourself? Or is it a door that is jammed and cannot be opened?

Lady — When he comes home from his work he is as cold as a chump of ice.

Sage — Lady, ice melts in a moment by the heat. If your heart is glowing with love, blazing with devotion, no ice can stay unmelted. Lady, do not even acknowledge all that seems undesirable to you. The best way to right the wrong is to look at it in the right light. It is we who cause our unhappiness and it is we who, if we happen to know the key to life, can find happiness.

Lady — Thank you, it is all too high for me. I'm going. *(Speculator comes behind her, as if he was taking her back. She pushes him away with her elbows; then he walks behind her, with outspread arms and bent knees, as if protecting her)*

Lover — My love, my love, I wish I could die. *(Lady and the two men rush at him)*

Speculator	Let us bring him to the bogeyman, telling him there is a soothsayer sitting here, we shall have your fortune told. *(he brings him to the Sage)* This man is lovesick. He said he had a disappointment and his heart broke. We cannot find where the pieces of his heart have dropped.
Modernist	Now we shall leave him to tell you his love-story. *(to the others)* Let us go out of Sarai.

(Sage and Lover left alone)

Lover	Please give me something that I instantly may die.
Sage	Why do you want to die?
Lover	I failed in love. She has abandoned me. Now there is nothing for me to live for. I want to die.
Sage	Have you failed in love? Love is the only real thing in life. For love is all that is. Love lives and all dies. If all failed you in life, love will not fail you. Perhaps you have not understood the meaning of love. Love that depends on being answered by the beloved is lame, it does not stand on its own feet. Love that tries to possess the beloved is without arms, it can never hold. Love that does not regard the pleasure and displeasure of the beloved is blind. Love that is demanding and self- asserting is dead. If you have love, you have all. What more do you want? Learn, my lad, to know what love is, before you profess to be a lover.
Lover	Then what am I to do? I am most unhappy. Life is miserable for me.
Sage	Your unhappiness comes from self-pity. Love is

	neither joy nor pain, it is both. If it is pain, it is as sweet as joy. If it is joy, it is as deep as pain. It is above joy and pain both. Love is the ladder by which you reach the highest ideal. Loving is living. *(remains in abstraction)*
Lover	No, no, I am most unhappy. I cannot endure it any longer. I will die, I must die. *(he puts a pill of poison in his mouth and falls dead near the feet of the sage)*
Sage	Ram, Ram, Ram, Ram.

ACT II

SCENE I

Scene: outside the hut of the sage. Chelas[2] *are beginning to gather. First chela is already sitting in silence. Two chelas enter.*

Second chela	He is always engaged in meditation, poor man.
Third chela	Perhaps he will hurry up his spiritual journey. There is a time for everything.
Second chela	Even God must get tired of hearing his continual prayer.
Third chela	He listens to the guru very much. For him every letter of the guru is a law. I suppose he is very good.
Second chela	Yes, too good to live. I can't be so good! I

2. For *chela*, see Glossary

	wonder if the path we have taken is the right one.
Third chela	There is no doubt about the path being the right one, but it is difficult to have patience to keep to it.
Second chela	I cannot go on much longer, for there are many other things to accomplish in life, not only this.
Third chela	"Seek ye first the Kingdom of God,"[3] is said in the scriptures. This is the principal thing to accomplish and all other things are secondary. If you take it as anything else, then you will be sure that you will never accomplish it.
Second chela	Yes, I suppose it is the work of such patient people as this one. *(pointing to the first chela. Enter fourth chela, hasting)*
Fourth chela	Has the class begun, has the class begun, has Guru come?
Second chela	Guru has not yet arrived, perhaps he has forgotten the time. There is no such a thing as time.
Fourth chela	The later the better. I'm only sorry I have left my notebook at home.
Third chela	Do you have to write down what is being taught here? Can you not take it all in?
Fourth chela	Oh, no, I can't do it. I must have it all on paper, for I need to chew the cud leisurely at home. *(he goes to the first chela)*
Fourth chela	*(to first chela)* Will you tell me please about

3. See Matthew 7.3

something I cannot understand? I have puzzled my head every day over it.

First chela — You must ask Guru.

Fourth chela — No, I dare not trouble Guru with my questions. Will you not tell me what it is? Guru said, all is one. If it is one, how can it be all, because all denotes plurality.

First chela — All sums up in unity.

Fourth chela — O! This I cannot understand.

First chela — You will understand one day.

Fourth chela — No never, I cannot. I can't be a hypocrite to my own self by imagining two to be one. Two is two, one is one. I have read hundreds of books on the occult sciences. And I have written fifty books on philosophy myself. I went from one occult school to another till I passed through perhaps twenty schools, but I have not yet got at the bottom of the thing I seek.

First chela — You will not get at the bottom as long as you feel you cannot get at the bottom.

Fourth chela — Explain to me please how many inner bodies there are. One school says there are five, another school says, there are seven. What I see is only one, this physical body. *(pointing to his body)*

First chela — This you must realize by meditation.

Fourth chela — I get tired of sitting quiet, even for three minutes. And tell me how many more times we have to come back here on earth. Shall we be born in other planets, and then what will happen in the end?

First chela — You need not worry about the end, for the end is the same as the beginning.

Fourth chela — What do you mean by beginning? Birth?

First chela — Whatever you imagine.

Fourth chela — That's what makes my head go round and round? It is like beating about the bush. You never come straight to the point. Everybody here complains of this.

First chela — Even if everybody did it, I suppose you don't.

(Fourth chela gets up and goes away. Enter fifth chela)

Fifth chela — *(goes to the first chela)* To me it is all vague, and in a mist; will you please explain something about the strange ways of the Guru.

First chela — The ways of the Guru are many, each subtle and incomprehensible. His moral conceptions, his philosophical thoughts, his lofty ideals, his realization of God, his wide horizon of vision and the flight of his consciousness in the higher spheres, all these cannot be put into words. He notices all things, whether he sees them or not, he feels all conditions, whether he knows them or not. He gives a bitter pill to one and a delicious sweet to another. He looks at one and thinks of another, he teaches one in words and the other in silence, he speaks to one and inspires another through his piercing glance. It is all his love whether it comes in the form of a heavy rainfall or in the form of a bright sunshine.

Fifth chela — *(to fourth chela)* The method that our Guru gives must be shaped according to the time. The time demands quite a different thing.

Fourth chela — I think you are right. But how do you think it must be done?

Fifth chela — Everything must be explained in words. And why is there necessity of secrecy? What is there to be kept secret in truth? If we know truth we can declare it before all people. What people are looking for is truth. And if we have it, it can answer their life's demand.

Fourth chela — I quite agree with you. It must be modified, and must be made to suit the modern world so that no scientist nor literary person can find any ground to criticize it.

(The first Chelas come nearer to hear the talk. Enter Guru, sees them conversing. They all greet)

Sage — What discussion is going on?

Second chela — My friend asks why truth cannot be given in the frame that may be accepted at the present time.

Sage — In the first place truth is vaster than any frame we can make to put it in. Besides, whatever frame we make for truth, for it to be presented in, an unawakened soul will never see it, but will only see the frame.

Fifth chela — But why must we keep secrecy about it?

Sage — God himself covers all beauty from the eyes of the unevolved. Beauty covers itself, or the unevolved close their eyes to it. In both cases, beauty remains veiled, and truth is the supreme

	beauty.
Fifth chela	Why must we not systematize spiritual knowledge?
Sage	What can be systematized cannot be spiritual knowledge. It is beyond all classifications. It is the earthly things that can be made cut and dried. The farther one goes in the spiritual path, the finer becomes his perception. Truth is most simple and most subtle. It is grosser than mountains and finer than atoms.
Fourth chela	Then how can we know occult laws?
Sage	By mystical perception.
Fourth chela	How can it be developed? It is twenty years since I have been reading occult books. Every day I have written down what you have said and yet I don't find I have arrived any nearer.
Sage	It is not study alone that brings you to the realization of truth. It often wraps your soul in many more covers. What gives you an insight into the hidden law of nature is meditation.
Third chela	That requires patience.

(Enter sixth chela)

Sixth chela	*(greets the teacher)* Excuse me for being late, Guru. I wish to tell you, last evening I went to a seance, and heard a spirit talk through the trumpet. He has told me so many things about what will happen in my life. Do you think it is true, all he said?
Sage	It is you who must know it.

Sixth chela — I have seen such a wonderful vision of you, Guru! You were all clad in blue and then you turned red. Then your whole appearance became scarlet and in the end it was a golden light; then your face altogether disappeared from my sight.

Sage — You may have seen someone else, not me.

Sixth chela — I saw the other day a lady who psychometrized things and told all their history. It was wonderful. When shall I develop clairvoyance? I have been your chela for several years. Now I ought to be able to work wonders.

Sage — I have not arrived yet at that stage myself.

Seventh chela — Guru, when first I came to you, things seemed to change, but now everything seems to go wrong with me. I have not been well for some time, money affairs have gone wrong and people make me agitated. Prayers annoy me, I cannot put my mind to meditation. I think there is no hope for me, Guru, and as my friend has left you, I feel I cannot go on any longer. Now I must do my own business alone instead of going after such things.

Sage — It is one's own attitude that changes life, but it is by patient pursuit that one arrives at the desired goal.

(Enter candidate)

Candidate — *(greets)* Will you take me as your chela, Guru? I have heard of you from my friend who said many good things about you. I have read much about these things and I have talked with many occultists. I think I am quite ready to take the spiritual path, do you not think so? I am sure you will not have much difficulty with me, because I

	am ripened. Do you really think there is a soul or a hereafter?
Sage	This, I suppose, you already know.
Candidate	Yes, but I would like to know what you think about it. *(little pause)* I will not belong to your group, excuse me for saying so. I don't wish to be bound by any vows, nor shall I make any promises, for I know if ever I did so, I should not be able to keep them. I don't want this to be known by my people and specially not by those of long robes. I'll be your chela, for I like you, but I hate to be among other chelas.
Sage	You do not need to be a chela, as you know already so many things.
Candidate	No, I have come to be your chela. Only I cannot have any discipline. Besides, I wonder if you agree with all I believe.
Sage	You keep on believing as you believe and go on the way you wish to tread. For this path is most difficult; it needs self-abnegation.

(Candidate greets and goes away)

Eighth chela	When I am before you, Guru, your inspiring presence gives me enthusiasm and faith. But as soon as I am away from you, I lose it all. When you speak to me, I believe it without any doubt, but when I go among my friends and hear them speak, then my mind becomes entirely confused. I get discouraged when people speak against these things, and doubt begins to creep into my mind.
Sage	The brick has to go through fire in order to become hard. You must learn to depend upon

your own feelings. It is then that belief becomes faith.

(Enter two policemen)

First Policeman — Is this not the bogeyman of whom people told us?

Second Policeman — I suspect this is the assassin of the young man at the Sarai.

First Policeman — Ha-ha-ha-ha-ha. And here he is preaching the gospel. Come along, bogeyman, you are wanted at the police station.

Second chela — *(to the third)* Look, here is the example of what is said in the scriptures, "You will know them by the result of their deeds."[4]

Third chela — It is also said in the scriptures, "Judge ye not, lest ye be judged."[5] We know not whether this is cause or effect. Sometimes what appears as effect may be the cause; sometimes what seems to be the cause may be the effect.

Fourth chela — I had thought so; there is nowhere in the world any good to be found. I now understand why there was all this talk of secrecy.

Fifth chela — This is the outcome of all that vagueness. If he had any truth, he could have put it in plain words. Look, even now he does not admit simply that he has killed the man.

---

4. Matthew 7.16
5. Matthew 7.1

First chela — *(to himself)* How time changes persons. True it is that "No one stands by you in your worst time." "Prosperity gathers friends, adversity scatters them."

(Sage stands up)

First chela — Guru, I will come with you.

Sage — No, you must not follow me in my disgrace. I must face it alone.

(First chela most unhappy)

Sage — *(turning to all his chelas)* My blessed chelas. Allow me to thank you most heartily for your response. Providence has brought us together here while I was on my way to the solitude from where I come. I have learned more from you than you have from me. And still you call me your Guru. Will you remember these my last words. Observe God in His manifestation, worship God in man, admire God in nature and love God in all living beings. Efface yourself continually and what will appear to you in the end will be God.

First Policeman — Cut short your sermon.

Sage — Continue to strive in the path of truth and be not satisfied with less than truth. In the light of truth you must see God and man, in the spirit of truth you must realize self and all.

Second Policeman — Now, that is enough.

Sage — *(stands up)* I will go where destiny will take me. Truth is victorious. God bless you. *(departs; all impressed and many sad)*

ACT III

SCENE I

Scene: Compound outside of the prison ground. Sage sitting in meditation. People come to greet him and depart.

One	*(among those who come to see him)* He must be a great sage. I wonder what has brought him to this prison.
Another	Many such saints sin in order to deserve life in prison.
Another	Look how deeply he is absorbed in his silence!
Another	He is as silent as the stork is while waiting for the fish to come.
Another	God's beloved he is. Such people care for no one, for nothing in the world. He is like a God on the earth.
Another	Psh, - God is in the heavens. When did you see him drop on earth? Don't speak so; it is sacrilege.
Another	I feel like sitting at his feet forever.
Another	Because you are so lazy.
Another	His atmosphere is so calm and peaceful.
Another	Look at his face, beaming with light. It is as if he were an angel.
Another	It seems lately angels have become cheap on the

	market; you can buy them at any price.

(Enter man, bringing a person who has lost the control of his nerves, and makes all sorts of faces and crooked gestures. When he departs, this person pulls his legs, saying, "Stay here")

Man	*(to Sage)* Will you cure him?
Sage	*(opens his eyes, touches his head and the man is well, all people amazed)*
Someone	Oh, he is a great healer!

(Enter a man and a woman, holding a woman between them)

Man	Will you please cure this person of obsession? *(to the woman)* Who is obsessing you?
Woman	I am a giant. I lived in the tree where this woman used to sit and sew. I looked and looked at her till I fell desperately in love with her. And now I have fallen I cannot rise. The woman possesses me and I obsess her. *(the woman moves her head round and round)*
Man	Away, you giant. Leave off controlling my wife.
Woman	No, I will not leave her.
Man	Do you know in whose presence you are? You will be driven out if you will not leave her, you will be burnt to pieces.

(Sage touches her)

Woman	Yes, yes, I leave her; I go, I am gone! *(the woman is well and they go out. All people there raving about the great sage)*

Another woman — Will you cure me of my illness? I get fits of temper. Then I tear my garments, I insult my friends, I torture animals, I quarrel with my neighbours. I fight with my husband, thrash my children. I throw at strangers anything within my reach. When I'm angry, I frighten devils away.

(Sage puts his hand on her head)

Woman — I'm cured, I'm cured, I feel I'm cured!

Everybody — Ah, what a great soul! This is the man I would follow with my eyes closed. To see a man like this is like seeing God. What power, he is a miraculous man!

(Enter two noblemen)

Noblemen — We have brought here the summons from our gracious queen to release you of your imprisonment. She has sufficient proofs now that you are innocent. We are asked to take you to the palace, where our queen is waiting to welcome you.

Sage — What have I, a wandering man, to do at the court? Prison or palace, are the same to me.

Nobleman — Great sage, if you would come, it would bless our queen and her palace.

Sage — Yes, I will come.

ACT IV

SCENE I

Scene: Palace veranda. The Sage is received, standing before the Queen, who is sitting near a little table with wine and glasses.

Queen — I am very sorry indeed, great Sage, that you were arrested in my kingdom. I apologize to you most humbly for this unjust treatment which you have received from our people. As the diamond shines out even if it is amongst garbage, so you have shown your light. I consider it my privilege to see you here and to receive your blessing.

Sage — All things that people do in life, good or bad, right or wrong, by these they build prison bars around themselves. Therefore at every moment of life their captivity becomes greater. Life itself is a prison, Queen, a prison which every soul experiences as it is dwelling in this mortal body of limitations. It is from this prison that I have sought freedom. Therefore no prison can bind my soul any more.

(The Queen offers wine to the Sage. She stands next to him, near the balustrade of the balcony. The Sage drinks)

Queen — I heard people talk so much about you and your wonderful healing power.

Sage — I never depend on popularity. People generally are like sheep; where one goes, all follow. They raise a person one day and throw him down the next. *(she puts her hand in his hand; he presses it to his heart)* I do not mean rare souls like you, fair Queen. It is the people I mean.

(People who had admired him pass by, looking and searching for the teacher and healer)

People O, he happens to be a false saint!

Others Look, look, he is drinking and making love to our beautiful Queen.

Woman *(who had come to get her head cured, holding both hands to her head)* He cannot cure my head, he cannot heal me!

Man *(comes in, limping)* I thought he was healing and he happens to be merrymaking. I have come from miles away, and it is all in vain.

Another Listen to what they say: it is all humbug.

Sage I had hardly uttered the philosophy when the example manifested before us. Every man weighs another soul in his own scale, and measures him with his own yard, not knowing the weight and length of the soul, neither comprehending its height nor its depth. Everyone judges all by himself.

Queen We must not remain here; we will go and have a quiet talk inside the palace.

ACT V

SCENE I

Scene: Room inside the palace. Queen and Sage, seated.

Queen *(with her hand on his chair)* The moment I heard of your presence here, I knew what was attracting me. Great Sage, I am hungering to understand life, thirsting for association with the Illuminated.

Sage	Yes, Queen, your hunger and thirst are of the soul. It is when a soul is born again that hunger and thirst begin.

(The Queen pours out wine and hands it to the Sage. The Sage drinks)

Queen	I should so much like to know about life and death, about rise and fall, about that which we see and that we do not see, about love and hate, about God and man.
Sage	Wonderful questions, Queen; your response draws you closer to my heart.
Queen	It is these questions that have attracted me to you, beloved Sage.
Sage	Your soul, beloved Queen, has waited for me, though it knew it not before we met. Life is one living stream, continually running without beginning nor end. Death is man's illusion. The change that covers from man's view his existence, he calls death. Life is still, but its flow which is ever moving, rises and falls in waves; it is this that created an illusion of rise and fall. All this we see is the manifestation of one Spirit in many and varied forms. Love, beautiful Queen, is the first will, the precedent cause. This whole manifestation is a phenomenon of love. Hate is the want of love; it has no existence of its own. God is the ideal. Man makes and raises him as high as he can for the expansion of his own soul.
Queen	How inspiring! It uplifts my spirit. How can I show you my gratitude, my devotion?

(The Sage holds her hand to his heart, and kisses her)

Queen — This is your home, since my heart has become an abode of your soul. You will bless me and my kingdom by staying here and will illuminate the chamber of my heart. I offer you, beloved Sage, my heart and soul and all I possess, though it is too small an offering to be made.

(She sends for a silk robe to replace the Wanderer's mantle, and gives him a pearl necklace instead of the old rosary. Gold-embroidered shoes are brought to replace the wooden ones)

Sage — This is all too rich for me.

Queen — Nothing is too rich for you, beloved.

(Enter Brahmins with two garlands of flowers and a tray with grain to give the blessing)

Brahmins — God bless this auspicious wedding.

(Entertainments are given to the Sage. Wine is brought and served by the Queen. Many courtiers come)

ACT VI

SCENE I

Scene: Dream—Wilderness

Sage — Wilderness, my dearest friend, why did I leave you? When did I leave you? Though I had left you, still you were always in my heart, — the memory of having meditated in the woods, of having wandered in the forests, of having talked with the trees of long tradition whose every leaf is a tongue of flame... Venerated trees, have I not taken refuge in your shadow from the hot sun, when tired of roaming about in the wilderness, bare-footed?...Little pools of water, I drank nectar from you...Joyful I felt under the vast canopy of the blue sky...Gentle streams of water, running from hills and rocks: I bathed in you and was purified of all infirmities...High mountains with a background of white clouds. No palace in the world could be compared with your beauty... Morning sun, you are most glorious in the wilderness. I have never seen your face so beaming anywhere else.

Ah, — am I really here, or am I in the midst of the world? Yes, there was a reason for being in the world. There is a reason for everything. Life is not without meaning, and all that one does, whether he knows or knows not, he only fulfills through it his life's purpose. The prison I was in was not a prison, for my conscience stood above it. The grandeur of the palace had no attraction for me. The only charm I felt there was my precious Queen. — Wilderness, you attract me, you call me. Though I long to be in the solitude, yet I never felt I was away from you.

ACT VII

SCENE I

Scene: Room inside the palace. Queen and Sage sitting next to one another. Courtiers present. The Prince is brought by the Governess and the Guardian. The Queen rises from her chair, kisses the Prince and brings him to the Sage.

Queen — Our little child, by the grace of God, is growing

marvellously, do you not think so?

Sage — *(takes the child and kisses it)* Yes, he is. *(holds him close to him)*

Governess — The Prince takes much delight in his play. He loves his little pony and does not allow anyone to touch it.

Sage — Does he put his mind to his studies?

Guardian — It is difficult to take the Prince from his play for his studies, but once he is studying he does it wonderfully well.

Queen — I don't know what would be the best way of bringing up our little child. I have been thinking much about it of late.

Sage — It is a great responsibility, beloved. Even a shadow of an undesirable person falling upon our child would make an impression upon him.

Queen — Does the child not bring with birth some inner tendencies and qualities?

Sage — Yes, he does, and yet they can be rubbed off by its experience on the earth. They can be covered by impressions it receives in coming here. To bring up a child is like moulding a new world. For it is man in whom God wakens to life.

Queen — Beloved, why are you looking sad today? Is there anything you need? I will procure all that wealth can bring, power can possess and love can supply — all you wish to make your life happy.

Sage — I am homesick, precious Queen.

Queen	Are you not at home then? I never thought that you had another home.
Sage	Yes, I had — solitude. It grieves me immensely to tell you, beloved Queen, that I have received a call to the wilderness which is my kingdom. I must go.
Queen	*(holds his hands and weeps)* You are not going, beloved, you will not go...
Sage	Now the hour has struck, precious Queen, that I should depart to roam about in the wilderness.
Queen	I will follow you to the end of the world!
Sage	No, beloved Queen, it is your duty to bring up this child to be the ruler of this kingdom. Destiny had arranged it so that he should be my son to reign over this country with wisdom and justice.

(The Queen weeps; all present are sad. The Sage embraces the Queen and kisses his son, takes off his crown and puts it on the head of the child. The mother cries and holds the child, weeping. Then he asks for his old mantle and takes off his kingly robe; he puts on his old rosary and his wooden shoes)

Sage	(*to himself*) This is the picture of life. Tarry here a while and then depart.

(He waves his hand and blesses all)

---

[1] THE LIVING DEAD

by Inayat Khan

CHARACTERS

Maharaja, an Indian king
Puran, his son
Maharani, the wife of the Maharaja
Naeka, a court dancer
Saheli, Naeka's maid
Bairagi, an ascetic sage
1st Courtier
2nd Courtier
1st Musician
2nd Musician
A page
1st Kazak)
2nd Kazak) Men who execute life's punishment
1st robber
2nd robber
3rd robber
4th robber
A fruitseller woman
1st farmer
2nd farmer
A boy with halva (a boy selling sweets)
An old man

Documents:
od.tp. = an old typescript of unknown provenance.
hw.IK. = handwritten notes by Inayat Khan written on the stationery of the White Star Line.

Notes:
1. Od.tp.: "Incomplete" added by hand

A woman with buttermilk (A peasant woman selling buttermilk)
A merchant with his wife
A mother with four children
A magician

ACT I

SCENE I

Scene: Maharaja is sitting on cushions. A servant waving a fan. 1st courtier sitting on his left hand, 2nd courtier on his right hand. Musicians singing and playing.

Maharaja *(after song)* Khan Sahab, which raga did you sing?

Musician It is Deepak, Huzur, the song of fire.

Maharaja But the fire has not yet broken out!

Musician Pardon, Huzur, it is just kindled; it will come to a blaze.

Page *(enters)* Maharaja! Naeka, a dancer of a most exquisite beauty whose skill has amazed all the great artists of the country, awaits your Majesty's orders.

Maharaja *(turning to 2nd courtier)* Do you know her? Is she really wonderful?

Courtier She is beauty itself. The colour of her skin is like a champak flower. With deer's eyes she penetrates the hearts of her admirers. Her swift movements are as graceful as the movements of the cobra. With nightingale's voice she sings, enchanting those who hear her.

Maharaja *(to page)* Bring her.

(Enter Naeka, greets Maharaja.)

Maharaja Have you caught your beauty from the rose?

Naeka Pardon me, Maharaja, the rose has borrowed its beauty from me.

Maharaja *(smiles)* Show me your wonderful skill, Naeka, I have heard so much about it.

(Naeka performs the dance of the flower girl, with gestures picking flowers and making them into a wreath; then takes a real flower garland, dances with it and at the end puts it on the neck of Maharaja. Maharaja takes her hands, holds them to his breast, drawing her nearer. She hangs down backwards, turning away her head. Enter page. Naeka leaves and goes back to her place.)

Page Your Majesty, Prince Puran is coming to pay his respects before going for a ride.

(Enter Puran, greets in the royal manner, saluting bending low, touching the ground. Naeka struck by the beauty of the prince, touches her heart while looking at him.)

Maharaja *(to Puran)* Are you going on horseback, son? Have your finished with your studies?

Puran *(embarrassed, with a half smile)* I intended taking some hours from my studies to be alone with nature.

Maharaja *(ironically)* Oh yes. Don't stay away too long.

(Puran leaves; Naeka shows her thrills by movement and expression, acting as if she felt inclined to follow him; walks two or three steps, then recovers her senses, moving her hand over her head as if to throw off her thought.)

Maharaja *(after Puran has left, to 1st courtier)* Why is it that he does not put his mind to study? What does he do?

Courtier He likes to be in nature; and when at home, he is frequently seen in his mother's company.

Maharaja I scarcely see him!

Courtier He does not enjoy hunting, wrestling, boxing; he is happy wandering alone in nature.

Maharaja We must keep watch over him!

Courtier Prince Puran is not addicted to any vices: drinking, smoking, or any other such habits. The prince is different from the young men of his age; he is not attracted to frivolities and stands for ideal and principle.

2nd Courtier It is natural; to what family does he belong!

1st Courtier He is simple but most intelligent at the same time; he does not care for reading or writing, but he thinks.

Maharaja *(smiles)* What does he think? Does he think of the moon?

(Wine is brought on a golden tray; Maharaja gives it to Naeka; the courtiers give it to the musicians and Maharaja passes the wine over to the courtiers.)

1st Musician To the glory of Maharaja. *(all present repeat)*

Maharaja *(to Naeka)* Now open your wings and fly, beautiful bird.

(Naeka dances. Maharaja moves his head on the rhythm of the dance. Naeka going round and round, gets into a swoon; raising her hands, balancing as if she might fall. Maharaja rises from his

seat and goes to her, makes a sign to the courtiers to leave the place. Courtiers and musicians depart. Maharaja holds Naeka to his breast. When she opens her eyes, she turns her head, swings her hands towards the door by which the prince had left.)

Maharaja One jasmine kiss. *(she responds, and he kisses her)*

ACT II

SCENE I

Scene: Drawing room in the new home of Naeka near the palace. Naeka putting kohl on her eyelids, touching her lips with red paint. Saheli holding a mirror before her, standing.

Saheli Bai, providence has granted you comfort, jewels, the sweet little pavilion Maharaja has given you; besides you have his love. Nothing more one could wish and yet I scarcely see you smile. Has an evil eye fallen on you? Maybe you are worrying about something. If only I knew what troubles your mind, I would give anything in the world to see you smile again.

Naeka Yes, I have everything that one could need, but I wish I could love him. I can't say I love him. His nearness is loathsome to me. Besides I cannot accustom myself to his expectations. He asks of me to abstain from every manner of frivolity.

Saheli Yes, because he loves you. You are a born artist, excuse me, Bai. *(smiling with an expression of funmaking and with gestures)*. You belong to those charming women who are inclined to love one and to like another, to smile at one and to wink at another, to caress one and to pet another, to kiss one and to embrace another.

Naeka Am I really charming?

Saheli — Certainly, Bai, you know you are. There is a woman who has a charm for many, and there is a woman who has a charm for one and there is another woman like I myself who has a charm for none. Your vanity has been fed, Bai, by the attention of many admirers.

Naeka — From my early youth I have grown up playing, chumming, singing and dancing with friends. I have attracted young men like a magnet and so I have been never starved of attention.

Saheli — This life must seem strange to you Bai, but you will grow to it.

Naeka — *(shaking her head)* No, never.

Saheli — You will change like the season when the time is there.

Naeka — This life is like a prison to me. I am like a bird in a golden cage. *(weeping)* I would rather be a free dancer than a queen in captivity.

Saheli — *(wiping her eyes and kissing her)* If I was admired by Maharaja as you are, I would walk to him on my hands. *(Naeka smiles)* You are yet too young to know what it is to be loved by Maharaja. Every dancer in the country envies your privilege. Now Maharaja has made you the court-dancer, but *(whispering in Naeka's ears)* one day you might become queen.

Naeka — That is all I want: to be queen one day. Yet I wish it was Puran and not he.

Saheli — *(holding her head with both hands in a great fright; then touching her lips with her finger)* Ah, seal your lips, it can be most disastrous.

Naeka — *(rises from her seat and looks out of the window)*

There he is going on horseback. Saheli, I pray, will you call him; say that I have something to talk over with him. Bring him here, won't you Saheli, please.

(Saheli gets up and runs to call the prince. Naeka acts when she is alone as if she wonders if he will come or if he will not come and how will she approach him and what she will say to him, embarrassed and afraid, enthusiastic and dumbfounded, she awaits his coming.)

Puran *(enter, to Naeka)* Did you call me?

Naeka Yes, I did call you, Puran; come in, sit here. *(giving him a seat next to her. He sits, shy, with downcast eyes)* I admire your beautiful horse. It seems to be proud of its handsome rider. Tell me, why is Maharaja not pleased with you? I would do anything to make him more favourable to you.

Puran Father's pleasure is all I seek; when I cannot please him, I realize my unworthiness.

Naeka You, unworthy, how can you say that? You are the worthiest son any father could have. If you were the king, people here would be happier than they have ever been. Our people will rejoice seeing you one day sitting on the throne with the crown on your head.

Puran May Father live and reign forever.

Naeka *(whispering)* I would be the one who stood by you if [2]struggle arose. *(with determination, raising her finger)* Know, Puran, that you always have someone to give your confidence to. I can be hard as a rock when it comes to a test.

---

2. Od.tp.: "To stand by you if ever" added by hand instead of "who stood by you if struggle"

Puran — *(looks bewildered)* What do you mean?

Naeka — Your mother must be most beautiful.

Puran — My mother's beauty cannot be observed by every eye.

Naeka — Is she old?

Puran — Her soul is older still.

Naeka — No doubt, she loves you very much.

Puran — She is for me God's compassion on earth.

Naeka — *(reluctantly)* I am your father's favourite *(smiling)* but I am young enough to be your love-mate. *(Puran still more perplexed)* Puran, why are you silent, why do you not talk to me? *(she puts her arm in his, caressing his hand, draws closer to his face)* Puran, have you ever known, or heard, or seen the outburst of the heart's volcano? *(Puran rises, she rises also and holds his hands)* Think what you will, say what you will, but let once my lips touch yours; what will be, will be. (*she throws her arms around him and kisses him; sees Maharaja coming behind the back of Puran. She looses her hold and*[3] *faints. Puran leaves hurriedly, not seeing his father)*

Maharaja — *(raises her up, one hand on his dagger, in rage)* What is this?

Naeka — *(throws her head on his breast and puts her hand on his shoulders)* Your son, your son!

Maharaja — My son, he is not my son. He cannot be my son. How dare he come here. Did he not know that I care for

---

3. Od.tp.: "pretends as if she were fainting" added by hand

you! He is a disgrace to my name. *(he lays Naeka down on cushions, she lies motionless)*

Maharaja *(to Saheli, outside)* Send for Kazaks [murderers]. (*He takes his own scarf and tears it)* Tear him, destroy him.

(Enter two Kazaks. Naeka sits up with staring eyes, listening)

Kazaks Command.

Maharaja Puran. Flay him, cut his head off, bury him alive, throw him into the sea, do whatever you choose, that I may never see his face again.

(Naeka trembles, falls down in despair. Kazaks depart)

Maharaja Saheli.

(Enter Saheli)

Maharaja Rosewater. *(Saheli runs and brings it, sprinkles it on Naeka's head. Maharaja, holding her with his left hand, fans her with his silk handkerchief)*

ACT III

SCENE 1

Scene: The jungle at sunset. A bitter cry of a woman from behind the scene.

Woman's cry My beloved son, my only son.

A deep voice Mother, mother, do not despair.

Crude voices — Come, come on. Linger no more, here.

(Puran is pushed on the scene by the two Kazaks, then stands calmly)

1st Kazak — Your head is to be chopped here.

2nd Kazak — Your bones will dry here in the sun.

Puran — I am perfectly resigned to father's command, if only you will allow me one moment to pray.

1st Kazak — No, it can't be done.

2nd Kazak — *(to 1st Kazak)* No, let him, let him.

1st Kazak — Do it quickly. We must return before sunset *(pointing at the red sky)* with your head to be brought before Maharaja.

(Puran kneeling down with palms joined, his head slightly raised)

1st Kazak — Let us take a little drop. *(they drink from the bottle)*

Puran — God, with a clear conscience and with pure heart, I lay before Thee the record of my life's deeds. No one have I ever offended, no one have I caused any harm. Clear away, Lord, my father's misconception of me; comfort the sad heart of my loving mother, and forgive the one who ignorantly brought this about. I pray Thee, Lord, bless them all. Amen. *(bends his head low. To Kazaks)* Now I am ready.

1st Kazak — *(to 2nd Kazak)* You do it.

2nd Kazak — You strike. *(both unsheathe their daggers)*

1st Kazak — You do it.

2nd Kazak No you.

1st Kazak *(goes to Puran, violently moves his weapon; when it nearly touches Puran's head, his hand becomes stunned. To 2nd Kazak)* No, you do it.

2nd Kazak I will. *(he twists and turns and passionately moves around, preparing himself to strike. He raises his hand with a great strength. When the dagger is near Puran's head, the Kazak's hand trembles and he throws his weapon away. Calls 1st Kazak, makes gesture)* Let him go.

1st Kazak *(with expression of fright, whispers)* No, what will Maharaja do to us?

2nd Kazak We shall see.

1st Kazak *(raises Puran up, holding his hand)* Now young man, we let you go; but go far, far away. *(Puran bows and leaves)*

1st Kazak *(to 2nd Kazak)* It's all right.

2nd Kazak He was innocent.

1st Kazak But what shall we say to Maharaja?

2nd Kazak He is dead and buried. *(both laugh, holding their stomach, looking in the direction where Puran has left)*

ACT IV

SCENE 1

Scene: The city gate at dawn. The moon still shining. A Bairagi [sage] *in Samadhi* [stage of meditation] *sitting on a tiger-skin, with a snake round his neck, between the road and the city wall. Two robbers sitting on a rock on the right, at the side of the road.*

1st Robber Thank goodness, we had some luck last night, and a good escape. But what about the other two; why did they not yet return? *(the 2nd Robber stands up and looks in the distance)*

2nd Robber They may come any moment.[4] There they are. *(pointing)* Do you see?

1st Robber They seem to have robbed a lot: see the heavy burden they are carrying. *(silence)* But it is a man!

(The two robbers rise, go some steps forward)

2nd Robber Hallo, what have your brought?

3rd Robber Brought our ill luck.

4th Robber We have never had such[5] a bad trip as this since we began robbery. When passing through the forest we saw from a distance the face of a beautiful woman. Our heart was delighted at the prospects of a good luck. As we went near, what do we find? This wretched man.

3rd Robber He had gone hungry, I suppose, for many days. He had nothing with him.

---

4. Od.tp.: Stage direction "Silence" added by hand
5. Od.tp.: "such" added by hand

4th Robber We thought to spare him from the wolves and picked him up in order to sell him at the slave market for twenty thousand dirams.

3rd Robber *(to other two robbers)* Yes, he *(pointing to the 4th robber)* had great dreams about this bargain but it all turned out to nothing.

4th Robber He was not so bad at first when we took him along with us.

3rd Robber We should have left him on the way when we saw that he was too ill to follow us; but you still persisted that we should carry him through the forest. Here we have tired our arms and legs and now he is worse than before, perhaps on the point of dying.

1st Robber *(frightened)* Be careful. If the police sees us with him, he will arrest us for his death.

(The four robbers, shocked, leave the body on the place and escape. An old fruitseller woman is hurrying on to go to the market with a straw tray of fruit on her head. She knocks against the body of Puran, is frightened and bends down)

Fruitseller What is it? Who is it? *(looks at him)* Poor man; he is dead perhaps.

(Two men pass with spade and harrow on their shoulders, going on their way to the fields. They stop to see what is going on)

Fruitseller Poor man, what has happened to him; is he dead? *(holds her finger near his nose)* He is still breathing.

1st Man What shall we do?

2nd Man Let us bring him near Bairagi; he will take care of him.

(Both men lift the branches on which the body was carried and

bring it before the Bairagi. The fruitseller woman takes her tray with fruit and runs quickly to follow the man)

Fruitseller — Baba, Baba, look at this man, help him, Baba, help him!

Bairagi — *(opens his eyes, bends low and looks at Puran, gently puts his hand in the centre of his breast and breathes on him. Puran opens his eyes)* Yes, awake, awake, awake. *(Puran moves head and body)*

Puran — Yes.

Bairagi — Now you rise, rise, *(he lifts him)* rise. *(Puran has risen and sits. Bairagi puts his hand in the brass pitcher next to him and wets Puran's forehead. Puran brightens up. It becomes light while all this happens*[6]*. People are coming from both sides: a boy with halva* [a sort of sweet], *an old man, a woman with buttermilk, a merchant with his wife, a mother with four children. They all stand still, curiously looking at the scene before them)*

Child — There is a tiger, it is looking at me. (*the three other children come nearer)*

Other child — *(frightened)* Oh, look at the snake. *(draws closer to his mother)*

Old man — *(with important voice to the children)* The snake is the sign of wisdom.

Wife — *(to husband)* What was the matter with this young man?

Husband — Life is a mystery.

---

6. Od.tp.: An indecipherable word followed by "break" and then "all" crossed out and "is happening" instead of "happens"

Old man *(important)* Life is a problem. (*looks at Bairagi for his opinion. Nodding head as if approving*[7])

Bairagi *(making gesture)* All this is a mazing Maya; there are four days of moonlight and then comes the dark night. The vision of Maya is the dream of mortality. *(Puran listens attentively)* When the screen will be removed from your eyes, you will see that nothing here belongs to you: the honour that cannot be sustained long, the name that will once be forgotten, the treasure that will one day be snatched from your hands, the comfort that will no more be yours, are of little value.

Merchant But the thousand rupies I have buried will not be taken away by anyone!

Bairagi You will say: this I hold, that I possess, but in reality nothing belongs to you, not even your own body.

Man with spade *(with an expression of doubt*[8]*)* Then we must have nothing?

Bairagi The day when you will have nothing, you will have everything.

Merchant So we must leave the pursuit of the world?

Bairagi When you cease to follow the world, the world will follow you.

Merchant Then what must we do?

Bairagi Realize the one, rising above all duality, burn your

---

7. Od.tp.: "Nodding head as if approving" added by hand
8. Od.tp.: "With an expression of doubt" added by hand

false ego to ashes[9] and powder you skin with them[10].

Merchant Do you mean to say we must give up all this?

Bairagi Hold on till it gives you up.

Man with harrow *(Ironically[11])* Then you think the whole life is meaningless?

Bairagi It is meaningless until you have understood the meaning of it.

Merchant Baba, is life on earth worthless?

Bairagi The moment you recognize its worthlessness, life becomes worth while.[12]

(A magician enters, his eyebrows painted white, his forehead painted red)

Old man Now you have spoken about life, Baba, but what about death?

Magician *(emphatically[13])* What are you asking him; what does he know of life or[14] death! Can he make the dead alive? *(with gestures[15])* I can cut myself and heal instantly; and I can kill myself and waken to life. I can drown myself and rise upon the water. Now you all who listen, leave him alone and follow me. I can get you anything: health, wealth, success, power, pleasure, all.

---

9. Od.tp.: "to ashes" crossed out by hand
10. Od.tp.: "The ashes" added by hand to replace "them"
11. Od.tp.: "Ironically" added by hand
12. Od.tp.: "while" crossed out and "living" added by hand
13. Od.tp.: "Emphatically" added by hand
14. Od.tp.: "or" crossed out and "and" added by hand
15. Od.tp.: "With gestures" added by hand

Old man — Let us see this fellow, what he is going to do. *(all, one after another, follow the magician)*

The boy with halva — *(the last remaining of the crowd pointing at Bairagi)* Nothing to do with him.

(Bairagi left with Puran)

Puran — They are like a flock of sheep.

Bairagi — Such is the way of the world.

Puran — Master, all you have said has deeply touched me. Pray grant me the privilege of your service, that one day I may deserve to live Vairag.

Bairagi — Vairag, my son, is a freedom from all bondage. Are you drawn by family ties?

Puran — No Guru, except the deep devotion I have for my mother.

Bairagi — Have you any ambitions of wealth or rank?

Puran — I have none, though I was born in a position to have it all.

Bairagi — The way of the mystic leads to the goal of annihilation. Will you keep to the path steadily in the face of all the earthly temptations, young man?

Puran — Yes Guru, by your help I shall gain the strength that will carry me through.

Bairagi — I will take you on probation, son, for a limited period during which you will pass through many tests.

Puran — *(bends down to the feet of the Bairagi)* I surrender myself to your inspiring guidance.

(Bairagi lifts Puran up, for a moment holds him, gives him his mantle to wear, the rosary he was holding he puts on Puran's neck, then touches his forehead with the water of his pitcher. And blesses him and hands [16]*.)*

ACT V

SCENE 1

Scene: Drawing room of Naeka. Naeka standing before the mirror putting on her earrings. Saheli holding the tray of jewels.

Naeka — Since the loss of his son, Maharaja is most depressed. Did you hear anything about Maharani?

Saheli — I have heard she hardly eats and never speaks and only moans during her sleep. While awake she calls the name of her son: Puran, Puran! She has aged so much that one can hardly recognize her and she has almost lost her sight by weeping. Did you hear about the garden of Puran, Bai, which was neglected for all these years Puran had gone. Many trees died and plants whithered away. Wolves were making their home in the place where the prince lived. But now they say that a wanderer has come there. He sits under the shade of a tree and since he has sprinkled a few drops of water from his pitcher, the whole garden has flourished again. People go in hundreds and thousands to see him. *(looking out of the window)* There he is going, do you see, Bai?

Naeka — Who?

Saheli — The sage of whom they talk so much in the city.

---

16. Od.tp.: illegible word added in handwriting

Naeka *(also looking out of the window)* He is the sort of man who can read one's fortune. Saheli, I pray, call him here.

Saheli *(fearing)* Oh Bai, if Maharaja knows I called a stranger here, he will give me to the vultures.

Naeka *(smiling)* Go, it will be all right.

(Saheli leaves. Naeka goes before the mirror and arranges her hair. Puran enters, wearing a growing beard, in the mantle Bairagi has given him, with the rosary on his neck. Both sit down)

Naeka When I saw you I thought you could see into my problem and help me out of it. *(Puran listens. Maharaja enters and seeing Naeka speak with a stranger is shocked and stands, looking what is going on)* The Maharaja who has loved me so long, I presume is losing interest in me.

Puran What do you think is the reason?

Naeka In the beginning he was blindly in love with me, but suspecting his son in connection with me, he condemned him to death and since then it seems as though his heart is becoming frozen.

(Maharaja holds his heart and hangs his head back with half closed eyes, remembering the incident)

Puran And what did Maharani do?

Naeka *(reluctantly)* She was most grieved at the loss of her son.

Puran Now what is she doing?

Naeka *(with hanging head, weeping[17])* She has almost lost her mind in his thought.

Puran I wish to see her. Will you please send for her.

Naeka Immediately?

Puran Just now.

(Naeka calls Saheli, whispers something in her ears)

Puran Now tell me, was Puran really in fault?

Naeka That I can't say, my lips tremble, my heart fails.

Puran *(looking into her eyes)* Tell me.

Naeka I could not have told anyone in the world, but I cannot keep any secret from you. I know you look in my soul. *(Maharaja is eagerly listening. Naeka weeps)* It was my fault; I wanted to be queen, but young Puran's wife and one day my heart burst out before him and he refused. But the impression Maharaja had was that he made love to me. In a fit of anger he condemned his son to death.

(Saheli brings Maharani, dressed simply; puts cushions for her to sit on the right side of Puran.)

Maharani *(as if she were in a dream)* Why did you bring me here? Why am I brought here?

Puran What have you to say?

Maharani *(nervously straightens as if hearing a familiar voice)* I long to see my son.

17. Od.tp.: "Weeping" added by hand

Naeka But he is dead.

Maharani *(agitated[18], irritated)* No, he is living.

Puran *(whispering)* He is living dead.

Maharani This voice, this is his voice. *(stands up, draws nearer to Puran, stretches out her hands)* I want to look at you. *(she feels his hand, cries)* My Puran, you are my Puran.

Puran Mother. *(they embrace. Naeka horrified[19])*

Maharani I wish to see you. *(Puran puts his two hands over her eyes. She looks at him, kisses him)*

Maharaja *(steps forward, Naeka faints[20])* Do my eyes deceive me; are you really there? My son, my Puran. I had never thought I would ever see you again. *(stretches his hands upwards)* Thanks providence. *(to Puran)* Will you ever forgive me? I can never forgive myself for the pain I have caused you.

Puran Father, I am always your son.

Maharaja What more do I want? I have had my days. Now you reign over this country.

Puran *(rises)* No father, I am going in search of another kingdom.

---

18. Od.tp.: "Agitated" added by hand
19. Od.tp. "Horrified" added by hand
20. Od.tp.: "Faints" added by hand

[In the file there is a photocopy of Inayat Khan's handwriting on paper headed WHITE STAR LINE which appears to be working papers for the play:]

And as swift as the [indecipherable word]

You know as well as I know do that I am naturally so disposed that while I have one and told to one and caress [indecipherable word] *like another, to talk to one and liken to another, to smile at one and to shed tears before another to caress one and to pale another to keep one and embrace another you know as well a I know I am naturally so disposed that while* [all previous crossed out]

I love one, I like another, to kiss one and to embrace another you know as well as I know I love one I like another while I smile at one I wink at another while I carace one I pale another, while I kiss one I embrace another.

[NEW PAGE]

A. He expects me to see no man, to talk to no man, to associate with no man, to appear before no man. Even my women friends have no exess to my home. I must veil my face - then passage which has been crossed out I think - from my earlier youth I have grown up with the tendence of running, jumping, dancing. I am well with all outdoor sports - I would rather be a free dancer than a captive queen (weeps).

Saheli: (wiping Naeka's eyes) You are yet too young to know what [privilege crossed out] *Is to be loved by a Maharaja, every dancer in the country envies your privilege*

Naika: Yes you are right it is a privilege which I have not yet grown to appreciate fully and yet I wish it was Puran and not he.

Glossary of Foreign Words 1924 II

The original language is indicated following each word in parentheses:

Arabic = A
French = F
German = Gr
Gujarati = G
Greek = Gk
Hindustani, Hindi = H
Persian = P
Sanskrit = S
Turkish = T
Urdu = U

The usual (dictionary) meaning of the word is given first; if the word has a special use in Sufi terminology, this meaning is given second, indicated by (suf).

Transliterations were made according to the following systems:

for Arabic: *The Encyclopedia of Islam* (New edition, Leiden, 1960-), except "k" and "dj" which have been replaced by "q" and "j".

for Persian: F. Steingass, *Comprehensive Persian-English Dictionary*, (8th edition, London, 1977).

for Sanskrit: M. Monier-Williams, *Sanskrit-English Dictionary*, (New Delhi, 1976; originally published in 1899).

A

ābi rū (P): freshness of countenance, radiance of face;
(suf): smiling forehead

ahīmsa (S, ahīnsa): harmlessness (one of the cardinal virtues of most Hindu sects, but particularly of the Buddhists and Jains; also personified as the wife of Dharma)

ā'īna <u>kh</u>āna (P): hall or palace of mirrors

ākāsha (S): open space, sky, accommodation;
(suf): receptivity, possibility

akhlāq (A): plural of khulq, morals, morality, good qualities, manners;
(suf): akhlāq Allāh, the manner of God

ālif (A): the first letter of the Arabic, Persian and Urdu alphabets (corresponding to alpha in the Greek alphabet); also, the number one

ānanda (S): pleasure, joy, bliss;
(suf): the soul's existence, happiness

āsaf (A): title generally given to a wazir; (upper case A) pen name of Mir Mahbub 'Ali Khan, 9th Nizam of Hyderabad

āsana(s) (S): posture; third limb of Patanjali's raja yoga

āvatāra (S): descent, appearance of a deity upon earth; the incarnations of Vishnu; incarnation of a deity;
(suf): God's Messenger, Prophet

B

baqā' (A): remaining; duration, permanence; eternity, immortality; life, living;
(suf): realization, an aspect of spiritual development; the ultimate stage of meditation; the life in God

bāy'at (A, T): pledge, allegiance; investiture; homage, fealty;
(suf): initiation

brāhmana (S) (English Brahmin): member of the highest Hindu caste of traditional priests, religious leaders and scholars

būddhi, būddh (S): wise or learned, reasonable, intelligent, having the power of forming and retaining conceptions and general ideas; source of the title Buddha

C

cherāg [cherāgh (U), chirāgh(P)]: lamp, light;
(suf): a person ordained to perform the Universal Worship Service

chēla (S): a servant, slave; one who serves a master; disciple

D

dār-al-salā'm (A): the gate of peace, shrine of God, the Holy City

darwīsh (P) (English dervish), religious mendicant, fakir

dhārma (S): morality, duty; the complex of values and law which identify any given (sub-)caste group

dhikr (A): remembrance, recital;
(suf): a spiritual practice of repetition of sacred words, especially the names of God

dīwān (P) (English divan): a collection of poems

dwīja (S): twice-born; one of the highest three castes, who are born again at their initiation, especially a title for a Brahmin, the highest caste

E

etekad, see ‘itiqā d

F

faqīr (A): beggar, mendicant, dervish

fanā' (A): passing away, perishing; mortality, death;
(suf): annilihation of the false self
fanā'-fī-sheikh: first degree of fanā, passing beyond empirical self-awareness into the initiator's viewpoint and attunement;

fanā'-fī-rasūl: second degree of fanā, absorption in a focus on a prophet/messenger;
fanā'-fī'llāh: third degree of fanā, absorption in the realization of God

fikr (A): thought, reflection;
(suf): a practice of silent repetition of a sacred word

G

gāthā (S): verse, song; part of the scripture of the Parsis;
(suf): series of teachings from Inayat Khan, intended as introductory lessons for *mureed*s

gāthaka(s) (S): chanting of a sacred poem;
(suf): a series of teachings, embracing several categories (religious, social, as preparation for candidates for initiation) in the teachings of Inayat Khan

guru (S): teacher, spiritual guide; a respected or venerated person

H

ḥadīth, āḥadīth (pl) (A): traditional sayings and recorded actions attributed to the Prophet Muhammad, held to have been recorded directly by those who knew him;

ḥadīth qudsī (A): a class of hadith giving words spoken by God (as distinguished from hadith nabawi, prophetic traditions, which gives the words of the Prophet Muhammad); hadith qudsi are considered by some as equivalent in authority to the Qur'an itself, and are especially prized by Sufis, who preserve some rejected by the four recognized authorities on hadith

hāmpta (P): equal, like, resembling;
(suf): etheric double

ḥaqq (A): justice, truth, God (one of the 99 names of God)

hijrat (A): emigration, separation;
(suf): Inayat Khan's departure from home in India on his way to the West, September 13, 1910, celebrated on its anniversary

ḥūr (houri in English), pl. of hawrā' (A): virgin of Paradise, female angel

I

īmān (A): faith in God, security, trust;
(suf): self-confidence produced by divine awareness

'itiqād (A): confidence, faith, belief;
'itiqād, rasm o ravāj, literally "beliefs, habits, and customs", translated as "Superstitions, customs, and beliefs", a series of lessons which form part of the Gatha papers, dictated by Inayat Khan

J

jalāl (A): majesty, power, greatness;
(suf): positive expressive power, energy, one aspect of which may be considered the masculine

jamāl (A): beauty, elegance;
(suf): the responsive principle, one aspect of which may be considered the feminine

jinn (A): a collective denoting fire spirits, occupying an intermediate plane between the earthly and the angelic

jīvan mūkta (S): freedom from the cycle of rebirth, the liberated soul or life

jñāna (S): knowledge, understanding, wisdom, important in Buddhist teachings

K

kaiser (Gr) (derived from caesar, Latin): emperor; (upper case K) the title of the German emperor

kārma (S): act, work, result

kamāl (A): completion, perfection

khalīfa (A) (English caliph): deputy, representative, successor

khawas (A): aristocrats, those regarded as special;
(suf): the initiated; a category in the teachings for higher initiates

khudā (P): God (from khud, self)

kshātria (S): second highest Hindu caste, warriors

L

laj (S): honour, sense of decency;
(suf): the determination to avoid shame

M

mahātma (S): literally, great swan; large-minded, noble, eminent, one of great soul

mahāraja (S): great king, a ruler with other kings under his authority

majdhūb (A): someone who has lost contact with ordinary life, often considered a madman, but also honoured as an advanced, if unconventional, spiritual seeker

majzub (P, U): see majdhūb

māntra shāstra (S): instruction, scientific work concerning sacred words mūni (S): ascetic, hermit, especially one who has taken a vow of silence

mureed, murīd (A, P, U): an initiate;
(suf): the eighth degree of initiation

murshid (A, P, U): a spiritual teacher and guide;
(suf, with upper case M): Pir-o-Murshid Inayat Khan

muwākkal (A): trustee, guardian, representative;
(suf): elemental, fine entity born of man's thoughts

N

nāda (S): sound

Nāda Brāhma (S): literally, sound God, meaning the Creator

nafs (A): self, ego, essence

naṣīḥāt (A): advice, admonition
(suf): a category in Inayat Khan's teachings for advanced initiates

nirvāna (S): extinguishment, annihilation, "going out", as of a candle, from the limitations and restrictions of outward selfhood into a state of abiding, elevated serenity;
(suf): without colour

P

prāna (S): breath, vitality, life

Q

qādir (A): measure, evaluation, fixed limit;
(suf, al-Qādir): one of the ninety-nine names of God, referring to the divine sovereignty

qāḍā' (A), qażā' (T, P, U): fate, destiny, destructive power; conditioning;
(suf): divine will

R

ṛājas (S): energy, action; middle of the three forms of energy

rasul (A): messenger, envoy;
(suf): the highest grade of the spiritual hierarchy, a messenger from God whose message is for all of humanity

rịāzat (A, P): abstinence, training, discipline, religious exercise;
(suf): one of the 'chapters' of the Githas, there translated as esotericism

rind (P): scamp, knave, rogue, drunkard;
(suf): in poetry, one whose exterior invites censure, but whose heart is sound

riyazat: see rịāzat

S

saf (A): clean, pure, precise

ṣālik (A): traveller, doctor
(suf): a Sufi walking the path of study, meditation, ethics; opposite to the rind

ṣāngam(a) (S): confluence of two rivers, especially the Ganges and the Yamuna

ṣāngātha (S): meeting place, confluence, consonance;
(suf): a category of teachings for advanced initiates

satī (S): perfect or divine woman; faithful wife who burns herself on her husband's funeral pyre

ṣāttva (S): energy, goodness; the highest of the three forms of energy

ṣāut-i sarṃād (S): eternal sound, the music of the angelic spheres

shaykh(a) (A): elder, chief (in a tribal, patriarchal, or scholarly sense);
(suf): an authorized teacher

shaf̣āyāt (A): healing process;
(suf): a higher initiation in the Healing Activity

siṛāj (A): lamp;
(suf): the title given to the person in charge of the Universal Worship for a country;
siraj-un-munir: munir means brilliant, shining; the person in charge of the Universal Worship worldwide

shūdras (S): the lowest of the four Hindu castes

sophīa (Gk): wisdom

sulūk (A): road, way, manner;
(suf): a category in the Gathas and Githas, translated as morals

T

talīm (A): teaching, instruction;
(suf): a category in the teachings for higher initiates

tāqwa tahārat (A): piety in purity;
(suf) a category in the Gathas, translated as "Daily Life"

tāmmas (S): darkness, error; the lowest of the three forms of energy

taṣāwwuf (A): literally, the wearing of woollen clothes;
(suf): the word translated as Sufism

tawajjēh (A): inclination, care, favour;

(suf): a method for promoting transformation of an initiate, involving "facing" the teacher

tō ōn (Gk. [from *to* the + *einai* to be]): the existent, that which is

U

'urs (A): wedding feast;
(suf): day of celebration, often the anniversary of the death of a Sufi saint; used also as a term of the Summer School in Suresnes, France

V

v̤āishyas (S): members of the third Hindu caste, merchants

v̤āiragya (S): growing pale; absence of passion; indifference, renunciation

Viladat (A): nativity, birth;
(suf): the birthday of Inayat Khan, July 5, 1882, celebrated on its anniversary

W

wahm (A): imagination, fancy, delusion

wājd (A): ecstasy, rapture; "finding", a condition of spiritual exaltation, often induced by music and/or poetry

wasīyat (A): precept, command;
(suf): a category in the teachings of Inayat Khan for advanced initiates

waẓīfa (A): daily worship;
(suf): a devotional text; a word or words for repetition

Y-Z

yaqīn (A): confidence, certainty

yōgi (S): practitioner of Yoga

zikr (P, U), zikar (Gu), see <u>dh</u>ikr

List of Persons, Places, Works, etc.

Aladdin, (A. 'Ala'-ad-Dīn, meaning "nobility of the faith") a character in one of the tales in *The Arabian Nights,* 7

Bahram, the name of a series of Sassanian monarchs, here referring to Bahram V Gur, known, among other things, for his skill in hunting onanger (*gur* in Persian), 218

Bedil (Abul-Ma'ani Mirza Abdul-Qadir Bedil) (1642-1720), a widely known Persian poet of Turkic descent, originally from Kabul province in present-day Afghanistan,161

Coué, Émile (1857-1926): French pharmacist who popularized the idea of autosuggestion, especially the phrase "Every day, and in every way, I am becoming better and better", 60

Darwin, Charles Robert (1809-1882), English naturalist who established the theory of evolution by natural selection , 51

Edison, Thomas Alva (1847-1931): American inventor and creator of the first industrial research laboratory, 92

Firdausi (Hakim Abu'l-Qasim Firdawsi Tusi) (935-1020), a highly revered Persian poet, author of the *Shah Nameh* (q.v.), the national epic of the Iranian world, 92

Hafiz, or Hafez (Khwaja Shams-ud-Din Muhammad Hafez-e Shirazi) (1315-1390), Persian lyric poet known to every Iranian, and recently popular in the West as well , 127

Hoeber, Mrs. Laura, was a mureed of Inayat Khan. In October 1924 he put her in charge of the Sufi Centre, Munich, Germany. See page 514 of the Biography for further details. 123

Jamsshyd Jamshid, figure in Persia's national epic, the *Book of Kings* by Firdausi, as one of the earliest and most glorious kings of the legendary Peshdadi dynasty, 218

Khayyam, Omar (1048-1131), Persian polymath (mathematician, philosopher, astronomer, physician, and poet) who wrote treatises on mechanics, geography, and music, in addition to his well-known collection of philosophical poems, *The Rubaiyat*, (Quatrains) 75

Khizr, Khadir, Khidr a mythological Sufi figure, the green man of the desert and the waters, sometimes identified with Elijah, and who is said to be the figure interacting with Moses in a Qur'anic story, 179

Leila (Layla, Leyli), the love object in a very well-known story (often called the Romeo and Juliet of the East), originally written by Nizami Ganjavi, but later retold by many other poets. A yong man named Qays falls madly in love at school with Leila, but because of class conflicts, her father forbids any contact. Qays goes mad from his love, and is hence called Majnun (madman, possessed). He lives alone in the wilderness, consumed with longing, 51

Majnun, see Leila

Masnavi (also known as *Masnawi-i Ma'navi* (Persian) or *Mesnevi* (Turkish), also written *Mathnawi* (Arabic), *Ma'navi*, or *Mathnavi*), vast poem written in Farsi (Persian) by Jalal-ud-Din Rumi, celebrated Sufi poet and saint, one of the best-known and most influential works of both Sufism and Persian literature; it consists of six books of poems, more than 50,000 lines, telling 424 stories to illustrate aspects of the human predicament in search for God; Rumi's poetry has become immensely popular in the West as well, 106

Nice, a city in France, the fifth most populous, located on the Mediterranean coast, 97

Paderewski, Ignacy Jan (1860-1941), Polish pianist, composer, politician, third Prime Minister of the Republic of Poland; Inayat Khan had a personal musical interaction with him at his home in Morges, Switzerland, described in Theo van

Hoorn's *Recollections of Hazrat Inayat Khan and Western Sufism* (Leiden, 2010, p. 320-30), 131

Rumi, Jalal-ud-Din (1207-1273), often considered the greatest of the Persian Sufi poets, widely read in the Islamic world, now well-known in the West as well, author of the *Masnavi* (q.v.) , 106, 127, 161

Sa'di (Muslihuddin ibn Abdallah Shirazi) (1184-1283/1291?), major Persian Sufi poet , 112, 127, 150

Sandow, Eugen (1867-1925), a Prussian pioneer bodybuilder, known as "the father of modern bodybuilding", 34

Shah Nameh, (The Book of Kings) enormous Persian poetic opus written by Firdausi around the year 1000, the national epic of Iran, 108

Shams-i Tabriz (died 1248), wandering Sufi mystic who greatly influenced Jalal-ud-din Rumi, 106, 161

Steindamm, Dr. became a mureed of Inayat Khan in 1924. In 1925 Inayat Khan initated him as Sheikh and he accompanied him on his tour through Germany that same year. For further details see p. 527 of the Biography.

Tansen (Tan Sen, Tanasena) (d. 1586 or 1589) famous singer and composer in the court of the Emperor Akbar (q .v.). Inayat Khan received the title Tansen-uz-Zaman from the Nizam of Hyderabad, 245

Universal Worship Service, religious service created by Inayat Khan and some followers in 1921, placing the scriptures of six main religions together on the altar (plus others as appropriate), lighting a candle for each, reading from each, reciting prayers, including a sermon and a final blessing, 120

Zarathushtra, also known as Zoroaster (dates in dispute, although most often considered to have flourished in the 6th century BCE), ancient Iranian prophet and religious poet whose writings form the basis of the Parsi religion; the majority of its followers now living in Western India. Inayat Khan had many friends among the Parsis in whom he took great interest both because of their religion and culture and because at the time they constituted the most anglicized and advanced social group in India, 134

Zeb-un-Nisa (1637-1702), eldest daughter of Mughal emperor Aurangzeb, remembered as a Sufi poet. A brief notice and copy of a miniature of her were published in "Sufi" a quarterly magazine, London April 1916 Vol II, No. I. 16

INDEX